Modern State Intervention in the Era of Globalisation

Modern State Intervention in the Era of Globalisation

Nikolaos Karagiannis
Nova Southeastern University, USA

and

Zagros Madjd-Sadjadi
Winston-Salem State University, USA

Edward Elgar
Cheltenham, UK • Northampton, MA, USA

Published by
Edward Elgar Publishing Limited
Glensanda House
Montpellier Parade
Cheltenham
Glos GL50 1UA
UK

Edward Elgar Publishing, Inc.
William Pratt House
9 Dewey Court
Northampton
Massachusetts 01060
USA

A catalogue record for this book
is available from the British Library

Library of Congress Cataloguing in Publication Data

Modern state intervention in the era of globalisation / Nikolaos Karagiannis, Zagros Madjd-Sadjadi
p. cm. — (New directions in modern economics series)
Includes bibliographical references and index.
1. Free trade—Economic aspects. 2. Globalization. 3. Economic Development.
I. Madjd-Sadjadi, Zagros, 1968- II. Title.
HF1713.K354 2006
339.5'2—dc22

2006025267

ISBN 978 1 84542 980 5

Printed and bound in Great Britain by MPG Books Ltd, Bodmin, Cornwall

Contents

List of Figures and Tables *vii*
Preface *ix*
Introduction *xv*

PART I: THEORETICAL ISSUES

1. Economic and Political Aspects of the State 3
2. The Role of the State and Government Expenditure 27
3. Globalisation: Problem or Solution? 55
4. Why Free Trade Isn't Free – and Shouldn't Be 79
5. Public Finance and Taxation 109

PART II: GLOBAL EXPERIENCES

6. Fiscal Policy and the Case of EC/EU 135
7. EC/EU Problems and Government 157
8. The Experience of Japan, South Korea and Taiwan in Retrospect 181
9. A Tale of Two City-States: Singapore and Hong Kong 207

PART III: MODERN POLICY

10. The Developmental State View 229
11. The Developmental State and the EC/EU 255
12. The Relevance of the Developmental State Today 283

Bibliography 305
Index 331

Figures and Tables

FIGURES

1. Non-Optimality of Total Free Trade xxii
2. Preferability of Local Regulation xxiii

TABLES

4.1 Typology of Internationalisation 107
5.1 The OECD List of Taxes 131
7.1 Main Regional Incentives: Distribution by Country and Incentive Type 165
10.1 Average Gross Saving (% of GDP) in the EC, USA and Japan: 1960-90 232
11.1 Two Opposite Policies to Regional and Industrial Development 256

Preface

The twentieth century has seen some profound changes in thinking about the economic role of government. During the twentieth century, the mixed economy emerged and grew probably as a result of both the expansion and increase in the scope of state activities which range from education, health, welfare services, and economic and social infrastructure to active industrial policy. Certainly, in every society, there is some form of government organisation which may, or may not, represent the members of the society collectively, but indeed plays an important role in the national economy. Governments are endowed with multiple functions and duties which involve expenditure and, consequently, revenue is required to finance them (Brown and Jackson, 1990, p. 154).

The preference for free enterprise dominated economic thought for a long period. However, economists found it increasingly uncomfortable to assume that the basic structure of the economy was that of free competition in which government activities represented only a minor aberration from universal private decision-making. This altered viewpoint partly came about due to the recognition that *laissez-faire* economic tradition was unable to explain the behaviour of imperfect markets. Similarly, a rapid post-war growth of the government sector, both absolutely and relative to the private sector, fostered a revision of the earlier presumption that favoured free enterprise (Bailey, 1995, pp. 12-13).

The Keynesian revolution in macroeconomic theory established a rationalisation for fiscal policy as a possible means of achieving (both) full employment and improved economic growth. Fiscal policy adds directly to aggregate demand, and in the event that private sector spending proves deficient, fiscal policy enables the economy to sustain a level of gross domestic product (GDP) consistent with full employment. Therefore, fiscal policy is capable of stimulating both employment and aggregate output, at least in the short run. On the other hand, *General Theory* has been the theoretical basis of fiscal policies in most mixed economies and concerning this, J. M. Keynes himself indicated the possibility and desirability of influencing the behaviour of economic aggregates through the deliberate manipulation of public expenditure and taxes (Allsopp, 1989, p. 181).

Since the mid-1950s, the theory and practice of public finance have changed drastically. A review of both the economic literature and the decision-making processes during this time reflect concern about the effectiveness or the ineffectiveness of state involvement on the size and composition of the national output, the allocation of resources, the income, distribution, etc. In recent years, an economic analysis of taxation policy has been supplemented by serious efforts to evaluate and appraise government expenditure alternatives. Public administration efforts reflect a concern for policy analysis and more or less systematic decision-making. A number of factors and phenomena have helped to clarify the conditions under which governments should intervene in the market economy and have provided guidance on the choice of instruments to accomplish social objectives (Brown and Jackson, 1990, p. 28).

Another factor influencing the development of public sector economics also needs to be mentioned. In the 1950s and 1960s, another concern, which was quite unrelated to public finance matters, caught the interest of economists. During this period, the field of economic development and growth, which focused on the low-income problems of the less developed nations, grew rapidly. In the search for meaningful instruments of national economic planning, criteria and the development of concepts and methods of public finance occurred which would not otherwise have happened (e.g., cost-benefit analysis). Some economists advised governments to depend substantially on unfettered markets to allocate resources and set prices. Another school of thought (i.e., the interventionist school) suggested that development was only possible with substantial government intervention. However, no single factor is responsible for development, or a lack of it, and no single policy or strategy can trigger the complex process of economic development.

Overall, the first quarter of the twentieth-century post-war period was largely characterised (at least among the OECD countries) by economic growth, high levels of employment alongside state activism, and a widely held belief in the beneficial powers of government action. State property, government intervention, discretionary fiscal and monetary policies, restrictions on trade and the like resulted in low unemployment and inflation, and economic stability and security.

The last quarter of the twentieth century, in contrast, has been characterised by much lower rates of economic growth in the Organisation for Economic Cooperation and Development (OECD) nations, though with rapid growth in the Asian Newly Industrialised Countries (NICs), persistent unemployment (even though unemployment declined in a number of countries, e.g., USA, UK) and a general decline of support for the role of government. Nonetheless, in many cases, the ratio of government spending to GDP continued to rise, and for much of this period governments ran substantial fiscal deficits. In country after country the state is being rolled back, and 'let the market decide' has become the main policy gospel for both developed and developing countries (Arestis and Sawyer, 1998, p. 1).

Since the late 1970s, most OECD nations have undertaken a reassessment of the role of their government sectors. The current debate on the role of government mainly concerns its economic aspects. The same broad debate may be behind attempts to reform public sector management and to control public spending better. But it would be undeniable that the intellectual and policy climate has shifted from one which saw an active role for state in economic and social matters towards a generally more sceptical view of the role of government. In all parts of the world, people are legitimately questioning what their governments ought to do, and all these questions ultimately raise the most fundamental questions of political organisation. At the same time, none of these issues can be decided on political principle alone; the issues are deeply philosophical and intensely practical.

Retrospectively, during the last two decades or so, free market policies have been over-emphasised and presented as the panacea for further development and prosperity, resulting in insufficient productive activity (through a lack of effective demand and inadequate levels of investment) and, thus, not effectively tackling the scale and diversity of problems that face modern societies. Despite this shortfall in endogenous growth, many still claim that the solution lies in a *laissez-faire* approach. Consequently, alternative development policy suggestions have been virtually ignored. A review of the global economy shows that all is not well, especially when one considers that global capitalism is experiencing one of its worst and most persistent crises.

Undoubtedly, the new millennium poses new challenges for national policy-making. Two challenges are fundamental. First, it is increasingly recognised that policy must be consistent, thorough and effective, and planning must be for the long term, as well as for the short and medium term. Second, governments, private sectors and social segments together must set the development agenda of tomorrow to meet the diverse and changing needs of consumers and producers (partly as a result of global competition). The appropriate role of government in the new millennium, in particular, appears to be an interesting and challenging one. Thus, if the future of modern economies and societies needs to be very different from the past, it will require a much sharper focus on radical development policy agendas.

When discussing the development experience of Japan and Asian Newly Industrialised Countries, there has been a tendency among economists to minimise the role of the state in these economies over the past two decades or so. This trend seems to be closely connected to the general support for the belief of free market forces with its direct consequence of rolling back the growth of government. Recent attempts to show that the East Asian experience illustrates why interventionist policies are not necessary for rapid economic growth have tended to focus the debate fairly narrowly on industrial policy. However, the whole array of state management activities needs to be considered. In this vein, the Developmental States of East Asian economies should be seen as both active planners and investors, and more cooperative arrangements between government and private business have marked their recent history. In fact, these countries managed to promote more orderly adjustments than the market would produce if left to itself.

Much of the discussion within this book relates to state involvement in the market system. In recent years, governments have assumed a more conscious economic role in societies. The primary goal of this participation has been in maintaining the economy along a low fiscal deficit/low inflation growth path. There has also been a lot of debate about the effectiveness or ineffectiveness of government actions (as a stabilising force), but one thing is evident, namely that the government's role is to keep the economy from 'swinging wildly' (Hadjimatheou, 1994, p. 323).

Today states require an alternative. They need to have strong policy instruments which will enable them to plan and finance their strategic goals such as job creation, higher mass living standards, endogenous competency and competitiveness, research and development, environmental protection, etc. This retooling of state policy-making requires a rethinking of the form of government intervention and, especially, an emphasis on its 'modern' developmental role. This is a crucial challenge facing countries today.

The book is composed of Parts I, II and III, or twelve chapters, which discuss theoretical issues, global experiences and modern policy issues respectively. Part I comprises Chapters 1, 2, 3, 4 and 5. The introduction of Part I poses a very interesting question: with globalisation reducing state sovereignty, is the era of the developmental state over? Surely, it appears that the power to shape markets is not what it once was, but does that mean that the state must passively accept the dictates of a New World Order? Chapter 1 provides important economic and political aspects of the state. Chapter 2 discusses features of the state, different approaches related to state activity and the impact of government expenditure as well as important social and political notions surrounding this expenditure. Chapter 3 examines the role of the state in modern capitalist democracy focusing on five interrelated concepts: capitalism, democracy, state, market and power. Chapter 4 seeks to provide a Post-Keynesian institutional theory of the state in this era of internationalisation and transnationalism. Chapter 5 discusses neoclassical and Keynesian approaches to public finance, and focuses on the incidence and macro effects of taxation.

Part II contains Chapters 6, 7, 8 and 9. Chapters 6 and 7 examine fiscal policy, economic, and other development-related problems in the European

Community/Union (EC/EU) area with respect to the role of the government. Chapters 8 and 9 discuss the success story of Japan, South Korea, Taiwan, Singapore and Hong Kong while exploring the interplay of important factors – historical legacy, the role of the market and the state, geopolitics, security, culture and social psychology – that have determined the structure of strategic centralised involvement in these countries' astonishing industrial development.

Finally, Part III is composed of Chapters 10, 11 and 12. Chapter 10 seeks to provide the Developmental State argument not only as a coherent theory but, more importantly, as a realistic development policy framework. Chapter 11 surveys regional and industrial policies in a number of EC/EU countries, and provides Developmental State policy considerations in the context of the European Union. The final chapter of the book critically examines the relevance of the Developmental State model today, and contends that parts of the Developmental State view are necessary for all modern governments regardless of their state of development.

This publication would not have been possible without the input of many persons. In preparing the section on Singapore, we wish to thank and acknowledge Justin Chee, who has given his permission to include material from a previously unpublished manuscript he co-authored with Zagros Madjd-Sadjadi, and the students at the College/University of The Bahamas (Spring 2006) for their valuable technical assistance. Special thanks go to the reviewers and advisers for their useful comments and suggestions as well as to Alan Sturmer and the staff of Edward Elgar Publishing Ltd. who have provided excellent support throughout the period it took to prepare this book.

Nikolaos Karagiannis and Zagros Madjd-Sadjadi
Nassau (Bahamas) and Winston-Salem, North Carolina (USA)
September 2006

Introduction

It has been 23 years since Chalmers Johnson (1982) introduced the concept of the developmental state in *MITI and the Japanese Miracle*. Three years later, Johnson (1985) extended his model to South Korea and Taiwan where he identified the developmental state having as key elements an autonomous bureaucracy, national planning overseen by both private and public interests that focused on long-term strategy, an emphasis on human capital, and an incentive and moral suasion approach that used market prices instead of administrated prices to produce results. Ha-Joon Chang (2002) argues the developmental state has always been with us: it is the way economies grow to dominate in the world economy.

Yet, with globalisation reducing state sovereignty, is the era of the developmental state over? Certainly, it appears that the power to shape markets is not what it once was, but does that mean that the state must passively accept the dictates of a New World Order? Adelman and Yeldan (1999) argue that the developmental state's era is over because the global market precludes the use of monetary policy to shape development, while Keng and Chen (2004), and Peng and Wong (2004), argue that East Asia may be 'growing out' of the developmental state by adopting more of a compassionate state model. More telling, however, is the rapid decline in household savings and the corresponding movement from an investment-driven to a consumption-driven economy, especially in South Korea which has seen a drop in household savings from a quarter of income in 1998 to around a twentieth of income in 2004. Similarly, the Japanese are now consuming a far greater percentage of their income than in the past. Indeed, the trade deficit that America continues to nurse cannot be traced to a lack of consumption on the part of Asian consumers; it is instead the result of overindulgent American consumers and a consumer credit system that is out of control. It is increasingly apparent that East Asians want to finally reap the rewards of their hard work and effort. And who could blame them? After all, the citizens of these countries did not engage in growth for growth's sake but rather for the desire for a better life for themselves and their children.

We believe that reports of the death of the developmental state have been greatly exaggerated. While it is true that some of the Asian nations may be interested in moving from a developmental state to a consumer-oriented state, the basis for promotion of development through the approach pioneered in East Asia is still very much alive and well. We are thus in line with the analysis of Bagchi (2000), who argues that the developmental state must merely change to meet new economic realities and new demands from the populace. The lessons learned from the developmental state are not necessarily the same ones that were once taught. The fact is that some of the tools of the developmental state need to be reshaped to meet the new globalised context as simple tariff protection and import substitution efforts may not be allowed in the new global trading regime. This means that states must become more creative in how they handle the process of 'creative destruction' (Schumpeter, 1934), which is an inevitable by-product of this framework that is the developmental state.

The world is becoming more interdependent. Regional trading blocs (ASEAN, EU, NAFTA), interregional cooperative bodies (APEC, NATO), and global organisations fostering the ideals of American-style capitalism (IMF, World Bank, WTO), are the first incursions into the traditional domains of the nation-state. Sovereignty is being chipped away as nations establish international rules of behaviour: the anarchic world is sowing the seeds of a leviathan.

Increasing interdependencies give some states increased power. The United States, for example, has engaged in extraterritorial jurisdiction in the application of its 'trading with the enemies' statutes. Under the auspices of punishing Cuba for the downing of two planes from the US-based 'Brothers to the Rescue' over international waters, the Helms-Burton legislation attempts to penalize foreign companies that do business with the island nation. The European Union, Canada and Mexico strenuously objected to this legislation. Canadian Trade Minister Art Eggleton forcefully stated Canada's position:

> We will not be bullied by the United States. . . I think it's a foregone conclusion that we're going to proceed [with an appeal to the North America Free Trade Agreement panel], because (the US Law) is a violation of NAFTA. (*Toronto Star*, 1996, E3)

Other states are on the peripheries of power. Canada is one of the richest countries in the world with a standard of living rivalling the United States. It has been one of the top-ranked countries in the United Nations Human Development Index for several years. However, it is a country that exists in the shadow of the United States because of its large trade dependence, and Canadians as well as outside observers have repeatedly questioned its role in the world:

> Canada has only one reason for existing, and that is, a lot of Canadians do not like the United States. If you leave that aside, it has no justification. Individual provinces normally have larger trade with the United States than they do with the rest of the place. The French do not like the English Canadians. The English Canadians do not like the French. . . If I were to offer them advice, I would suggest that they just disintegrate. (Tullock, 1992)

And yet, the 'New World Order', an outgrowth of globalisation, has both positive and negative connotations. One benefit is the establishment of the rule of law in international discourse through treaties that carry known penalties for those who choose to violate their terms. This greater certainty brings stability and a sense of 'fair play' to the world of international relations. A downside is that it represents an unprecedented 'war' against differing ideologies, and it does not limit its attacks to those areas falling in the traditional realm of foreign policy. With increasing interdependence, items formerly under the purview of domestic policy have international implications and carry international consequences. Several countries object to Japan's closed markets and whale hunting. The United States tells China to establish rules protecting intellectual property rights. Australia and Canada denounce the United States' agricultural subsidies. The United States wants Mexico to engage in greater environmental protection and questions Canada's cultural policies. On the other hand, there is a high degree of tolerance for violations of basic political rights, as if economic rights were sacrosanct. Indeed, even in the popular press more attention is paid to those who abuse religious freedom than political freedom. The persecution by China, Vietnam and Saudi Arabia in the realm of religious rights overshadows the fact that many more countries fail to respect democratic systems of governance.

Even in the case of egregious violations of political rights such as the detention of Dang Ang Suu Kyi by Myanmar, the economic pressure can hardly be considered overwhelming as the country has received special economic deals from ASEAN and curries favour with international investors (MacIntyre, 1994; Stackhouse, 1995). China, the rising new darling of the international economic community, successfully convinced advanced industrial countries, eager to gain access to what is potentially the world's largest market, to accept a policy of not linking human rights abuses to trade. The one case where comprehensive international pressure secured political rights (South Africa) is a special one: not a moral commitment to human rights by other nations, but an example of the influence of domestic pressures on foreign policy. Every other country since World War II which has faced international sanctions on 'non-economic' grounds faced such threats because of one of four reasons:

1. invading another country;
2. committing terrorism against another country;
3. engaging in communism; or
4. practicing genocide.

The first two reasons are fairly obvious ones for imposing sanctions; to do otherwise would be to say that borders are meaningless. The third is an economic reason: communist countries do not have free markets and so deny basic economic rights. The fourth reason has a spotty record of enforcement at best (witness the half-hearted attempts by the UN to keep the peace in Rwanda and Bosnia-Herzegovina and Serbia).

This duality of interest is obvious: in any trade, both sides benefit. Otherwise, autarky results; for there to be a price, the item must have value with the price being set equal to the value placed upon the item by the buyer and the seller. When there is no trade, both sides lose. As the justification for sanctions in the economic sphere is to open up trade, the sanctioning country hopes these future benefits will outweigh the present costs. The justification for sanctions in the political sphere is a moral one, not an economic one. While the cost accrues to both sanctioned and sanctioning countries, the sanctioned country can reduce this cost in so many ways that sanctions are rarely effective.

This does not mean that trade agreements do not have political consequences: interest groups engaging in rent-seeking behaviour will find their benefits diminished and will seek to have enforcement of these provisions delayed or stymied. There may also be serious repercussions when standards in different countries are not in concordance with one another, resulting in substandard products entering the country. Similarly, constraints on the national government may filter to the locality in some cases but not in others. A federal system of governance, with division of powers between levels of government, makes enforcement of global provisions more costly and difficult (if not downright impossible). Other countries however, expect federal governments to live up to the obligations of the treaties they sign without regard to the nature of their governmental structure. Federal governments must keep tabs on their subnational governments, just as parents must monitor the behaviour of their children and are sometimes liable if the child breaks the law. This analogy is a valid one. The need for two incomes and a breakdown of traditional sources of moral support in the community and religious institutions impair the ability of parents to monitor their children. Similarly, federal governments find it increasingly difficult to constrain the actions of their subnational governments due to budgetary constraints, increasing interdependence, transnational corporations, and an increasing legislative role of these sub-nationals.

METHODOLOGY AND PROBLEM FORMATION

This study employs a neo-institutional methodology combined with some post-Keynesian economic theory. We examine the change in the world through the concept of the *developmental state*, which seeks to maximise benefits for the nation-state in the context of rising globalisation. The analysis focuses on these systems as *evolutionary* institutions with their own national purpose policy preferences. These preferences derive from nation-states (within the case of the global economic system) but they are more than the sum of the constituent preferences.

The neo-institutional view focuses on institutional change by examining the organisational structure in addition to the values, norms and preferences of institutions. It assumes the following (Pederson, 1991, p. 126):

1. Institutions *and not states* are the actors in the system (although states can be an institution).
2. The history of an institution guides its actions.
3. Institutions react to other institutions and learn and adapt their reactions based on feedback from those institutions.

Therefore, nations are not unitary actors; nor are the global or federal systems merely compilations of their constituent parts. The systems and nation-states act due to their organizational structures and institutionalised preferences. Federal states interact with the system and with one another in a similar fashion but there are other institutions underneath the nation-state that affects its policy outcomes. These other institutions include non-governmental organisations, multinational corporations, political parties, labour unions, the international economic market, the markets of various countries, various religious and philosophical traditions, the political cultures of various regions, which all influence each other and the nations as a whole. The above is not even a comprehensive list. Of course, the number of variables in a truly complete institutional analysis would be enormous so this book concentrates only on the individual nations as units of analysis and treats all the others as parameters.

THE CENTRAL RESEARCH QUESTION

Scholars have allied themselves on opposite sides of the debate. The first chapter, which provides background material to this debate, positions this study within the context of the literature. However, a little foreshadowing is in order. Laxer (1993, p. 2) argues that globalisation is a 'false god' that will destroy the nation-state 'if its commandments are followed'. Laxer (1993, p. 2) goes on arguing that the advocates for globalisation have as their 'highest priority' the task of convincing 'that this is the age of globalisation and that its dictates must be followed'. The liberal left often echoes this theme. Lang and Hines (1993) believe that free trade means lowest common denominator regulation and increasing income disparity. Daly and Goodland (1992) state that the concept of comparative advantage is meaningless because of increased capital mobility and that free trade destroys both the environment and social welfare. Even John Maynard Keynes (1936) argued against the free flow of capital.

Writers such as Lipsey (1986) and Watkins (1987) discuss how free trade limits national sovereignty. Simeon (1986) and Schockman and Madjd-Sadjadi (1994) emphasise that free trade may place strains on the federal system. Authors on the right tend to dismiss such allegations and some even argue that free trade extends sovereignty (Reisman, 1986; Crispo, 1986a, 1987)! Others contend that free trade and globalisation processes benefit governments *because* they limit sovereignty: they see government intervention as being wholly incompatible with the free market. David Frum (1995), son of late leftist journalist Barbara Frum, argues right-wing governments win because their policies (tax and spending cuts, the classic ingredients in conservative platforms) obey 'the economic equivalent of the law of gravity, the laws of the market'. On the other hand, left-wing governments, according to Frum, openly defy 'the laws of the market'. To Frum, it is necessary to bow to an economic orthodoxy that calls for free trade, international (not national) standards (MacInnes, 1994), and fixed exchange rate monetary policies (Rueff, 1972; Kindleberger, 1986; Triffin, 1968). At the same time, it should be noted that some attack this last doctrine (Johnson, 1962; Yeager, 1976; Corden, 1977; Friedman, 1953).

This manuscript takes the middle ground (that is, a dynamic mixture of inward and outward orientation). There are benefits to free trade. If there were none, there would be no trade. Free trade has great economic benefits, but it does have its costs. These costs (cultural,[1] political,[2] social,[3] and economic) ensure that the optimal level of free trade is only partial (see Figure 1) or may not be achieved.

Costs and benefits of free trade can change. Local and national regulation may be more efficient in a global economy than global regulation for two reasons. First, global agreements typically devise 'one size fits all' regulations, while national and local governments are more flexible. Second, national and local governments can make regulatory changes at lower political cost as the interests of its constituency align more closely at the local than at the global level (and localities hold similar advantages over national governments). Effectively, this flattens the cost curve (see Figure 2), leading to more benefits (as shown by correspondingly higher isobenefit lines) at the same cost. At the same time, local regulation may be more efficient than national regulation for an additional reason: national governments examine other national governments more closely than they examine subnational governments. In the end, local regulation may end up costing only slightly more than other forms of regulation but the inframarginal benefit from such regulation outweighs the inframarginal cost.

On the other hand, local governments often lack the capacity to implement what would otherwise be the preferred policy. For this reason, we focus most of our attention in this book to the developmental state at the national level. However, it should be noted that the analysis given in this study would naturally extend to the locality if sufficient institutional capability were found there.[4]

As evidence of the point that total free trade is non-optimal, the global economy shows stresses. Managed trade is on the rise. It is typified by 'a sharp increase in the use of quantitative restrictions: quotas, voluntary export restraints (VERs) and orderly marketing agreements (OMAs), typically negotiated on a bilateral basis outside the safeguard provisions (*Article* XIX) of the GATT and in clear violation of its letter or spirit' (Trebilcock, Chandler and Howse, 1988, p. 78). At the same time, competing visions of global governance appear. Some, such as Ohmae (1990) and Reich (1991), articulate a vision of pseudo-anarchy where the nation-state is powerless to stop the forces of natural economic law and can only act as a developer of quality workers for the international economic system. Others, such as the Commission on Global Governance (1995), argue international organisations should have increased powers while preserving the nation-state as a political unit within a reconstituted international community. Louis Pauly (quoted in Knox, 1995, D5) echoes this opinion: 'There is a global economy, but no move towards a global polity'. Another view expressed by Horsman and Marshall (1994, p. 267) is that while the state is not going to disappear, it must increasingly transfer power both up to international organisations and down to subnational governments. It will also have to find a way to champion both 'equality and justice where the economic system sees only efficiency' (Horsman and Marshall, 1994, p. 267). Although agreeing with this analysis on the proper role of the state in the new economy, the study argues that those states that temper their responses with proper respect for institutions within their countries will best be able to champion such a policy.

In keeping with traditional neoclassical economic analysis, the first graph below (Figure 1) reflects the following key assumptions:

1. that benefits from free trade are always increasing;
2. that there are diminishing marginal returns to free trade; and
3. that there are constant costs to negotiating trade agreements.

So long as costs are constant or increasing to trade agreements, the analysis would hold although increasing costs would actually provide for a lower level of overall free trade. The constant costs to negotiating trade agreements are a simplification that aids in the analysis from a graphical standpoint. If the marginal cost of free trade is a linear function of its provision, while the marginal benefits decline as the level is increased, the axis for free trade costs can serve as well as an axis for free trade provision. In fact, this analysis shows that, under these assumptions, there will be some finite point where MC = MB. If this case exists anywhere on the curve, total free trade must be suboptimal under neoclassical assumptions, i.e., some (minor) restriction on free trade would be Pareto superior to absolute free trade. Thus, even free trade is not a free lunch.

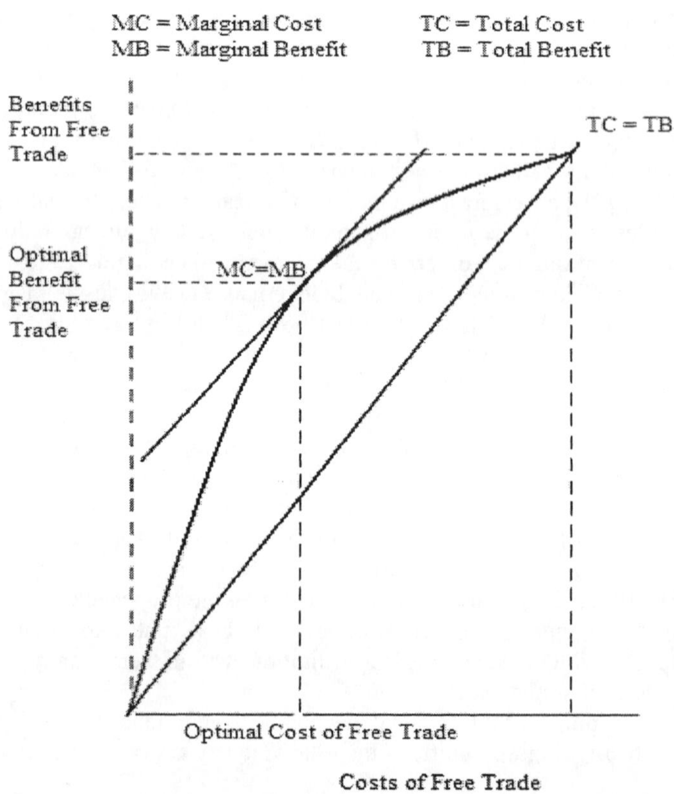

Figure 1 Non-Optimality of Total Free Trade

(B_L, C_L) - Benefits and Costs From Local Regulation

(B_N, C_N) - Benefits and Costs From National Regulation

(B_G, C_G) - Benefits and Costs from Global Regulation

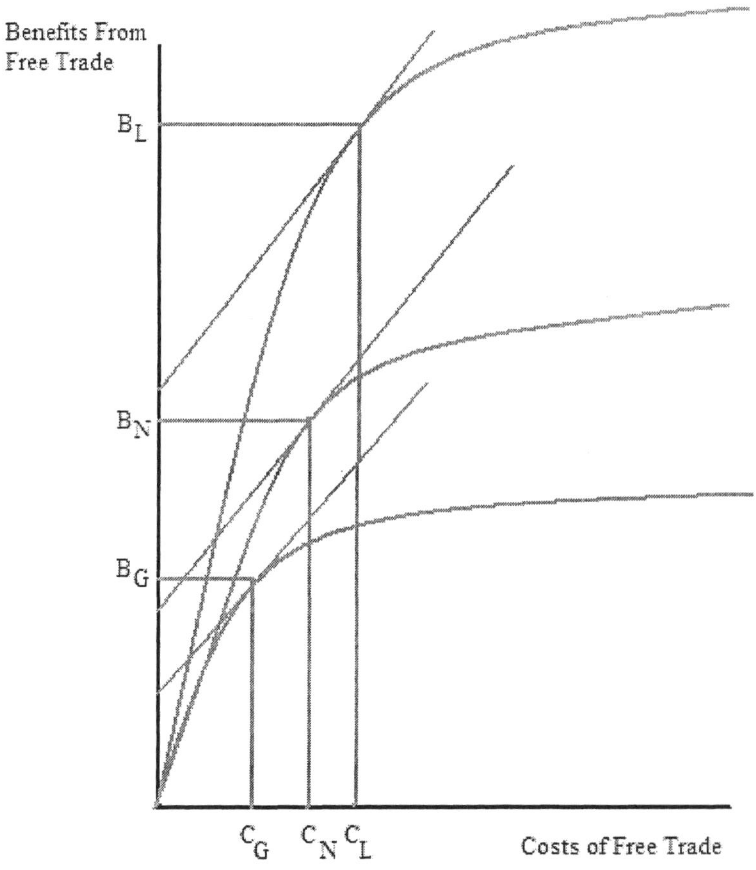

Figure 2 Preferability of Local Regulation

Each parallel line represents an *isobenefit* curve and is drawn parallel to an imaginary line that equates benefits and costs and thus would be a ray extending from the origin at a 45-degree angle. As such, higher isobenefit lines represent higher net benefits, and each isobenefit line represents a constant level of benefit based on combinations of benefits and costs of free trade.

NOTES

1. The importance of culture in maintaining identity is well known in the literature but less emphasised is the degree that culture influences public policy. For a study of this in the area of foreign affairs, see Saul, 1994.
2. In Canada, significant political barriers have traditionally obstructed free trade. These barriers include the sovereignty of individual provinces and the historic anti-American sentiment expressed towards closer ties with the United States. For an examination of this in relation to trade policy, see Muirhead, 1992.
3. Canadians, for example, still trade more with each other than with the United States, despite the free trade agreement:

   > If the border were as inconsequential as national borders are supposed to be in this supposedly globalised world, trade with the US should be much more important than trade within Canada. . . But it isn't. On average, Canadian provinces trade with each other 20 times . . . more than they trade with American states. (Watson, 1995, p. 11)

4. One possible explanation (not given by Watson) is that the social fabric of the nation is such that Canadians prefer to do business with other Canadians, all other things being equal.

PART I

Theoretical Issues

1. Economic and Political Aspects of the State

A state can be universally represented as the official incorporation of political power. The state can be conceptualised or defined on a variety of levels which emphasise either universal characteristics or ideological-specific roles. There is the well-known Weberian emphasis on the state as the institution which can lay claim to the use of legitimate force. But this view may raise problems in assuming legitimacy for the state in all circumstances.

On surer grounds are those views which identify on technical bases those structures and functions that are universal properties, irrespective of ideology or efficiency criteria. Indeed, all states perform executive, law-making, judicial, administrative and coercive functions. At the minimum, the structural requirements include a political directorate, an administration and a military force. Greater degrees of differentiation could involve distinct judicial and parliamentary bodies. Therefore, the state's principal activities can be categorised as:

1. regulating behaviour (law and coercion);
2. managing and deploying resources (administration);
3. rationalising or legitimising actions (ideology); and
4. defining goals and means of attainment (policy).

Approaches to the classification of states are based on the following basic factors:

1. the methods followed in choosing political directorates;
2. the style or manner in which power is exercised;
3. the main class forces identified as guiding the paths of political directorates; and
4. the ideological direction of policy.

Neoclassical economics has had an influence in redefining the role of the state in recent years. The so-called 'Washington' school has trumpeted the virtues of free markets and free trade, and economic consultants have embarked upon the world to spread the gospel of the orthodoxy in economic thought. At the forefront of this paradigm have been proponents of three schools of thought that have reshaped economic policy. Prior to the 1970s and the collapse of the Breton Woods agreement, most policy-makers would have been thoroughly in the Keynesian camp, whereas many neo-classical economists had moved on to other explanations.

However, the insufficiency of microfundamentals to explain Keynesian economics had lain bare a profession that had prided itself in having a unified theory, and elements of this insurgency were being felt in the writings of the Public Choice theorists who were arguing to apply economic rationality to the political scene. After all, why is it that we should automatically assume that governments were interested in maximising social welfare when the interests of politicians would seem to be contrary to this insofar as it did not advance the probability of reelection. Indeed, regulatory capture and the need for vast sums of money for campaigning could ultimately lead to short-sighted policies that favoured one group in society over another so that share-enlarging, rather than pie-enlarging, behaviour was paramount (Olson, 1971, 1982).

Moreover, the traditional import substitution industrialisation advocated by radical development economists was being challenged by academic economists who argued that trade barriers were ultimately self-defeating, and that the infant industries that were being protected were never allowed to venture forth into the world. Thus, these industries increasingly grew dependent on subsidies and never blossomed into the agents of dynamic comparative advantage that Listian political economy sought (Bruton, 1998). The minimalist state was seen increasingly as the ideal one, echoing the sentiments of not only Adam Smith but Thomas Jefferson who argued that 'government is best which governs the least' even as he presided over an unprecedented expansion of government through the Louisiana Purchase.

Based on the above argument, the collapse of Breton Woods and the rise of OPEC triggered a mass disillusion with the Keynesian 'cross' and its ability to dampen both expansions and recessions in such a way as to tame the business cycle. Instead, a belief in the hyper-rationality of individuals as seen in the rational expectations models that began to appear argued that the state could really do nothing right in the long run. Far from allowing a Philips Curve relationship that served as a menu of choices between inflation and unemployment, the rational expectations school of Lucas argued that, in the long run, the Phillips Curve was vertical. Monetarist policy that would be governed by rules rather than discretion was given credence by these models since the Phillips Curve's short-run phenomenon was merely the imbalance between expectations and reality. Consequently, the monetary authorities advancing Keynesianism were simply creating disturbances in the economy rather than alleviating them, according to economists who sided with Lucas and Friedman in the debate.

Developing countries were seen to be the catalyst for these changes. Multilateral institutions such as the International Monetary Fund (IMF) and the World Bank increasingly required debtor countries to implement changes in their economies so as to encourage the free flow of goods across their borders. These requirements mirrored the desires of the developed countries that were more interested in expanding market opportunities for their own products than in encouraging the development of industries that could compete successfully against them.

These goods were often desired by elites in developing countries and thus the two groups cooperated to open the spigot of trade, and the policy prescriptions often benefited the upper and middle classes of society to the detriment of the vast lower classes that made up much of the developing world. This cooperation, however, was based on mutually shared goals rather than a conspiracy to harm others. Yet, the very nature of these common aims served to blind the wealthy in each country to the social ills that they were creating and the potential for social instability (Perkins, 2004).

These actions have continued to encroach on the ability of the nation-state to be autonomous. The IMF's Structural Adjustment Programmes, for example, try to regulate virtually all aspects of economic policy within a country, both external and internal in nature. Although understandable from the perspective of donor nations in the aftermath of the debt crisis of the early 1980s, these policies so severely constrained the state that alternative visions could not be considered, and their 'one size fits all' policy prescriptions failed to consider either the social milieu in which they would operate or the need to change direction if the policy prescription failed to work as anticipated. Instead, it often served to lock successive governments into a policy platform by 'starving the beast' of government for funds when the changes failed to deliver economic growth. Things only spiralled out of control from the perspective of small autonomous states in the 1990s.

Recent World Bank publications attempt to define the 'appropriate' role for the state (the 'middle ground' position of the World Bank) as

> [O]ne that limits it to always being, by and large, a pure facilitator of the private sector (through its corrections of market failures in general). Such an approach, although it seems to be pragmatic, is quite conservative, [highly partial and passive] and may be illustrated by asserting a 'Geisha model' for the state (which is expected to know how to walk lightly, keep the man – i.e., the private sector – happy, and stay subordinate in her relation, with little or no outside the box, strategic agential role to play in the relationship).
> The World Bank's ideal for the role of government is clearly one of yoking of apparently unequals, and the relational model is a fairly strict division of duties

> (or labour) with little allowance for entrepreneurial action by the 'Geisha-state' – because of an expected show of 'Geisha-government failure' – and little encouragement is thus given to do otherwise than her narrowly circumscribed 'Geisha-government' role. (Northover, 2001, pp. 77-8)

What's more, many donor governments and multilateral institutions were requiring debtor countries to agree to various 'good governance conditionalities' in accepting funds, which served to change not only economic policy but also introduced changes in political, legal, and social institutions (Chang, 2003, p. 2). Some of these changes might be regarded as being a net benefit to all sides such as an insistence on transparency and the rule of law, but other policies, such as implementation of so-called intellectual property rights that served to lock in protections via the Copyright Act for 70 to 95 years, may have a deleterious effect on competition and on the ability of nations to improve themselves through education.

Indeed, the expansion of copyright in this fashion had little to do with economic efficiency since the works that were being protected, by and large, already existed and had come into being despite not having these protections. While it might be true that such enhancements would lead to the creation of more creative works going forward, they certainly did nothing but harm economic efficiency with regard to current copyrighted material.

Thus, even after various extensions of protection, these were the ones that carried no net economic benefit to the world and, by retarding the rise of public domain releases based on these works, ended up creating a net economic harm to the poor, causing a net welfare transfer from poor underdeveloped countries that, by and large, lacked large quantities of copyrighted materials that were popular on the global stage to rich industrialised countries.

This is just one concrete example of how neoliberal policies have not only failed to produce the desired result of enhanced growth but they have actually increased economic inequality and created economic instability that has led to the disintegration of the social fabric that holds many societies together. The economic crises faced by Russia, Indonesia and Argentina can be directly linked to neoliberal policies pursued by policy-makers in these respective countries.

Neoliberalism was supposed to usher in a new era of economic growth and prosperity for all concerned and was supposed to narrow the gap between rich and poor nations. From 1960 to 1980, the world's per capita income grew at a rate of 3.1 per cent per annum with developed and developing countries growing at about the same pace. However, developing country economic growth slowed dramatically in the 1980-2000 period following the ascendancy of neoliberalism, tumbling by 50 per cent to just

1.5 per cent per annum. This is all the most disconcerting when one realises that the fantastic economic growth of China and India is included in these lackadaisical numbers which, combined, account for one third of that growth, while the economies of Latin America, the former Soviet Union and Sub-Saharan Africa have either stagnated or are actually in active retreat. A more accurate picture would be to say that neoliberalism fails to deliver even on its most basic promises (i.e., efficiency and growth). Yet, despite rising social discontent in the developing world, much of the Washington consensus continues to believe the fairy tale.

The public sector is neither the bastion of excellence that was heralded as maximising some social welfare function by a perfectly competent social planner nor is it a catastrophic failure due to selfish individuals desiring to further only their own utility. Instead, when we choose between market and state, we must distinguish between them based on the results that each provides rather than our speculation about their potential failures (Wolf Jr., 1988). Instead of blindly following neoliberalism, the 'developmental states' of East Asia and the 'social corporatists states' of Scandinavia provide viable and worthwhile options for state intervention in the economy. Though born of very different historical, cultural and political contexts and using very different policy instruments and economic institutions, each of these two models have served their own regions very well. Culture does matter and without understanding the differences in the locality and its unique needs, any system of governance is bound to failure.

Such an alternative approach focuses on the role of the state as the designer, defender, and reformer of many formal and informal institutions in the context of national purpose, industrial development and structural change. Two roles are particularly important: first, its role as an entrepreneur that provides the vision for the future and builds the necessary institutions; and, second, its role as the manager of conflicts which arise in the process of economic transformation and structural change. But the role of political constraints and globalisation in the performance of such functions must also be taken seriously into account.

While the WTO has brought about significant changes to global trading rules, there is still much room for national policy intervention. Industrial strategy is still very important and relevant: it can promote particular industries with an array of policies with a view to increasing the production and productivity of the national economy in the long run.

State supervision of national development, investment coordination among potential competitors within key dynamic sectors, 'socialising risk' through technically proficient industrial planning, and focus on targeted investments, capacity, skills and research and development (R&D) can help the economy achieve faster industrial growth and structural change. This alternative development policy framework is what modern economies (especially the developing ones) need (Karagiannis, 2002).

DEFINING AND MEASURING STATE INTERVENTION

Neoliberal analysis draws heavily on the First and Second Theorems of Welfare Economics. The First Theorem of Welfare Economics states that competitive markets produce Pareto optimal results, although the results of that competitive market may not be to the liking of individuals: markets may distribute goods in a manner that produces large-scale disparities in wealth. The Second Theorem of Welfare Economics states that it doesn't matter that competitive markets produce disparities in wealth because these can be corrected by altering the initial endowments that everyone has. Neoliberals sell the concept of growth based on the First Welfare Theorem and discount the drawbacks by holding out hope with the Second Welfare Theorem. But states are often told to reign in their redistributive roles as reallocators of social progress and thus the equilibriums that are created are inherently unequal in allocation.

Additionally, there are important caveats that limit the applicability of the First Welfare Theorem. Markets must be perfectly competitive, agents must act in a competitive manner, there cannot be any externalities in consumption or production, and information in the economy must be costless with no transaction costs interfering with the smooth functioning of markets. Not only are none of these conditions satisfied in the real world, they are also violated to a far greater extent with developing countries than with developed ones. Information is nonexistent in many economies about competitive prices, unlike in developed countries where marketers freely advertise and compete on price. In Jamaica, for example, prices can vary widely between two stores that are no more than a block away and yet these price variations not only persist but sales continue at both entities. Essentially stores end up attracting and capturing clientele who rarely stray to be the tipping agents in a market towards a rebalancing of supply and demand through competitive means.

However, neoliberalism has becoming a mantra for far too many. While disagreement can persist over what is 'good' or 'bad' state intervention, neoliberalism castigates any intervention as uniformly bad. Yet, without government intervention, such social institutions as slavery and child labour would persist, and without guarantees like minimum wages and labour standards, the inherent lack of power that labour has via a *vis-à-vis* capital would be unmasked.

Each of these policies serves to restrict entry into the labour market but is considered socially desirable (to a greater or lesser degree) by the population of most advanced industrial countries. At the same time, consensus has not yet developed worldwide on these practices, and at the time Adam Smith was writing the *Wealth of Nations* in 1776, each of these policies would have been considered to be a state intervention that 'artificially' restricted labour market entry throughout the world.

As Chang (2003, pp. 81-2) notes, while OECD countries have accepted that children have a basic right to education and therefore the rights and obligations of individuals have been altered by social circumstances resulting in restrictions on what were once clear and obvious property rights, many developing countries view restrictions on child labour as part of a legitimate policy debate. Similarly, as noted by Commons (1931), the US developed labour legislation and hamstringed the so-called free market at the turn of the century as social covenants changed. Property rights are not eternally static in definition but alter with the passage of time and the distance of space. Consumer protections in Japan differ dramatically from those in the United States. Indeed, most of the worldviews may find laughable the various warnings that the litigious system in the USA has produced where a sunshade for a car must have the warning label 'Remove this from dashboard before driving', and individuals must be properly cautioned that eating large quantities of fast food can make you fat.

Similarly, the US has criticised on the grounds of trade distortion the European bans on genetically modified crops, while few in Europe would regard these as market 'interventions' that call into question the validity of their free markets. Similarly, asbestos regulations in the United States and Europe have been considered trade distortionary by Canada. Essentially, any rule that serves to restrict trade in a product will find it challenged by a country that holds a comparative advantage in that product. In the global political economy, the OECD countries have the deck stacked in their favour and are able to change the rules by which the world trades to favour themselves. Clearly, while capital freely flows throughout the world, labour does not.

Therefore, the very definition of a free market is not universally acknowledged. It means, as Humpty Dumpty in *Alice in Wonderland* might have put, only what the individual society chooses it to mean, leaving us to understand that rights and obligations exist not in a vacuum distinct from society but rather are generated by society through its institutions and social conventions (Chang, 2003, p. 83).

Thus, since different individuals define state intervention differently, it becomes difficult to sort out exactly how large the state *ought* to be, if even that is the correct question to be asking in the first place. And while the percentage of GDP that is comprised of government expenditure may be an indicator of how much fiscal spending occurs in an economy, it is unclear that this is necessarily a measurement of the amount of intervention. Asian economies have been traditionally labelled as non-interventionist (World Bank, 1991, p. 40); yet the economies of Taiwan, South Korea, Singapore and even Hong Kong have all been highly interventionist when one considers how much these states distort the normal functioning of the market.

The reason for this is that these societies have much lower spending on transfer payments than Western economies, and they have sometimes used veiled mechanisms to influence business without necessarily directing it. For example, instead of subsidising an infant industry, the East Asian economies might engage in the antithesis: raising the costs of those industries that are in disfavour, but this has the effect of causing favour to all industries not so hampered by the extra costs.

Similarly, the US government through its federal procurement policies set standards for the industry that have innovation-distorting effects that are not readily quantifiable in terms of government expenditure. The rhetoric of the Bush White House might be on free trade and free markets, but when it comes to homeland security and national defence, its actions have repercussions that cascade throughout the economy and cause distortions that are not readily seen. For example, the calling up of the national guard can have a disproportionate effect on certain localities where the reservists are stationed. Increased scrutiny in ensuring homeland security has imposed enormous costs on private individuals and businesses, and the research and development of military technology has had spin-off effects that have aided the development of various consumer industries. Radar, the computer, the cell phone and GPS technology all owe either their initial development or their improvements to research and development in the service of the military – industrial complex, and yet none of these would be considered interventions in the free market by even the most ardent neoliberal economists in the USA. Definitions have meaning only in regard to the social, cultural, and economic climate that they inhabit but these definitions often underpin specific ideological viewpoints.

STATE INTERVENTION AND PUBLIC ENTERPRISES

Why is it that we have public enterprises? There are several possible reasons that have been given standing and the argument in favour of such enterprises is more clear-cut among developing countries:

1. Where capital markets are incomplete or underdeveloped, the domestic private sector may be unable to undertake investments that would be necessary to develop the local industry to a sufficient extent. This is particularly true where industries have significant scale economies and

the costs of entry are high or when the investment is in a natural resource such as oil or bauxite. This would usually not prevent foreign entities from being about to fund these activities but the political repercussions from selling out to these companies may prove to be too high for a government to accept.

2. Where there is a natural monopoly, the choice may be between regulation and ownership. In such cases, there is an inherent potential problem of regulatory capture and so, to protect itself, the government may decide to own the monopoly outright since it would then have access to its actual cost information. Without that information, it is difficult to regulate the entity, and a cost plus 'reasonable return' regulatory framework may evolve. In such cases, costs may be inflated in order to garner larger profits since the rate of return is based on expenditure. This will also serve to defeat incentives to economise and become more efficient. Thus ownership, if properly managed, may be economically preferable to natural monopoly.
3. Through cross-subsidisation, public enterprises can achieve important public policy goals. For example, rural areas are subsidised by urban centres in the US in terms of mail service. It costs the same to mail a letter in the city as it does to send it across the country or to a rural area and letters are carried by postal workers to every corner of the country in two to three days time. Rural electrification projects in most countries (hydroelectric power in Quebec, the development of a province-wide telephone system in Saskatchewan) all have been accomplished by public enterprises in a far more efficient and faster manner than would have been the case with private enterprise, which would tend to 'cherry pick' in order to achieve profitability in the absence of regulation.
4. Similarly, public housing and transportation in Hong Kong and public education in many countries help to achieve policies that would have otherwise left numerous individuals incapable of bettering their lives or supporting themselves.
5. The public enterprise can serve as a 'window on the industry' allowing it to provide information to the government for the setting of policy. In addition, by becoming a price leader, it can have a far greater impact than its own size through competitive pressures on private entities.
6. When there are significant externalities, a public enterprise can respond in a socially desirable manner as it need not be a profit-maximising enterprise. By explicitly incorporating externalities into the decision-making process about how much to produce, the public enterprise can reduce negative externalities or increase positive ones.
7. Since public enterprises have access to the public purse, the paradox of thrift can be eliminated and such enterprises can serve as important levers to ensure stability of demand.

8. In light of complete uncertainty, investors generally view the future through the lens of the present and therefore a bias exists whereby individuals disproportionately factor in present circumstances in the formation of long-term expectations. For example, Hurricane Katrina has dramatically altered expectations of hurricane damage to New Orleans. The actual probabilities of a hurricane strike have not changed but the mere fact that a hurricane has recently struck and done widespread damage has moved an issue that was previously of low concern to the forefront of public policy and debate. However, this issue can be even more foreboding because, in some cases, present actions may make it *less* likely for similar results to occur. For example, a large earthquake can relieve stress in the earth's mantle and tectonic plates that will make it less likely that such a catastrophic event will occur in the immediate future. Similarly, even for non-disasters but still unpredicted circumstances, capacity is only likely to be created in so far as its use appears to be profitable at the existing state of effective demand. The additional production generated in the future by the sum of the investment decisions of the present will itself increase the demand of commodities in comparison with the present level – a factor which private investors cannot take into account, or can do so only imperfectly, since they take their decisions independently of each other. Investments by public enterprises, on the other hand, can take the comprehensive effect of all investments into account in judging the social profitability of any particular investment project. In fact, when public investment is part of a national plan, it is possible to take into account all kinds of criss-cross effects, which would not be possible with private investment. It should be noted, however, that a state plan is capable of doing this even when the investment is undertaken by private enterprises, as the Japanese example shows.
9. What is required is that there should be a fairly comprehensive state investment plan for industrial development, and the state should be capable of giving effect to this plan through the 'administrative guidance' of the privately owned firms (provided that, as in Japan, these are indigenous and not foreign-owned firms).
10. When the First and Second Welfare Theorems' basic premises are violated, the Theory of the Second Best comes into play that argues that if we cannot obtain a maximum in all dimensions, we should seek no maximum in any. Thus, to achieve maximum social efficiency, we must not achieve private efficiency unless we can achieve maximum private efficiency. Where barriers exist, market restrictions have a place and public enterprise can be one of the tools to ensure that regulations are followed by providing market discipline as opposed to regulatory discipline.

11. Regulations themselves require considerable expenditure to implement and administer. Regulating 'through the market' via a 'window on the industry' can have significant public benefits in terms of greater efficiency since there is increased transparency between public policy objectives and the meeting of those objectives. The public enterprise must implement public policy while private enterprise may attempt to give only the appearance of compliance.
12. Public enterprises can help alleviate coordination failure. In cases where the factors of production are interdependent in use but dispersed in ownership, endogenous development or effective structural change may require coordinated changes in many components of the economy. While standards setting can be performed by industry, the various battles between VHS/Betamax, Internet Explorer/Netscape, IBM/Apple and QWERTY/Dvorak typewriters call into question whether market-driven standards always provide the most efficient solution – it may just be the best marketed. That doesn't imply that public enterprises will necessarily choose the best standard, whatever 'best' might mean, but with input from all stakeholders, selection is less likely to be caused by lack of information or path-dependency. Indeed, Hirschman (1958) argued that economic development depends not so much on finding optimal combinations for given resources and factors of production as on calling forth and enlisting for development purposes resources and abilities that are hidden, scattered, underutilised or badly utilised (Chang, 2003, p. 52).

On the opposite side of the aisle, neoliberals argue that no matter what the best intentions of public enterprises, they suffer from the fact that there is no profit motive, and the managers who are put in place may not have the same interests as their political bosses. This is not exactly true and there is a bit of deception because private enterprise also suffers from a principal – agent problem in form of separation of ownership from control. Managers of private enterprises may even find themselves having greater incentives to deviate from the interests of their shareholders – owners because they are usually insulated from the risks of their mistakes (and thus are overly risk seeking in their behaviour, generating a survivorship bias in the market-place).

Yet, their compensation is not necessarily tied to their performance (many managers have received bonuses and extravagant pay even while companies were floundering on the grounds that it is unusually difficult to find individuals capable of running large enterprises) and may even be tied to goals that are contradictory to profit maximisation (such as sales growth or industry share). Indeed, the real problem for private enterprise is that the direct bosses of the managers (the board of directors) are often managers in other companies and they may not have the proper incentives themselves to ensure profit maximisation. Meanwhile the shareholders of the corporation, when it is widely held, are so small relative to the entity that they lack power to effectively subjugate managerial intent.

Managers of public enterprises, on the other hand, usually are closely monitored by one or at most a handful of individuals and, as a result, their compensation is not only a matter of public record but also public scrutiny. Thus, their rewards are given not in terms of monetary gain but rather in terms of following the policy dictate of the political overseers in the hopes of receiving honours (such as a knighthood) or promotions (such as an ambassadorship).

Then the question comes down to whether or not the politicians are acting in the interests that have been specified. While undoubtedly it is true that they might not be, it is equally clear that significant deviations from the public trust can endanger a politician's career in a democracy. Public enterprise is increasingly about transparency, and if social goals are not being met, the press and the public have the levers to put the squeeze on errant politicians.

Furthermore, since each of these above listed goals encompasses a particular desire of public policy or is a response to market failure, it is unclear how reversion to markets will make the situation any more tolerable. If markets are the problem in the first place, the question is not whether or not the public enterprise is perfectly efficient; it is whether it is better than the market alternative.

Moreover, as Chang (2003, p. 212) notes, public servants may view themselves as being part of the 'guardian of public interests', and their preferences may be endogenously formed through traditional cultural values or social psychology. But more contradictory is that neoliberalism has been championed by politicians who are, it is claimed by neoliberalism, self-interested. In that case, if politicians are self-interested and are running public enterprises for their own personal interests rather than the public interest, and the public interest would be better served by getting rid of the public enterprise (and, correspondingly, the interests of the politicians would *not* be served by doing so), why would self-interested politicians get rid of the public enterprises in the first place?

In reality, the question of public enterprises being inefficient is not supported by the facts. South Korea, Taiwan and Singapore all have vibrant and thoroughly efficient public enterprises which can compete with the private sector without difficulty (World Bank, 1983; Amsden, 1985). Hong Kong with its Independent Commission Against Corruption (ICAC) has been highly effective in cleaning up corruption in the public sector. Indeed, one striking similarity between East Asian countries is the low level of corruption in its public sector ranks. High levels of corruption would be consistent with the notion of self-interested individuals in the public sector, but due to both social conventions and policies which ensure that public sector employees are adequately, though not extravagantly, compensated, East Asia has been able to enjoy an extremely competent civil service.

An additional indictment against public enterprises is that they do not face the rigours of the free market. Since they are usually monopolies, they have all of the various defects of private sector monopolies in that their customers have few, if any other, options. In the first instance, this argument is defective as the same is true in the case of private monopolies. Contrary to what some believe, public enterprises can be taken over and frequently are through a change in government or a rationalisation of the private sector that causes entities to merge or reorganise. They might also go bankrupt facing the additional challenge that they can be privatised. In any case, large corporations in the private sector are often not allowed to go bankrupt as the government will seek to stop contagion in the case of financial corporations or will bail out major employers so as not to cause widespread unemployment. For example, the US government bailed out Chrysler Corporation some years ago for exactly this reason. Indeed, in some ways, public enterprises may face greater pressures to perform than private enterprises. Private enterprise frequently must only answer to its own shareholders and, with widespread holdings, it may be very difficult for an individual shareholder to challenge a decision made by the corporation's managers.

Furthermore, much of the decision-making process in the private sector is shrouded in the mystery of corporate secrecy. On the other hand, public enterprise must often ensure their decision-making process is transparent. Public enterprises face increased scrutiny from the public and the media because their actions are often matters of public record and therefore the concerns of the public can be given, in the words of Hirschman (1970), 'voice'.

The supposed virtue of firm discipline through the market for corporate control (i.e., the capital market) has been the main point of the arguments for privatisation of nationalised firms in the UK. In brief, the suggestion is that even for privatised natural monopolies, where by definition the product market discipline is bound to be inadequate, the forces of competition in the capital market (principally through the takeover mechanism) will ensure efficiency. However, this line of reasoning is seriously flawed. First, there are important a priori reasons which suggest that, even in theory, the market for corporate control may not work efficiently. Second, empirical studies show that selection for survival in the market for corporate control takes place only to a limited extent on the basis of efficiency or profitability but to a far greater extent on the basis of size.

On the basis of the above findings, Singh (1971, 1975) had suggested that instead of disciplining large firms whose managers seek growth for empire building or power motives, the market for corporate control may encourage them to seek a further increase in size. Paradoxically, such large firms may be able to achieve that end through the takeover mechanism itself by acquiring smaller but relatively more profitable firms. Hence, the capital market discipline may not just be inadequate, but it may very well be perverse (Chang, 2003, pp. 214-15).

To add to these Keynesian worries which derive from the role of speculation, the volatility of stock market prices, and the fact that such prices may not be efficient, some economists suggest that the takeover mechanism may, in a number of ways, further encourage a 'short-termist' outlook on the part of management to the detriment of long-term productive investment, industrial competency, economic growth and competitiveness (Keynes, 1936; Karagiannis, 2002).

THE 'EFFICIENCY' / 'INEFFICIENCY' OF PUBLIC ENTERPRISES

This section examines the arguments and evidence which are available concerning the efficiency of public enterprises in the non-centrally-planned, mixed-economy, developing countries.

The *World Development Report* (1987) observed that the performance of state-owned enterprises varies widely between countries, but their record has frequently been poor, particularly in developing countries; they have often put large burdens on budget and external debt. Such unfavourable assessments of public enterprises and the role of the state in the economic sphere have also been echoed by some influential mainstream economists (e.g., Balassa, 1986). Similarly, Vernon (1988) suggests that privatisation today is being driven by a spirit of pragmatic reaction to at least three decades of failed experiments in public enterprise. However, the allegation that public enterprises are invariably inefficient or that most of them perform badly cannot survive even an elementary examination of facts.

Public enterprises are ubiquitous in mixed economies throughout the world – they have not simply been confined to left-wing regimes or under-developed or poorly performing countries. Indeed, aside from the relatively few communist states, there is no empirical support for the notion that public enterprises represent any sort of drag on the economy.

Massive privatisation of enterprises have never resulted in dramatic upswings in economic performance and often firms that were once privatised fall back into the hands of the government after an unsuccessful run as a private sector entity. Air Jamaica, for example, was recently rescued by the government at a cost far greater than the government originally received when it privatised the entity in the first place. At the same time, many economies that have been on the fast track for growth have done so predominantly through state-owned enterprises, including Singapore, South Korea, Taiwan, China, Austria and France. Indeed, Austria is a good case in point, being both one of the fastest growing economies in the world and yet having one of the highest concentrations of public ownership (Sawyer, 1996).

One must also recognise that private enterprise and public enterprise are not supposed to be established with the same goals in mind. If one's sole criterion for success is profit maximisation, many public sector entities may fall short of this goal. But to the extent that they seek to increase profit in the scope of some government objective function, they may be doing more from a public policy perspective to improve the state of affairs in an economy than any private firm could have done. There have been many examples of successful public enterprises as well as many examples of unsuccessful private ones.

Indeed, the choice between market intervention or *laissez-faire* is not a dichotomous one wherein either market or state has a monopoly on competency but rather one in which neither is fully competent, and we must resolve to address the problem by choosing among various imperfect alternatives. In doing so we must consider exactly what is the purpose of market intervention. If it is to serve some public policy goal in addition to or as a replacement for the profit maximisation criterion used in the private sector, then it could very well be worthwhile to do so.

Take another example. The most efficient steel company in the world is the giant Korean enterprise POSCO (Pohang Steel Company). POSCO is state-owned; it produced 467 tons of crude steel per head in 1986 compared with an average of 327 tons for Japan's five biggest steel producers. The efficiency advantage of POSCO is passed on to its Korean customers. It charges its domestic steel consumers $320 per ton – far less than American or Japanese car makers who pay $540 and $430 per ton respectively (see *The Economist*, 21 May 1988). Hence, if public enterprises are viewed as inherently poor performers, the POSCO example does raise the important analytical question – why should that be so? If POSCO is an exception, the obvious question is – what makes it so? (Chang, 2003, p. 204). Although POSCO is not a typical case, it is not that much of an exception either.

Empirical evidence on the poor performance of public enterprises relative to private firms in properly conducted comparisons – which control for the effects of industry, size, market power, age, etc. – is far from being either universal or conclusive (Wolf Jr., 1988). It must be noted here that even in countries where the public enterprise sector is not viewed as being generally successful in the mainstream accounts, there are nevertheless acknowledged outstanding cases of efficient public enterprises. In Sub-Saharan Africa, for example, notable cases of successful public enterprises include the Kenyan Tea Development Authority, the Tanzanian Electricity Supply Company Limited, the Ethiopian Telecommunications Authority and the Guma Valley Water Company of Sierra Leone (World Bank, 1983).

Yet, still privatisation calls persist and there is a general perceived bias against private enterprise. But to understand this one merely needs to look at who is calling for the changes. Most of these complaints come from the private sector, which might look at public enterprise with suspicion and even outright hostility when they must compete directly with it.

Therefore, it is unclear whether the general public really thinks much about the debate or, if it does, whether it has been unduly influenced by the temper of rhetoric emanating from the private sector. Still, the private sector has no such belief in the free market when it fails to serve its interests. One has only to witness the persistent calls for 'Buy Jamaican', 'Buy American', 'Buy Canadian', or similar buy local campaigns spearheaded by the private sector to see that firms seek to eliminate competitors through any means necessary and truly believe in a completely uncompetitive market with their firm as the sole supplier.

THE 'MARKET PRIMACY' NOTION

While neoliberals champion the market, they often forget that it is the state that created the environment upon which the embryonic market was able to develop. Prior to the Enlightenment, few, if any, of the structures that typify a free market were present in society (Xing and Hirsch, 2004). It is government that created property rights. They were not handed down by God nor were governments created in the aftermath of a free market. Rather, they were necessarily pre-existent because they solve the one vexing problem that confounds free markets: how to ensure that property rights are secured. Indeed, what neoliberals have traditionally lacked was a creation myth to go along with their beliefs. Madjd-Sadjadi (2003, p. 211) provides this for them in the form of a play on Genesis: 'In the beginning God created supply and demand . . . and no intersection was upon them. And the invisible hand moved upon the face of the waters. And God said, Let there be equilibrium: and there was equilibrium. And God saw the equilibrium, that it was good'.

Indeed, the notion that economics and, by extension, neoliberalism is religion and economists and policy-makers of the 'Washington consensus' are the high priests is carried forth in great detail by Nelson (2001). Besides, neoliberalism suffers from a problem associated with many religions: it has internal inconsistencies that can only be resolved by faith. But faith isn't science and therein lies the rub.

While neoliberalism would like to prove the inherent superiority of the market system, the market cannot survive without the state. It is completely dependent upon it for enforcing contractual obligations and for the granting of various property rights. For example, the early American book industry thrived predominantly by stealing from English book publishers. Popular books would be bought and then quickly set up on printing presses so that a new American edition could be brought out without paying a single cent in royalties (Epstein, 2002, p. 97). That the US major book publishers were originally copyright thieves may surprise people given their current stances on such matters of public accessibility of out-of-print texts.

At this point, we must emphasise that the fact that someone attributes institutional primacy to the market does not necessarily mean that he/she supports a minimal state view, as the problem here is not really about where the right 'boundary' between the state and the market should lie. There are many who start (at least implicitly) from the market supremacy assumption but are clearly aware of the failings of the market and willingly endorse a relatively wide range of government interventions. Indeed, if open-minded neoclassical economists began to take their own logic to the limit, they could end up endorsing all kinds of state intervention. However, they would still see state intervention, or for that matter any other solution based on non-market institutions, as 'man-made' substitutes for the 'natural' institution called the market (Chang, 2003, p. 91).

Economic historians have repeatedly shown that, except at the very local level (in supplying basic necessities) or in luxury trade, the market mechanism was not an important part of human economic life until recently. In fact, the emergence of markets was almost always deliberately engineered by the state, particularly in the early stages of capitalist development. Karl Polanyi's (1957) classic work shows how, even in the UK where the market economy is supposed to have emerged spontaneously, state intervention played a critical role in the process. Indeed, the road to the free market was opened and kept open by an enormous increase in continuous, centrally organised and controlled interventionism.

Also in the US case, early interventions by the state in establishing property rights, providing critical physical infrastructure, especially railways and telegraphy, or the funding of agricultural research etc., were critical for its success in early industrialisation. Even the World Bank has recently recognised this (World Bank, 1997, p. 21, Table 1.2). Most importantly, the USA was the home of the idea of 'infant industry protection', and was indeed the most heavily protected economy among the industrial countries for around a century until the Second World War (World Bank, 1991, p. 97, Table 5.2).

Looking elsewhere, we see that virtually every single country has had significant experiences with state intervention. As early as the 2nd century BC, the Chinese government instituted a supply management mechanism to ensure the supply of rice was sufficient to allow the peasantry to purchase it and yet not so ample as to destroy the incentives for farmers to produce it. Canada, France, Italy, Japan, South Korea, Hong Kong, Singapore, China, Germany and many other countries have used the levers of the state to increase the productive capacity of the nation.

These interventions range from the provision of mass transportation and affordable housing through its direct control of land allocations in Hong Kong to a nascent welfare state under Bismarck in Germany to Canada's numerous crown corporations. Indeed, since virtually all now-advanced countries developed in some 'unnatural' way, which involved heavy state intervention, it seems questionable whether there is any point in calling the market a 'natural' phenomenon. Moreover, the massive privatisations of Eastern Europe have failed to bring forth prosperity, and have instead plunged much of the area into deep recessions, rescued only by entry into the European Union, itself a non-market creation.

Yet, the establishment and distribution of property rights and other entitlements differ from society to society; so, there is no clear directive on how they could ever be thought of as 'natural' as opposed to political in nature. An individual receives standing to sue based on a defective item sold to him in one country (Canada) and fails to receive this consumer protection in another (Japan). Property rights might legitimate illegal behaviour (the Kennedy family did not have to give up their bootlegging profits after Prohibition ended) or force certain individuals to begin life with a limited endowment (the freeing of the slaves neither gave them claim to the goods and services of their former masters nor did it come with the proverbial 40 acres of land and mules supposedly granted them by the US government). Each of these institutional changes created a different society: more able to react in certain circumstances, less able in others.

Efficiency cannot be abstracted from the institutional environment in which it is present. Thus to argue that a particular distribution of property rights is correct under every set of assumptions is baseless; yet multilateral organisations and donor countries operating on the 'good governance' criterion suggest that anything that imitates the Western powers is good and anything that deviates from it is bad.

Indeed, the whole functioning of the market cannot be accomplished without political processes. Interest rates, whether determined by rule or discretion, are fundamentally political. As the joke goes, the difference between a liberal and a conservative is that the liberal is always willing to sacrifice inflation to save jobs and the conservative is always willing to do the latter. In this case, as in so many others, the economic theory that breeds neoliberalism has a tangibly conservative bent (Waligorski, 1991).

Constructing an institutionalist political economy is surely a difficult task. However, without a radical restructuring of the ways in which we conceptualise the market, the state, and politics, as well as the ways in which we analyse the relationships between them, we will not be able to overcome the neoliberal worldview, which has dominated the intellectual and political agenda of our time and has had many negative consequences.

MARKET FAILURE THEORY

Market failure is judged in neoclassical economics by one *and only one* criterion, and that is deviations from Pareto optimality. Since neoclassical economists cannot make value judgements lest they become normative (although the very concept of efficiency as paramount is laden with a value judgement), they do not judge as unacceptable *per se* deviations from a regime of perfect equality that may have harmful effects on the social structure of society. Their chief concern is to ensure that their efficiency criterion holds, and they utilise the Second Welfare Theorem in reaction to those who argue that a market mechanism produces an unjust distribution.

Simply to have a 'non-distortionary' system of income transfer, in the minds of many neoliberals, we will have to 'rob Peter to pay Paul'. Once this is achieved, everything will be better; but that is simply not the case because any form of taxation of such kind, if anticipated, will be planned for and steps will be taken to minimise exposure, while if unanticipated this risk will be factored into future tax evasion or avoidance strategies. Since tax evasion or avoidance itself consumes countless resources that result in deadweight losses to the economy, no income transfer system can truly be non-distortionary. In such cases, it may be better to use the market because of the difficulty in avoiding its grasp.

In addition, by trumpeting allocative efficiency to the exclusion of all else, neoclassical economic analysis ignores X-inefficiency: that level of inefficiency that arises not out of the inability to properly combine resources but rather the ability to properly utilise them. By trying to dismiss all trade barriers and other impediments to growth, neoclassical economics might be able to add 5 per cent or so to gross world product (GWP); but eliminating X-inefficiency could raise living standards by significantly more (Leibenstein, 1966).

Moreover, competitive markets are inherently technologically stagnant since innovation requires the protection of ideas from competitors in order to flourish. Without such protection, investment in research and development will diminish or even stop. Indeed, competitive markets are, by definition, failures according to the Schumpeterian view because they fail to provide breeding grounds for innovation. From the perspective of an institutional economist, markets may subjugate the engineer's sense of technological progress for the betterment of humanity to the price system's desire for conformity. Thus, the whole Veblenian dichotomy between instrumental behaviour that seeks to solve problems and ceremonial behaviour that seeks to maintain tradition can be seen as a tension that operates in the world of the market.

Therefore, depending on one's perspective of the market (Neoclassical, Institutional, Schumpeterian), one's perspective on market failure changes. How much does 'market failure' matter, however we may define it? The short answer is that it would matter greatly for the neoclassical economists, whereas it may not matter so much for other economists (especially the institutionalist economists). Neoclassical economic analysis is an analysis about the market mechanism or more precisely not even that; it is really about the barter exchange economy where there are, to use Coase's (1992) analogy, 'lone individuals exchanging nuts and berries on the edge of the forest'. In neoclassical theory, even the firm exists as a 'production function' and not as an 'institution of production'. Other forms of institutions that make up the modern capitalist economy (e.g., formal producer associations, informal networks, trade unions) appear only as 'rigidities' that prevent the proper functioning of markets (Chang, 2003, p. 88).

To the extent that the neoclassical economist discusses institutions, such as the firm (Williamson, 1975) and the state (Krueger, 1990), it is always couched and considered in the absence of any real power in the market. To institutional economists, the economy is a system of power (Tool and Samuels, 1980); but neoclassical economists gut these institutions of this important dimension and, instead, examine them as though they were market mechanisms devoid of any power relationship. They thus lose 'the forest for the trees' because they see institutions not in a holistic sense but rather from the narrow perspective of orthodox economics. Besides, their own biases trap them into not realising that the economy itself cannot be abstracted away from the power, whether it be condign, compensatory, or conditioned power, with only the second being recognised formally by neoclassical economists (Galbraith, 1983, pp. 4-6).

THE STATE IN DEVELOPING COUNTRIES AND THE COMMONWEALTH CARIBBEAN

Public administration in developing and less-developed countries is rooted in the colonial systems that were inherited from their colonial governments.

Indeed, the government sectors of developing and less-developed countries can be characterised as following the traditional bureaucratic model of public administration (although the model of Japan and Newly Industrialised Countries (NICs) has exhibited significant differences). These systems were based on highly centralised authorities using bureaucratic means to govern their colonies, and despite the different models of economic development followed in Africa, Asia, Latin America, the Caribbean or in the Pacific, the familiar Weberian precepts were to be found. The Weberian bureaucracy was a successful export to developed and lesser-developed countries alike. 'This approach included the various features of the best administrative practice available in the developed nations and this, naturally enough, was the traditional model of public administration' (Hughes, 1998, p. 213).

In the period following World War II, in particular, development administration for less-developed and developing countries was the most powerful institutional factor. The idea was 'to apply to [less-developed and] developing countries the administrative procedures derived from the former colonial countries' to modernise their economies and accelerate development in order to catch up with the leading ones (Hughes, 1998, p. 213).

Indeed, bureaucracies were particularly important in developing and less-developed countries (even though there is a sharp contrast between a bureaucratic state as left in the colonies and a developmental state). These bureaucracies often operated at a remove from their own societies and constituted an elite with more in common with their counterparts in the developed nations and with foreign corporations than their own people. As a result, in the less-developed and developing world, most bureaucracies served themselves and often looked after their own interests first. In fact, public administration itself has been susceptible to corruption since officials exercise a substantial amount of power. Of course, this is not limited to the less-developed and developing world since, even in developed countries, the concentration of power with technical 'experts' can lead to abuses of power.

Most social science writings in the Caribbean region in particular, like elsewhere, are in one way or another related to the structure and functions of government. The state as the centrepiece of the political system is impacted upon the domestic and international environment. Broadly and over time, emphases in the literature concerning the state have been of three kinds:

1. mainly historical accounts of the colonial origins and constitutional-administrative evolution of states;
2. contemporary studies of political opinion and electoral behaviour, treating with alignments of party, race and class, in addition to the

role of leaders and parties in managing the linkages between society and state; and
3. generalised interpretative-ideological analyses about the structures, functions, and powers of contemporary 'state systems'.

Much of the work done, essentially on constitution making, has been descriptive and has tended to assume the legitimacy and appropriateness of Westminster-style structures. But authors like Singham (1968) and Munroe (1972) have been much more analytical and critical of the relevance of the British model for political transformation in the region. Their analysis was based on the view that earlier descriptive writings had failed to locate constitutional-administrative systems within sets of socio-economic and ideological interests of the wider society. Later, studies of political attitudes and voting behaviour sought to illustrate the process of class coalition and conflict that shapes the real character of contemporary Caribbean states.

In addition, left-wing theorists argue that imperialism and the play of local class forces combine to subvert formal democracy into class rule. The main concerns of Caribbean writings are to be found in the following areas:

1. propositions concerning matters of class and the political power of classes (composition, collaboration and conflict of classes, ruling class, the political power of the petit-bourgeois class, working class or working people);
2. propositions regarding types of states or 'state systems' (such as liberal democracy or authoritarian states);
3. propositions concerning the power of states in relation to social forces; and
4. propositions relating to the ideological functions of states (such as protector of existing relations of domination).

Arising from various combinations of factors, at least three approaches to classification of states in the Caribbean can be identified:

1. bourgeois-democracy, national-democratic regimes and socialist states (Munroe, 1986);
2. liberal-democracy, authoritarian states and socialist-democratic states (Thomas, 1984); and
3. democratic-pluralist states, authoritarian states and popular-statistic regimes (Stone, 1986).

Clearly, most of the existing states could be classified under the one or other of the categories depending on the classifier's view. Thomas's (1984) 'liberal democracy' equates with Stone's (1986) 'democratic pluralism', both stressing political rights of association, expression and election as fundamentals. By contrast, the traditional Marxist-Leninist view emphasises the hegemony of the international bourgeoisie over both local economy and state, in the interest of the survival of private capitalist relations of production.

The Westminster model, in particular, adopts an outlook which tends towards conserving status quo interests within the social system. According to Stone (1986), a strong emphasis on order, stability and unity makes such a state naturally conservative and often a natural enemy of the working class and the underclasses, resulting in social revolution or anti-colonial movements where a political vanguard leadership seeks to protect the interests of the majority classes as the main priority.

A key task of state development in the post-Independent Caribbean has been the development of functional state institutions capable of undertaking expanded and more complex policy and administrative functions. These functions raise the crucial issue of the technical-managerial competence of states in relation to their capacity to carry out any selected ideological programme. Technical competence is indifferent to ideology, even though competent personnel are hardly devoid of ideological dispositions. Studies of the sociology of bureaucracy in the Caribbean have shown how civil administrations have been infected not only by excessive proceduralism but also by class and colonial values which inhibit the success of transformative programmes.

Moreover, the political, bureaucratic and military capabilities of states are the dimensions along which their overall strength or power are to be evaluated. One of the fundamental concerns of theory is the extent to which states may be relatively strong or weak *vis-à-vis* domestic and international forces with which they have to contend. The concepts of 'sovereignty', 'over-development' and 'relative autonomy' have been applied to measure the strength of states. They cover both domestic and international aspects of the environment of classes and interests surrounding the operations of the state in peripheral societies. However, discussions of the capacity of states to exercise relative autonomy in the Caribbean context have neglected the dimension of relative size in demographic and resource terms.

At the other end, the smallest states in the Eastern Caribbean area are even more deficient in resource endowments and administrative capacity. There are also greater levels of dependency that seem to amount more to differences of kind than of degree. In these smallest states, greater state intervention in the local economy was followed by even greater state ineffectiveness.

At present, the central factor governing the world of nations is their division into a super-ordinate state system and a sub-ordinate state system, in which technological domination is decisive. In essence, there are two dynamic forces at work, which undermine the sovereignty of Caribbean states. First, the generalised acceptance of the programme of 'investment by invitation' means that the political elites perceive their main function as securing political and social stability, and creating an atmosphere conducive to even greater investment. Second, the spread of transnational corporate power is a major threat to small nation-states in the Caribbean in terms of both power and policy space. These dynamic forces are therefore extremely important challenges facing Caribbean nation-states at the turn of the century.

2. The Role of the State and Government Expenditure

In recent years, the capitalist state has experienced continual growth. One of the most remarkable changes which has occurred in industrialised capitalist economies during the twentieth century has been the growth of both the scale and range of state activities. In every single one of the OECD countries, government receipts and outlays, as a percentage of the gross domestic product (GDP), increased dramatically between 1960 and 1985. But since then, most governments have tried to arrest the growth of government expenditure. The growth rate varies considerably between countries over time. For example, in the USA, government outlays have increased from 27 per cent of GDP in 1960 to 36.7 per cent in 1985; in the Netherlands, from 33.7 per cent to 60.2 per cent; in Japan, from 18.3 per cent to 32.7 per cent; in the UK, from 32.3 per cent to 47.8 per cent (in 1984); and in Sweden, from 31.0 per cent to 64.5 per cent, the highest in the OECD countries (Mueller, 1989, p. 322).

The state plays a central role in the provision of public goods and contributes to economic and social development. All societies, from those organised under *laissez-faire* principles to those organised under socialism, require a public sector because the market mechanism cannot perform all economic functions desired by households. The market alone cannot satisfy all consumers needs and fails entirely in the provision of public goods. In macroeconomic theory, there is a lot of debate about the impact of the level of public expenditure (and taxation) on the level of economic activity, and the relative efficacy of fiscal and monetary policy in the achievement of the objectives of government macroeconomic policy (Sawyer, 1989, p. 298).

The first main section of this chapter provides some features of the state and different approaches related to state activity. The following sections discuss a variety of theories related to the role and impact of government expenditure as well as important social and political notions surrounding this expenditure.

STATE AND PUBLIC SECTOR: AN HISTORICAL OVERVIEW

According to the market failure approach (Pitelis, 1991a, p. 325), the state exists because of market failure. On the one hand, evidence cannot support a general preference for markets only; but on the other hand, there is no answer to the question as to where the economic borders of the state ought to lie. Although the nature of the state has not been given a great deal of attention by orthodox analysis, there have been close links between certain areas of conventional economics and the role of the state. Discussions about the role of the state in market economies go back as far as Adam Smith (1776). In his view, the duty of the state was to protect its citizens from external threats, from oppression by each other, and to provide public works and institutions that were not profitable for individuals to undertake. The state should guarantee property rights, provide for defence, keep law and order, and maintain the value of the currency. For Smith, redistribution of income was largely left to charity and the raising of revenue was restricted, in the main, to customs and excise, monopoly and commodity taxation. Although his name is normally associated with the theory of markets, Smith sets out the functions of the state as he saw them to be:

> According to the system of natural liberty, the sovereign has only three duties to attend to, three duties of great importance, indeed, but plain and intelligible to common understanding: first, the duty of protecting the society from the violence and invasion of other independent societies; second, the duty of protecting, as far as possible, every member of society from the injustice or oppression of every other member of it, or the duty of establishing an exact administration of justice; and third, the duty of erecting and maintaining certain public works and certain public institutions, which it can never be for the interest of any individual, or small number of individuals, to erect and maintain because the profit could never repay the expense of any individual or small number of individuals, though it may frequently do much more than repay it to a great society. (*The Wealth of Nations*, 1961, IV ix. 51)

Smith's rejection of state intervention in the market did not mean that the state had no role to play, or that political economy was indifferent to the state. On the contrary, the purpose of Smith's analysis of the economic system was to define the proper role of the state. Smith criticised vigorously the commercial, fiscal and financial policies of the state, but this did not lead him to criticise the political constitution of the contemporary state. Buchanan (1949, 1975), following Smith, refers to the collective wants, which could be taken to include defence, justice, law, order and delineation and enforcement of property rights as well as the provision of public goods (Buchanan, 1975, pp. 21-6).

Neoclassical Analysis

Neoclassical economic theory views the state's activities as limited to cases of correcting market failure. One type of market failure recognised by neoclassical economists is the provision of public goods. A public good is defined as a good that is both non-rivalrous and non-excludable.

A non-rivalrous good is one where the consumption of a good by one consumer does not preclude its consumption by another. An apple is a rivalrous good. If one person eats an apple, another person cannot. On the other hand, the light of the sun is non-rivalrous. The fact that one person is enjoying the light of the sun does not preclude others from using it as well. Public goods have an ethereal nature to them as opposed to a physical nature. One result of this is that public goods are goods for which the marginal cost of supplying an extra unit to any particular consumer may be zero.

Non-excludability means that one cannot easily stop an individual from consuming the good or service. The degree of excludability will determine whether a good is considered to be a 'club good' (where the good is non-rivalrous but excludable) or a 'public good'. For example, a TV station that broadcasts over the air in an unencrypted manner cannot exclude anyone who owns a TV but a cable TV broadcast can be scrambled so that it cannot be received by anyone who lacks an authorising descrambling device. The former case is an example of a public good, while the latter is an example of a club good. Club goods are not considered examples of market failures but the inability to exclude those who fail to pay for provision of a good, coupled with the non-rivalrous nature of the public good, combine to ensure that the Pareto optimal amount of a public good will not be provided by the private sector except under very specialised circumstances.

Many goods are supplied by the public sector as well (e.g., education), but are not public goods because they lack these two characteristics. Indeed, some public goods are supplied by the private sector; typically, they are not provided in sufficient quantities without government support. Therefore, it is important not to confuse the term public goods with goods supplied by the public sector (which also include merit goods), those supplied by nationalised industries, and so on. Thus the concept of public goods, in contrast to private goods, is an attempt to explain at least part of the range of activities undertaken by governments by arguing that the market will fail to provide public goods in the way in which private goods are provided (Sawyer, 1989, p. 306). However, the nature of the degree of under-provision and how much *ought* to be provided is the subject of debate among neoclassical economists, and some economists have even decried the concept that the private sector cannot provide a proper amount of public goods on its own. The former problem is found in the definitions of marginal cost by three different authorities. Musgrave argues the marginal cost is equal to the sum of individual prices. Bowen and Samuelson state the marginal cost is equal to the sum of marginal rates of substitution. Buchanan contends the marginal cost is equal to the sum of marginal valuations. If these three values do not add up to the same result, the 'proper' amount that the civil authorities should provide will be in doubt. Still, Coase (1974) argues that the 'classic' example of a public good, the lighthouse, does not imply market failure and that the British lighthouse system, which relies on 'light dues', paid by ships that dock at British ports is an example of how public goods can be provided by the private sector. His analysis does not preclude the rationale of public provision of some public goods but does serve to call into question the *necessity* of government action in the case of lighthouses.

Neoclassical analysis also assumes that the aim of the state is to maximise the utility of the consumers (the public). At one level, the state is seen as operating in the public's interest, which is often discussed in terms of some defined objectives such as the maximisation of social welfare (Ng, 1983, pp. 279-82). States grow because the demand for their services by consumers increases, which explains the growth of the government sector in market economies. Other important reasons for market failure are the following:

1. the existence of externalities which give rise to a divergence between social and private benefits and, consequently, Pareto efficiency cannot be achieved even in the presence of perfectly competitive markets (Arrow, 1963, 1970); and
2. the presence of oligopolistic or monopolistic market structures, which implies the absence of perfect competition and thus the possibility of prices exceeding competitive prices.

In the presence of distortions in markets, states will be faced with second best situations and a first best optimum will not be attainable (Lancaster and Lipsey, 1956, p. 12).

Neoclassical theory indicates substantial intervention by governments to correct externalities and restrain monopolies in order to try and create the nirvana of general equilibrium. However, even in these cases, neoclassical economists have disagreed as to the viability of private provision in all cases and therefore have ventured towards more extreme infatuation with private market provision. Positive externalities, for example, exist where social benefit exceeds private benefit. The classic example of a positive externality is the beekeeper and the farmer. Each receives a benefit from the provision of the other's good and neoclassical theory traditionally argues that there will be underprovision of both flowers and bees because the benefits are not distributed in such a form as that they all accrue to the provider of the good or service. Similarly, negative externalities, such as pollution, exist when private benefit exceeds social benefit and economic theory would suggest that too much pollution would exist. However, economists such as Coase (1960) and Cheung (1973) have argued that both types of externalities can be rectified through the market mechanism.

Even in the case of monopoly, some economists suggest that the possibility of entry can deter monopolies from acting in an egregious form (Schumpeter, 1942; Baumol, 1982). Furthermore, the source of monopoly is often seen as being the responsibility of government in the first place. Thus, neoclassical economics commits itself to a small state, even as it carves out limited exceptions that might be seen as possibly providing the basis for government action. Yet, these exceptions are increasingly being challenged from within neoclassical economics itself. They are thus coming closer to the views espoused by New Right economic theorists.

New Right Views

New Right economic theory (i.e., the Austrian approach, the Public Choice view and Monetarism) recommends a free market, as left to itself; the market economy has a self-correcting mechanism, which does not involve macroeconomic instability (Pitelis, 1987, 1991a; Sawyer, 1989, 1990, 1992). The New Right views governments with suspicion and argues that there is little that governments can do which is beneficial, as its intervention into market operations is usually harmful.

The Austrian approach is an extreme *laissez-faire* view. Hayek (1944, pp. 25-8) advanced the view that the expansion of state activities is the 'road to serfdom'. The basis of his argument is that state activity combines legal coercion with a monopoly supply; therefore, the power of the state over individual behaviour is enhanced. The market is seen to promote individual freedom and economic efficiency and the state is viewed as restricting (at least eventually) liberty and undermining efficiency. The appropriate role of the state is seen to be a minimal one, often being restricted to the provision of defence and a legal framework. The Public Choice view supports the fact that the state is not operated in the social interest, but is managed by politicians and bureaucrats for the maximisation of their own personal interests such as salaries, promotion prospects, and the size of the budget and staff, which they control. In effect, members of the bureaucracy are interested in its expansion, which builds in a basic tendency for the size of governments to expand. This maximisation of personal interests is considered as the main reason for the growth of the state, and it also helps to generate a political business cycle whereby employment and output are stimulated prior to an election (Buchanan, 1984, pp. 16-21). This school of thought thus argues that the state cannot effectively correct market failure because of systemic issues that result in government failure. New Right theory criticises the concept of a disinterested state operating in the social interest and the Public Choice School rejects the neoclassical assumption that states have no interests other than those of their citizens, whose collective will they reflect.

Keynesian Analysis

For Keynes, the distinguishing characteristic of the state was motive. State action is related to those decisions, which are not made if the state does not make them. The Keynesian approach recognises that the market system is not necessarily self-correcting (Keynes, 1936, pp. 25-6) but it can be saved from collapse by a little guidance and support from the state (Keynes, 1936, p. 89). The government should inject aggregate demand into the economy when there are signs of slack and recession, but restrain demand when inflation threatens (this does not involve interfering directly in markets). So, aggregate demand management is the Keynesian solution to stabilising the economy (*Collected Writings*, VII p. 19; XXIX p. 80 and p. 215).

Keynesian interventionism does not involve any significant extension of the power of the government over private capital, but only a closer coordination of the independent investment plans of the private and public sectors in which public investment is more closely tailored to the needs of the private sector. On the other hand, it sometimes envisages a much greater role for the state in the regulation of wages. The main role of the state is to influence aggregate demand in order to achieve a full employment equilibrium that would not necessarily be achieved by a complete unfettered market system.

Keynes saw unemployment as a deficiency of demand. At the macroeconomic level, the classic failure for a closed economy was the potential failure of coordination between the savings decisions of households on the one hand, and the investment decisions of firms on the other. Keynes (1936) concluded that, 'Apart from the necessity of central controls to bring about an adjustment between the propensity to consume and the inducement to invest, there is no more reason to socialise economic life than there was before.'

Changes in government expenditure and taxes bring about changes in output and income. Government expenditure adds directly to the level of aggregate demand in the economy, as an increase in government spending means an increase in aggregate demand. The Keynesian analysis supports the view that by controlling the level of aggregate demand for goods and services in the economy, the government can exert a large influence over the economy, and it suggests that the most effective way of doing this is to employ a fiscal policy. Thereby, the government obtains nearly all its revenue by levying personal income taxes, company income taxes and indirect taxes and it may be seen as a spender, investor and income redistributor. Consequently, the size of the government budget is of great importance, for the larger the budget, the larger the impact on the economy, and vice versa.

The multiplier has also been at the heart of the Keynesian analysis. The value of the multiplier is influenced by fiscal variables. Fiscal changes are capable of influencing an open economy's income or GDP fluctuation in a manner that compensates for any adverse change in exports and imports. Moreover, the value of the multiplier is influenced by many other factors, for example, even though income is high, considerable excess capacity may reduce induced investment; the distribution of income may raise or lower it; and international transactions, monetary policy, policy-makers priorities, etc. may also exert an influence.

Different types of government expenditure may have different effects on the GDP and its growth rate. Governments devote a substantial amount of their resources to educational development and health services, which improve the quality of human resources and are an essential ingredient of a quality life. Both education and health are very important components of human capital, which plays an important role in the process of growth and development. Human resource development has an important bearing on economic growth and development and investment in human resources helps to accelerate economic growth. In a fast-changing global economy, the skills of labour are a very important means of production. Housing satisfies a basic human need and a lack of housing creates important social problems. In terms of the objectives of insurance, income support, and redistribution, social security is very important.

Marxian Approaches

In Marxist theory, the state exists in order to ensure the maintenance of the capitalist mode of production. The objective of the dominant class in this system (capitalists) is to derive maximum possible profits. States exist and grow because capitalists' needs for state functions increase. In the Marxian tradition, the growth of state expenditure is viewed in terms of capitalism's laws of motion. According to Marxists, the following three broad functions of the state exist (Sawyer, 1989, p. 318):

1. Accumulation: the accumulative role of the state is to preserve and reinforce the conditions for profits; capitalism is only viable as an economic system if profitable accumulation is possible.

2. Legitimation-repression: the legitimate role of the state is to maintain social order and control, which includes conditioning and persuading workers to accept the capitalist system.
3. Social reproduction: the capitalist class needs well-educated and healthy workers.

Within the Marxian framework, the state has no general determination. The theoretical issues relating to the capitalist state are not combined into a single, coherent theory but summarise the various ideas which recur in the writings of Karl Marx, Friedrich Engels and Vladimir Lenin. Miliband (1969, p. 7) notes that Marx himself 'never attempted a systematic study of the state'.

The modern state (and its expenditures) can only be explained by locating them in relation to the historical development of capitalism. In capitalist society, the state has to be seen in relation to the reproduction and accumulation of capital, and to the class relations of workers and capitalists (Poulantzas, 1980, pp. 35-6). Capitalist class influence on state policy is also fostered by certain widely shared ideas and beliefs, which tend to coordinate state decisions in a line favourable to the class interests of capital. In extreme cases in advanced capitalist countries, and routinely in underdeveloped countries, capitalist influence on state policies is exercised through coercion, violence and sabotage (Baran and Sweezy, 1967, pp. 179-83).

Furthermore, Poulantzas (1980, p. 167) argues that the agenda for state action and the major pressures on state policy bring 'the state increasingly to bear on the heart of the reproduction of capital'. Poulantzas (1980, p. 168) goes on to argue 'its economic functions are directly articulated to the specific rhythm of the accumulation and reproduction of capital'. On the other hand, 'the capital accumulation process directly dictates the rhythm of state activity' (Poulantzas, 1980, p. 169).

While capitalists in general, and large capital in particular, are seen as having a generally decisive advantage in their conflicts with the working classes, there is no reason that the state and its policies should be reduced to a simple expression of the dominance of the capitalist class or one fraction of it in modern society (Poulantzas, 1980, pp. 127-9). Jessop (1987, pp. 75-6) writes that the mechanisms through which classes struggle over state policy are complex and historically specific, and the particularity of those mechanisms plays a real role in determining the outcomes.

Marx and Engels (1848) were emphatic: 'The executive of the modern state is but a committee for managing the common affairs of the whole bourgeoisie'. Jessop (1977) distinguished six different approaches in the traditional Marxist thought:

1. The state as a *parasitic institution*: The state becomes the private property of its officials who further their own interests, favouring particular sectional groups at the expense of the common interest.
2. The state and state power as an *epiphenomena* (i.e., simple surface reflections) of the system of property relations and the resulting class struggles.
3. The state as *a factor of cohesion*, with the function of regulating class conflict and using the techniques of repression and concession in a way which mediates but does not undermine the rule of capital.
4. The state as *an instrument of class rule*, which is often assumed to be neutral and capable of being used by any class.
5. The state as *a set of institutions or public power* which develops at a certain stage of the division of labour, and which is characterised by a distinct system of government involving officials who specialise in administration and/or repression.
6. The state as *a system of political domination* which conditions the results of class struggle through the forms of state intervention and of political representation which are adopted.

The Welfare State

The roots of the concept of the Welfare State go back far into the past, and the scale and nature of the Welfare State, at a particular time in a particular country, reflect the outcome of the interaction of economic, social and political pressures. During the nineteenth century, the general prevalence of *laissez-faire* beliefs (in the virtues of free enterprise and free competition) was unfavourable to the development of welfare services and, consequently, there was general hostility to government intervention in the working of the economy. However, a number of factors led towards a more positive attitude towards state action for social welfare and this constituted the foundations of the Welfare State in the first decades of the twentieth century. These included the rapid rise of the population, industrialisation and urbanisation, the needs of an industrial society for education and health, an experience of the inadequacy of the market to provide for urgent social needs, pressures for greater equality, the recognition of social rights to welfare services, etc. (Sleeman, 1973, pp. 10-14).

The design of the Welfare State is based on a number of theories that were developed in the interwar years and concepts of the state that are particularly relevant in the area of welfare economics (Ng, 1983, pp. 240-41). The term Welfare State came into general use in the years after World War II to describe the government's responsibility for the provision of social services in order to positively promote the welfare of all its citizens (Johansson, 1991, pp. 61-8). After World War II, the two main aims of governments were state intervention in industry and a macroeconomic role for the state in coordinating individual behaviour. The third aim was the government's commitment to guaranteeing a minimum standard of living for the poor via the Welfare State and providing the basic social primary goods (education, public health, social security, pensions, etc.). Therefore, social expenditure was a significant part of government spending after World War II, in both Europe and the USA (Helm, 1989, pp. 27-31).

Until the mid-1980s, the perceived macroeconomic role of the state tended to expand and represented, in part, responses to new problems that arose in the immediate postwar years. According to Sleeman (1973, pp. 14-22), the reasons for state intervention in the welfare field were:

1. the inability of private welfare organisations to carry the entire burden, particularly in times of depression;
2. the difficulty of achieving equitable treatment of all the victims of poverty through private channels;
3. the absence of organised relief agencies in rural areas;
4. the inverse relationship between income and the incidence of social and economic risks associated with modern industrial life, with the result that those most likely to be at risk can least afford to protect themselves through private savings and private insurance;
5. the influence of egalitarian ideas;
6. growing recognition of the fact that poverty and slum conditions entail social costs for the entire community; and
7. other factors, such as the influence of Keynesian economics.

The new welfare economics pointed towards a positive set of rather simple criteria (based on widely acceptable value judgments) to provide a rationale for the Welfare State and intervention as a mechanism for the achievement of social justice.

Overall, mainstream economic analysis assumes that social interest and social welfare can be measured using techniques like cost-benefit analysis, and that the state may intervene to correct cases of market failure. Within a lot of macroeconomic analysis (particularly that of the Keynesian variety) the role of the state can be described as 'the puller of levers' (Sawyer, 1989, p. 307). As the discussion about the Welfare State suggests, its scale and nature at a particular time in a particular country may reflect the outcome of the interaction of economic, political and social pressures. Sawyer (1989, p. 331) argues, 'Many aspects of the welfare state represent a replacement of the market and the market ethos (allocation according to the ability to pay) by non-market mechanisms and an ethos of allocation according to need'.

From a Marxist perspective, the fundamental intent and effect of social welfare programmes is to expand productivity, production and profits and to maintain capitalist profitability. Moreover, an analysis of the state cannot be undertaken in a historical vacuum but it should include a discussion about the social and political background against which a specific state operates.

STATE ACTIVITIES AND PUBLIC EXPENDITURE

During the 20th century, the general trend has been for the role of the state to change from one which largely involved defence and the maintenance of law and order into an involvement with extensive income transfers (through the welfare state), the provision of social services, and the ownership of production facilities (nationalised industries). The market appears to have failed to deliver an adequate performance in a number of crucial areas. Thus, state activity increased and was able to achieve much that was not possible through the market mechanism. For example, the transport of goods requires the provision of roads, but the private provision of roads is generally unprofitable (not least because of the difficulties of charging for use) (Sawyer, 1989, p. 297).

The notion of public goods does not provide an adequate explanation for the size and growth of the public sector, since public goods are an important part of any economy. Government expenditure reflects the policy choices of governments and represents the costs of carrying out these policies. In other words, public or government expenditure can be defined as all outlays from the fiscal budget. As they appear in the national accounts,[1] government expenditures are represented by the following two main categories of government activity. First, there are exhaustive public expenditures, which correspond to the government's purchases of current goods and services (i.e., wages and salaries, consumables, etc.) and capital goods and services (i.e., government investments in roads, schools, hospitals, etc.). Exhaustive public expenditures are claims on the resources of the economy and their use by the public sector precludes use by other sectors. Second, there are transfer payments (i.e., public expenditures on pensions, unemployment benefits, subsidies, etc.). These expenditures do not represent a claim on the society's resources by the public sector, as is the case with exhaustive government expenditures. Instead, transfers are a redistribution of resources between individuals in society, with the resources flowing through the government sector as intermediary (Brown and Jackson, 1990, pp. 160-61).

The OECD study provides the following classification of public sector activities (such as reflected in government expenditure):

1. defence and general public services (justice, law, order, etc.);

2. education, health, housing, community and social services (many of which have a strong income maintenance component);
3. pensions, sickness benefits, unemployment compensation, family allowance; and
4. public debt interest in addition to various economic services not included elsewhere.

Three main fiscal functions are conventionally regarded as comprising stabilisation policy, allocation policy (e.g., externalities, property rights, decreasing cost industries, etc.), and distribution policy (e.g., distribution of income, redistribution policy). By conventional budget and GDP measures, the government's role in the allocation and reallocation of resources has increased considerably over the last century, and the growth shows no sign of abating. The public expenditure/GDP ratio is a variable of prime analytic interest.

During the second half of the twentieth century, this ratio increased for most OECD and EC countries (OECD, *National Accounts*, various years; OECD, *Historical Statistics 1960-1990*; and OECD, *Economic Outlook*, various issues). Major increases can be seen to arise from the growth of transfer payments by the government. About half of a typical developed country's public expenditure in the mid-1990s went on direct transfers (OECD,*Basic Statistics: International Comparisons*, various years; OECD, *Economic Outlook*, various issues; and OECD, *National Accounts*, various years).

There are evidently good reasons why the size of the public sector is a subject of constant controversy. Public expenditures are a large proportion of GDP and the corresponding tax burden affects everybody in the society. State activities arise for both ideological reasons and from governments' attempts to deal with allocative and distributional market inefficiencies. Therefore, governments provide public and quasi-public goods along with transfer payments. Below is an examination of some of views and models that are related to the growth of government.

The Organic State View

Adolf Wagner was concerned with explaining the share of GDP taken up by the government sector, and this has been formalised in what is referred to as Wagner's law of expanding state activity. We will follow Musgrave's interpretation and refer to Wagner's law as an expression of the growth of the relative size of the public sector. In Wagner's own words (Musgrave and Peacock, 1958, p. 8):

> The law of increasing expansion of public and particularly state activities becomes for the fiscal economy the law of the increasing expansion of fiscal requirements. Both the state's requirements grow and, often even more so, those of local authorities, when administration is decentralised and local government well organised.

The basis of Wagner's statement was empirical as he recognised that when an economy became industrialised, public sector services (like legal services, police services and banking services) become necessary. In other words, the development of an industrialised economy is accompanied by a rising share of public expenditure in GDP.

The growth of government expenditure on education, health and welfare services, recreation and culture was explained by Wagner in terms of their income elasticity of demand. For Wagner, these services represented superior or income-elastic needs. Thus, as real incomes in the economy rise, public expenditure on these services rises more than in proportion, which would account for the rising ratio of government expenditure to GDP.

Wagner's law of expanding state activity concentrates upon a demand side explanation of government expenditure growth. In the crudest terms, Wagner's law is viewed as implying an income elasticity of government expenditure greater than 1 and furthermore, that government services are to be regarded as luxuries in that sense. Government expenditure, at least in industrialising countries, often tends to increase at a faster rate than output, and Wagner argued that social progress brings increased state activity, which in turn means more government expenditure. He gave three reasons for this growth of state activity. First, economic and industrial development requires more police and legal services resources. Second, new technology creates the need for large amounts of capital in production, which can only be provided by state banks to those who have the best investment opportunities. Finally, society demands health and education services. Thus, the state is assumed to grow like an *organism*, making decisions on behalf of its citizens. Besides, an important role is given to the rise in population density, whilst some empirical studies (Baumol, 1967; Dunne, 1992, 1993; among others) often lead to a consideration of a relative price effect on (changes of) public expenditure.

Moreover, a tax has an impact on aggregate demand which, as a result, influences the level of economic activity. Taxes are an integral part of a government's fiscal policy being used to stabilise aggregate demand. Wagner supported the view that taxes must be used to obtain revenues in order to finance public expenditure (in research, the estimate of taxation as a proportion of GDP is commonly used).

Bird (1971, p. 3) has pointed out that Wagner's law can be regarded as 'a positive theory of an expansion of cultural and welfare expenditures'. An alternative view of Wagner's law lays emphasis on 'the transformation of the traditional society into the industrialised society with its contemporaneous shift from the family to the public sector of education, health and elderly care etc' (Lybeck, 1988, p. 30).

The Political Constraints Model

Peacock and Wiseman (1967, 1979) founded their analysis upon a political theory of government expenditure determination, namely 'that governments like to spend more money, that citizens do not like to pay more taxes, and that governments need to pay some attention to the wishes of their citizens'. Their 'displacement-concentration hypothesis' (1967, p. 25) implies that an increasingly centralised state produces a large and growing government expenditure. This hypothesis is based on a statistical study that showed that government expenditure rises rapidly during wartime. Factors such as wars and other uncertainties create a break or 'displacement' in the pattern of government spending and taxation. The authors argue that during periods of war, the government is able to increase taxation to fund its defence spending; however, after a war, the government does not reduce the level of taxation to its pre-war levels. People get used to paying higher taxes and, hence, governments are given a larger budget to produce goods and services that people did not necessarily vote for. The displacement effect (created by such shocks) leads to a break between tax and public goods and this divergence is narrowed by large scale 'social disturbances', such as major wars. Consequently, a divergence may emerge between ideas of desirable expenditure on the one hand and tolerable levels of taxation on the other. The authors argue that such a disturbance must also be explained in relation to changes in government attitudes and ideas (1967, p. 67).

Bird (1970, 1972) and Musgrave (1969) have both questioned the long-run significance of Peacock and Wiseman's displacement effect. Moreover, the increases in government expenditure of the 1960s and 1970s do not easily fit into a theory of social disturbance.

Leviathan and Micro Models

Discussions about the determination of the optimum level of public goods or the growth of government are far from new. Terms such as the political bargaining process, marginal-equilibrium analysis, the Pareto criteria and others have been widely used by different views or schools. As far back as 1896, Wicksell examined the mechanisms of political decisions and argued that none of them could satisfy the Pareto criterion, because they express the preferences of one or more groups against other(s). Assuming that the distribution of income is fair, the Pareto criteria may only be satisfied when there is general agreement among different social groups, which is almost impossible in practice. Lindahl (1919) looked more closely at the relationship between efficiency norms and political decision-making, and supported the view that the contributory share of each social group to the cost of production of a public good plays the same role as prices in the market. This is what makes the supply and demand of such public goods equal to each other and determines their quantity, for which all the social groups should be in agreement. Downs (1957) supported the view that collective decisions for the production of public goods do not usually satisfy the Pareto criteria. Political parties (due to political competition) present optimum programmes and society can reach an optimum position if the political party in power keeps its promises. However, Downs argued that such a solution seems to be unrealistic due to a lack of public information. The preference of consumers for private and/or public goods is affected by monopolies, which advertise private goods while consumers or voters tend to underestimate the benefits of public goods. Downs also argued that the budget may be too small in a democracy; hence, collective decisions, which are made through various political mechanisms, lead to levels of production of public goods which are lower than the optimum level (Galbraith, 1987, pp. 180-87).

Wicksell's work provided the basis for some of the later theoretical and empirical developments, and a number of scientists examined the behaviour of bureaucrats in addition to that of voters. In this respect, the Public Choice view is rooted in the tradition that was established by Wicksell. Public Choice has been defined by Mueller (1979, p. 1) as follows:

> The economic study of non-market decision making is simply the application of economics to political science. [The research agenda of neoclassical public choice theory is concerned with designing or explaining the mechanisms through which individuals make collective choices. The theoretical premises of public choice theory are precisely those of individual private decision-making.] Its subject matter is the same as that of political science: the theory of the state, voting rules, voter behaviour, party politics and the bureaucracy. Its methodology is that of economics, however.

The interaction of voters, politicians and bureaucrats together produces final outputs (in terms of the levels and mixes of public outputs and taxes). Buchanan and Tullock (1962) both argued that the activities of pressure groups can result in an overexpansion of the size of the public sector, while Tullock (1982) alone emphasised the role of voters and politicians in a government, since the voting process connects the public and politicians. The authors examined the majority principle, which is an important feature of political democracies, and argued that it directs collective decisions to the production of public goods at higher levels than the optimum one (according to Pareto efficiency). This happens as a result of compromises and agreements between different groups; consequently, the public sector produces too much output and there is an overexpansion of government expenditures (i.e., the production of public goods exceeds their optimum level). The benefits of government expenditure are enjoyed by particular groups, whereas taxation is general. The authors concluded that political votes (and the bureaucratic state) have significant weaknesses; and the market mechanism, although not perfect, is more efficient, reliable and preferable than any political mechanism or the state, which, in general, is more likely to perform worse than the market mechanism. Therefore, an improvement in efficiency can be achieved from a reallocation of resources from the public to the private sector.

In a rather similar vein, the political business cycle approach (Nordhaus, 1975; Frey and Schneider, 1978) emphasises attempts by governments to bribe the electorate just before an election through changes in both public expenditure and taxation. The key proposition about political business cycles is that economic activity tends to revolve around election dates, with governments seeking favourable economic outcomes just prior to an election and postponing unfavourable outcomes to after it. Nordhaus (1975) focused on the short-run trade-off between inflation and unemployment. In the Nordhaus model, the electorate was assumed to only be concerned about the level of unemployment and the rate of inflation, and the government elected depended on the outcome of these two variables. Immediately after an election, the government follows economic policies to raise the level of unemployment which, in turn, lowers the rate of inflation and depresses inflationary expectations (in accordance with Phillips curve).

In some of the more recent work, the emphasis has been placed on interest group activity. Mueller and Murrell (1985, pp. 125-45) found a positive relationship between the number of interest groups and the scale of state activity whilst Lindbeck (1985, p. 310) suggested that 'fragmented horizontal redistributions' lead to vote trading and that such vote trading has some bearing on the growth of government. 'When such activity is small group specific, then the average tax costs relative to the benefits may be small' (Hadjimatheou and Tackie, 1992, p. 70). In Mueller's explanation of government growth, bureaucratic power and the state can both be seen within a framework where the state is placed above the citizens and only the preferences of the state or of the individuals in the government are decisive (Mueller, 1989, p. 344).

Pigou (1928), Dalton (1936), Samuelson (1954) and others all used marginal analysis to determine the optimum level of public goods. According to Samuelson's rule (which is a general equilibrium model or a neoclassical generalisation of the earlier views of Wicksell and Lindahl), public goods should be provided up to the point where the marginal costs are equal to the sum of marginal benefits to individual consumers.

Other scientists have emphasised either the relative price effect or the degree of centralisation to explain public expenditure growth. The work of Baumol (1967) led to a consideration of the relative price effect in studies of government expenditure growth. The Baumol formulation (Baumol and Oates, 1975) can be adapted in the following way. Let the output of the government *Got* be produced at a constant level of labour productivity *Lgt*, where *t* is a time subscript. Productivity in the private sector *Lpt* will rise exponentially (where *r* denotes growth rate) also producing exponential growth in output in the private sector *Pot*. Then:

$$Got = aLgt \tag{2.1}$$
$$Pot = bLpt(1+r)t \tag{2.2}$$

The ratio of government output to total output *Not* is represented by the formula:

$$Got/Not = aLgt/aLgt+bLpt\ (1+r)t \tag{2.3}$$

where $Not = Got+Pot$.

If one assumes that public expenditure on goods and services *Get* is equal to the labour costs of producing government output and that the wage rate *w* is the same in both the public and private sector, the correspondingly private expenditure on goods and services *Pet* will be equal to the labour costs of the producing output. Consequently,

$$Get = wLgt \tag{2.4}$$

$$Pet = wLpt \tag{2.5}$$

Again, the ratio of government expenditure to total expenditure *Net* can be expressed as follows:

$$Get/Net = (wLgt)/w(Lgt+Lpt) = Lgt/(Lgt+Lpt) \tag{2.6}$$

If one further assumes that the labour supply is constant, *L* will be equal to *Lgt+Lpt*.

From Equation 2.3 it follows that as $t \to \infty$ then, with a constant labour supply, the only way in which the ratio of government output to total output can be maintained constant is by transferring labour from the private to the public sector. However, in the process of doing so, given the assumptions of the model, then with an equal wage rate *w* the ratio of government spending to total expenditure must rise. This proposition is clear from Equation 2.6

for, as $t \rightarrow \infty$ then Lgt increases while $Lgt+Lpt = L$ is constant. In other words, if government goods and services (in real terms) are to remain as even a fixed proportion of total goods and services (in real terms), public expenditure as a proportion of the total expenditure must rise through time.

Baumol's theory of unbalanced growth is the modern counterpart of Wagner's law of increased state activity. According to Levitt and Joyce (1987, pp. 7-8), the Baumol formulation postulates the existence and importance of the relative price effect.

The role of the degree of centralisation of power has been used to explain the growth in the relative size of the government sector. Greater centralisation may enable governments to keep a tighter control on spending whilst decentralisation may also lead to lower public spending because of the closer link between taxation and spending decisions.[2] Recent evidence on this issue (Wilensky, 1975; Giertz, 1981) suggests that centralised systems tend to spend more that decentralised systems.

The relationship between the degree of (de)centralisation and the growth of public sector activities has also been explored by Oates (1972; 1985). In his study 'Fiscal Federalism', Oates (1972) used a sample of 57 US county governments to search for a positive relationship between the degree of fiscal centralisation and the size of the government. In a more recent study, Oates sought to provide an empirical assessment of *Leviathan* as suggested by Brennan and Buchanan (1977), with the aid of an international sample of 43 countries and a sample consisting of the 48 contiguous states of the United States (Oates, 1985). Specifically, Oates tested the following two alternatives to the Leviathan hypothesis:

1. There is no systematic relationship between fiscal decentralisation and the size of government; and
2. Greater decentralisation is positively associated with public sector size.

The presumption here is that the loss of economies of scale would increase cost and, therefore, the level of public expenditure. Alternatively, citizens in smaller communities may empower their local governments with more functions and responsibilities. However, Oates's findings failed to uncover evidence linking fiscal decentralisation to the size of government. Moreover, Friedman (1962, 1980) regarded concentration of power as a great menace to freedom: 'The greatest threat to human freedom is the concentration of power, whether in the hands of government or anyone else' (Friedman and Friedman, 1980, p. 309).

Political Scientists' Views

Political scientists have offered their own explanations concerning public spending growth. For Peltzman (1980, p. 211), the literature on the size of the government uses two modes of analysis to explain public expenditure growth. The first one focuses on specific historical events as the primary cause, while the second focuses on a market for public goods. One widely known example of the historical mode of analysis is Peacock and Wiseman's (1961) study of the growth of British government spending.

Peltzman's (1980, pp. 220-21) basic hypothesis is that incentives to redistribute wealth politically are the more important determinants of the relative size and growth of the public and private sectors; consequently, incentives to redistribution drive the size of governments. Moreover, the author does not ignore the role of political institutions in the growth of governments, especially in the three Anglo-countries: Canada, the USA, and the UK.

For Wildavsky (1985, p. 349), the size of the government in any given society is a function (or consequence) of its combination of political cultures. The important decisions that individuals make are simultaneously choices of culture; therefore, the size of the state today is a function of its political culture yesterday. Wildavsky supports the view that budgetary balance is a function of regimes. There are only four possible ways in which governments can manage spending in relation to revenues, namely, the following ones (Wildavsky, 1985, p. 354):

1. Governments can manage neither their spending nor their revenues.
2. Governments can manage their spending but not their revenues.
3. Governments can manage their revenues but not their spending.
4. Governments can manage both their spending and their revenues.

Starting from the presumption of fiscal balance, Wildavsky (1985, pp. 354-5) identifies the following five strategies for relating public revenues and expenditures:

1. Do nothing.
2. Increase spending.
3. Increase revenues.
4. Increase revenues and spending.
5. Decrease revenues and spending.

The first strategy is a fatalistic regime where balance is achieved when spending equals revenues. The second is a sectarian regime where balance is achieved when high spending greatly exceeds low revenues. The third is a hierarchical regime where spending marginally exceeds revenues with both at high levels. This follows from the notion that where government has money, it will find the means to spend it. The fourth is a social democratic regime where there are impulses towards equality of both taxes and spending at maximal levels. The fifth is a market-based regime where expenditure exceeds revenues at low levels of spending. Interestingly, Wildavsky does not recognise the notion of a state that consistently incurs a public surplus rather than a deficit, although this characteristic is found among several East Asian states.

It can be inferred from the above literature that the view of the state and its activities, which is implicit in most conventional economics, is a rather simplistic one. The overall impression is that, 'Through most of this literature there also runs the strong presumption that free enterprise and the operation of the market will tend to maximise efficiency' (Smith and Aaronovitch, 1981; quoted in Sawyer, 1989, p. 305). In sharp contrast to this, the Keynesian analysis postulates that by varying the levels of public expenditure and taxation, the government can control the level of aggregate demand and so the levels of output and employment. In addition, fiscal policy and its associated multiplier effects can be used to 'crowd in' private spending and to promote economic development through, for example, government spending on human capital and on infrastructure.

We will return to our critique of other theories of these states as we build an institutional framework for understanding its operation in Chapter 3.

PUBLIC EXPENDITURE: SOME ECONOMIC AND SOCIAL NOTIONS

Social expenditures are a part of public expenditures and are defined by the OECD as direct government expenditures on education, health services, pensions, unemployment compensation and other income maintenance programmes and welfare services. Since housing is a social problem of great importance, housing should be included in this term but is not. What people usually mean when they speak of housing as a necessity is that some minimum standard of accommodation is a necessity of life as we have come to expect it in any modern society.

Social expenditure has been the fastest growing component of total government expenditure over the last four decades. According to the OECD (1992b), its share has increased on average in the OECD countries from 47.5 per cent of the total government outlays in 1960 to over 59.7 per cent in 1990. Of the remaining categories, which include government expenditure on public administration, defence, law, order, housing and economic programmes, only the cost of servicing the public debt (with high levels of interest rates and sizeable new borrowing) has grown rapidly.

Government expenditure on education grew rapidly during the 1960s and early 1970s in the OECD countries. From the beginning of the 1970s, the growth of education expenditure slackened due to demographic developments and tighter spending policies. The latter tended to be directed towards capital expenditure rather than current expenditure (OECD, 1985, *Social Expenditure: 1960-1990*).

In terms of its indirect beneficial effects on the economy, government intervention in education has been successful (OECD, 1992b). However, underlying inequalities in the distribution of income, wealth and power has placed limits on the redistribution that can be achieved through expenditure on education. For example, severe inequalities among regions and social classes characterise most school systems. The correlation between national income levels and education spending is strong and state provision aims at achieving, among other things, equality of opportunity in education. Societies set both efficiency and equity objectives for the education system. The former usually requires the adoption of a system that yields the maximum social benefits (which are less tangible), while the latter (equity objective) requires equality of opportunity in education.

During the 1960s and early 1970s, public expenditure on health also grew rapidly but continued growing at a slower rate until the mid-1980s. During the 1960s, public health programmes expanded to cover the whole population, while the 1970s were marked by the introduction of major public health programmes in a number of countries and by the extension of existing programmes in others.

Governments' responsibility for public health and health care originates 'in the realisation that individuals, voluntary organisations and the private sector are unable to meet all health needs through their own efforts alone. Indeed, the fundamental problems of resource allocation apply just as much in the field of health as they do in any other area of life' (OECD, 1992b). There are two principal objectives that a society might have with respect to health care: efficiency and equity. Certainly, in some countries, increasing health expenditure in the late 1960s and 1970s was not accompanied by the equity gains made in earlier years, while in other countries, notable progress was made where state provision aimed at achieving equality of access to health care (OECD, 1985, *Social Expenditure: 1960-1990*).

In general, health services tend to be unevenly distributed among the population, and capital cities and other major urban areas usually have several times as many doctors, hospitals and hospital beds in relation to the population as rural areas (Eurostat, *Rapid Reports: Population and Social Conditions 1990-97*). On the other hand, health, medical services and income are highly correlated both at the individual and at the national level. In many countries, conscious attempts have been made to control the growth of health expenditure, and real expenditures and the average real benefit have grown much more slowly than during the last two decades.

Clearly, economies can, and should, devote increasing resources to the improvement of educational and health standards (and, therefore, to the improvement of human capital), since an improvement in the quality of human resources leads workers to be more productive. It should be noted that some economists and sociologists (radical critics) altogether reject the idea that education raises productivity. An element in their critique is that education acts as a screen or sieve to select the fortunate few who are then 'credentialed' to hold elite positions in society. More radical critics add that the school system essentially reproduces the class structure from generation to generation. The solution to all this lies not in any conceivable reform of the school system within the framework of capitalist society, but in the radical reform of the social structure and economic system.

Most governments in the OECD area have used social security systems as means of supporting and redistributing income and insurance. A wide range of insurance benefits has been provided, and where private market alternatives are available, they have failed, in many respects, to match the quality attained by public arrangements. Most OECD and EC countries have tried to reduce inequality of income through social security benefits. For example, in general, social expenditure on pensions did not grow at a significantly slower rate over the 1975-90 period compared to the 1960-75 period. Surprisingly enough, even though the elderly population has continued to increase in size relative to the population as a whole, pension coverage has continued to expand, and so have average real benefits (OECD, 1985, *Social Expenditure: 1960-1990*).

According to the OECD (1992), social expenditure on unemployment compensation programmes grew fairly rapidly in the period 1960-75. But since 1975, the growth rate of unemployment compensation has declined, despite the increase in the unemployment rate for the OECD and EC countries from 5.2 per cent in 1975 to 12.1 per cent in 1994; this is largely because coverage has declined. In most OECD and all EC member countries, the ratio of pension and unemployment payments to GDP rose substantially over the period 1960-75. However, in the same period, there was a widespread decline in the importance of family and child allowances, whose share in GDP has reduced in most countries, and where the level of benefits, relative to per capita GDP, has declined in all cases. On the other hand, in the period 1975-90, the growth rates of pension and unemployment payments in most OECD and EC countries have declined, but less than the growth rates of family and child allowances. It could, therefore, be argued that governments have put a rather greater emphasis on the active relative to the inactive population (OECD, *Social Expenditure: 1960-1990*).

When assessing the macroeconomic costs and benefits of an increase in publicly provided pensions, it is important to bear in mind that these are transfers and that an increased scale of benefits has virtually no real resource cost, because the transfer which is made is essentially from people to themselves at a later point in their life cycle. To a very large extent, therefore, not only are these expenditures simply transfers to and from the same individuals, but the state is also merely acting as a substitute for what could have been obtained by most people, if with less security and transfer ability (and perhaps at a higher real cost), by private savings and insurance arrangements. Therefore, the income effects of redistributive and/or social policies are, indeed, of great importance.

THE ROLE AND IMPORTANCE OF GOVERNMENT INVESTMENT

Firms, states, households and non-profit institutions undertake investment. It includes the acquisition of human and intangible capital as well as physical capital (Kolb, 1988, p. 5). However, investment may be inadequate in failing to provide sufficient resources for future production and, if it is insufficient, to bring about the full utilisation of existing resources. This latter problem has received major attention as a consequence of the work and influence of Keynes (1936). In a similar vein, Kalecki's approach to the explanation of business cycles was based on the view that fluctuations in investment expenditure are the major forces generating macroeconomic fluctuations (Kalecki, 1971).

The state as a direct player in the organisation of investment was very much at the heart of Keynes's thinking and constitutes an explicit long-term policy proposal to be found in the *General Theory*. Keynes viewed the state as 'taking an ever greater responsibility for directly organising investment expenditure' (Keynes, 1973, p. 164). A collective decision-making body set up to regulate huge funds for more socially desirable investment purposes could be construed as a mechanism of *socialising* investment spending, i.e., 'the democratic control of capital formation' (Seccareccia, 1994, p. 377). Keynes's proposal in favour of government investment has to do with the *composition* of public expenditures and not about whether the share of total government expenditures out of GDP (or GNP) should rise so as ultimately to monopolise all investment spending in the economy (Seccareccia, 1994, p. 379).

Therefore, public investment is one of the components of total public expenditure and means spending on fixed assets (land and buildings, vehicles, machinery, etc.) by central government and local authorities, less sales of fixed assets, plus the increase in book value of stocks and work in progress of central government and public corporations. The public sector is involved in many activities that have the character of investment, ranging from the construction of schools, universities and hospitals to defence-related industries. The capacity-creating aspect of government investment is considered very important since investment spending adds to the productive potential of the economy. Following the Keynesian tradition, investment expenditure not only creates additional income (the 'multiplier principle') but also increases and improves the productive capacity of the economy. Indeed, capital formation enlarges a country's capacity to produce goods and, therefore, capital accumulation is central to technical progress as it adds to both demand and capacity.

Any capital investment project, especially when it is undertaken in the public sector, requires careful consideration (economists have tried to elaborate criteria to enable public sector decision-makers to reach the best decisions about potential investment projects, and equate the theory of optimal public sector project decision-making with cost-benefit analysis). Since public sector outputs (and public investments too) are not allocated via markets (i.e., instead they are provided via the budget), then the benefits are likely to be much wider within the government sector. Perhaps, without the undertaking of large investment expenditures by the public sector in basic (at least) infrastructure projects, the rate of growth of an economy would be smaller than what has in fact been achieved. Moreover, it is argued that public projects are less risky than private projects. So, there is a good argument to be made for it to engage in high risk projects that normal capital markets would fail to support. But, on the other hand, government capital formation is the result of government (and/or political) decisions.

GOVERNMENT EXPENDITURE AND DEVELOPMENT

Many definitions exist for the term 'development' but it is defined here as a dynamic procedure with economic and social characteristics which has a strong political affect, with emphasis on:

1. the satisfaction of human needs; and
2. the process that brings about changes in economic and/or social structures, if necessary, for the achievement of substantial regional growth and further industrial development.

The question that arises from this concern is which kind of government expenditure is related to economic and social development. We argue that government expenditure (related to socially sensitive development) may include the following categories:

1. social needs and programmes for human welfare (in both urban and regional areas): education and its relationship with new technology and know-how, health, housing, social security (i.e., pensions) and other income maintenance benefits;
2. economic plans and investments in strategic economic sectors and activities, special pilot-programmes, etc;
3. the improvement of infrastructure and modernisation; and
4. protection of the environment and natural resources.

Indeed, human resource development is considered to be of paramount importance for economic growth and development. On the one hand, economies can, and do, devote increasing resources to the improvement of educational and health standards; but it is also apparent that investment in human resources helps to accelerate economic growth. It does this by increasing labour productivity, since an improvement in the quality of human resources leads workers to be more productive. On the other hand, all economies must follow a defined pattern of educational development in order to obtain the kinds of trained people they will need.

As with education, health services improve the quality of human resources, now and in the future. Economic development tends to improve health status, whereas better health contributes to economic growth and development. This clearly arises out of the recognition that healthy people are more productive and essential for economic development. Good health increases human potentialities of all kinds and is rightly regarded as a basic human need. The ability of countries to invest in social development is no doubt influenced, to a great extent, by trends in their economic performance and development. However, according to the OECD (1992b) figures, many governments have not seriously taken up the strategic actions which are required to generate and mobilise all possible resources for education and public health. Evidently, the elaboration of well-defined plans of action is an essential part of any strategy that aims at attaining a better human capital and further social welfare (OECD, 1985, *Social Expenditure: 1960-1990*).

So far, the importance of the relationship between the government sector and regional development/policies and industrial policies/strategy has been ignored. The term 'industrial strategy' means that 'the government adopts a strategic view of future industrial development in the economy concerned and provides a range of support mechanisms to those sectors deemed to have a key role to play in the future' (Sawyer, 1992a, p.8).

According to Yuill and Allen (1987, p. 37), the following four major areas of activity reflect the economic needs of a region (and a nation as a whole):

1. the promotion of technical development and innovation;
2. the provision of risk capital for trading companies;
3. supplying training courses and development programmes; and
4. investment in infrastructure and industrial and commercial property.

The argument put forward in this book is that industrial intervention is based on remedying the inefficiencies of the market system. The public sector should play a key role in identifying social needs and inadequacies of the market mechanism in addition to developing new operations, but not necessarily controlling or owning them. Where the government participates in the market it should benefit financially, but its primary role should not be to maximise profit. The public and private sectors can cooperate 'in a range of different arrangements, each contributing what it does best and both participating in the financial returns within the context of a socially defined agenda' (Sawyer, 1992a, p. 15). The key point is the need for a strong developmental role for the state in order to raise the momentum of industrial change and to ensure that such change fully reflects broader national interests (a developmentalist industrial strategy).

Within such an approach, regional development and growth is not aimed at promoting one area against another. Rather, investment activity is designed to add to the sum total of investment capital and infrastructure, training, workspace and the available services; must add to product ranges; create better quality output and employment; provide finance, services and opportunities where none properly exist; and must support technical innovation where the market is deficient. On the other hand, in all countries, there are some certain sectors with growth potential at the regional and even national levels. Technology programmes must not only add value to a particular sector; they must also bring opportunities to a region. As well as being commercially viable, investment expenditure, training and technical development must add to the opportunities for local economic growth and development (Yuill and Allen, 1987, pp. 36-8).

Radical scientists argue that social efficiency is intimately bound up with economic democracy and the decentralisation of political power, as economic democracy is fundamental to maximising a society's economic welfare. To this end, people and communities have to possess a significant degree of direct control over the dominant centres of economic and political power (Sawyer, 1992a, pp. 12-3). While the private sector can ignore all of these, the state as public entrepreneur cannot. Thus, the above parameters must be part of a meaningful role for the public sector in its policies for industrial investment.

CONCLUSION

In most capitalist economies, the state undertakes a range of functions. Its role can be defined either in terms of institutions (i.e., legislative bodies, executive bodies and judicial bodies) or in terms of its functions (e.g., to maintain law and order, to levy taxes, etc.). But in both cases, the government has a certain role to play with substantial effects on the economy and society. There are also many cases where the range of state activities extends beyond the passage of laws and the levying of taxation.

Two areas of state intervention are of particular importance. The first one covers the range of public services such as education, public health, pensions and housing, which tend to be underprovided for by the private sector. There are many well-known reasons why an unfettered market system would not perform as well as one involving (some forms of) state intervention, and there are many well-known examples where the difference between private and social returns would lead the private sector to under-provide public goods or engage in underinvestment. The second area relates to the fact that government expenditure increased massively during the twentieth century, and major increases are seen to have arisen from the growth of government transfer payments. In addition to the above facts, government intervention can range from facilitating or promoting industrial development to its direct involvement in the productive process (Ham and Hill, 1984).

According to New Right views, the existence of what they see as excessive state intervention threatens personal freedom and introduces arbitrariness in the activities of the government; opens the door for the appropriation of the state apparatus by interest groups including the government bureaucrats themselves; and creates rigidities and inefficiencies in the economy that harm its performance. In complete contrast, the Keynesian approach supports the fact that government intervention has multiple economic effects on the economy.

Clearly, Keynesianism and Monetarism differ sharply in their theories of aggregate expenditure. The Keynesian analysis suggests that any increase in government spending increases aggregate demand. Therefore, government expenditure adds directly to the level of aggregate demand in the economy. On the other hand, monetarists support the view that an increase in government spending (which increases aggregate demand) will increase the money supply and will push the price level up (i.e., inflation).

Theoretical perspectives suggesting that bureaucrats, politicians and voters are interrelated do not seem to offer a powerful explanation of the role of the state and the growth in public expenditures. By focusing on methodological individualism, they tend to ignore systematic considerations, which are taken up by radical political economists. The interests of bureaucrats and politicians are only part of the influences on the state, and the power of others, especially the capitalist classes, has to be taken into account.

NOTES

1. Other alternative indexes are:

   (a) the ratio of public expenditures for goods and services only to GDP;
   (b) the ratio of public expenditures for goods and services that related to consumer goods to GDP; or
   (c) the ratio of total public revenues to GDP.

2. Centralisation: current revenues of national government to current revenues of all levels of government in the year indicated or the closest year for which data is available; in other words, current revenues of the central administration and government to current total public revenues.
   Growth of centralisation: log change of centralisation.
   Growth of government/GDP: log change of government/GDP.

3. Globalisation: Problem or Solution?

> No point blaming [then Canadian Finance Minister] Paul Martin for that budget of his. It wasn't his fault. . . The market made him do it. . . The previous Tory government, the NDP at Queen's Park or in Saskatoon or Victoria, they all take their orders from the same place. . . (Ewener, 1995, A15). We never see the shooting of the baby hippo. No hippo blood and guts on national television. . . The camera cuts to a little schoolgirl assuring us that the baby hippo has indeed been shot. . . Eric Malling explains: 'What, shoot the baby hippo? That's right. No room at the zoo and they couldn't expand the hippo pen because the government has no money.' Death: the ultimate deficit solution. . . What choice is there but to shoot the baby hippo? The government is in debt. . . Hippos, line up. Bam, bam, bam. You can almost feel the confidence of international investors growing with each shot. (McQuaig, 1995, p. 1)

The modern forces of neoliberalism would have the state abandon its traditional role as nurturer of markets. Yet, the state plays a vital role in the operation of the economy and what type of economy ensues. It is through this structure that agents attempt to secure their position using power. Too often governments surrender their sovereignty to globalisation's hidden agenda, which is to trumpet the notion of government for capital, of capital and by capital. Yet this very concept increases the concentration of wealth and power in the economy by stripping the public of one of its potential weapons against the avarice of business by constitutionally limiting the role of government in the economy using trade agreements and globalisation. At the same time, Marxian and Keynesian economics provide only partial solutions to this problem. In order to understand the role of the state in modern capitalist democracy, we must deal with five interrelated concepts: capitalism, democracy, state, market and power.

OPERATIONALISING THE CONCEPTS

What are capitalism, democracy, the state, the market and power? Many would argue one knows each concept when one sees it, but this is not a satisfactory answer. What Galbraith (1983, p. 2) has said about power works equally well for all the other concepts: 'However diversely the word is used, the reader or listener is assumed to know what is meant.' But defining these works precisely allows us to better understand the process by which states can intervene in the marketplace for the betterment of societies.

We will define capitalism as any economic system where markets allocate goods through a price mechanism. Democracy is a political system where power rests in the collective and by a voting system of one person, one vote, the collective exercises power either through representatives elected for a finite term or direct voting. A market is an institution that translates economic decisions into transactions by a system of voluntary exchange conducted between two or more independent parties, each having a property right establishing domain over the item exchanged. The state is an institution whereby collective decisions translate into action. Power is 'the possibility of imposing one's will upon the behaviour of other persons' (Weber, 1958, p. 323).

Operationalising the final concept of power requires a more in-depth discussion as the operational definition used in this study is the heterodox one proposed by John Kenneth Galbraith. Power finds itself implemented in one of three forms: condign, compensatory and conditioned (Galbraith, 1983, p. 4). Condign power is the imposition of one's will through '. . . The ability to impose an alternative to the preferences of the individual or group that is sufficiently unpleasant or painful so that these preferences are abandoned. . . [It] wins submission by inflicting or threatening appropriately adverse consequences' (Galbraith, 1983, pp. 4-5).

This is in contrast to compensatory power, the imposition of one's will by

> . . . The offer or affirmative reward by the giving of something of value to the individual so submitting. . . And as personal or public rebuke is a form of condign power, so praise is a form of compensatory power [as is] pecuniary reward – the payment of money for services rendered. (Galbraith, 1983, p. 5)

On the other hand, conditioned power is the imposition of one's will through ' . . . [C]hanging belief. Persuasion, education, or the social commitment to what seems natural, proper or right causes the individual to submit to the will of another or of others. Submission reflects the preferred course; the fact of submission is not recognised' (Galbraith, 1983, pp. 5-6).

The sources of power, according to Galbraith (1983, p. 6), are property, personality and organisation. Personality will always exercise power, since it is impossible to systematically connect the strength of this power to a measurable objective quantity. However, it is not a very important source on its own. Only through the combination of an organisation can power manifest itself to the heights expressed under a Hitler or Napoleon. Besides, property as a source of power is quantifiable. Under a system of power-neutralisation, alleviation of property-based power can occur using high marginal taxation. Eradication of this power requires the abolition of private property. However, such a power, when not combined with organisational power, is only economic in scope. There is no automatic translation of economic power into political clout. This study will concern itself primarily with the third source of power: organisational. Galbraith (1983, p. 54) states 'property and personality have effect only with the support of organization'. Other scholars, such as Lindblom (1977), Berle (1969) and Stinchcombe (1968) reach similar conclusions.

Do the systems proposed by different schools of thought act as enhancers of the ability to combine the organisational power of the state with the other two sources of power? If yes, they violate the equality tenant of democracy. Given the difficulty of locating the position of personality in the placement of power, we will only deal with property in combination with the state apparatus.

Property is not just monetary in origin. It includes a much broader definition accounting for an individual worker's 'ownership' of his labour-power. The socialist alternative of abolishment of private property is an insufficient means of power-neutralisation as it neglects the property value of the individual's labour-power. In so doing, socialism assigns higher value to those who make greater contributions to society. On the other hand, capitalism assigns higher value to those who have more wealth. Yet neither socialism nor capitalism can solve the Veblenian dichotomy because each preaches resistance to change once its own system is in place. Each society must determine for itself the method that is best for its own use and no adherence to one specific philosophy will prove useful in all institutional environments.

GLOBALISATION PROCESSES

Globalisation is the ultimate expression of the will of the marketplace. Increasingly, this world is moving towards a 'borderless economy' (Ohmae, 1990, p. 18) through a process driven by institutional change, technological change and modernisation. International pressures transform the traditional roles of the nation state:

> Increasingly, functions normally associated with nation states are being passed 'upward' to international regulatory agencies, to multilateral monitoring agencies, to free trade arrangements and, for Europe, to a supra-national political structure. . . [G]lobalisation is . . . decentralising both in the consumer sovereignty sense (i.e., Citizens everywhere are acquiring 'rights' to access consumer goods and services regardless of country of origin) and in the sense of heightening citizens' awareness of their local communities where they live and

> work and play since, in this interdependent world, this is about all that remains under their control. (Courchene, 1992, pp. 108-9)

It is this lack of control that is particularly disconcerting. No one asked whether collective rights ought to be abolished, but globalisation is about the 'emancipation' of the individual from the collective. Globalisation encourages capital movement to countries having an abundance of 'cheap, exploitable labour and away from areas with high direct and indirect wage costs, high taxation and attempts by states to impose some control over investment decisions' (Warskett, 1990, p. 122). Governments initiated this process but they often regret the results. In the pursuit of greater prosperity, governments undertook to champion free trade and economic integration. However, these actions have fallen victim to 'the Law of Unintended Consequences [which] is based on the observation that a course of action undertaken in the hope and devout belief that it will produce a particular outcome often ends up leading to a very different one' (Chodos, Murphy and Hamovitch, 1993, p. 8). Governments, in using their power to shape the international trading system, find their power diminished as a result. Thus, 'the perception – and, at least in part, the fact – is that the nation-state is not only being eroded by the development of the forces which it unleashed and nourished but actually stands in contradiction to the further development of those forces' (Chodos, Murphy and Hamovitch, 1993, pp. 12-13).

Another problem, as seen by liberal writers such as Robert Reich (1991) and Christopher Lasch (1995), is the elites of society do not wish to produce policies beneficial to all, but only ones that aid their small segments of the population. Reich's (1991) 'symbolic analysts' (the well-educated, well-remunerated professionals who form the basis of the new elite) are not beholden to any flag but instead will travel to gain the best deal possible for their personal interests. They seek low taxation primarily, given that they enjoy a high benefits package that insures them against needing to avail themselves of social services provided by the state. Similarly, Lasch (1995) argues that the elites are in revolt over high tax levels and as such demand a lowering of taxes or else emigration will result. He argues that under such circumstances there is a 'betrayal of democracy' in that the politicians must adapt to the desires of these elites to protect the tax base. This analysis makes a great deal of sense on the surface.[1] As echoed by Galbraith (1967, 1973), there is private affluence and public poverty. The insistence that individuals be allowed to keep their earnings and decide what to do with them is an idea that runs counter to the liberal viewpoint that spreading the wealth makes for a better society. A discussion of this point occurs later in this chapter when dealing with the problem of equity versus growth.

Governments have created this process and can change it. International financial markets may demand less state intervention, balanced budgets and greater liberalisation of property rights, but the World Bank appears to retreat from the view that such actions are a panacea for growth and sees market intervention as playing a role in development (World Bank, 1993). Others, such as Amsden (1989; p. 8), speak of successful development as a process where '[T]he state intervenes with subsidies deliberately to distort relative prices in order to stimulate economic activity. . . In exchange for subsidies, the state has imposed performance standards on private firms.' Porter (1990) argues globalisation means nations must build a 'competitive advantage' through industrial policy, a theme also echoed by Reich (1991) and Thurow (1992).

Ironically, even conservatives find solace in globalisation. Globalisation is in concert with conservative economists who argue for dismantling the welfare state (e.g., Buchanan, 1986, pp. 178-85) and against government interference in the marketplace (Hayek, 1973; Buchanan and Wagner, 1978; Brittan, 1975, 1977). These writers believe that non-market failure is wide-ranging and symptomatic of democracy (Olson, 1982; Buchanan, 1986, pp. 210-21; Hayek, 1976) and want to eliminate fiscal deficits.

However, the choice between market intervention and *laissez-faire* is not a dichotomous one

> as Galbraith and Friedman sometimes imply . . . between relatively perfect governments and imperfect or inadequate markets (i.e., the Galbraith view) or between relatively perfect markets and imperfect or inadequate governments (i.e., the Friedman view). The choice in actuality is among imperfect markets, imperfect governments, and various combinations of the two. The cardinal economic choice concerns the degree to which markets or governments – each with their respective flaws – should determine the allocation, distribution and use of resources in the economy. (Wolf, 1988, p. 6)

Unfortunately, globalisation clouds this issue by reinforcing the mystique about the perfection of the marketplace in ordering society. However, perfect markets have never existed in the real world, being the creations of simultaneous linear equations in a general equilibrium framework on the blackboards of economists. Furthermore, no market mechanism is the same in any two countries or regions: authority relations, path dependencies, culture and a myriad of regulatory constraints and laws have created a patchwork of conflicting standards for marketplace performance. The question is not to create a 'free market' but whose 'free market' to accept? Even such relations as property rights cannot be universal nor are they 'natural rights' that predate government: 'Property is itself a form of authority created by government. . . Property rights are consequently grants of authority made to persons and organisations (by) governments (which) authorise such an arrangement' (Lindblom, 1977, p. 26). Even if one accepts the notion of an intellectual property right (and not everyone does), for example, to what extent are these rights enforceable? For how long are they enforceable? In what mediums? How close to the original should something be before it is infringing? Each of these questions is in the domain of the legal framework, not of economics, and appeals to 'universal' principles fail to adequately answer them. However, a different legal environment will create a different outcome and it is impossible to be certain as to the results *a priori*.

Similar questions occur when attempting to reconstruct the role of the state, given globalisation, in labour policy (Martin, 1986; Johnson, McBride and Smith, 1994) and tax policy (Razin and Slemrod, 1990). Should a government concern itself with maintaining balanced growth or maximising total welfare? How can a government achieve transparency of operations? What is the appropriate role of government in alleviating labour market disruptions, if any? Appeals to 'universal' principles fail to answer these questions as well. However, one can assert that they are worth asking and debating instead of resigning to the 'inevitability' of globalisation and its effects on everyone's lives. To paraphrase Shakespeare, 'there are more institutional matrices which are possible in a globalised world than are dreamt of in our current expression of globalisation.'

WHY NOT ACCEPT GLOBALISATION?

The best way to see this is by analogy. Suppose that there exists an economy with no inflation in the beginning and a theory states that a rise in the demand for capital creates an increase in a demand for labour over the 'natural level', which creates upward pressure on the price level. The central bank does not like inflation. Suppose there is another competing theory saying if the central bank raises interest rates, this action will reduce demand for capital, which will reduce the demand for labour, resulting in a decrease in inflation. Suppose that the central bank overshoots the target and creates deflation. Now the theory works the cycle in reverse and lower interest rates raise demand for capital. There should be an observable increase in the demand for labour to correct the deflationary spiral. But sometimes this does not work. What if a large percentage of consumers derive the bulk of their income from savings? Cuts in the interest rates lower their return and cause lower consumption. This consumption causes a decrease in the demand for goods, causing a decrease in the demand for capital, decreasing the demand for labour and creating more deflation. At some future point, the system might switch again. Thus, society's make-up, the 'institutional matrix', has much to do with how individuals react in the system. Neoclassical economists assume all of this away when they decide to write theories denying the importance of the assumptions and attempting to ascribe universality to their theories. A theory can be universal only when consistent with all possible institutional matrices. As the above simple case shows, this is not the case with some parts of contemporary economic theory.

The standard response is 'all other things must remain equal'. However, this is never the case. Economic theory must recognise that isolation of economic events is nearly impossible.[2] Individuals will take the predictions of economists and (according to economic theory) will discount them in their own determinations. If this is the case, then economics cannot usefully predict anything: 'If an economist were so smart, then, she would be rich' (McCloskey, 1990, p. 123).

When one leaves the confines of theory, one sees that the medicine of neoclassical economics is not a naturally superior way of ordering society. Many take solace from the collapse of the former Soviet Union and its East European satellites as confirmation of the 'error' of socialism. However, policy prescriptions of neoliberals have failed to prove to be vastly superior to other, more moderate, prescriptions of Post-Keynesians. Witness New Zealand, a textbook example of neoliberal theory in action. After attributing incorrectly the actions of the government as being a necessary response to hitting the debt wall, neoliberal economists ignore the devastation left by this experiment. The unemployment rate doubled and New Zealand suffered the worst decline in GNP among the OECD countries between 1985 and 1990 (Hewlett, 1993), while the debt to GNP ratio rose both absolutely and in relative terms to other countries in similar circumstances (Colgate and Stroombergen, 1993). Instead, a brighter example is the first Canadian province to balance the books, Saskatchewan, which did so not by the Alberta experience of cutting expenditures in a scorched earth fashion but a minimum of expenditure cuts and heavy tax increases. Despite this, the government recently coasted to an easy victory in the provincial elections.

Neoclassical economics is fundamentally based upon a value-laden judgment of human behaviour called rational self-interest. This hedonism does not account for the observation that humans appear to be creatures of habit and suggestion (Downey, 1987, p. 49). Prior purchases by individuals or their parents are strong indicators of future purchases. The billions of dollars spent on advertising demonstrate the power of suggestion. Yet, neoclassical economists persist with the claim that advertising is mainly informational in content (Stigler and Becker, 1978).

In so doing, the 'change in tastes' seen when people respond to advertising is reducible to an incomplete information problem: as consumers gather more information about a product, they can better formulate their purchasing decisions based on their existing pattern of tastes. By doing that, their buying patterns change. Advertising does not manipulate tastes; it informs consumers. Even the most ardent institutionalist admits that their argument is elegantly parsimonious. This does not mean it is correct. Occum's razor is not a proof.

A second problem with the self-interest claim is that individuals will delay for the future gratification today in anticipation of some future utility (Downey, 1987, p. 50). While one may seek a concrete object, it is wrong to speak of anticipated utility. The utility to consume of a particular individual differs depending on that individual's personal circumstances, the time of day and his mood. There is no reasonable way to calculate future returns as the individual cannot be certain of any of these things or even if they will be physically present to experience them. An individual can only receive utility in the present. Perceptions of the future may influence feelings of happiness or sadness in the present, but one feels these emotions in the present. Discounting is not a reasonable formulation of utility in this case because the realisation of utility is in the present.

So how is it the individual decides to pursue a particular object? It is the basis of desiring the object itself, not utility derived from it, which drives people (Downey, 1987, p. 50). However, once one removes the abstract notion of utility, this leaves economists back at a neo-institutionalist means of ascribing purchases which are made on the basis of habit, suggestion and impulse, and rational calculus operates on a subset of the choices made by individuals. As Downey (1987, p. 53) states, should the theory be deprived of its hedonistic content it is reduced to the unobjectionable statements:

1. that men will not buy a thing unless they want it;
2. that a commodity cannot be sold for more than someone is willing to pay for it; and
3. that in a perfect market situation no one will pay more for a given commodity than anyone else.

Assume, however, the neoclassical economists are correct (and even if they are not, perhaps human nature will change to suit the economics image[3]) that man is self-interested. What then? From such a model must the public sector naturally evolve into a government of limited interference in the marketplace? Must governments only check the most egregious of behaviour such that would cause the market system to fall into disrepair (such as enforcement of contracts and property rights)? No, not at all. It is because neoclassical economists not only state that individuals are self-interested but also that they *ought* to be self-interested that springs this trap. By assuming self-interest is good, they select individual welfare over group welfare. They subordinate all group activity as being the accumulation of individual activity, not as Commons (1961, p. 69) would simply describe institutions as being 'Collective Action in Control of Individual Action'.

Collectivism advances the group; individualism advances the individual.[4] Group identity is a necessary foundation for any society. By creating autonomous agents in the economy, the implication is that government is alien to the individuals; it is some nefarious plot by certain groups to gain undue control over others. However, individuals are not autonomous; the culture of their native society has a profound influence on their behaviour. Similarly, it is impossible to abstract the government from the governed in a democratic society. Governments derive the power to govern from the citizens, and the institutions of the state give citizens the power to influence those who govern. Government is not derived from citizens; citizens are not derived from the government: each is derived from the other.

One possible way of reintegrating 'hedonism' with the discourse established previously is that done by Margolis (1982), who presents a solution based on the notion individuals have a *bi-dimensional* personality based on both altruism and egoism. Individuals thus allocate their actions (either towards group-oriented or self-oriented behaviour) based on what Margolis calls the 'fair share' rule:

> The larger the share of resources I have spent unselfishly, the more weight I give to my selfish interests in allocating marginal resources. On the other hand, the larger benefit I can confer on the group compared with the benefit from spending marginal resources on myself, the more I will tend to act unselfishly. (Margolis, 1982, p. 36)

However, in each and every case, the important aspect is that if people are driven not by self-interest but by other forces as well, the ability of the state to enter into the market becomes clear. The First Theorem of Welfare Economics may state that all market equilibria are Pareto efficient but this only occurs when market participants are self-interested. Destroy that and the market criterion becomes impotent. No longer can we prove that the market will present us with the proper allocation of goods. Furthermore, as goes the First Welfare Theorem, so too, goes the Second Welfare Theorem, which states that markets can achieve any Pareto efficient allocation. Things get even more complicated when issues such as national pride occur wherein people desire governmental services and goods, not because of their inherent efficiency but because of their power as national symbols. We must never forget the power that such symbols may have on the productive spirit of the nation.

All of this is mired in the phenomenon known as X-Efficiency, a term coined by Liebenstein (1966) to discuss why firms persistent fail to use resources properly. It differs from allocative efficiency, which can be cured through market intervention ('by getting the prices right') and focuses instead on the wastefulness and inefficient use of resources. The vastness of this inefficiency is critical and may be up to thirty times greater than that which would be cured if all markets were completely free. It is also that form of inefficiency best tackled by examining institutions, as Leibenstein (1966) argues that it has more to do with incomplete contracting, a failure to work to one's full capacity and satisfying, as opposed to maximising, behaviour among managers.

Another critical problem of neoclassical economics is the fundamental assumption that markets tend towards equilibrium. Equilibrium assumes a state of rest; to deviate from that position of rest requires an external shock. If markets are perfectly in equilibrium then there would never need to be any worry about the transition period. However, what is there that is external to cause so many changes on a minute-by-minute, nay second-by-second basis? With everything interconnected and the time lags differing between events, it is better to state that the markets are never in a state of equilibrium but are constantly on the move searching for equilibrium without finding it. If markets were truly self-regulating in that they moved immediately towards equilibrium, there would be no need for arbitrageurs (those agents that seek to minimise differences between markets at a given time). Instead, the markets are not self-correcting but have developed instrumental mechanisms (such as computers) to push the system towards balance. This is one way whereby profits are possible.

However, not all markets move with the rapidity of computerised arbitrage. Some variables, such as wages or interest rates, cannot adjust rapidly without command and control structures:

> To suppose that a flexible wage policy is a right and proper adjunct of a system which on the whole is one of *laissez-faire*, is the opposite of the truth. It is only in a highly authoritarian society, where sudden, substantial, all-round changes could be decreed that a flexible wage policy could function with success. (Keynes, 1953, p. 269)

Worse still, the neoclassical economists have ample proof on their side that the self-correcting nature of the market is faulty. If a self-correcting system is closed and experiences continuous change, it cannot have disequilibria at any point. However, some closed systems exhibit only a tendency towards 'equilibrium' followed by a distancing as they approach the critical point: they are not self-correcting. The system tries to converge but always fails. This is an example of chaos. The human mind always attempts to find order in disorder; so it tries to present convergent systems for divergent phenomena. If economic systems are chaotic (and evidence by Day (1993b) and Anderson, Arrow, and Pines (1989) suggests that they are) then equilibrium is an invalid concept.

Even their own theory is internally inconsistent. Suppose that people are self-interested and markets self-equilibrate. Their own theory suggests that no government intervention of any kind should be necessary. Oh, but they do not like this! The development of inventions stagnates unless there is a guarantee of inventor compensation. Authors only write books if intellectual property rights exist. Buyers fail to go to the market, if they are afraid of thieves and brigands. Thus, intervention, to a limited degree, is necessary. Buchanan (1975, p. 18) tries to address the scope of this intervention when he argues that 'economic exchange among persons is facilitated by mutual agreement on defined rights'. However, there is a problem:

> The presence of ambiguity and conflict [means that] adjudication of claims is necessary. . . [Indeed,] adjudication by the state is designed to prevent the introduction of physical force by the parties. [Besides,] well-defined rights require enforcement; violations must be policed and violators punished even when each person's rights are acknowledged by everyone. (Buchanan, 1975, pp. 88-9)

However, each jurisdiction defines property rights in different ways. An individual receives standing to sue based on a defective item sold to him in one country (Canada) and fails to receive this consumer protection in another (Japan). Property rights might legitimise past illegal behaviour (the Kennedys did not give back their bootlegging profits after Prohibition ended) or force certain individuals to begin life with a limited endowment (freeing of slaves did not give them claim to the goods and services of their former masters). Each of these institutional changes will create a different society: more able to react in certain circumstances, less able in others. Efficiency cannot be abstracted from the institutional environment in which it is present. To argue a particular distribution of property rights is correct under every set of assumptions is baseless.

Who is to say that defining property rights based on state ownership of all resources is any less efficient than defining it on the basis of individual rights? Communism may have failed, not due to some inherent problem, but because the necessary indoctrination of individuals was not sufficient to overcome what the members of the society saw on the outside. Max Weber (1958, p. 159) argues that Protestantism created the work ethic: 'Labour came to be' and considered in itself the end of life ordained as such by God. St Paul's 'He who will not work shall not eat' holds unconditionally for everyone. Unwillingness to work is symptomatic of the lack of grace.

Without this ethic, it is doubtful that any system of control or free market could have accounted for the accumulation of the Western nations. China, India and the Islamic world were far ahead of the West in developing markets, engaging in trade and implementing technology. The state did not control markets any more than the West; indeed, Eastern markets were probably a good deal freer. The one thing they all lacked, according to Weber, was the Protestant work ethic. Yet, as we will see in our chapters on East Asia, this 'work ethic' that Weber is so in love with may not be all it is supposed to be because other philosophies may prove more amenable to economic growth.

Indeed, markets seem to need something beyond the market to gather momentum and grow. To argue that the *Marshall Plan* acted as a retardant on growth seems to be disingenuous but that was market intervention. Even more compelling is the success of the Japanese Ministry of International Trade and Industry (MITI).[5] As Johnson (1982, p. 199) notes, the economic miracle of Japan produced results 'unprecedented for Japan or any other industrialised economy' due to its industrial policy

> derived from the government's selection of industries for 'nurturing,' perfection of measures to commercialise the products of these chosen industries, and development of means for regulating the cut-throat competition that the first two sets of policies generated. The tools in the hands of the economic bureaucrats included control over all foreign exchange and imports of technology, which gave them the power to choose industries for development; the ability to dispense preferential financing, tax breaks, and protection from foreign competition, which gave them the power to lower the costs of the chosen industries; and the authority to order the creation of cartels and bank-based industrial conglomerates which gave them the power to supervise competition.

Although it is impossible to determine if neoclassical economists are right in stating such measures could only retard economic growth, not enhance it, it is equally awe-inspiring to imagine Japan, Singapore or China under their model. There seems to be no reasonable explanation how three of the world's fastest growing industrial economies during their periods of ascendancy could possibly have grown any faster. It would appear that the prescription that the market system is inherently superior to the government is faulty. Indeed, Frank Hahn (1982, p. 16), one of the most voracious critiques of heterodox approaches to economics, has pointed out that the conditions under which the invisible hand works are almost non-existent in the real world, resulting in a process which is 'occasionally downright arthritic'. Furthermore, as the theory of the second best demonstrates the neoclassical fairy tale collapses under its own weight whenever any of the stated or unstated assumptions of the model are violated. Allowing markets to work independently without interference from the government does not guarantee efficiency. In fact, achieving economic efficiency without market intervention is decidedly the exception and not the rule.

Markets fail. Markets undersupply public goods and ration goods using the price system (although the degree to which they do so is in dispute in the economics profession). However, public enterprises distort market allocations and may supply goods at a higher price.

Markets fail because their efficiency is in allocation. When there is a diminishment of competition (such as has been occurring over the past hundred years) so large corporations increasingly find themselves with large market shares and very few competitors, the dynamics of competition that drives companies down to competitive pricing begin to unravel. As corporations become larger, there becomes a gap between the ideals of the owners (represented by the shareholders) and those of the managers. To argue that the interests of the shareholders and the managers are the same (to maximise profitability) is incompatible with neoclassical theory, except under very special conditions. If every individual seeks to maximise his income stream, then it would be likely that the individual manager will engage in the same behaviour. If he receives a fixed salary, he might concentrate on increasing the size of the corporation or, perhaps, market share to accentuate his power. If he receives his payment in stock, he may wish to increase the volatility of the stock price, to be able to sell it for a higher return. If the stockholders desire security of income stream, they might seek to increase the stock price each year even if it is below what it could be under more volatile conditions. As Galbraith (1967) and Caves (1970) have noted, the tendency is for large corporations to become more risk-averse with increases in size, which is exactly the type of behaviour one would expect from managers seeking to limit exposure to failure.

The neoclassical economists hammer away at the bureaucratic state: 'Unfortunately, a unidirectional bias towards expansion of fiscal accounts seems to be present. . . Ideologies aside, persons may be attracted to politics because they intrinsically place high value on the power to make decisions affecting the lives of others' (Buchanan, 1975, pp. 157-8). Hayek (1988, p. 44) contends 'governments have more often hindered than initiated the development of long-distance trade'. In addition, Becker (1983) claims that the pressures of different interest groups determine whether government intervention occurs, while Krueger (1974) worries that bureaucrats engage in rent-seeking. However, none of these problems make a case against government intervention. They only point out that government intervention is not a perfect solution any more than market non-interference. There is no perfect market and no perfect government; there are only institutional arrangements that have different allocations of market-government mix.

Lending credence to this analysis is that the firm is not organised as a free market. It is more like government, using a model of command and control (Coase, 1937). This is because there are transaction costs associated with markets. Command and control minimise these transaction costs. However, transaction costs can change with changes in technology and what was once a burdensome cost (such as transportation) may become a trivial component in the overall cost over time. Similarly, transaction costs that go up over time (such as medical malpractice fees) may become an increasingly large component. Without the ability of government to reshape itself and react to these changes, there is an ever-present danger of stagnation. The problem of the rigidification of the state by a 'once and for all' alternation in its property rights scheme through the implementation of a global trading system also constricts the market by making it impractical or impracticable to reshape the 'working rules' of the system.

Neoclassical economics has embarked on a curious path: embracing the liberal banner of 'natural rights' to authorise an unprecedented restriction on the adaptability of government. Neoclassical arguments boil down to this: government is best that governs the least, and that does not expend more than it receives. The quasi-libertarian attitude they take is one that, at its extreme, has no room for minimum wage laws, health and safety standards, public education, universal health care, unemployment insurance or public highways. Government services ought to be privatised and left in the hands of free enterprise for it is more 'efficient' to do so. However, this begs the most serious of questions: why is it that efficiency is so desirable?

Efficiency has three major problems: the first is defining what it is; the second is whether the market is efficient; and the third is deciding if it is desirable based on the definition. What is efficiency? Which is being dealt with: allocative efficiency (the efficient allocation of goods and resources over a range of choices); or X-efficiency (the congruence of objectives between workers and owners within an organisation (Liebenstein, 1966)? What about the distortionary effect of normal interest rate fluctuations on economic behaviour (the time horizon declines as the interest rate increases, yielding the possibility for inter-temporal inefficiency)? Is it dynamic or static efficiency that is of concern?

Far more serious is that in using the market mechanism as the basis for selection criteria, one ignores non-market utility, thereby making the market inefficient. If a market does not price an externality, the decision calculus ignores the externality. Of course, some of these, such as pollution, can be priced (Thayer et al., 1993) and a market can be created after careful delineation of property rights (Cason, 1995). However, these are imperfect measures. Emission control permits assign a fixed cost to society and require polluters to pay a fixed amount but the cost is not equalised across individuals (characteristic of all public bads; with public goods, the benefit is not equalised across individuals), leading to potential inefficiency.

Then there are those items that are not measurable. A choice once taken cannot be undone. The extinction of a plant or animal species may prove to be a fatal blow in the future to an entire ecological system. The resource extinguished today might hold the cure for cancer tomorrow. It is impossible to know and so, under conditions of uncertainty, the 'rational choice' may not be the best one had all information been available. Of course, the counter to this argument is that such information, being unavailable, is impossible to consider. This is not a valid counter in cases where extinction is the likely outcome: the marginal social benefit of the extra unit of resource is not likely to be worth the marginal social cost (marginal social cost rises as the resource approaches extinction while marginal social benefit remains constant or falls).

More puzzling is the cost of intangibles. To arrive at a price, one must be able to quantify the item under consideration. How does one quantify the cost of an accident? One can determine the actual cost of treatment and it is possible to make an educated guess (using actuarial figures) about the accounting cost of an injury (lost wages and productivity). However, one cannot determine the utility cost of pain and suffering due to asymmetric information (only the victim knows the extent of the pain and suffering, while outsiders cannot verify it).

Even within the market there are problems. There is the problem of price rigidities associated with administrated prices (Means, 1935). Carlton (1986) argues that 'alternatives to price allocate goods efficiently where price rigidities occur', and Galbraith (1952) argues in favour of wage and price controls as a means of controlling inflationary pressures. Coordination failures provide another source of inefficiency due to spillovers and strategic complementarities (Cooper and John, 1988; Shleifer, 1986). Other problems include self-fulfilling expectations, path dependencies (Arthur, 1989; David, 1985), adverse selection (Akerlof, 1970), and increasing returns (leading to natural monopoly). All these areas are potential ones for government intervention (although there is the problem of non-market, i.e., government, failure to consider as well). method

The third dimension of this problem is whether efficiency arguments are paramount. There is, it appears, a trade-off between efficiency and equity (Okun, 1975) and societal norms of distributional equity may not be consistent with market outcomes. This can lead to stresses and controls placed on the market by democracies that view the distribution of income to be unfair (Viner, 1960). Wolf (1988, pp. 28-33) stretches the idea of efficiency to its limit in classifying income distribution as a public good. Consequently, he argues that this is a question of market failure and not a repudiation of efficiency. Of course, as *The Economist* (1994) has indicated, the trade-off between equity and efficiency may be a false one. Not only is there the possibility of work stoppages and other measures taken by the lower classes (such as unionisation) to ensure a rise in their wages but also one must examine how taxation policy enters into the discussion.

In a progressive tax system, redistribution can alleviate the trade-off between equity and efficiency. In such a way, a 'Pareto optimal' solution is reachable. Indeed, such a system has a way of 'flattening' the inequality curve by transferring additional dollars of income generated at absolute high levels to those with absolute low levels of income. However, when the tax system is neutral with respect to income or even regressive (as many taxes in society now are; the sales tax and the payroll tax come immediately to mind), the effect is to leave intact the inherent inequalities of the market or even to exacerbate them.

Clearly, there are problems when attempting to transfer the concept of efficiency to the non-market realm. Even granting (a very generous grant) markets are 'more efficient' than governments in providing these services, there are the twin issues of accessibility and accountability. The public holds government to a higher standard of conduct than private enterprise. Bribery of public officials is illegal but not bribery of private officials when given the innocuous term of 'transaction'. An example is frequent flyer mileage: federal government officials must turn over frequent flyer mileage to the government but many private firms allow employees to accumulate miles in their personal accounts.

The state is also a 'deep pocket' and is potentially liable for unlimited damages. Private concerns can go bankrupt to relieve themselves of their obligations. In California, this has meant a government that is 1 per cent liable might be responsible for 100 per cent of the costs, if the other responsible parties are lacking the fiscal resources. Citizens expect and demand 'fairness' from elected officials and these officials must deliver it: if the government treats a citizen poorly, the citizen can use the complaint mechanism to secure a favourable response. The government always knows that the electorate will be around next time to vote for or against it (or some may decide not to vote, sending an entirely different message). The used car salesman who sells a clunker might be less accommodating. He knows the likelihood of repeat business is low in any case.

The second major aspect of governmental control is accessibility. A private company creates a library and can limit access to it to those who pay a fee. The government, although able to charge a user fee, subsidises part of that fee and may even make it free. If the government charges too high a user fee and excludes an important voter segment, there will likely be a cross-subsidisation plan offered to aid that group. Accessibility is clearly paramount. The private company does not care about the individual who lacks funds. If an individual does not have enough money to buy a Nintendo, then he cannot buy the Nintendo. Barring government regulation, there will be no cross-subsidisation. He may have the right to buy the game but he lacks the wherewithal. This fundamental difference between the right to do something and the ability to do it means that some rights are not exercisable. In such cases, they are not 'rights', but are instead a permission or license.[6] This study shall now examine how different schools of economic thought resolve the problem of government versus the market, beginning with the Keynesian-welfare school approach.

THE KEYNESIAN-WELFARE SCHOOL

Keynesian-welfare theorists argue that government intervention may be beneficial. By dropping the dogmatic approach to economic policy, they approach political economy from a pragmatic viewpoint. To a Keynesian-welfare theorist, democracy acts as a brake on the excesses of the capitalist system. Keynes (1953) viewed the capitalist system as being capable of generating an 'underemployment' equilibrium and government was the only vehicle for kick-starting the economy. However, many acknowledge the limits of government involvement. Olson (1982), for example, argues societies can have their governments 'captured' by special interests. His solution is to have a government that can regulate these interests and reinvigorate the society suffering from 'institutional sclerosis'. The key question of government intervention, for Keynesians, however, still uses an 'efficiency' criterion.

The institution that is most efficient ought to be the one called upon to perform the task, and the goal is always to minimise market distortions when using state intervention (Howlett and Ramesh, 1992, p. 37). As these actions are often second-best solutions, the question of efficiency is not an easy one to answer: when deviating from the market structure, no one can be certain that a small deviation will produce a better result for society than a large one. Keynesian-welfare theorists, in assuming the least deviant solution is the best one, might cause more harm to the economy than if they adopt a radical solution. Worse, Keynesian-welfare theorists ignore the problem of power in the system. By failing to recognise the unequal power distribution of the market system, they do not see that their 'solutions' to market problems are merely treating the symptoms and not the disease itself.

MARXISM AND SOCIAL DEMOCRATIC THEORY

Marxists at least realise the inherent problem of power in the system and try to correct it. However, their solution is no better than the neoclassical one. In attempting to correct the imbalance of power that favours capital, the Marxists call for the elimination of private property. In so doing, they strengthen labour's hand too much. While worker cooperatives theoretically ought to be more efficient than capitalist firms (Mill, 1917), they suffer from a public goods problem. As noted by Coase (1937) and Williamson (1985), the firm has evolved to solve the problem of how to coordinate transactions when a market structure is lacking. As unions and other cooperatives tend to have multidimensional utility functions, they lack the single-minded drive for profit that allows the market mechanism to select the best product. Worse, if one eliminates markets along with their built-in incentives, there is no mechanism for rewarding increased or superior performance. Though one could theoretically compensate workers based on the labour value of product, quality might suffer. Worse, from a Schumpeterian viewpoint, is that by stifling competitive processes, innovation suffers as inventors do not realise the full benefit of their creations.

In theory, Marxists ought to be the most enthusiastic supporters of democracy, though they despise capitalism. Indeed, some of the most ardent advocates of communism (such as Rosa Luxemberg) have stressed the need for democratic control in both the workplace and the state. However, theory and practice do not seem to be in congruence. Instrumental Marxists view democracy as an additional 'opiate for the masses' allowing the public to think they are changing the system; they fail because the interests of capital exercise the true power in the system (Mandel, 1970; Castells, 1980). Structural Marxists argue the capitalist system requires the state to perform certain functions and it is imperative the state acts in these interests to ensure the economy continues to work (Althusser and Balibar, 1977; Gough, 1979). Others assume that the state will simply wither away after a socialist revolution (Bobbio, 1987). Marxist-Leninist regimes (such as Cuba and the former Soviet Union) have little commitment to free expression of ideas because they believe the ideal form of government is a 'dictatorship of the proletariat' (Lenin, 1939b).

Central to their theories is a belief that modern capitalism represents a continuous shift of power from labour to capital, embodied by the replacement of skilled labour with unskilled labour through the assembly line. Mass-production capitalism, known as Fordism, has led to increased unemployment and increased income inequality, according to Marxists. Nevertheless, it is unclear whether one can dismantle the capitalist state. Without a simultaneous revolution in the advanced industrial countries (probably precipitated by a major economic depression), the likelihood of the abandonment of the capitalist system is approximately zero. Any major country that attempted to change its system would find other countries pressuring it to readopt capitalism. Also, the growth rate of the economy would likely fall as no other economic system could duplicate capitalism's success in producing so much wealth in such a limited amount of time, given the current structure of the world economy. The cost to overthrow the economic system is simply something citizens in most major countries would not wish to bear.

Social democrats try to combine Marxist conceptions of power (in that labour's power relative to that of capital is weak) with Keynesian-welfare economics. They differ from Marxists on two main points. First, they believe democracy is a social good. Second, they seek to assist labour and curb the power of capital without fomenting a revolution of the current economic system. However, since their prescriptions use a class-based perspective, they are unable to view globalisation as the catalyst for tearing society not along just capital/labour lines but also between manufacturing workers and 'symbolic analysts' (Reich, 1991).

NEO-INSTITUTIONALIST AND POST-KEYNESIAN THEORY

Post-Keynesianism and neo-institutionalism seek to redress these imbalances of power. Noting that power is inherent in the system (Galbraith, 1983), some neo-institutionalists have sought relief in the idea of empowering certain groups with a 'countervailing' power (Galbraith, 1967). Cornwall and Maclean (1984, p. 54) argued for pursuing a long-term industrial policy, allowing for 'cooperative industrial relations [and increased] investment in the manufacture of goods with high income elasticities of demand'. Laxer (1984) argues for a selective incentive policy to promote the growth of sectors in the economy with the highest potential for growth. Eichner (1980) argues that large corporations have changed capitalism so that they set administrated prices. Power exists in the system and it is relative power, not the ordinary mechanisms of free markets, which sets the prices in the system so that now the system can no longer self-equilibrate. However, post-Keynesians do not view their solutions as being anti-market. Instead, they view them as being market friendly (Wade, 1990; Karagiannis, 2002). They argue for increased cooperation between labour, capital and the state, a political process known as *corporatism* and practiced in Scandinavia, Japan, and many of the NICs. Modern national policies may combine an inward focus with an outward orientation, and should allow for the 'co-evolution' of market and state:

> The political system must then devise means – *outside the system of markets* – to restore access to that system when competition drives workers or owners or managers out. . . The market system must be imbedded in a framework of institutions that provides for its own modification in response to social-economic pressures, that monitors the decentralised process so as to identify the human costs of change and that responds creatively to new social problems as they emerge. . . If this lesson is not learned, the preconditions of socialism will be recreated and the history of the 19th and early 20th centuries will be repeated. (Day, 1993a, pp. 76-77, emphasis as in original)

As noted by Choi (1994), Amsden (1989), Johnson (1982), Lim (1983) and Wade (1990), the respective governments of Hong Kong, South Korea,

Japan, Singapore and Taiwan all massively intervened in their domestic economies to promote certain sectors of the economy over others. Each of these countries vastly outperformed the economies of other developing nations, and rank consistently among the most competitive and fastest growing economies in the world. Howlett and Ramesh (1992) attempt to throw cold water on the post-Keynesian fire by charging that, if such actions were taken, it may be possible to correctly predict market trends. They argue 'markets are notoriously unpredictable and formal cooperation among societal groups and the state must be highly flexible to respond efficiently to changing market conditions' (Howlett and Ramesh, 1992, p. 41).

However, this is a misrepresentation of post-Keynesian argument. Post-Keynesians do not put all of their eggs in the proverbial basket but merely attempt to facilitate market adjustment towards desired aims and objectives. To assume that the market is all-knowing and all-powerful is as great a threat to understanding the process of economics as to assume that governments can plan every detail (as is attempted in a communist society). Markets can be adjusted: witness the recent push by California for a major increase in the number of cars that do not pollute the atmosphere. Because of California's initiative, carmakers are scrambling to build new cars that run on electricity. California effectively created a new market and demand for a new product by *bypassing* normal market mechanisms and, instead, modified the market. Similarly, industries employing high-skilled labour receive assistance through indirect means. Grants to universities, moral suasion campaigns aimed at increasing the relative concentration of students in technical fields, and mandatory worker retraining programmes for those on welfare are three examples of completely viable options under the existing rules of trade that generate a shift towards specific industries meeting the post-Keynesian criteria of being 'strategic' and away from less productive sectors of the economy.

The second major objection to post-Keynesian thought is that such collaboration between labour, capital and the state is difficult because the various groups may simply be loath to cede decision-making authority to a consensual body. However, it is not necessary to have a formal process of making everyone accept a common policy. Government, through the coercive power, can enact laws that make it in the interests of both labour and capital to cooperate. This leads to the elder sister of post-Keynesian thought, neo-institutionalism.

Neo-institutionalism does not adopt the viewpoint that neo-Keynesianism does regarding the preferred economic system. Neo-institutionalists are not interested in debating the relative merits of capitalism or socialism but in making whatever economic system is chosen better: 'Ideological adherence and allegiance to a particular type of social structure, whether market capitalism or socialism, are seen as institutional encumbrances that limit the range of human discretion' (Albelda, Gunn and Waller, 1987, p. 264).

Neo-institutionalists measure development policy in both qualitative and quantitative terms, and seek to improve the ability of societies to change. However, the Veblenian dichotomy between 'ceremonial' (tradition, habit, and other 'cultural' variables) and 'instrumental' (technological progress) behaviour of institutions threatens to get in the way. Government policy attempts to break down these barriers to change and ensures that the domestic society can control its destiny (so it does not substitute one form of ceremonial behaviour for another). Neo-intuitionalists view suspiciously the idea that all technological advancement is good because some forms of technology may lead to a reduction in the quality of life while stimulating the quantity of consumables. Therefore, the neo-institutional perspective justifies some resistance to change. Similarly, changes constraining future choice are unnecessarily restrictive from this perspective. Neo-institutional theories are fundamentally value-laden and attempt to solve problems, and their theory of behaviour includes concepts such as status, power and invidious comparison.

In so doing, neo-institutionalist prescriptions tend to be power-neutral but they are also time and culture-dependent. If any factor of production takes precedence, future changes have a tendency to move in the direction of the benefiting factor of production. Thus, neo-institutionalists agree with post-Keynesians and Marxists on the need to limit the power of capital that is increasingly dominant. Unlike Marxists, if labour gains the upper hand, neo-institutionalists would side with capital. Unlike post-Keynesians, neo-institutionalists see nothing wrong with replacing capitalism if a better system exists. However, neo-institutionalism and post-Keynesianism are not incompatible so long as one does not push the comparison too strongly. This study borrows the tools of post-Keynesians because it appears that creating a social and industrial policy along their lines is a positive step at this time in human development. Neoclassical economics seeks to destroy the welfare state and embrace globalisation, but ignores institutional and political realities. Marxism would require an *autarkic* viewpoint thoroughly incompatible with the modern world. Similarly, Keynesian-welfare political economy, by ignoring power and emphasising only economic variables in trading relationships, lacks the ability to tackle the social consequences of increased globalisation.

All that being said, we ought to understand that seeking to limit future changes to the system is counterproductive. Marxian, Neoclassical and Keynesian-welfare policy perspectives do not have room in their analysis for systemic change from one form of economy to another. Instead, they stake out a claim of superiority for their viewpoints.

Government is a countervailing force to the 'free market'. Bringing this actor to bear against the 'invisible hand' allows for the neutralisation of power. Small businesses cannot always withstand the onslaught of the new industrial state and need to appeal to the force of government to halt actions taken by larger competitors. Government must be able to act in terms of accessibility and equity, which are the two major criteria for determining governmental efficiency.

At the same time, globalisation is a fact that modern states cannot ignore. As the ability of states to alter their competitive advantages is limited by globalisation's tenants, each state must become more creative in how they approach industry and social policy. For example, while positive interventions in the marketplace, such as subsidies, may be closed off as options, negative interventions, like raising the cost of labour by increasing the minimum wage, a policy undertaken by Singapore in an effort to move from a labour-intensive economy to a more capital-intensive one, are not only possible but are likely preferable. It is easier to 'pick losers', those industries that you do not wish to have, than it is to 'pick winners'. After all, when everyone is courting the same industries, industrial policy may become a zero-sum game wherein each country is simply contributing money to the bottom line of those industries. Yet, when one is actively discouraging the establishment of a particular industry, all non-discouraged industries stand to benefit because competitive advantage is truly a relative, not an absolute, concept. Indeed, even if one 'loses' by retaining such an industry, the active negative intervention will ensure that the industry ends up subsidising society, instead of the other way around.

NOTES

1. However, it is unclear whether individual elites have a 'credible threat' to move. Capital can move more easily than individuals can.
2. Experimental economics attempts to bring controlled experimentation to the science. However, when dealing with human subjects, Harvard's Law applies: 'Under the most rigorously controlled conditions of pressure, temperature, volume, humidity and other variables, the organism will do as it damn well pleases' (Bloch, 1991, p. 114).
3. As pointed out by McCloskey (1990, p. 140):

> Some economists imitate the role of *ipse homo economicus* they have created. Any one who has administered economists will report that a third or so of them behave in selfish ways, justifying their behaviour when challenged by smirking reference to the economic model of man. . . Historians and doubtless professors of literature have their own occupational diseases, but cheeky selfishness is not one of them. It's not done in their circles; it is in economics, because of the market stories the economists tell.

4. There is a significant literature dealing with so-called 'common ownership' which suggests that private ownership and control lead to better allocative efficiency. However, these studies suffer because all deal with societies having at least some basis for individual property rights in other venues. It is not clear whether the hedonistic impulse is innate or learned; however, evidence from psychology suggests the later is true. In any case, even if private ownership does provide better incentives for private gain, it is unclear whether such systems equally serve other societal goals, such as equity.
5. Japan is not alone in this. All the newly industrialised countries of East Asia had significant government intervention in their markets during the time that the 'miracle' fostered their significant growth rates. Japan (Johnson, 1982), South Korea (Amsden, 1989), Singapore (Lim, 1983), Taiwan (Wade, 1990), and Hong Kong (Choi, 1994) have all been shown to be significantly interventionist in their economies at the time of their economic 'take offs'. The difference between East Asian and other developing countries seems to be that East Asian governments have relied on pragmatism and not politics in formulating their economic policies.
6. Only the power of the state can limit a legal right. Third parties, on the other hand, can restrict a license. Therefore, a concealed weapon license gives one permission by the state to carry a concealed weapon and this permission can be rescinded or limited via either the courts (by taking away the license) or by a third party (private property owners can prohibit the carrying of weapons on their premises). On the other hand, only the state can limit the right to vote (using citizenship, age or residency requirements). Thus, a license is merely a grant of permission whereas a right is a granting of an enforceable power.

4. Why Free Trade Really Isn't Free – And Shouldn't Be

Damien King, an economist at The University of the West Indies, Mona, in Kingston, Jamaica, is fond of saying that if free trade agreements were written by economists, they would be a single page with just one sentence on it: 'There shall be free trade'. However, things are not always so simple. The world trading system is biased towards states that have significant power in the marketplace, such as the United States, and the rules of trade reflect that power. To take one example, intellectual property rights have come to dominate the discourse on international trade, with the United States and its media companies seeking to extending copyright protections even on products that have already been produced. Such an extension, while possibly laudable from the perspective of the creation of future works, is positively laughable from the perspective of works that have already been created. All it does is create monopoly rents and limits the free flow of information because nothing can be created in the past that was not already in existence at the time of the copyright extension.

Thus, such extensions provide no material benefit to society and only serve to enrich monopoly capital concerns. Yet, although the vast majority of orphan works receive no benefit and the action will cost developing countries potentially billions of dollars in terms of economic innovation, the desires of a few large media companies have allowed the USA to turn international intellectual property rights into a Mickey Mouse concern. This is especially ironic because in the 19th century it was the United States that was the leading bastion of flagrancy in terms of copyright violation, so much so that Gilbert and Sullivan entitled their operetta the Pirates of Penzance as a reference to those US opera companies that routinely put on Gilbert and Sullivan's plays without paying so much as a sixpence in royalties to the duo. Yet, beyond power concerns, there is an economic rationale against free trade, but before we examine that, we must examine the case for it.

THE ECONOMIC CASE FOR THE FREE FLOW OF GOODS

International economic integration began with foreign trade. Indeed, early mercantilist writers, such as Mun (1986), argued that a country's wealth lay in the gold and silver it held and that it was important to use trade to accumulate a surplus. Such an argument is not entirely without merit. Gold and silver were, after all, the only universal mediums of exchange. While China might have no use for English port, it would always take gold in exchange for its silk. However, this was not the reason cited by the mercantilists.

Hume (1951) attacked this line of reasoning. Hume argued that the price level in a country would rise in direct proportion to the supply of money. Thus, if a country constantly imported bullion, the price level in the country would invariably rise, eventually turning the balance of trade against the importing country, causing an outflow of gold and making a long-term favourable balance of trade unsustainable.

Quesnay (1970) would coin the term '*laissez-faire, laissez-passer*' in describing the physiocratic embracement of increased trade; this came from the perspective that all wealth sprang from so-called 'productive classes', specifically agricultural interests.

Adam Smith (1976, I:468-9) believed that the principal advantage of engaging in foreign trade was to dispense of goods that were oversupplied within a country's borders:

> The importation of gold and silver is not the principal much less the sole benefit which a nation derives from its foreign trade. . . [Foreign trade] carries out that surplus part of the produce of the land and brings back in return for it something else for which there is a demand. It gives a value to their superfluities, by exchanging them for something else, which may satisfy a part of their wants, and increase their enjoyments.

Thus, foreign trade for Smith is a means of extending the market. In this way, the manufacturers in a small country need not limit the scale of production to serve only their market. With trade, their market is the world, but their competitors are not just merchants in their own country, but also those of foreign countries as well. Besides, Smith (1976, I:472) felt that the mercantilist solution of engineering a favourable balance of trade gives the government 'two great engines for enriching the country, restraints upon importation and encouragements to exportation'.

Import restraints manifest themselves as either import duties or outright prohibition used on imported goods that compete against domestic products. Another target of such deliberate actions are countries that persistently have a favourable balance of trade with the country deciding to impose the duties. Such actions should not be unfamiliar: 'fair trade' is usually just a call for trade balancing. As a member of the European Community trade delegation to the United States said, 'Americans seem to feel that they have a God-given right to a trade surplus; anytime they don't have one, they complain that someone must be cheating' (private communication with confidential source, January 1995).

Smith believed that such restrictions gave the home-grown industry a 'monopoly' in the domestic market. In this regard, Smith uses the term 'monopoly' in an unfamiliar form. In contemporary economic thought, a monopoly consists of a single company with total productive control over a single market. However, Smith's notion of monopoly is fundamentally the same. The duties and prohibition created a situation that limits free entry and exit. It is this limitation that is at the heart of market power. Without the ability to limit entry and exit from an industry, there usually exist conditions where a 'rent' or 'profit' (in the modern sense of the words) is earnable.

Smith (1976, I:477) believed an individual feels affinity towards his country and will choose to keep capital employed there, all other returns being equal:

> By preferring the support of domestic to that of foreign industry, he intends only his own security; and by [maximising his returns], he intends only his own gain, and he is in this, as in many other cases, led by an invisible hand to promote an end which was no part his intention.

Smith, however, believed that duties and prohibitions create incentives to produce at home, items that are importable for less. Smith (1976, I:478) states the granting of such a position to home markets is either a pointless exercise in the flagrant use of power or an act that will actually hurt the nation:

> It is the maxim of every prudent master of a family never to attempt to make at home what it will cost him more to make than to buy. . . What is prudence in the conduct of every private family can scarce be folly in that of a great kingdom.

Smith went on to argue that restrictions *may* aid the country *if*, while the monopoly is in force, the industry secures an absolute advantage (i.e., it produces a good at a lower cost than another country can) in the making of that good. However, such circumstances are rare, temporary, and, to Smith, always serve to diminish the revenue available to a country in the short run. The short-run diminishment will cause capital accumulation to slow over the whole country and, according to Smith, negates any benefit from granting the monopoly to the industry.

Another case where it is possible that such import restrictions may be beneficial, according to Smith, is when foreign ownership would negatively affect national defence. After all, it would prove to be a disaster if the supplier of defence equipment turned out to be an enemy. Another reason for duties, according to Smith, is where there are taxes imposed on the home industry in that manufacture. In such a case, to not impose a tax would be to grant to the foreign producer a material advantage over its domestic rivals and the problems of duties would reverse, encouraging individuals to invest overseas to a greater extent than would exist in a 'regime of perfect liberty'.

Smith also stated other reasons to deviate from the general principle of universal free trade. When other countries refuse to lower their barriers to trade, Smith (1976, I:489-90) believed:

> Revenge . . . naturally dictates retaliation, and . . . we should impose the like duties and prohibition upon the importation of some or all of their manufactures into ours. [This action is prudent] when there is a high probability that there will procure the repeal of the high duties or prohibitions complained of. The recovery of a great foreign market will generally more than compensate the transitory inconvenience of paying dearer during a short time for some sorts of goods.

Smith called for a slow transition to a universal free trade *if* such a change would throw a large number of individuals into the lines of the unemployed. Smith suspected this would not occur, pointing out that export-competitive wares have an advantage at home (because they must compete against protected commodities in other countries) and most workers displaced would likely find jobs quickly in other businesses.

Smith argued that from a political viewpoint the transition to free trade would be slow and incremental. This was due to domestic laws (corporate privileges, apprenticeships and the laws of settlement) that made relocation of the workforce unlikely, coupled with the fact that such a move to total free trade would benefit the majority at the expense of the wealthy and powerful.[1] Such men opposed any move to diminish their power and privilege and held greater sway over the politicians who would vote on these matters than the silent majority ever could: 'To expect, indeed, that the freedom of trade should ever be entirely restored in Great Britain, is as absurd as to expect that an Oceana or Utopia should ever be established in it' (Smith, 1976, I:493).

Smith saw how disadvantageous it was to slap restrictions on countries against which England had a trade deficit. He noted that having a negative balance of trade with one country could actually improve the *overall* balance of trade. Taking the example of France and England, and supposing for the moment that free trade gave England a trade deficit with France: 'If the wines of France are better and cheaper than those of Portugal [Great Britain should] purchase . . . the wine . . . of France. Though the value of the annual importations from France would thereby be augmented, the value of the whole annual importations would be diminished' (Smith, 1976, I:498).

Smith argued the balance of trade argument lacked substance because countries would only trade when they found it advantageous. It is the amount of savings in an economy (production less consumption), not the trade balance that determines prosperity for Smith. He argued there was little value in hoarding metals because a country could always acquire them through trade.

On drawbacks of duty (being the recompense given to a merchant so, upon re-exportation of a good, the duty previously paid to the government is returned), Smith agreed with the principle but argued the whole duty, not merely a portion, should be returned. Thus, the 'natural balance of industry, the natural division and distribution of labour, which is always more or less disturbed by such duties, would be more nearly re-established by such a regulation' (Smith, 1976, II:8).

Smith attacked bounties (export subsidies) as taxing the home market to pay for the consumption of foreigners. Although exports may increase in one industry by such means, it will be to benefit an industry that ought not be exporting. This places a burden on the other industries that would naturally export and on the citizens who must forgo consumption in the home market.

Finally, Smith noted that trade treaties are often detrimental to one, or both, signatories. By forcing countries to admit goods from another country at a preferential rate (compared with other countries), it may prove to be a counterbalance to the monopoly of the home market by the local producers. But such allowances give the country granted the preferential standing an advantage not accorded other exporters. Thus, imports from such countries (as Viner (1950) would later point out in his classic work on customs unions) crowd out those of others and will result in an overall lower rate of production and consumption than would naturally occur in a regime of perfect liberty.

Mathematician Stanislaw Ulam once stumped Paul Samuelson by asking for 'one proposition in all the social sciences which is both true and non-trivial' (Jones and Neary, 1984, p. 3). Samuelson later suggested Ricardo's comparative advantage theory. That it is logically true need not be argued before a mathematician; that it is not trivial is attested by the thousands of important and intelligent men who have never been able to grasp the doctrine for themselves or to believe it after it was explained to them (Jones and Neary, 1984, p. 3).

Ricardo begins his exposition on foreign trade by refuting Smith's 'vent for surplus' argument (Ricardo, 1911, p. 77): 'No extension of foreign trade will immediately increase the amount of value in a country, although it will very powerfully contribute to increase the mass of commodities, and therefore, the sum of enjoyments'. Smith argued the ability of firms to use the foreign market since a 'vent for surplus' allows them to combat the tendency for profits to decline by allowing them to shift the surplus goods overseas. As the profit rate tends to equalise across industries, Smith went on, the profit rate rises across industries because of this ability to export. Ricardo attacks this and purports to show Smith to be in error because profits can only change with a change in the wage rate, which requires a drop in the cost of subsistence. If foreign trade allows the subsistence wage of labourers to drop, profits will rise 'but if the commodities obtained at a cheaper rate . . . be exclusively the commodities consumed by the rich, no alteration will take place in the rate of profits' (Ricardo, 1911, p. 80).

Instead, it is comparative advantage that justifies trade. Under Ricardo's theory, a country trades that which it is relatively more proficient in producing for that which it is relatively less proficient in producing. This also works in everyday life: Woodrow Wilson was a better typist than his secretary, but Wilson was comparatively far better at the affairs of state. Thus, it was advantageous for Wilson to conduct affairs of state and leave typing to his secretary. The fundamental assumptions of this theory are:

1. one (fixed in supply) factor of production with constant returns to scale;
2. no deficit spending on commodities by either country;
3. an absence of transportation costs;
4. only two countries with two commodities to be traded;
5. pure (not necessarily perfect) competition;
6. countries are absolute, not relative, gains maximisers; and
7. the factor of production cannot be moved between countries (this is what actually differentiates international trade from national trade for Ricardo).

What makes the Ricardian model so rich is the ease of extending it without loss of clarity. For example, the result that countries completely specialise follows from the constant returns to scale assumption. If one industry faces (relative to the other) increasing costs (meaning that the other, relative to the first, is a decreasing-cost industry), the country will face a sloped production possibility frontier. In increasing its importation of a good, it must export an ever-increasing amount of the other. In such a case, where the terms of trade imply that goods are traded in a fixed ratio of one to the other, countries will produce part of their domestic consumption for each good.

Another reason that a country may be unable to supply the entire world is production limitations. In the case where one country cannot produce all the demand for both countries (a so-called 'small country' case), the smaller country will produce up to its needs and will export the rest to the limit of its productive capacity. The large country will then find it necessary to produce the remainder of its consumption.

The Ricardian model can be extended for multiple countries. Although the derivation is too long to give here, the result is:

> If all countries are ranked according to their labour-productivity ratios, . . . [t]he country with the highest ratio will export good 1, the country with the lowest ratio will import good 1. Countries in the intermediate range may export or import good 1, even though all countries exporting good 1 will have higher labour-productivity ratios than all countries importing good 1. (Bhagwati and Srinivasan, 1983, p. 36)

The model is extendible for multiple goods using a similar methodology (Bhagwati and Srinivasan, 1983, p. 43). Transportation costs are not independent of the goods themselves and cannot be included in the model by simply adding a third good, 'transportation'. Instead, one can use either of two methods. Either the good can have its transportation costs explicitly included in the price or it can be implicitly included using Samuelson's 'iceberg' principle. This principle states that, of the original quantity shipped only a fraction is received. Just as an iceberg melts, transportation costs can be viewed as consuming part of the produce in the process of transport. In either case, there is an international and a separate domestic price that governs trade. Only when the domestic price is higher than, or equal to, the international price will trade occur. Import tariffs have the same effect by causing the international and domestic prices to diverge. Therefore, with such constraints, trade is reduced or possibly eliminated. With the lowering of these artificial (tariffs) and natural (transportation costs) barriers to trade, trade activity increases. Transportation costs, in this manner, encompass both the direct (freight) and indirect (spoilage) costs associated with the transport. Storage and distribution costs can also be subsumed to this concept.

Ricardo's international trade theory does more than refute the vent for surplus argument and advance comparative advantage. Ricardo showed '[a] bounty on the exportation of corn tends to lower its price to the foreign consumer, but it has no permanent effect on its price in the home market' (Ricardo, 1911, p. 201).

Smith had made the remark that the bounty had the effect of pushing up the price of corn as the bounty caused there to be a higher price abroad than at home. The effect was not to increase production, but profits, and this caused the farmers to desire to sell overseas to a greater extent than in the home market. The effect is supply would contract at home, driving up the price so wages, being fully regulated by the price of corn, necessarily rise. It is this 'tax' that was referred to earlier. As Ricardo acknowledges, Smith presupposed the critical assumption of the argument: production would not rise in the face of a bounty. Ricardo does not push this point and counters instead (1911, p. 204):

> If nothing were consumed by the labourer but corn, and if the portion which he received was the very lowest which his sustenance required, there might be some ground for supposing that the quantity paid to the labourer could, under no circumstances, be reduced – but the money wages of labour sometimes do not rise at all, and never rise in proportion to the rise in the money price of corn because corn, though an important part, is only a part of the consumption of the labourer.

Ricardo returns to devastate the Smith's fundamental assumption. After granting wages might rise, he notes:

> Wages are paid by the manufacturer, as well as by the farmer, and . . . must be equally affected by a rise in the price of corn. But they are unequally affected in their profits, inasmuch as the farmer sells his commodity at an advanced price, which the manufacturer sells his for the same price as before. (Ricardo, 1911, p. 205)

To Ricardo, since profits tend to equality, capital flows out of manufacturing and into agriculture. This causes corn production to rise and manufacturing production to fall. However, the price of manufactured goods does not rise; more can be gained in exchange for the exported corn. Ricardo (1911, p. 205) argued if a bounty raises the price of corn in conjunction with a rise in the price of all other commodities, then there can be no greater profits for the farmer. The manufacturer will not be harmed because though he 'pays a greater price for his corn, he is compensated by the greater price at which he sells his commodity, with which the corn is ultimately purchased'.

Ricardo (1911, pp. 210-12) saw bounties as 'divert[ing] a portion of the capital to an employment which it would not naturally seek. [In so doing, it might] lower in a small degree the value of money'. It is this aspect of a bounty that harms. Ricardo, like Smith, supported free trade but was more willing to argue for a gradual reduction in tariff barriers, recognising adjustment costs were associated with the transition from protectionism to free trade.

There was little real progress until after the First World War. Heckscher (1919) and Ohlin (1933) showed that countries tend to export products using relatively abundant indigenous factors of production intensively, while Lerner (1952) and Samuelson (1948, 1949) showed that free trade in finished goods tended to equalise factor prices after accounting for factor productivity. Many of these studies only served to confirm the Ricardian argument that free trade was welfare-enhancing. Even the New International Economics of Helpman and Krugman (1985) shows that, under a number of circumstances (although not all), free trade is preferable to autarky. To deviate from free trade would mean a lowering of allocative efficiency. However, it is unclear whether free trade is the first best solution to the problem of X-efficiency that is the long-run managerial efficiency of production (Liebenstein, 1966; Tirole, 1988). This would suggest that the state could play an important role in developing industries by inhibiting free trade.

THE ECONOMIC CASE AGAINST THE FREE FLOW OF GOODS

One of the attacks on the theory is the division of the gains from trade. If the country is a relative gains maximiser then it accepts free trade so long as this trade increases its world income *vis-à-vis* the rest of the world to a greater extent than the increase in bilateral income for the other country.

The one common thread of the liberal free trade supporters is the belief that government interferes with the growth of the economy. Adam Smith (1976) went so far as to ascribe that government should only provide mechanisms for justice, defence and public works. However, another group of intellectuals was creating the first threads of industrial policy. Alexander Hamilton (1928) and Frederich List (1977, 1983) saw that government could have a role in *creating* comparative advantages where they were heretofore nonexistent. This 'infant industry' argument was the first acknowledgment of a political dimension to the economic integration spreading throughout Europe and the newly founded United States.

Given Ricardo's emphasis on dynamic analysis in the rest of his book, it has always been a wonder why he never tackled the dynamic aspects of foreign trade. Perhaps it was because he was an economist from 'the dominant country' as List called England. Frederich List was a German economist who exaggerated and frequently misstated the work of Adam Smith, leading someone to wonder whether he ever read *The Wealth of Nations*. List had not read Ricardo's book when he wrote *The Natural System of Political Economy* in 1837. The manuscript was a submission to a contest question proposed by the French Academy, 'If a country proposes to introduce free trade or to modify its tariff, what factors should it take into account so as to reconcile in the fairest manner the interests of producers with those of consumers' (List, 1983, p. 191).

List makes no reference to Ricardo in the submission nor does he make more than two brief references in his other book, *The National System of Political Economy*, published in 1841. However, references to Adam Smith abound.

List begins by criticising classical economists, including Smith, for advocating a 'cosmopolitan' economics as opposed to one that centres on the state. In this regard, he is obviously in error. Smith never advocated the state must look after the interests of the world but stated the interests of the world and the interests of the state were the same in many, but not all, cases. Smith (1976, I:487), for example, looked upon national security as being an adequate reason for restricting imports, and noted that without adequate defence the wealth of the nation would soon be lost.

There is justification for List's refutation of the more extreme of Smiths adherents, who believed universal free trade was not only proper, but in its absence, unilateral free trade is the preferred course. In addition, List attacked Smith's notion of 'unproductive classes' a full eleven years before Mill did. He notes the theory of absolute advantage (and, by extension, comparative advantage) neglects dynamics. He notes that there is a difference between production and the productive powers of the state. Beginning, as does Smith with the individual, List (1983, pp. 34-5) writes:

> A father who spends his savings to give his children a good education sacrifices 'value' but substantially increases the productive powers of the next generation. But a father who increases his savings and neglects to educate his children increases the 'exchange value' at his disposal by spending the interest on his capital at the expense of the future productive powers of the country. . . A planter who raises slaves is 'productive' in the sense that he increases the wealth of the nation but he weakens the productive powers of the state. There are many products, such as alcoholic liquors, which increase the 'exchange value' of a nation but weaken its productive powers.

This is List's fundamental *dynamic* argument for the use of a tariff. He notes the country may have to sacrifice by consuming objects of poorer quality in the short run but that it is in the long-term interests of the state and its citizens to engage in these manufactures.

List was writing after the industrial revolution had already taken root. He watched as England attempted to drive commerce off the continent after the Napoleonic Wars and how protective tariffs enabled French industry to survive. Not one who believed in protectionism to the extent that some would make him, List concerned himself with events in Germany and viewed the introduction of a tariff as a means of fostering national unity. He was instrumental in the formation of the German *Zollverein* (customs union) and looked at internal free trade as necessary for a nation to prosper.

However, he did not believe that the same privileges ought to be accorded to outsiders.

Although aware these actions would mean that the country could not consume or produce at the highest possible level *at the moment*, List believed a nation that failed to develop industry would forever be a backwater, forced to ship raw materials to other countries and unable to foster its own economic growth.

List was the first economist to discuss economic development using fundamental stages through which a country must go. In the first stage, the state is in its infancy. Agriculture is dominant, but it is an industry lacking technical knowledge. In terms of class structure, there are only the landholders and the landless. There is no capitalist class to speak of, and all knowledge and productive means lie in the hands of the landlords. During this stage, List argues that there is a need to develop the means of production and to free these from the hands of the landed class. To acquire the tools necessary to enter the second stage of development, countries become providers of raw materials and food for countries that can send them technology and manufactured goods.

As the means of production flow into the country and the productive powers of the country increase, it is first necessary to engage in a process of the expansion of agriculture. After this occurs, it is possible to move on to the second stage of development where small manufacturing firms are first established.

List notes as a country enters this second stage of development (and indeed while it is in it), it faces a difficult choice as to the future on which it will embark. He believed small nations lacked the ability to set up large-scale manufacturing firms and therefore ought to conduct treaties with other nations, allowing them the benefits of a customs union (and eventual political integration).

For countries able to set up such manufactures and compete, the course on which they embark must come from their political reality. Although List was quick to criticise countries engaging in prohibitive practices in the first stage of development (it being necessary to gain the means of production in the shortest possible time), he did acknowledge that such a situation is possible:

> [I]f the country already operates a system of prohibitions or high import duties . . . the rates of the duties should gradually be lowered until protection is afforded only to those branches of manufacture which appear to stand a good chance of being profitable at some time in the future. (List, 1983, p. 192)

He is like Smith, who noted a tariff might prove beneficial if removed at some point in the near future. However, List rejects Smith's contention that such a case is the exception, not the rule. List argues if the country lacks a tariff, it should implement one to allow the country to 'protect and to foster the development of those branches of manufacture which appear likely to be successful in the future' (List, 1983, p. 192).

As the country industrialises, the policy should be to gradually reduce the tariff. Eventually, tariffs should only serve to protect domestic industry from countries seeking to drive out the manufacturing base by dumping their products (selling below cost) and to allow for the base to remain even if there is some temporary setback causing the industry to lag behind its foreign competitors (for example, if the foreign competition comes up with a novel new invention).

In the last stage of industrialisation, List argues that the barriers to trade should be withdrawn and the country's industries should be forced to compete on an equal footing both at home and abroad:

> [A]n industrialised country in which manufacturers have developed to such an extent that – even though it adopts a policy of free trade – it [can] compete successfully with any other country . . . should gradually reduce its import duties so as to allow foreign . . . goods to . . . compete with native products. (List, 1983, p. 192)

List believed barriers to trade should never exist in agriculture, only in manufacturing. He argued that capital does not move from agriculture in the process of industrialisation but is *created* in the process instead. He noted that natural resources available for use in industry have little or no value to the agricultural community. He was one of the first economists to note that land used in manufacturing is more valuable than land used for farming. He argues that most technological expertise will be drawn from other countries and the development of industry allows for a greater development of agriculture, and was one of the first commentators to see that 'factories provided employment for a type of labour that is useless on the land – namely the labour of women, children and old people' (List, 1977, p. 78).

List challenged Smith's notion of a tariff as producing a monopoly of the home market for the domestic industry and that this is ruinous to the consumer:

> Is it really right to attack as a 'monopoly' a measure to ensure that our 20 million industrialists enjoy a legal right to supply our 20 million agriculturalists with manufactured goods – especially when one remembers that our agriculturalists enjoy a natural monopoly to supply our 20 million industrialists with foodstuffs? (List, 1977, p. 81)

List goes on to state that there are good and harmful monopolies. He points out that the monopoly granting an investor exclusive rights to his creation for a given period of time helps to encourage the development of such inventions. In addition, he reminds the reader that the monopoly merely excludes the entry of foreign competition, in a sense, closing the market. Still there are no prohibitions on the ability of citizens to establish their own manufacturing firms. Indeed, though List does not explicitly state as much, the tariff provides for the ability of many to enter the market when before they could not. List argues that the only justification for objection is if the goods produced under such a system cost more in the internal market than they do abroad. However, List argues, this state of affairs is only a temporary one. The increase in the productive powers of the nation (i.e., expansion of the production possibility frontier) will more than make up for today's loss of 'exchange value'. The result is lower production costs and increased exports.

List argued agriculture needed no protection as it benefited from a natural monopoly (in the Smithian sense) while industry did not. He argued restraints placed on the consumption of manufactured goods would hurt only the standards of living in the present, but would not affect the populace's physical well-being. However, agricultural protection would hinder the very programme he envisioned:

> To increase the cost of food by the imposition of prohibitions or import duties is to defy the natural law of national survival. It gives to those who already monopolise a country's land a second monopoly by permitting an artificial increase in the cost of agricultural produce, which harms the welfare of society as a whole. On the other hand, to protect industry by the imposition of a tariff provides the working class with jobs and with food and enables it to escape from the consequences of any increase in the cost of manufactured goods.

Only the protection of industry by means of a tariff will enable the country to buy food from abroad if the harvest at home should fail (List, 1983, p. 89). Thus, List was not a diehard protectionist. Indeed, in a long-range dynamic sense, he was not even a mild protectionist.

List's arguments were dynamic in nature and *did not represent* a return to mercantile thought. List was correct in asserting this was a new form of political economy, although his form was more a derivative of classical methods than a revolutionary idea. List ignored the trade balance and never associated precious metals with wealth. His arguments have the same rigour as those of other classical economists and he is closer to Smith in tone than to Locke or Mun.

List made many mistakes that took the form of incorrectly reading some of Smith's arguments; his enthusiasm to refute the claims of the master often got the better of him. Considering his correct understanding of other sections of *The Wealth of Nations*, List was probably more the victim of poor notetaking than of purposeful deception or ignorance. In addition, his interpretation of history is slanted but List was an advocate, rather than an expounder, of possibilities. Germany was a newcomer to development and England did have the advantage of being the first to industrialise. List was never afraid to take jabs at the orthodoxy and, on occasion, was prone to wild misses.

Although the theory of comparative advantage was probably unknown to him, this does not diminish the ability to use his arguments as an attack on static comparative advantage as well. His development of stages of industrialisation presages Rostow's (1960) theory by more than a century, and differences in how societies ought to approach economic processes are a clue as to a course that economics might have taken.

There is a progression from Smith's challenge to the hegemony of the mercantilists to Ricardo's elaboration of comparative advantage to List's formulation of the theory of development. This progression is natural and could only occur in this sequence. Smith would be unable to gather up the ideas of the physiocrats and organise and dispose of them into a unified theory of economics had there been no mercantilists or physiocrats. Ricardo would have been unable to come to grips with political economy or develop the theory of comparative advantage had there been no Smith. Similarly, even if List did not know of Ricardo at the time of his writing, Ricardo popularised the ideas List attempted to refute and Ricardo influenced the actions that England was taking at the time.

List was virtually forgotten as an economist for many years and only in recent times has the case against free trade again resurrected many of his ideas in new form. These economic objections[2] to free trade usually concentrate along ten lines of attack:

1. the Listian 'infant industry' argument;
2. high adjustment costs;
3. economic externalities;
4. the need to pressure others to open up their markets;
5. imperfect markets (including oligopoly);
6. protection of 'high-wage' industries;
7. backward linkages;
8. 'strategic' industries;
9. the terms of trade; and
10. incomplete information or uncertainty.

There are at least two additional economic lines of attack: declining marginal benefit to trade coupled with high transactions costs for concluding agreements; and the most powerful players in the market make the 'rules' governing trade.

Infant industry protection is an old argument that both Mill (1917) and Marshall (1926) favoured. GATT recognised its validity with article XVIII

(B). Essentially it is an argument of *intertemporal* market failure, a market failure correctable only if an industry receives protection during the period of time when market forces would force a premature exit. Often it is argued that the industry is one that benefits from scale economies in production (Krugman, 1984) although, in this case, it is only worthwhile to have protection if there is no retaliation (Krugman, 1992). According to Corden (1984, pp. 91-2), market failures used to justify infant industry protection include ones involving capital market imperfections (such as investment myopia), labour market imperfections (such as an inability of firms to recoup the investment in labour due to labour mobility), and network externalities (such as knowledge diffusion and growth stimulation in other sectors of the economy). In all cases, the first best policy is one that attacks the central problems (either correction of the market imperfection or direct financing to compensate firms for the loss of labour or to create knowledge[3]) as opposed to using tariffs or export subsidies.[4] There are four key problems with the infant industry approach[5]:

1. determination of which industry will likely develop to be dynamic and competitive in the future is problematic;
2. political considerations can often enter into the determination of which industries receive protection;
3. complacency may set in the industry because the premise of the infant industry argument, learning-by-doing, must be based on the conditions that surround the learning process;[6] and
4. the longer an industry needs protection the greater the future benefits are required to be for the protection to be economically viable.[7]

On the other side, during periods of 'late' industrialisation it may be possible to pinpoint these issues more accurately (this is the so-called 'young country' argument). However, this still makes this better suited for developing, rather than developed, countries to justify protectionism.

Then there is the question of adjustment costs. If the gains from trade are small or have a lengthy transition period and adjustment costs are sufficiently high, the continuation of protection is justifiable. Put it another way, trade liberalises if and only if the discounted future value of the gains from trade is greater than the discounted future cost of adjustment (that invariably occurs before the gains from trade). Thus, if adjustment costs are high and short term and the payback from trade is long term, a case for protection may be justifiable.

Economic externalities may exist. If the price of a good does not reflect its true social cost, free trade may not be warranted. For example, one may need to inspect imported fruits and vegetables to ensure that no insects are imported into the country (the Mediterranean Fruit Fly, for example). The government may impose a tariff equivalent to the marginal cost of inspection to compensate for this cost. Similarly, there may be a case where a product has consumption externalities (such as cigarettes or gasoline that cause pollution) warranting tariffs.[8]

Protectionism can force others to open up their markets. This is an argument against unilateral free trade but in favour of bilateral free trade. It works if power exists in the system to allow for countries to use the *threat* of protectionism to extract favourable trade conditions or if the cost of introducing punitive tariffs is less than the benefit from opening the new markets (if the future discounted return to tariff protection exceeds the future discounted cost of the same, tariff protection is the optimal strategy). In practice, such strategies tend to be anything but temporary measures and instead create a situation where foreign tariffs are a given. However, for political reasons, tariffs may be answered with tariffs. In such cases, it is an unfortunate circumstance but one that restores equity within a country (at a lower level of efficiency and overall income).

The so-called 'strategic trade policy' of the new international economics promoted by Helpman and Krugman (1985) shows that where there exist imperfectly competitive markets (such as in oligopolistic industries), *laissez-faire* is suboptimal.[9] Also, Hagen (1958) argues that, in the presence of distortionary pricing in the labour market (found in either discriminatory wage payments or labour union power), a laissez-faire policy is not the optimal policy.

Reich (1991) says one must protect 'high wage' industries. This is unlike the pseudo-economic argument in that Reich does not argue that competition with 'low wage' countries will drag down wages. Instead, he believes a country needs to maintain its base of 'high wage' industries (those that require high levels of skill and are thus 'high wage' industries in all countries) to maintain a high standard of living in the country. This, and its related argument, the strategic industries case, share the same defect: if a country is going against its competitive advantage, it will lose business to other countries and the 'high wage' jobs that are saved will be saved only at the cost of higher unemployment and greater efficiency losses in other industries.

Some commentators emphasise 'backward linkages'. There are linkages between various sectors of the economy so the development of one industry is dependent upon the development of another. The car industry supports the steel industry so if one is lost, the other will be lost as well. While one can argue economics of agglomeration are important, this is an argument for subsidisation of the generation of linkage benefits and not for tariff protectionism.[10]

Then there is the 'strategic industries' argument. This is a political argument veiled as an economic one. Proponents believe certain industries are 'strategic' as they are required for a country's viability. The points made against the 'high wage' industries argument are equally applicable here as being variations on the same theme. Cohen and Zysmen (1987), and Karagiannis (2002) argue 'manufacturing matters' in that manufacturing and services are linked in such a tight and concrete way that if one removes the manufacturing base, the service sector may fail to develop. Kaldor (1966) argues manufacturing industry is important as it is more technically progressive than service industries. Libicki (1989, p. 1) argues strategic industries are 'those that best foster the systematic application of knowledge to generate more and better outputs from inputs'.

Johnson (1958) and Bhagwati (1958) note that economic growth can be 'immiserising': a deterioration in the terms of trade is generated by growth such that overall welfare falls because the terms of trade decline causes a greater reduction in welfare than the overall growth rate adds to welfare.[11] There are two paradoxes that an optimal tariff[12] can fix: the Metzler paradox and the Lerner paradox. Under normal conditions, the demand curves of both countries are elastic so the introduction of a tariff has the effect of protecting the domestic industry. On the other hand, if the domestic curve is inelastic and there is the introduction of a sub-optimal tariff, the Lerner paradox can occur leading to a deterioration of the terms of trade. If the foreign curve is inelastic, the Metzler (1949) paradox may ensue leading to a reduction in the price of imports.[13]

The presence of uncertainty and incomplete information is perhaps the most persuasive argument of all. Under uncertainty, in the extreme, autarky may be Pareto-superior to free trade (Newbery and Stiglitz, 1981) leading to tariffs as insurance against the uncertainty of the market system (Eaton and Grossman, 1981).

The last two arguments are ones of political economy as opposed to pure economics. The first is the conclusion that trade agreements have certain costs and there is a declining marginal benefit to each additional widening (addition of countries) or deepening (reduction of trade barriers) of trade relations.[14] The second of these arguments is that the country with the most 'power' is the one that makes the rules. This uses the concept of the economic hegemony (Kindleberger, 1981, 1986; Keohane, 1980). While it may be beneficial to conclude free trade agreements nonetheless, it is not entirely clear that the following of the hegemon's rules would be the best course of action for increasing world welfare. Thus, multilateral free trade may be preferable in order to reduce trade dependency and harmonisation of policies in accordance with the hegemon to bilateral trade agreements. Thus, diversification and greater worldwide welfare may result from having small countries choose to liberalise trade with other small countries before liberalising with the hegemon.

THE FREE FLOW OF CAPITAL

It is in the area of the free flow of capital in that the strongest attack on free trade is being waged. Free trade, in the traditional Ricardian-Herschker-Olhin sense, is purely a static theory. Trade and production, however, are fundamentally dynamic and equity concerns must play a role. Kuznets (1955) argues rapid industrial growth has a positive correlation with rising income inequity. However, the Newly Industrialised Countries' 'East Asian Miracle' has produced a far different result. Recent research (for example, *The Economist*, 1994) even suggests inequity is inimical to growth.

Although this 'miracle' was a case of state-driven industrialisation based on the selective application of investment incentives and disincentives, it is incorrect to assume all actions by the state are fundamentally beneficial. But who makes the decisions if the government does not? The answer is the multinational corporation.

However, there is a paradox in this entity. Although these corporations have stockholders from many different countries, the price to earnings ratios differ considerably across nations, even for comparable firms. The great leveller of profit maximisation is not a universal concept since it is unclear which profit is to be maximised: short, medium or long term. Japanese firms fundamentally and structurally differ in management style (Pascale and Athos, 1981) and their relationship to the state (Johnson, 1982). This has produced a corporate structure that favours retention of employees over the American-style expansion and contraction of the workforce to fit with the current state of the economy. Japanese corporations are far less profitable by measures of return on equity, assets and sales than American companies (*The National Times*, 1994); however, they are far more stable in their profit patterns, indicating that the reliance on long-term, as opposed to short-term, outlook has a positive effect on their ability to manoeuvre effectively.

Governments can, through the establishment of the 'working rules of going companies' (Commons, 1957), alter the economic foundations of their capitalist systems to produce growth economies. Kaname Akamatsu's (1961) analysis of development likened economic development among regional players to a flock of 'flying geese' with each country losing lower echelon industries to their neighbours such that all countries in a region will develop together with the dominant player taking the lead. Such an approach would lend itself to a product cycle-based industrial policy so that regional free trade will prove to be the springboard to investment decisions that would create the appropriate backward linkages in the economy (Vernon, 1966).

The springboard for this investment is the multinational corporation (Vernon, 1971). Levitt (1970) and Gilpin (1975) argue the multinational corporation acts primarily in the interest of the country where its home office is located and thus it is an extension, not a restriction, of state power. This is not to say corporations serve directly the commands of the national government but there are bridges between government and enterprise facilitating the exchange of personnel between the two sectors. The two share a commonality of interest. Problems occur when the firm faces a conflict between states (e.g., when its country of origin attempts to impose extraterritorial requirements). The firm has divided loyalties: the home country's desire for extraterritoriality of its laws and the host country's desire for territorial sovereignty.

It is also important to realise the notion that private corporations will continue to operate in the national interest without coercive action being in decline. As corporations internationalise (as opposed to being multinational), indications are that the principals will come from all the firm's branches. Localisation strategies and the efforts to promote advancement opportunities for the best workers, regardless of nationality, are making these linkages increasingly tenuous over time. Also, with international shareholders, the possibility of using corporations as tools of national power is decreasing every day. This does not mean that there are no opportunities for states to continue to influence the behaviour of firms. The tax codes of an individual country may direct them to engage in a different ordering of priorities. However, multinational corporations hold a good deal of power in the system. They can choose to relocate their head offices (for example, Jardine Matheson, one of the major Hongs (trading companies) in Hong Kong, moved its corporate headquarters to The Bahamas in order to avoid Chinese retribution after the 1997 takeover), can exercise power within the domestic political system to change government objectives or they may set up their entity as a transnational corporation which lacks a clearly identifiable national identity.

Marxist theorists and neo-Marxist dependency theorists (Lenin, 1939a; Galtung, 1986; Wallerstein, 1976) believe the world system of capitalism creates uneven patterns of development, enslaves the masses to the capitalist mode of production, and makes labour part of the machinery. Lenin argued the potential for profit was what drew multinational firms to invest and that these profits are extracted from poorer countries. However, such an analysis would conclude that most of the profits are patriated, a condition not supported by the evidence.

Another view is firms act the same because each is rationally attempting to maximise profit. It is unclear whether one can make such an assessment. Even if individuals maximise utility (that may not be the case, see Downey, 1987; Simon, 1983), it does not immediately follow that firms will maximise profit. Given absentee ownership, the desires of the shareholders for further profits may conflict with the desire of managers to further their own interests

(Veblen, 1954). Incentive-based manager compensation systems somewhat mitigate this. Such systems emphasise short-term profits and lead to actions that temporarily boost stock values when complete information is lacking. This brings up other problems: is profit maximisation concerned with short-term profits, long-term profits or an intermediate concept? What is the benchmark discount rate for future profits? What happens when tax policy causes distortions? However, these questions are beyond the scope of this study.

Further, Hymer (1976), coming from the Marxian tradition, concludes that international investment has more to do with trade barriers than with exploitation of labour. Transaction cost economists (also known as the New Institutional Economics) argue the same thing in that such investment allows firms to bypass market mechanisms that have high transaction costs (Coase, 1937; Williamson, 1985; Ethier, 1986). Nevertheless, there is an apparent paradox working here: although trade barriers are coming down international investment is increasing. Of course, this is explainable at least partially from the transactions cost perspective in arguing that barriers to international investments are coming down faster than trade barriers. Technological factors could drive the process or network externalities associated with such investment may exist.

We assert something different is happening. If institutions matter, they must have the capability to change the working rules of the society to create incentives that advance the national interest (Chandler, 1992; Scaperlanda, 1992, 1993; Schockman and Madjd-Sadjadi, 1994). The role of the state is to engineer policies that support the development of national-based firms and speed up the development of competitive advantage. However, it is not possible to reverse the natural course of the free market without facing dire economic consequences (World Bank, 1993). The reason for national-based firms is important. Although home governments do not directly control their firms, firms do bring the culture and methods of their society with them when they invest abroad. Just as 'cultural capital' can explain the success of various diasporas (Sowell, 1994), corporations may be thought of as having a form of 'cultural capital' based on their origins. When they are transnationals, they use leverage given to them by the world system to extract payments from other national governments.

A national-based firm faces three important obstacles to the use of power against its own nation. First, history guides its actions, and its values, norms and preferences are compatible with the nation. To change head offices may require a number of changes in corporate culture that, although possible to undertake, result in considerable cost. Second, the firm creates numerous backward linkages in the national economy and aligns its organisation of production and distribution with the national system in mind.

Third, the firm employs large numbers of individuals within the country, creating a vast institutional memory that would be lost after such a move.

GLOBALISATION AND THE NATION-STATE

Globalisation is merely the latest phase of this process of international economic and political integration. The nation-state has been under attack for more than four hundred years,[15] and this attack has gone through five clearly distinctive stages: Colonialism, Imperialism, Multinationalism, Internationalism and Globalisation (see Table 4.1 at the end of the chapter for a typology of these periods). These stages are not mutually exclusive nor can they be clearly delineated by boundaries of time, for as Marx has said, the seeds of the old regime carry forth into the new regime. The first stage was typified by the colonial expansion that began with the rediscovery of the New World by Christopher Columbus and the rise of the Spanish and Portuguese Empires and ended with the American revolution. Besides, it was typified by the internationalisation of security. This was the height of the nation-state and yet also the beginning of its demise. No longer was a country subject to attack merely at its borders. It now had to defend its colonies in far distant lands as well. This led to the first international arms races, large alliance structures, and the first attempt to divide the resources of the world using international agreements (the Pope divided the world between the Spanish and Portuguese at the start of the 16th century).

The revolt of the American colonists led to reclamping by the European countries, and an attempt to conquer through imperial force, instead of through colonisation, Third World countries. This period is the age of Empires that ended with the beginning of World War I, and was typified by the internationalisation of production. After the American experience, there was little attempt to displace native populations by a large-scale exodus from the home country. Instead, the natives were exploited and denied the democratic institutions given to colonists and this allowed order to be maintained. To ensure this subjugation, the first corporations came into being. At first, they were instruments of the Crown and were monopolies allowed to operate in a geographic region. A classic example of this was the British East Indies Company which controlled India. Gradually, these corporations acquired private identity and competition grew. In almost all cases, interests in the home country controlled the corporations. Thus, the great Hongs of Hong Kong had almost free reign over the Crown Colony for most of its existence. Cloth from India and silk from Hong Kong made their way to British shores. British industrial factories turned them into fine garments while opium was sold to placate the Chinese.

The weakening of empires after the First World War led to another form of domination, multinationalism, where the branch plant model came to dominate. This is typical of a multipolar world where no country can easily dominate others. It also brought forth the internationalisation of money. Trade occurred between countries with different currencies, necessitating a system that allowed the exchange of goods at a price converted into local money. The gold standard ensured that each country would have a fixed exchange rate mechanism, so the transfer of goods into money went smoothly. However, this regard for the need of a system of exchange to handle increasing trade flows did not find its way into practice on other fronts. Trade barriers were high and, despite heavy rhetoric calling for free and open markets, little progress was made in reducing protectionism. After the United States heavily increased its tariff structure following the *Smoot-Hawley Tariff Act of 1930*, the rest of the world followed suit. International trade between countries diminished considerably and it appeared that the internationalisation of the economy and polity was rapidly ending. But this was not the case. Internationalisation merely changed form, not substance.

The Great Depression was the most significant economic event of the past century. It ushered in changes to domestic and international economic institutions and its ramifications continue to this day. Black Thursday did not merely wipe out economic fortunes; it nearly wiped out the economic science. Several writers (Rowald, 1976; Cleveland and Britain, 1976; Kindleberger, 1986) argued it was Britain's decline as a world power that resulted in the Great Depression. Weakened by the First World War, Britain was unable to recover its premier position in the world economy and refused to establish a viable exchange rate because of political considerations. They lamented this and argued for a hegemon. However, the lack of a hegemon was a necessary, but not sufficient, cause of the retrenchment. The Great Depression was inevitable because the international system that preceded it used undemocratic and inegalitarian principles while the nations of the world were increasingly democratic and socially responsible in the conduct of domestic affairs.

Polyani (1957) noted that there is no self-regulating mechanism and, to impose a regulatory mechanism, one must destroy the free market myth. There is nothing inherently 'free' about free trade in a regulated society. If one regulates exchange rates or attempts other measures of stabilisation, one inherently alters the incentives derived from the market. However, this is precisely what the different powers were doing with their international gold standard. Imperfections are inherent in any economic system, but the correction of these imperfections only draws one farther away from the theoretical model and enhances some groups at the expense of others.

In a multipolar world, the desires of individual countries take on greater importance. Even as free trade waned (although not in the rhetoric of nations), the balance-of-power system disintegrated (in the First World War), and the self-regulating market system proved to be driven by the state regulation. The gold standard was an inviolate principle accorded the status of divine inspiration. Maintenance of the gold standard was no longer an attempt to impose a series of conditions on the players in the system but a commandment from the invisible hand of God in the capitalist religion. From this, all else follows: fiscal balance is mandatory as is a commitment to protect the currency from inflation. However, as in all religions, even those of faith are subject to interpretation. The legacy of the era was that nations discovered that, just as on the national scene the market was not perfect, so too, it was imperfect internationally. Therefore, when economic conditions dictated, it was inevitable that countries would turn to gold sterilisation policies, and these policies are what directly led to a collapse of the world monetary system and the Great Depression.

After World War II, one country, the United States, became the first superpower reshaping the world in its image. This led to internationalism in a bipolar world through the internationalisation of politics. International law received its most prominent place during this period, and the establishment of the United Nations and World Court gave countries a real ability to manage the international system. Countries increasingly ceded sovereignty to these organisations instead. The WTO, IMF and World Bank furthered this. However, the international system only mirrored American interests. Again, the hegemon continued in an inegalitarian fashion. While the global boom aided many in the developed world and launched several newly industrialised countries (NICs), many other countries, particularly in Africa, struggled.

The oil price shocks provided the first indications of a regime change. The Breton Woods agreement on fixed exchange rates collapsed under the weight of the cartel's increase in the price of oil. However, only with the collapse of the Soviet Union in the late 1980s and early 1990s was there confirmation of the new era of globalisation. No longer is America the hegemon and, just like the period leading up to the Great Depression, the players in the system worry about their relative payoffs. Despite increased international linkages, the world economy moved lethargically, especially from the mid-1970s to the late 1990s, compared to the 1960s.

Transnational corporations and multilateral organisations hold increasing power over sovereign nations. A series of books (Naisbitt, 1994; Wriston, 1992; Ross and Trachte, 1990; Ohmae, 1990; Lang and Hines, 1993; Barnet and Müller, 1974) analyse the problems caused by this. Extraterritoriality is impinging upon national sovereignty as nations sign various binding global agreements having more to do with reforming the economic system within countries (a traditionally domestic function) than breaking down barriers to free trade.

THE MULTINATIONAL CORPORATION AND THE ISSUE OF SOVEREIGNTY

Globalisation can be broken down into two fundamental areas: governance structures and industry practice. Most of this book will be concerned with the former and industry practice will be taken as a given. This analysis will now briefly turn to the latter issue to understand the process of globalisation at the firm level and how it is driving all the changes seen thus far. There are several reasons why nations and subnational governments seek foreign investment. These include increased capital formation, technology transfer, job creation, the gaining of new production and management techniques, network externalities resulting from such transfers, enhancement of regional development, and an improvement in the balance of payments. There are also several reasons why governments do not welcome foreign investment. These include concerns over foreign industrial dominance through increased concentration, the fear of technological dependence on another country, changes to the corporate customs and practices in a country, and issues of extraterritoriality (Behrman, 1970).

Increased capital formation can come domestically or from foreign investment. Foreign investment may be preferable to domestic investment for two main reasons. First, foreign investors typically have a longer time reference than domestic investors because of additional uncertainty over exchange rates. Foreign firms (that invest in a domestic economy) tend to be larger (than the typical firm in that domestic economy), translating into a longer time horizon for investments (Schumpeter, 1928). Second, foreign investors do not vote and therefore their leverage in the political system is not as great as the domestic investor.[16]

Foreign investment brings technology transfer. This allows a country access to the scale economies of other nations' technological advances to advance its own research and development (Lindsey, 1986). Technology transfer can occur at the national level, but then the technology tends to be evolutionary for the firms and not revolutionary. By importing technology, new industries can arise in a fraction of the time it takes to build them from scratch.[17] Similarly, production and managerial techniques are transferred, although these sometimes fall victim to a need to adapt to local culture. These transfers produce network externalities and allow local companies to gain expertise.

Another desire by host governments is to use foreign firms to promote regional development:

> If the incentives are sufficient to offset the long-run costs and inconveniences [but this is not always the case, as some firms have concluded], the officials of the multinational enterprise are quite willing to be cooperative with government

> officials in regard to location. . . Since this dispersion increases demand for transport services and local construction and raises local employment and income, both local and federal authorities are pleased. Cooperation in location tends to reduce other demands from the government on operations of the affiliate. The multinational enterprise thereby obtains an additional return for its cooperation. (Behrman, 1970, p. 20)

Foreign competition can also substitute for domestic competition. When entering a new market, foreign competitors often bring with them cultural baggage from their origin. They come with new ideas and ways of doing business which allow them to compete in areas other than pure price competition, thus developing new products and services. They can import successful designs found in other countries that may not be developed by domestic companies due to scale restrictions or cultural ignorance. Rapid technological change in any society often coincides with external influences. Still, the most important difference between domestic and international competition is cultural.

Last on the list of beneficial consequences of foreign investment is the balance of payments effect. As technology transfers involve the elimination of transaction costs over a market-based mechanism (one of the principal reasons for the creation of a multinational corporation in the view of Williamson, 1985), they can result in a favourable shift in the balance of payments for the host country.

Balancing these benefits are several concerns about the effect of foreign competition in the domestic realm. The first is a fear of foreign industrial dominance based on the belief that foreign firms are either acting as agents of their countries of origin or they otherwise lack the same commitment to the domestic market as do their domestic counterparts. However, this fear is often unfounded as firms, both foreign and domestic, often have investors in several different countries and are answerable only to their shareholders. Countries can try to engage in extraterritorial action but the company might leave.

The second major fear is foreign competitors can change corporate customs and practices. This fear is a paradox in the thinking of the host government: on the one hand, they welcome the managerial and production techniques from abroad insofar as these raise productivity; but on the other, they fear the dislocations and complications that the changing working environment can cause.

The third major fear is that of becoming technologically dependent on another nation. This fear is not entirely baseless. When there was a revolution in Iran, the United States imposed a trade embargo against the country. In so doing, the USA denied to Iran spare parts needed to keep its American-built helicopters and airplanes in service. Once problems began to develop, Iran was in a tenuous situation: enforce its sovereignty or cater to American demands for changes in its domestic and foreign policies. By choosing the former, Iran was condemned to take a giant step backwards in the development of its aviation programme.

The issue of extraterritoriality becomes a problem when considering the multinational as an entity. And which set of laws does it follow: its host government's or home government's? This problem is not always one that is onerous. If the home government attempts to extraterritorially usurp control over business decisions in another country, the company can always move its head office. Of course, the choice is similar for the company facing restrictive practices by the host government, but such activities eliminate the potential for profitable ventures in that country (moving the head office only transfers corporate control to another location and does not necessarily inhibit the capacity of companies to actively pursue economic gain in that country; exceptions to this include areas of investment regulated by the country but these restrictions could be circumvented by creating subsidiaries or joint venture operations that have a 'majority interest' held by nationals of the country). However, it is simply not practical to move one's head office at the slightest hint of extraterritoriality. Often, the cost of doing so outweighs the cost of compliance; so, the company complies with the imposition of extraterritorial restrictions (while usually decrying such actions as placing it at a competitive disadvantage in the world marketplace).

Host governments have several possible responses to these changes.[18] They can place restrictions on new entrants (by requiring a majority stake to be held by nationals). They can demand exit payments (as is done in Europe) if the company chooses to leave. They can set performance requirements (requiring a certain amount to be exported or specifying a certain percentage of value-added that must come from within the host country). Finally, they can simply deny foreign ownership in certain sectors of the economy.[19]

NOTES

1. Ironically, several left-wing writers now maintain that free trade in the modern era does exactly the opposite, concentrating wealth in the few at the expense of the many.
2. There are several non-economic and pseudo-economic objections to free trade. Root (1984, pp. 281-3) lists examples of pseudo-economic arguments that commonly find expression in the popular media, on 'buy domestic' campaigns and in labour union advertisements. These include the mercantilist argument that money spent on foreign goods goes overseas and thus impoverishes the nation; the 'buy domestic' argument that states that money spent on domestic goods creates domestic jobs while similar expenditures on foreign goods only create foreign jobs; the 'equalisation of costs' argument that asserts that tariffs should equalise costs so as to ensure a 'level playing field'; the wage disparity

argument that maintains that price and wage differentials will force domestic 'high wages' down to foreign 'low wages'; and the 'prevention-of-injury argument' that attempts to shield domestic industry from harm by allowing the raising of tariffs if the market share of foreign firms increases too quickly or to a level that threatens the domestic industry's survival.

3. See Baldwin (1969) for an explanation of why tariffs cannot be justified as creating incentives for greater knowledge diffusion by individual firms.
4. Grimwade (1989, p. 27) incorrectly argues that subsidies are economically more efficient because they lower prices, as opposed to raising them through the tariff. The reason subsidies are Pareto-superior is that the deadweight losses are lower than for the tariff.
5. As pointed out by Johnson (1971, p. 147-8), the argument against initially extending infant industry protection, which asserts infant industries often continue to be protected after they have matured, is technically invalid because the gains from protection may lead to a social gain, despite the continuance of such protection over the non-introduction hypothesis.
6. As there is a difference between the conditions surrounding a protected market and those surrounding a free trade zone, the outcome will differ (Bhagwati, 1988, p. 97). Indeed, competition may be a lubricant for industrial change. For a good institutionalist argument about the merits of competition, see Auerbach, 1988. For an evolutionary discussion, see Nelson and Winter, 1980.
7. As pointed out by Johnson (1971, p. 146), there is a present cost to protection that must be at least matched by the future stream of income generated after the removal of protection for the policy to be economically efficient.
8. In such cases, domestically produced goods should also be taxed and affected leading to the possibility that an excise tax should replace tariffs. However, it is important not to discount the possibility that the social cost of imported goods may be higher than the domestically produced goods, rendering the need for a tariff.
9. This argument differs from the proposal that a country could attempt to use monopoly power *temporarily* by imposing a tariff (the temporary nature being because the rest of the world would retaliate) and the short-term exploitation would more than compensate the long-term loss. Johnson (1953) showed this is not generally the case while Rodriguez (1974) showed it is the case if quotas substitute for tariffs (showing as well that the long-stated equivalence property between tariffs and quotas is not valid). Thus, under GATT, certain non-tariff barriers were allowed if they are converted into 'equivalent' tariffs, but the reverse is not allowable.
10. This all comes down to a question of path-dependency. Dynamic protectionist arguments (i.e., arguments for subsidisation) assert that path-dependencies exist while those who give static free-trade arguments are implying that these are path-independent variables.
11. Neither Johnson nor Bhagwati argued for protectionism in these papers. They merely noted theoretical possibilities for declining welfare following growth in both open and partially open economies. Furthermore, Johnson (1967) and Bhagwati (1968) argue the presence of tariffs does not alleviate this problem.
12. An 'optimal' tariff is one that reconciles the terms of trade such that the net national gain is maximised. Optimal tariffs correct distortions in the world

market. These distortions are only correctable with a tariff and not a subsidy (which corrects distortions in the domestic market). Johnson (1965a, p. 4) goes so far as to say that the 'only valid argument for protection as a means of maximising economic welfare is the optimum tariff argument, [while] all other arguments for protection [are] arguments for [taxes or subsidies]'.

13. Jones (1989) shows that an optimal tariff may not resolve the Metzler paradox.
14. One could argue there is a rising marginal cost to concluding trade agreements. This is easily demonstrated: widening carries with it the costs associated with securing agreement among an ever increasing number of market participants (hence costs increase with the number of participants) while deepening requires a more involved political process as ingrained interests are increasingly attacked as the process continues (the first 'casualties' from the viewpoint of those who 'lose' under trade agreements of trade agreements are usually those that have marginal constituencies). In either case, the results are the same.
15. There is no indication that the nation-state is in any danger of extinction, commentary by writers like Anthony Giddens (1995), notwithstanding. Indeed, one might say the opposite as 192 nations are now in existence, the largest number in the history of the world. These states range from the tiny Pacific Island nation of Palau (the smallest country in the United Nations with a population of only 16 000) to China (with 1.2 billion people).
16. Of course, this is also well known by the international investor. There is supposed to be national treatment of foreign firms but there remains an additional political risk associated with these investments that is not present to the domestic investor (see Johnson (1965b) for an exposition of this problem in new and developing countries).
17. Of course, this point is not lost on the countries that hold the lead in the technology game. From their perspective, the transfer is a cost to their future competitiveness. Thus, the United States has certain export restrictions and has sought to ensure that its patent protections are enforced internationally.
18. The host country might also erect legislation that prevents the compliance with the extraterritorial legislation. When the United States attempted to enact laws requiring the Canadian subsidiaries of American firms to reveal financial records to the United States, the governments of Quebec and Ontario rapidly passed laws prohibiting this transfer. The USA later dropped the requirement.
19. For example, Air Canada at one time owned 25 per cent of the voting rights in Continental Airlines but had American 'allies' who control 41 per cent of the stock, giving it effective control of the airline. Ford Motor Company similarly holds a controlling interest in Japan's Mazda Motor Company despite having only a third of the voting rights.

APPENDIX

Table 4.1 Typology of Internationalisation

PERIOD	COLONIALISM	IMPERIALISM	MULTINATIONALISM
What Globalised?	Trade; Security	Capitalism; Production	Money; Management
Age of:	Colonies	Empires	Realignment
Orthodox Economics	Mercantilism	Classical Economics	Neoclassical Economics
Heterodox Economics	Physiocracy	Marxism	Institutional Economics
Unit of Analysis	State	Class	Producer
Time Period	1500-1775	1775-1918	1918-1945
Major International Institutions	The Papacy		League of Nations

PERIOD	INTERNATIONALISM	GLOBALISM
What Globalised?	Politics; Investment	Authority; Consumerism?
Age of:	Cold War	'New World Order'
Orthodox Economics	Neoclassical-Keynesian Synthesis	?
Heterodox Economics	Post-Keynesian Economics	?
Unit of Analysis	Consumer	Individual/World Community
Time Period	1945-1990	1990-Present
Major International Institutions	United Nations World Bank IMF International Court of Justice Bretton Woods (to 1973) GATT NATO Warsaw Pact OSCE COMECON European Community	European Union NAFTA WTO APEC ASEAN CSCE International Criminal Court

5. Public Finance and Taxation

During the last forty to fifty years, governments have been involved in altering the income distribution whether deliberately or as a secondary effect of taxation policies. Some have assigned more functions to government sectors while others have preferred to encourage social welfare services. For example, health programmes transfer resources from those who are healthy to those who are not; social security transfers income from those who are working to those who are retired or unemployed; income can be redistributed between general taxpayers and bond holders. Thus, it can be expected that the level and structure of taxation will have implications for the distribution of income and for levels of economic activity (Sawyer, 1989, p. 332).

In the previous chapters, the discussion about the state was largely concerned with the range of activities undertaken by the state. In this chapter, the focus is on revenue, i.e., taxation. Governments levy a wide range of different taxes, and a particular tax may cause changes in people's behaviour and have an impact on the distribution of income and aggregate demand, which influences the level of economic activity. There is only space to consider public finance briefly here, and the focus is on macro effects and the incidence of taxation.

PUBLIC FINANCE: A BRIEF RETROSPECT

Concern with public finance may well be the oldest branch of economics and fiscal analysis has followed (and in some cases led) advances in economic science. Ricardo, Mill and the marginalists, namely, Marshall, Pareto and Pigou all left their stamp on the economics of public finance along with Keynes and the emergence of stabilisation as a goal of budget policy. The next phase of the development of public finance theory emerged with Pigou's (1920) analysis of externalities. External costs and benefits remain unaccounted for by the market and thus call for correction by public policy. Pigou (1928) did not develop this theme in his treatise on public finance. But fiscal economics has also added to the general body of economic analysis. 'Its concern is not limited to the effects of fiscal operations on the market, and market responses thereto' (Musgrave, 1987, p. 1055).

Fiscal analysis discussions took a new turn in the 1880s when utility analysis grounded value theory on the demand side. It was argued that public services, no less than private ones, are provided to meet the preferences of individual consumers and this provision, through the budget, could be viewed in analogy to the exchange mechanism of the market system. Taxes were viewed as price payments that were paid by the consumers. Therefore, a voluntary exchange model of the tax-expenditure process emerged (Sax, 1887; Mazzola, 1890). However, Wicksell rejected this vision of the fiscal process. Both Wicksell (1896) and Lindahl's (1919) studies made use of the benefit principle of taxation in order to determine the principles and decision-making rules that democracies should adopt when deciding upon a just distribution of the tax burden between individuals. Though the simplistic hypothesis of voluntary exchange was rejected, Lindahl (1919) developed an exchange formulation that had an important role to play. Lindahl's formulation, '. . . with its vertical addition of demands, thus anticipated a significant feature of Samuelson's later formulation' (Musgrave, 1987, p. 1055).

Since the 1950s, a new perspective has emerged and attention has turned to how public policy behaves and how such behaviour is determined. In the process, emphasis shifted from concern with market failure and focused on problems in public policy (Buchanan and Tullock, 1962). Efforts to develop a theory of public-sector behaviour were made within a Marxist framework and viewed the State as an instrument of exploitation by the ruling capitalist class. Recent analysis in mainstream economics has proceeded with an analogy to microeconomics, involving the self-interested behaviour of voters, bureaucrats, and politicians.

THE NATURE OF PUBLIC FINANCE AND ITS SOURCES

Public finance is concerned with the income and expenditure of public authorities, and with the adjustment of one to the other; with adjustment not necessarily being equal to equality. Public authorities include all sorts of territorial governments, from parish councils up to national, federal and even international governments. They differ widely, of course, as regards the magnitude of the areas and populations that they govern, the range of functions that they exercise, their methods of obtaining income, the objects of their expenditure and their financial relations with other public authorities, 'superior or subordinate to themselves' (Dalton, 1954, p. 7).

The main division in public finance is between public income (revenues) and public expenditures. The neoclassical perspective, for example, refers to the 'Principle of Maximum Social Advantage' (spending whatever is necessary in order to get the best results attainable), but of course, its practical application is often very difficult. Within such a perspective, all the operations of public finance resolve themselves into a series of transfers of purchasing power, or of variations in total purchasing power, and of consequential changes in the use of economic resources. These transfers are made by taxation or otherwise from certain individuals to public authorities, and back again from these authorities (by way of government expenditure) to other individuals. Some of these individuals (for example, policemen or contractors) render services in return, while others (like old age pensioners) do not (Dalton, 1954, pp. 12-13).

The sources of public income may be classified, but many of the distinctions involved are not clear-cut. However, in the long run, the first and most important practical distinction is between taxation and other sources of public income.

TAXES, TAXATION AND PRINCIPLES

Taxation is part of fiscal policy and also the main financing mechanism for public expenditure. Taxes are collected by governments in order to finance their expenditures and also for purposes of stabilisation, distribution and allocation. Particular taxes may cause changes in people's behaviour and have an impact on aggregate demand that, therefore, influences the level of economic activity. Taxes are the instruments through which governments redistribute income and wealth and, moreover, they are an integral part of a government's fiscal policy as they are used to stabilise aggregate demand.

Taxes are commonly classified into direct and indirect taxes. Broadly speaking, direct taxes are taxes levied directly on the income, profits, capital gains, and wealth of individuals, households, firms, etc., while indirect taxes are taxes levied on transactions, goods and services and, hence, are paid for indirectly. Apart from the above two classifications, we can also distinguish the following kinds of tax:

1. Progressive or Regressive taxes impose relative burdens on the wealthy and on the poor and such taxes include income, spending, net worth taxes (regarded as progressive in terms of their rate schedules), flat rate payroll taxes and sales taxes (regressive). The degree of progression can be calculated for both individual taxes and for the tax system as a whole. A progressive tax takes a higher proportion of an individual's income as that income itself increases; a neutral tax takes a constant

proportion; and, a regressive tax takes a declining proportion (Vickrey, 1987, p. 1021).

The most important issue concerns the bases to which the burden of taxation can be related. The tax base defines the activity taxed and falls into one of three categories: income, expenditure, and capital. The base is usually taken to be income, but alternative bases for evaluating progression (or regression) are consumption expenditure and capital. Although these latter two have been used as alternative bases for taxation, income has received the most attention (Vickrey, 1987, p. 1021).

A frequently used measure of overall progressivity is the change in some overall index of inequality. One such index is the area between the Lorenz Curve (which plots for each lowest x per cent of the population the per cent y of total income received by that group) and the diagonal; this index has a range from 0 to 1/2. An equivalent index of inequality is the Gini Ratio, defined as the ratio of the mean of the income differences between all possible pairs of incomes to the mean income; this has a range of from 0 to 1, always just 2 times the Lorenz area. Fundamentally, the question of how far one can or should go in the pursuit of progressivity in taxation (and redistributive outlays) is a political and social matter as much as one of economics.

2. In its most comprehensive form, Property Tax encompasses within its base the value of all property including land, any structures on the land, producer and consumer durable goods, business inventories and holdings of government bonds and cash. Effectively it is a tax on capital or non-human forms of wealth, and as such, it has been a significant source of tax revenues in numerous countries. In most of these countries, its distinguishing characteristic is its role as a primary revenue source for local governments (i.e., local finance and regional incidence). Property taxation may affect the supply of capital, and exert a depressing effect on the real wage and, second, it may affect resource allocation (Oates, 1987, p. 1034).
3. Two issues concern taxes on income from capital. The first one centres around the arguments for efficiency and equity while the second one centres around the various views put forward on the appropriate choice of an economic model and its parametric values that are relevant for policy. In most economies, the tax on capital discriminates between different sectors, corporate, capital, housing, etc. (Chamley, 1987, p. 598).
4. Industrial countries levy a profits tax on the earnings of corporations. In most OECD countries, the statutory rate of tax is typically close to 50 per cent; interest paid on corporate debt is deducted from the tax base; dividends earned on corporate equity are taxed at the household level

under the personal income tax; and, capital gains on corporate equity are taxed on a realisation basis at a preferential rate of tax. Most systems of corporate taxation include a variety of special provisions: accelerated depreciation, investment tax credits, preferential tax treatment of specific industries and depletion allowances. As corporations undertake most industrial investments and save through retained earnings, the effects of corporation taxation on economic growth and employment are of special interest to policy makers and academics (Mieszkowski, 1987, p. 600).

5. The income tax represents the single most important revenue source in most developed countries. For example, in 1992, (OECD, 1994) taxes on income and profits accounted for 45 per cent of government tax revenues in the USA and Japan; 44 per cent in Canada; 38 per cent in the UK; and 34 per cent in Germany. France was unusal among the leading industrialised countries in raising only 18 per cent of its tax revenues from these sources. Income tax requires a more developed government infrastructure than other revenue sources, as it is a direct tax on individuals, rather than an indirect tax on transactions (Auerbach, 1987a, p. 604).
6. Taxing wealth (on an annual basis) may be viewed as equivalent to taxing its return at a rate sufficient to produce the same tax revenue. There are four types of wealth taxation: property taxation, net worth taxation, estate taxation and capital levies (Auerbach, 1987b, p. 607). The basic requirement of a good tax system is that the tax burden should be distributed in an equitable fashion and this requirement has taken the following two forms, with one calling for taxation in line with benefits received, and the other calling for taxation in line with one's ability to pay (Brown and Jackson, 1990, pp. 298-300):

   a) The 'benefit principle' of taxation examines the costs and benefits of public sector activities facing individual citizens. In other words, this principle examines how much benefit an individual has received from government expenditure, and taxes are levied in accordance with the benefits arising from government services which are financed by the taxes.

   b) The 'ability to pay principle' applies to the levying of taxes according to how much an individual can afford to pay. In other words, the more an individual earns, the more he pays; thus, taxes are heaviest on those with the highest incomes and/or wealth. According to this principle, unequals should be treated unequally while equals are to be treated equally. This equity principle of taxation was originally based upon a particular notion of justice, namely, that equality in tax payments implied equality in sacrifice (Brown and Jackson, 1990, pp. 298-300).

CLASSICAL AND NEOCLASSICAL APPROACHES TO TAXATION

As stated above, there are two main principles relating to taxation and the latter one, the ability to pay principle, has its foundations in the writings of both Adam Smith and John Stuart Mill. In the *Wealth of Nations*, Smith (1776) pointed out:

> The subjects of every stage ought to contribute toward the support of the government, as nearly as possible, in proportion to their respective abilities; that is, in proportion to the revenue which they respectively enjoy under the protection of the state. The expense of government to the individuals of a great notion is like the expense of management to the joint tenants of a great estate who are all obliged to contribute in proportion to their respective interest in the state. In the observation or neglect of this maxim consists what is called the equality or inequality of taxation. (E. Cannan (ed.), 1937, Vol. II, p. 130).

Smith goes on to argue '[i]t is not very unreasonable that the rich should contribute to the public expense, not only in proportion to their revenue but something more than that proportion' (1937, Vol. V, ii e. p. 6). Smith's basic principles of taxation were the following ones:

1. Equity: individuals ought to contribute 'as nearly as possible in proportion to their respective abilities' (Smith, 1776, p. 310).
2. Certainty: tax liabilities must not be arbitrary or uncertain (visibility and compliance cost considerations).
3. Convenience: the manner and timing of tax payments should be convenient to the taxpayer.
4. Economy or efficiency: the excess burdens (or welfare costs) of taxation should be minimised. Included under this heading are the administrative, collection and psychic compliance costs of taxation (Smith, 1961, p. 310; p. 348 and further).

Mill founded his argument firmly on questions of justice and fairness, as can be clearly seen in the following extract from his *Principles of Political Economy*:

> Government must be regarded as so pre-eminently a concern of all, that to determine who are the most interested in it is of no real importance. . . As in a case of voluntary subscription for a purpose in which all are interested, all are thought to have done their part fairly when each has contributed in accordance with his means, that is, has made an equal sacrifice for the common object. (Book 5, Chapter 2)

If one looks carefully at Smith's basic principles, one can spot some inconsistency because his opening sentence appears to suggest that he also believed in the benefit principle. For Smith, the ability to pay was considered only as an addition to the more basic benefit rule. However, Mill definitely rejected the benefit principle because he believed that it would result in regressive taxation, since the poor were more in need of the services of the state than the rich. For Mill a tax system based on the benefit principle was not just and, instead, all individuals should be treated equally under the law with equality being the rule in all affairs of government. Mill's interpretation of the ability to pay principle led him to propose a system of proportional taxation, however, he made no attempt to prove this case. As a utilitarian, he assumed that the absolute loss in income to the rich man would represent a smaller welfare loss than it would to a poorer man. For Mill, 'equality in taxation meant equality of sacrifice'. Consequently, according to Mill, a just distribution of tax shares prevails when all contribute to the common good so as to incur equal sacrifice (Mill, 1921, pp. 187-8 and p. 804).

David Ricardo presented his view on the general-equilibrium theory of tax incidence, ' . . . with the desire to solve the *puzzle* of tax incidence that confronted him, thus, formulating a general theory of income distribution' (Musgrave, 1959, p. 385). Having determined the theory of factor shares, Ricardo considered the incidence of taxes on wages, rent, and profits, as well as on various kinds of product taxes (Ricardo, 1951, pp. 157-8, 182, 213-15 and 222).

A second attempt at a general-equilibrium theory of tax incidence was made almost seventy years later by Wicksell (1896), who focused primary attention on the relationship between output and the length of the investment period. As in the Ricardian case, Wicksell's theory reflected the structure of a very specific model of distribution theory and 'Wicksell's line of reasoning took an important step toward a marginal-productivity theory of factor shares' (Musgrave, 1959, p. 392). His results on tax incidence reflect the assumption of a fixed wage fund. In a competitive market, the tax must be shared by the factors in proportion to their marginal productivity; hence, the production tax and the income tax become equivalent in their effect on output and disposable incomes (Wicksell, 1896, pp. 21-75).

Following Wicksell, Lindahl (1919) divided the requirement for justice in taxation into 'the socio-political problem of creating a just distribution of income and the purely fiscal problem of providing for the satisfaction of public wants' (Musgrave, 1959, p. 74). According to Lindahl, its solution was in accordance with individual preferences and involved three factors:

1. the total amount of public expenditures and taxes;

2. the allocation of total public spending among goods and services providing for the satisfaction of various social wants; and
3. the allocation of total taxes among various individuals (Musgrave and Peacock, 1958, pp. xiv-xvi).

In other words, Wicksell and Lindahl analysed tax revenue and public spending as an integrated system (Brown and Jackson, 1990, p. 12).

Also, as social goods become available, various taxpayers value them differently. The benefit principle is met because each taxpayer equates his marginal rates of substitution between goods supplied for the satisfaction of social and private wants with their respective price ratios. 'On the basis of a given proper state of distribution, total utility derived from public services is maximised thereby' (Musgrave, 1959, p. 77-8). According to Lindahl, the ability to pay principle is satisfied, because each taxpayer purchases social goods at a different price reflecting his particular ability to pay (Lindahl, 1919, pp. 16-20 and 48-59).

For Marshall, public finance was confined to theories of tax shifting and tax incidence. Alfred Marshall used tax shifting in the context of a partial equilibrium analysis to illustrate the principles of price theory: 'There is scarcely any economic principle which cannot be aptly illustrated by a discussion of the shifting of the effects of some tax.' Marshall's comparative static analysis provided a positive theory for analysing the relative price and output effects of alternative taxes on individuals and firms (Brown and Jackson, 1990, p. 11).

In addition to Marshall's positive theory of tax incidence, the period leading up to the 1950s saw the emergence of a normative theory of taxation based on Pigou's utilitarian approach to the question of how the tax burden should be allocated between individuals (Brown and Jackson, 1990, p. 11).

Walras in his *Elements of Pure Economics* (1954) also analysed tax incidence by considering an economy made up of landowners, workers and capitalists. He considered that the government could collect its taxes directly by cutting into the income received by these three groups, or alternatively:

> It may collect the tax in advance from the entrepreneurs prior to the distribution of earnings to the factors, it being clearly understood that the entrepreneurs will reimburse themselves by adding the amount of the tax to the prices of the products which they sell to landowners, workers and capitalists. In this way, the reduction in rent, wages and interest is made indirectly. Direct taxes are levied on services and indirect taxes are levied on products. (Walras, 1954, p. 450)

According to Walras, a personal tax on wage income cannot change the price obtained for a given supply of labour in the market. As a result of the tax, the supply of labour may rise or fall; if labour supply is unchanged, the burden of the tax will fall entirely on the workers. An exception arises where wages are at the subsistence level and the tax is passed on to consumers through a reduction in the labour force (Musgrave, 1959, p. 400).

Walras further argued that a tax on rent falls on the income of the landowner. When the tax is introduced, the owner of the land loses a part of his income as well as a part of his capital. After the land has changed hands, the tax is said to be paid by no one (Walras, 1954, p. 385).

According to Walras, if a tax is imposed on the income from all capital goods, the income of capitalists is reduced, resulting in a rise or fall of savings. If savings remain unchanged, then the tax falls on the capitalist. However, the situation differs if the tax is imposed on income from selected capital goods only. Accordingly, if capital only in industry Y is taxed, then the supply of capital to this industry decreases, the price of product Y rises and the consumers of Y bear the tax with a portion of the tax being borne by the capitalists. Capital will then flow to other industries, resulting in a general decline in capital income and a reduction in the prices of other goods, thus enabling consumers to recover part of the loss suffered from the rise in the price of product Y (Walras, 1954, pp. 385-9, 450 and further).

The emergence of neoclassical growth models, such as the one put forward by Solow (1956), also added to classical economic analysis and 'invited a reformulation of long run tax incidence in the classical tradition' (Musgrave, 1987, p. 1060). When analysing the impact of taxation on steady-state and equilibrium paths, neoclassical economists look at the effects of taxes on:

1. the rate of growth in the long run;
2. the level of *per capita* income and consumption;
3. the income distribution among factors; and
4. the income distribution among individuals (Atkinson and Stiglitz, 1980, p. 229).[1]

Tax incidence under steady growth is shown to depend on savings propensities as well as the elasticities of factor supplies (Krzyzaniak, 1967; Feldstein, 1974).

Modigliani and Miller (1958, pp. 261-97) noted that the presence of a corporate tax meant that firms would have an 'incentive' to issue additional debt. Since interest payments on debt are excluded from corporate taxes, substituting debt for equity allows firms to pass returns to investors with a lowered tax cut to the government. Consequently, firms would be all debt if the tax authorities still recognised such debt payments as excludable from taxable corporate income. Modigliani and Miller further argued that the only way to stop this expansion would be the real costs of dealing with the inevitable bankruptcies of high debt firms. Although it is logically possible, it would be at the expense of reducing corporate finance to the study of the trade-off between the tax advantages of debt and the costs of bankruptcy.

Several classical and neoclassical theories relating to taxation have been presented above and the starting point is considered to have been Wagner's law in which the state was to intervene in the market economy through a paternalist social policy and a redistributional tax policy. As a result of what he regarded the 'social-welfare principle of taxation', Wagner advocated progressive income taxation as well as wealth, luxury, inheritance and capital gains taxes (Wagner, 1880, pp. 282-92).

KEYNESIAN VIEWS AND MODELS

A quite different macro-perspective on public expenditures and taxation emerged with the Keynesian models and analysis. The classical framework had left the budget aggregate-demand *neutral*, but deficit and surplus finance now became a source of aggregate demand expansion and restriction. Tax reduction (increase) was now seen to be an alternative way of achieving similar results, with the emphasis on fiscal expansion (restriction) directed at an increase (decrease) in government spending.

According to Kalecki, in the general case of an open economy with a government sector, the income view of GNP (at market prices) and the expenditure view of GNP can be written as follows:

GNP = profits (net of direct taxes) + wages and salaries (net of direct taxes) + taxes (direct and indirect) (5.1)

GNP = capitalists' consumption + workers' consumption + government expenditure on goods, services and transfers + gross investment + export surplus (5.2)

Kalecki assumed that government transfers were paid to workers and can here be presented with wages and salaries in the income-GNP and to workers' consumption on the expenditure-GNP. Consequently, the equality between income-GNP and expenditure-GNP (or between Equations 5.1 and 5.2) yields the following:

Gross profits net of taxes = capitalists' consumption + gross investment + export surplus + budget deficit – workers' savings (5.3)

This can be rearranged to give the following:

Gross profits = capitalists' consumption + gross investment + government expenditure on goods, services and transfers + export surplus – workers' savings – taxes on labour income (5.4)

Interpreting Equation 5.3 as an equation for the determination of the level of post-tax profits, it can be seen that gross investment, export surplus and budget deficit are equivalent in terms of their effects on profits. Thus, a government budget deficit helps support profits and this would appear to lead to capitalist support for budget deficits as leading to profits (Sawyer, 1985, pp. 77-9).

Kaldor regarded taxes as the best available instrument for improving the income distribution (as well as for altering the composition of production and expenditure). A change in the structure of income tax affects some income groups more than others and, consequently, such a change has an effect on the distribution of income.

One consistent theme was equity as between different sources of income, and specifically the need to ensure that income from property bears a fair (but not penal) share of the tax burden. This motivated, among other things, Kaldor's well-known pioneering proposal to change the basis of progressive personal taxation from income to expenditure, which better covers capital gains and other windfalls.

The equity of a tax system is to be judged by whether people with the same taxable capacity, the ability to pay, contribute the same amount of tax. If a tax system is to be fair between individuals according to their ability to pay, the first requirement is a just and comprehensive definition of income. The problem that preoccupied Kaldor was finding a definition of income that would be fair to all taxpayers. The essence of the problem is that however comprehensively income is defined for tax purposes, it remains an inadequate measure of ability to pay because it ignores taxable capacity that resides in property as such. This constitutes an argument for measuring one's ability to pay by spending power rather than by income. Kaldor considered two kinds of tax: capital gains taxation and an expenditure tax (see also Thirlwall and Targetti, 1989, pp. 113-17 and 120-28).

According to the Kaldorian theory of income distribution savings are composed of:

$$S = (s_1 W) + (s_2 P) \tag{5.5}$$

where s_1 and s_2 are the propensities to save out of wages and out of profits respectively. Since I=S, Equation 5.5 can be written as follows:

$$(s_1 W) + (s_2 P) = I \tag{5.6}$$

With government activity, Equation 5.6 can be written as follows:

$$(s_1W - s_1t_1W) + (s_2P - s_2t_2P) + T = \mathrm{I} + \mathrm{G} \qquad (5.7)$$

This expression (Equation 5.7) can be rearranged to give the following:

$$(s_1W + s_2P) - (s_1t_1W + s_2t_2P) + T = \mathrm{I} + \mathrm{G} \qquad (5.8)$$

where T is total taxation (equal to $t_1W + t_2P$), t_1 and t_2 are the rates of tax levied on wages and profits respectively and G is government expenditure. Equation 5.8 can be rewritten as follows:

$$(s_1W + s_2P) + (t_1W + t_2P) - (s_1t_1W + s_2t_2P) = \mathrm{I} + \mathrm{G}$$

According to Kaldor, an increased tax on wages would raise the national income, lower the post-tax wages but raise the pre-tax wages. Moreover, capital gains and profits accrue to only a small minority of property owners, which means that the exemption of capital gains and profits from taxation should widen the post-tax distribution of income, and in this sense is doubly inequitable. The effect of a change of profits tax on national output is seen to depend on the response of the mark-up of price over unit cost (*m*) to the tax change, and an increase in profits tax could reduce national output if dm/dt_2 was sufficiently large (Sawyer, 1989, pp. 333-5).

As one can see from the above review, aggregate demand effects of fiscal operation have remained of major concern throughout the twentieth century and have joined the issues of allocation and distribution as a third dimension of fiscal economics.

THE INCIDENCE OF TAXATION

Taxes have effects on both the demand and the supply sides of the economy, changing real disposable income and altering demand; different kinds of tax have different effects on economic activities.

New Classical and Monetarist economists have suggested a minimum role for the state in economic affairs because they strongly believe that the part government plays in the economy should be as small as possible while the part played by the private sector and the market should be as large as possible. Individuals are said to be the best judges of how their incomes must be used and, accordingly, taxes should be low. According to Wilkinson (1992, p. 36), those taxes that must be collected to provide essential public goods should be raised as efficiently as possible, and disincentives and distortions should be minimised. In addition, according to New Classical and New Right economists, fiscal budgets should be balanced; government management of aggregate demand is undesirable and unnecessary. This is because market mechanisms are able to bring the economy to equilibrium at full employment (and a stable money supply provides stable prices). Monetarists see the economy as basically stable and have argued that, if markets are permitted to operate freely, supply would equal demand, in the labour market as well as in the goods market (Wilkinson, 1992, p. 13).

Changes in taxation may be used as incentives on the supply side of the economy, rather than the demand side, as they affect incentives to work, to save and to invest. It is argued that when taxes are reduced, incentives to work and to employ are encouraged and employment and output rise. But most empirical studies of the effects of tax policies on investment or savings have failed to find strong incentive effects (Gemmell, 1986, 1987).

According to monetarists, higher wage rates induce more hours of work and thus encourage more workers into the labour force. In addition, lower income taxes and lower benefits make workers more willing to work, and the reduction of higher rate taxes and the abolition of capital transfer tax make entrepreneurs invest, expand, and take on more workers. It is also argued that investment in new equipment makes workers more productive, and average and marginal productivity of labour subsequently rises.

There are other fiscal and non-fiscal measures which, supply-siders argue, make employers more willing to employ. These include the reduction of taxes on labour paid by employers; a reduction of union power; the weakening of employment protection legislation; and skills training. An increased quantity of employment means increased total output; however, aggregate demand management is regarded as unnecessary, because the economy tends to full employment, and undesirable, because demand expansion via tax cuts (or by increases in government expenditures) leads to budget deficits which are financed through inflationary increases in the money supply (Wilkinson, 1992, p. 41).

Keynes and Keynesians have argued that there is a role for government to compensate for what happens in the private sector. Taxation can reduce the private sector's claims on an economy's resources so that they are released for use by the public sector in a non-inflationary way. This is the allocative role of taxation. Taxes are also used to redistribute income; and for Keynesians, they have a role to play in the management of demand in the economy (stabilisation). If private demand is deficient, if investment is less than saving, then the public sector should make good the deficiency and restore full employment. If the government increases taxes in order to finance an increase in its own expenditure, then, a higher government expenditure will increase aggregate demand, whereas higher taxation will reduce the private sector's disposable income, and therefore its expenditure (especially consumption spending). In general, when taxes rise, the private sector does not reduce its consumption spending by the same amount, but by less than the extra tax payments. Consequently, when disposable income falls due to higher taxation, consumption is reduced by less than the fall in income and savings are also reduced. This implies that the reduction in consumption expenditure is less than the increase in government spending (a net increase in aggregate demand). With increased/reduced government expenditure, the effect on aggregate demand is direct; with increased/ reduced taxation the effect is indirect (through lower/higher disposable income).

Taxes and transfer payments involve the redistribution of national income, since they represent pure redistributions and not the real use of economic resources. The taxing function of the government is crucial to the achievement of the desired distribution/redistribution of national income between public and private consumption, between consumption and saving, and between foreign borrowing and saving from domestic resources. It is also important in achieving the desired allocation of resources. The purpose of the stabilisation branch of the government is to adjust the levels and the composition of taxation and expenditure so that aggregate demand will fully utilise the productive capacity of the economy without generating inflationary pressures (Musgrave, 1959, pp. 6-26).

Keynesian tax and spending policies are undertaken to compensate for what is happening in the private sector as aggregate demand can change both by government expenditures and by tax changes (Wilkinson, 1992, p. 48). If aggregate demand in the economy is insufficient to support a full employment level of output, the government should increase demand by spending more or by reducing taxes or both. Conversely, if demand exceeds the productive capacity of the economy (resulting in inflationary pressures), the government should reduce aggregate demand by spending less or by increasing taxes or both (note the emphasis here on fiscal policy). What Keynesian policies against unemployment effectively came to be in practice were increases in public expenditures, or tax cuts to promote consumption, or both of these together. Hence, tax changes should be directed to both the demand side and the supply side of the economy. It is also important to recognise that the overall level of taxation can be used to offset inflationary or deflationary tendencies in the economy (Wilkinson, 1992, pp. 48-9).

CONTROVERSIAL ISSUES AND EMPIRICAL EVIDENCE

Neoclassical analysts have argued when taxes are reduced, incentives to work and to employ are encouraged and employment and output rise. Also, the possibility of taxes influencing savings-consumption choices is guarded against by the assumption of 'homogeneous' marginal propensities to consume, which prevents income redistribution from affecting the savings-consumption choices. The theoretical basis of neoclassical tax incidence analysis is the marginal productivity theory of income distribution (see Mieszkowski, 1969, 1972; Kotlikoff and Summers, 1987).

Within neoclassical theory, whether taxes are levied on commodities, incomes or wealth (property), they ultimately affect the demand for, and supply of, factors and factor returns. This tax incidence is independent of who pays the tax (whether producer or consumer). In neoclassical models, the tax incidence can only be used to produce results under the specific conditions of perfect competition and disaggregated markets with single products. In post-Keynesian tax incidence analysis, the macroeconomic impact of taxation is considered and the legal incidence of taxation is shown to differ from the economic incidence. Central to the post-Keynesian view of tax incidence is the notion that variations in broad based taxes have significant macroeconomic demand effects which alter the level of economic activity and the distribution of income. Kalecki (1937, 1971) analysed the macroeconomic effects of taxation on the level and distribution of income and employment (under some assumptions) and argued that the incidence of taxes will, through their effects on the income distribution, alter the level of aggregate demand (this stands in contrast to various 'crowding out' effects).

Within the post-Keynesian analysis, the theory of tax incidence considers the relative strengths of the various effects of any tax, allows a fuller appreciation of the macroeconomic affects of tax changes, and can operate successfully under conditions of less than full employment. It is based on the post-Keynesian theory of income distribution which is also empirically testable (Kalecki, 1937; Asimakopoulos and Burbidge, 1974; Reynolds, 1984; Laramie and Mair, 1992, 1993 and 1996; and others).

Kaldor (1955, pp. 21-53) divides taxes into their effects on resources and their effects on incentives and the comparison made is often between an income tax and an expenditure tax. An income tax is imposed on both the income when it is first received and any interest paid when the income is saved. On the other hand, an expenditure tax only taxes savings once, namely, when they are spent (Kaldor, 1955, pp. 79-101 and p. 223). Hence, an expenditure tax allows a more favourable return to savings as interest can be received on the gross amount of any income saved (i.e., the 'double taxation of savings' by an income tax).

As well as affecting savings and investments, taxation may also affect the level of enterprise in the economy. According to Kalecki (1937, p. 444), the analysis of the influence of various types of taxes on effective demand leads to ' . . . quite unexpected results, which are of practical importance'. Also, Asimakopoulos and Burbidge (1974) have reproduced and extended

Kalecki's conclusions in a short-period post-Keynesian model for both competitive and non-competitive markets, in which taxes may have macro-economic effects even during a short period; in post-Keynesian terms, the long-run incidence of taxation (or other government measures) can differ from the short-run incidence.

Laramie (1991, pp. 583-94, 1992) integrated the structure of taxation into Kalecki's analysis of income distribution and national income determination and has suggested that the structure of taxation has an impact on investment and growth. As tax revenues change, the factors which determine the distribution of income change too; but the impact of taxes ultimately depends on the type of tax levied and on the method of tax finance used. Furthermore, Laramie and Mair (1996, p. 16) argue that the incidence of taxation on profits is determined by the following two sets of effects:

1. a public sector effect which depends upon the government's budget stance; and
2. a private sector effect which depends upon: a) the reaction of personal savings to the tax/fiscal budget stance; b) the reaction of investment to the tax in the long period; c) the change in corporate mark-ups with respect to the tax; and d) a foreign sector effect.

Laramie also reintroduced the political dimension into the analysis of the conflict over the distribution of income and extended the analysis of class struggle to other activities of the state, particularly the revenue side of the budget. Consequently, the economic effects of taxation depend upon the following:

1. the structure of taxation and the relationship between the type of tax revenue and the direction of government spending; and
2. the power that economic classes can exert in reaction to being taxed (O'Connor, 1973; Laramie and Mair, 1992).

A lot of empirical evidence exists concerning the effects of taxation on labour supply and incentives, and it tends to suggest that the work behaviour of men responds very little to changes in income taxation; however, there is much greater variation in the evidence about the labour supply responses of women. The studies have covered many different groups of taxpayers in different countries and at different times, and most of them point to the fact that, for primary earners, taxation does not have a large effect (Brown and Jackson, 1990, pp. 442-51). An important result is that there appears to be no substantial disincentive effect from increased taxation, and taxation influences in the aggregate supply of effort seem to be relatively unimportant

(Barlow, Brazer and Morgan, 1966; Brown, 1968; Chatterjee and Robinson, 1969; Fields and Stanbury, 1970, 1972; Godfrey/OECD, 1975; Institute for Fiscal Studies, 1976). On the contrary, evidence suggests that it is possible that an increase in taxation could stimulate the working population to greater efforts. Consequently, it is impossible to say on theoretical grounds alone whether or not taxes influence the amount of work done (Brown and Jackson, 1990, p. 456).

There has also been considerable interest in the idea that tax revenues can be increased by lowering tax rates, a concept reinforced by the so-called Laffer Curve that points out that a 100 per cent tax rate collects as much as a 0 per cent tax rate, that being nothing. The bone of contention between various economic theories is where the inflection point that determines maximal revenues from a given tax rate exists. Supply-side economists argue that it is at a low level of taxation, but evidence suggests that revenue increases will not follow cuts in the basic tax rate (Brown and Levin, 1974; Hausmann,1985; Brown et al., 1986; Burtless, 1987; Brown, 1988).

It would appear to be valuable for a government to have a system of taxes that is elastic with respect to income (one desirable feature of a tax system). Whether or not the tax system is, in practice, elastic with respect to national income growth depends both on the structure of the tax system and on the distribution of existing income and of increases in income. A more progressive tax structure could help to mitigate the maldistribution of increases in income, if such increases are received by the richer classes of the population, and can also generate more elastic tax revenue. The degrees of progressivity of the tax and the tax incidence and shifting are of interest because of the income distribution consequences of any tax or tax system. Therefore, the most likely ways to obtain extra revenue from high-income people are changes in the methods of payment, reductions in avoidance and evasion, and the effects of a progressive tax system where real incomes are rising (Brown and Jackson, 1990).

MEASUREMENT AND PROBLEMS OF TAX REVENUES

It is obviously useful and convenient to have a classification system that is used as widely as possible, and for this reason the OECD classification of taxes has been chosen as its list is preferable to many classifications (see Table 5.1 in the Appendix to this chapter). The definition of taxation of the OECD-UN system of accounts is 'current receipts of government' consisting mainly of direct and indirect taxation, and social security contributions paid by employers and employees. One of the significant advantages of the OECD list (which is updated annually) is that 'the OECD has undertaken a major exercise [which is] to compare the tax structures of all OECD countries using a single consistent set of definitions. The estimate of taxation as a proportion of GDP is commonly used' (Brown and Jackson, 1990, pp. 306-7).

OECD estimates show the ratios of Taxation/GDP (per cent, at market prices) of European Community/Union countries for the years 1960, 1980, 1990 and 2000. The ratio Taxation/GDP has increased considerably for all OECD and European Community countries since 1960, and Denmark, the Netherlands and Belgium had consistently had a high ratio of tax revenue to GDP.

Also, recent OECD estimates show percentage shares of tax revenues of European Community/Union countries since the early 1990s as well as the importance of various broad groups of taxes relative to tax revenue. Of course, this importance differs from country to country and it depends on where these countries put the most emphasis. Within a rising taxation/GDP ratio, there has been a decreased reliance on consumption taxes and an increased reliance upon income taxes and social security contributions. The OECD study observed that the long-term trends slowed down after 1975, with the 1980 structure being virtually identical to that of 1977.

Denmark (56 per cent) put the greatest reliance on taxes on income, profits and capital gains while France and the Netherlands (both 43 per cent) put most emphasis on social security contributions. Portugal (48 per cent), Greece (45 per cent), and Ireland (44 per cent) have emphasised taxes on goods and services (*Revenue Statistics of OECD Member Countries 1965-1980*; OECD, *Revenue Statistics*, various years).

The tax burden can be analysed in a number of different ways, each providing distinctive insights, and a relatively simple analysis, based upon the same set of OECD comparative statistics, is sufficient to support the conclusion that there have been major changes in the composition of tax revenues and these have taken place without being consciously planned. For example, unprecedented inflation rates have distorted the tax structure so that the burden of taxation has shifted in ways not intended by policy makers (Heald, 1983, p. 283).

Many of the parameters of the tax system are set in nominal terms and without regular adjustments to allow for inflation, there will clearly be 'a marked drift towards existing taxpayers paying a higher proportion of their income in income tax and towards the creation of new taxpayers as the nominal incomes of hitherto untaxed individuals cross the unchanged threshold . . . Governments are ambivalent about such *fiscal drag*' (Heald, 1983, p. 285).

So far, two separate problems of tax revenues have been ignored: avoidance and evasion. Avoidance, which is legal, means that the individual organises his financial affairs in particular ways so as to reduce his tax liability. Avoidance occurs when the data supplied are correct, but give a misleading impression, since the transaction has been recast in a way that gives a substantively identical result but a different tax treatment.

Evasion, which is illegal, means that the individual does not declare his full income to the tax authorities and this is simple tax fraud. In other words, the taxpayer reports inaccurate information to the authorities, or fails to report at all. Tax evasion is part of the Black Economy and it is widely believed that the black economy, which operates mainly in cash, has expanded but there is no agreement as to its extent. Participation is open to all social classes and the coexistence of taxed and untaxed sectors diverts resources into the latter, even when these would have been more usefully employed in the former (in Greece, for example, the Black Economy forms one-third of GNP).

Moreover, redistributive policies become much more difficult to operate when major uncertainty begins to attach to the declared income of many individuals. Therefore, the appropriate public policy is a sharp reduction in tax evasion. Attempts to draw direct links between the level of taxation and compliance underestimate the role of cultural factors. For example, France and Italy have long been believed to suffer far more severely from non-compliance than the UK, even though their overall levels of taxation have appeared broadly comparable (Heald, 1983, pp. 292-3).

TAXATION AND MACROECONOMIC EFFECTS

Changes in the structure of taxation impact the aggregate level of activity. Taxes are imposed on the private sector of an economy in order to transfer purchasing power to the government sector unilaterally. In most countries, taxation is among the stronger weapons of economic policy. With the dissemination of the points of Adolf Wagner (with relation to the social and political role of state-government), taxes started to be used to moderate the economic inequalities. In addition, after the prevalence of Keynes's theory, taxes have been among the stronger sources of economic policy used for stabilising an economy.

During the post-war period, taxes became the way of influencing the distribution between consumption expenditure and planned investments so that the social rhythm of economic growth and development could be achieved. Consequently, economic development became the conscious social objective and aim of countries and people. Indeed, taxes can be used to achieve the following aims (Karageorgas, 1979, pp. 124-9):

The Transfer of Productive Means to Public Sector

Governments can decrease the private sector's disposable income and its expenditure (especially consumption expenditure), as a large part of it can go to consumption expenditure and the rest to savings. Firms and enterprises may decrease the quantity of their products, and some means of production are released for use by the public sector in a non-inflationary way (i.e., this is the reallocative role of taxation which can reduce the private sector's claims on an economy's resources). The state becomes a producer itself, or buys from the private enterprises and firms, or subcontracts public goods (roads, guns, traffic lights, etc.) to other companies. Therefore, the state can use more means of production for the production of public goods (either directly or indirectly).

The Stabilisation of the Economy

Taxation is a strong economic policy tool for confronting problems in any economic system. First of all, tax policy can be applied efficiently in order to help the economy to come out of an economic recession. A decrease of aggregate demand in an economy causes economic recession, and if the economy is to come out of the recession the aggregate demand has to be raised by increasing public expenditures or decreasing taxes. An increase in consumption motivates private enterprises to increase production, which results in increases of incomes and demand. Therefore, both production and income are increased in relation to the first (starting) increase of demand, which was caused by a decrease of taxes.

The opposite tax policy may be applied by the government in periods of inflation which results from surplus demand. To this end, governments can decrease government expenditure or increase taxation. Besides, a decrease in consumption decreases aggregate demand. The final conclusion is that when the state tries to decrease surplus demand and efface inflation, it must apply a policy of increasing tax revenues. The most effective kinds of tax are probably personal tax on expenditure and indirect tax on consumption as these kinds of tax affect consumption directly.

The Moderation of Economic Inequalities

Adolf Wagner, the German theoretician of public economics, was one of the first scientists to support that taxes must not only be used to obtain revenues in order to finance public expenditures but also to lessen economic inequalities among a country's citizens.

One of the most effective taxes for the moderation of inequalities on the income distribution might be the progressive tax on income, depending on tax incidence. The more progressive the tax factor the more governments may lessen economic inequalities. Other effective taxes for the moderation of economic inequalities may be the property tax and indirect taxes on consumption (income distribution effects of any tax or tax system).

The Speeding-up of Economic Growth and Development

Taxes are usually suggested as an effective way of obtaining the following two main conditions for speeding-up economic development and growth:

1. the mobilisation of social saving on the level that is required for a socially desirable pace of development and
2. the promotion of the types of investment expenditure that speed up economic development.

The following three procedures can be used for the achievement of the above aims:

1. policy of *protective tariffs* imposes taxes on foreign products which compete with domestic products (e.g., sectors of high potential);
2. policy of *tax motivation* contributes to economic development either by using tax exemptions or by decreasing the tax charge on savings and investments; and
3. *excessive tax charge* of non-productive types of spending attempts to decrease overconsumption or non-productive spending, thereby, redirecting these public revenues to: a) finance the infrastructure and current government expenditure on development; b) give loans and subsidies to enterprises which (wish to) invest in the desired sectors of production (in some cases the state can direct investments to special areas of production) (Kindleberger, 1973, Chapt. 7).

CONCLUSIONS

In this chapter, we have presented the theoretical issues relating to public finance and discussed the second main component of fiscal policy in order to clarify what the different approaches can offer. Tax incidence is very important because of its implications about the impact of state economic policies; but empirical work on 'tax incidence' does not seem to support the 'apostles' of *laissez-faire*. Taxation has been emphasised because it is an important economic policy tool, and some important problems relating to it have been examined within this chapter. A sophisticated understanding of the needs for government action is a requisite to the appropriate selection of a useful and well-timed economic policy-making.

The next chapters will present fiscal and other state economic policies in the EC/EU area, and discuss the successful experience of the Asian 'tigers' (Japan, South Korea, Taiwan, Singapore and Hong Kong) in retrospect.

NOTES

1. Samuelson (1954) used a marginal income-utility model by taking the amount of tax paid into account.

APPENDIX

Table 5.1 The OECD List of Taxes

1000 TAXES ON INCOME, PROFITS AND CAPITAL GAINS
- 1100 Individual taxes on income, profits and capital gains.
  - 1110 On income and profits
  - 1120 On capital gains
- 1200 Corporate taxes on profits and capital gains
  - 1210 On profits
  - 1220 On capital gains
- 1300 Unallocable as between 1100 and 1200

2000 SOCIAL SECURITY CONTRIBUTIONS.
- 2100 Employees
- 2200 Employers
- 2300 Self-employed or non-employed

3000 EMPLOYERS' PAYROLL OR MANPOWER TAXES

4000 TAXES ON PROPERTY
- 4100 Recurrent taxes on immovable property
  - 4110 Households
  - 4120 Other
- 4200 Recurrent taxes on net wealth
  - 4210 Individual
  - 4220 Corporate
- 4300 Estate, inheritance and gift taxes
  - 4310 Estate and inheritances
  - 4320 Gifts
- 4400 Taxes on financial and capital transactions
- 4500 Non-recurrent taxes
  - 4510 On net wealth
  - 4520 Other non-current
- 4600 Other

5000 TAXES ON GOODS AND SERVICES
- 5100 Taxes on production, sale, transfer, leasing and delivery of goods and rendering of services
  - 5110 General taxes
    - 5111 Value added taxes
    - 5112 Sales taxes
    - 5113 Other
  - 5120 Taxes on specific goods and services
    - 5121 Excises
    - 5122 Profits of fiscal monopolies
    - 5123 Customs and imports duties
    - 5124 Taxes on exports
    - 5125 Taxes on investment goods
    - 5126 Taxes on specific services
    - 5127 Other international taxes
    - 5128 Other taxes
- 5200 Taxes on use of or permission to use goods or to perform activities in connection with specified goods
  - 5210 Recurrent taxes

5211 Paid by households in respect of motor vehicles
5212 Paid by others in respection of motor vehicles
5213 Paid in respect of other goods
5220 Non-recurrent taxes
6000 OTHER TAXES
6100 Paid solely by business
6200 Other

Source: OECD, *Revenue Statistics of OECD Member Countries: 1965-1980*, Paris, 1981, pp. 35-6.

PART II

Global Experiences

6. Fiscal Policy and the Case of the EC/EU

During the post-war era, many European countries experienced the growth of social welfare expenditure and the accompanying increases in taxation. According to Sawyer (1989, p. 297) the expansion of the government sector during the post-war period in Europe seems to have been caused mainly by expenditures incurred for redistributive or growth purposes. In virtually all the EC states, the most important reason for the increase in the government expenditure/GDP ratio has been government transfers to households due to demographic changes and the advent of social security programmes. The more general causes of the rapid growth of transfer payments are the relative decline of traditional 'pure' public goods (i.e., defence) and the increasing demand for 'merit' goods (i.e., education, health, social security) in most European countries. Clearly, the welfare arrangements are more developed in some countries than in others and the nature of government involvement is also different among different countries; but in general, during the 1980s and 1990s, the attempt to control government spending by setting ceilings on budget deficits has resulted in a decreasing expansionary effect of public expenditures (OECD, *National Accounts*, various years).

Similarly, different EC/EU countries focus on different forms of taxation, but the compulsory nature of social security contributions leads to the treatment of these contributions as a tax. However, there are differences among the EC countries in the ratio of total tax revenue to GDP, and many factors are important in understanding not only inter-country differences in overall tax shares and tax structures but also the various patterns of public expenditure growth, structure and policy in Europe (Sawyer, 1989, p. 297).

This chapter examines some of the controversial issues related to the role of fiscal policy in the EC/EU, highlights the recent macroeconomic environment therein, and discusses the two components of fiscal policy (i.e., government expenditure and taxation). In other words, it provides background material on the public budget in EC countries but is not detailed enough to serve as a basis for assessing the effects of different fiscal policies that were applied in different countries at different times. One would assume that the forms of government intervention, the nature of public services provision, the characteristics of tax systems, etc., would have become (almost) similar across the EU area following economic integration. However, at an aggregate level of public expenditure or tax trends, inter-country differences do not appear to have declined significantly through time; but it is extremely difficult to accurately assess this due to frequent shifts in the boundary line between public expenditure and other forms of government intervention. Accordingly, only a semi-complete picture of the changes that have occurred since 1970 and onwards is provided and the aims of economic policy (especially fiscal policy) in the EC/EU are only outlined in broad terms.

GOVERNMENT AND FISCAL POLICY: SOME CONTROVERSIAL ISSUES

The conflict between the market and the state has always been at the heart of all the major debates in economic theory. Classical and New Classical tradition is associated with various attitudes towards government, and it shares with *laissez-faire* a belief in a competitive market system and limited government intervention in the economy (Cagan, 1987, p. 496). In contrast, the Keynesian analysis supports government intervention in the economy, for various reasons. The advocacy of deliberate state action to regulate the level of aggregate demand is the hallmark and the essential novelty of the Keynesian perspective (Keynesians also look at the effects of government expenditures on the supply potential, e.g., education).

Economists at the Federal Reserve Bank of St Louis have contested the superiority of Keynesian models over monetarist ones in regard to the significance of fiscal components. Andersen and Jordan (1968) reported the results of a study that tested the response of economic activity to fiscal and monetary actions. They tested the 'St Louis equation', in which changes in nominal GNP depended on current and lagged changes in the money stock, current and lagged changes in government expenditures, and a constant term that reflected the trend in monetary velocity. They concluded that their equation, fitted to US data, showed a strong effect of money on GNP, thus contradicting the Keynesian claim that fiscal policies were more important than monetary economic policies. However, the St Louis equations were widely criticised on econometric grounds. For example, Modigliani and Ando (1976) pointed out that the coefficients of the fiscal variables were positive whereas the coefficient of the monetary variable was negative. They concluded that the St Louis equations, with regard to the US economy, overestimated the impact of monetary influences and underestimated the impact of fiscal influences. According to them, the results were unreliable.

Artis and Nobay (1969) attempted to estimate the St Louis equations with UK data similar to that which Andersen and Jordan (1968) used. They explained that, at the formal level at least, fiscal policy works faster and performs better in explaining changes in GDP than measures of monetary policy.

One consequence of the St Louis equation was that it helped to bring Monetarism to the public's attention. Monetarism is generally associated with a *laissez-faire* and anti-big-government philosophy, a desire to avoid active government and a belief in the inherent stability of the private sector. Friedman (and other monetarists) took the view that the quantity of money has a major influence on economic activity and the price level in the short run only. They advocated that control of the money supply was superior to Keynesian fiscal components for stabilising aggregate demand. Therefore, monetary theory of aggregate expenditures is based on a demand function for monetary assets and the belief that fiscal effects on aggregate demand are small because of the low interest elasticity of money demand (Cagan, 1987, p. 494).

The Keynesian analysis postulates that by controlling the level of aggregate demand for goods and services in the economy, the government can exert considerable influence over the economy. The Keynesian analysis further suggests that the most effective way of doing this is to employ fiscal policies. Any increase in government expenditure adds directly to the level of aggregate demand in the economy. According to this approach, there is a shift in the command of resources towards the public sector and away from the private sector. Consequently, the Keynesians favour fiscal policies.

Monetarists support the view that an increase in government spending (which also increases aggregate demand) increases the money supply and pushes the price level up. In other words, budget deficits or an increase in government expenditure creates inflation. The Keynesian response is that:

1. budget deficits are not necessarily money-financed;
2. money supply is related to bank policy; and
3. it is very important to specify the type of government spending we are talking about as different kinds of government expenditure have different effects on the GDP and its growth.

Keynesian analysis focuses on the determinants of the components of aggregate expenditures and assigns a minor role to money holdings. In monetarist theory, money demand and supply are paramount in explaining aggregate expenditures.

The variety of views linking fiscal and external deficits as following the two main perspectives, neoclassical and Keynesian, is another controversial topic. According to the neoclassical analysis, an increase in the fiscal deficit raises the lifetime consumption of the present generation while shifting tax liabilities onto future generations. Further, in a closed economy with full employment, the boost to aggregate demand produces higher interest rates and crowds out investment. In contrast, in an open economy the widened budget deficit has some degree of impact on the exchange rate and therefore on net exports and, in a small open economy that takes world interest rates as given, all the adjustment is borne by net exports.

On the other hand, Keynesians assume that the economy starts in a position of underemployment and the increased government budget deficit leads to an increase in aggregate demand and national income. As a result of the latter effect, aggregate national savings may or may not decline; consequently, crowding out via domestic investment or net exports need not occur (Perry, 1987, pp. 762-4).

The fundamental difference between these two schools and traditions is their view on the self-equilibration of the economy. The Keynesian school starts from a position of less than full employment that, barring a change in fiscal policy or some other shock(s) to spending, persists. In contrast, in the neoclassical and New Right models, forces are at work to move the economy back to its full employment position, regardless of the stance of the fiscal authorities.

It is necessary to manipulate the balance of spending and taxation in the budget in order to produce the desired result for output and employment. This is entirely in tune with the income-expenditure analysis of the determination of income which formed the central idea of Keynes's *General Theory*. Because output is driven by demand, it can be altered by a government's action to raise or lower its own expenditures and to raise or lower, via taxation, private sector spending. Government budget deficits directly affect the level of aggregate demand and its composition, and it is in this sense that deficit finance and Keynesian economics are closely linked together. The effects of deficits on the level of aggregate demand became an important focus of governments' budget planning after Keynesian fiscal policy and stabilisation analysis was absorbed into policy-making (Artis, 1987, p. 764).

Another argument against fiscal changes affecting GDP is the so-called Ricardian Equivalence Hypothesis (REH), which focuses on higher future taxes implied by a deficit spending programme, and asserts that deficits directly bring forth an offsetting change in private savings (the REH was first stated by Ricardo in the early 1800s and restated by Barro in 1974). The REH is the proposition that the method of financing any particular path of government expenditure is irrelevant. Changes in the pattern of taxation, which keep the pattern of spending unaffected, do not affect the inter-temporal budget constraint of the private economy and thus may have little effect on private spending. But this argument, known as the 'Ricardian equivalence of debt and taxation', holds only if taxes are lump-sum (Ricardo, 1960, pp. 87-9, 102-5, 173, 213-15 and 222). Some taxes, which induce strong intertemporal substitution, such as an investment tax credit on firms, will have stronger effects if they are temporary. For most others, such as income taxes, changes in the intertemporal pattern may only have a small effect on the pattern of spending. Changes in the pattern of government spending obviously have real effects. But again, various forms of direct 'crowding-out' may be at work. Public spending may substitute perfectly, or imperfectly, for private spending so that changes in public spending may be directly, and either fully or partially, offset by consumers or firms. Even if public spending is on public goods, the effect will depend on whether the change in spending is thought to be permanent or transitory. Therefore, one should not expect any change in taxation or public expenditure to have 'a one-for-one effect on aggregate demand' (Blanchard, 1987, p. 728).

The starting point of the crowding-out discussion is the IS-LM model, in which fiscal expansion raises aggregate demand and output. The smaller the fiscal multiplier is the lower the elasticity of money demand to interest rates. Fiscal expansion crowds out the interest-sensitive components of private spending, but the multiplier effect on total output is positive. As output and interest rates increase, it is quite possible for both investment spending and consumption to increase. When dynamic effects are taken into account, other channels arise for crowding-out. But the analysis of these dynamic effects, taking into account the dynamics of debt accumulation, was initially conducted under the maintained assumption of fixed prices and demand determination of output. When prices are also allowed to adjust, the effects of fiscal policy become more complex and crowding-out becomes more likely. On the other hand, not every increase in aggregate demand translates into an increase in output. This is clearly the case if the economy is already at full employment when fiscal expansion can have adverse effects on output (Blanchard, 1987, p. 729).

The crowding-out thesis is presented as an additional critique against an active economic role for the state: the public sector is not only inefficient and incapable of stabilising the system, which is fairly stable anyway, but it is also ineffective in influencing overall aggregate demand and the level of economic activity in the real sector of the economy. Furthermore, some aspects of this debate have provided valuable insights into the effects of different categories of government expenditure and of alternative ways of financing such expenditure (Hadjimatheou, 1994, p. 321).

Bacon and Eltis (1978) raised the point about the effect of government expenditure on the economy. Their thesis on government spending focuses only on a particular aspect of the general proposition that any government attempt to stimulate aggregate demand is futile in that any effect on the economy of the extra government spending is fully offset by displacement, or crowding-out, of an equivalent amount of private expenditure. They suggested that the growth of government was mainly at the expense of capital that was finding it increasingly difficult to maintain adequate levels of capital formation.[1] Moreover, Landau (1983), Marlow (1986), Grier and Tullock (1989), Scully (1989) and Barro (1991) all concluded that the growth of government hurts overall economic performance. That is, growth of the government results in significant reductions in long-term growth and employment.

Although the REH appears to have some empirical support, it applies more clearly to different methods of financing a given level of government spending rather than a change in the level of public spending. Barro (1974, pp. 1095-117) put forward a forceful argument against deficit finance. His idea presumed that consumption decisions were based on an optimising strategy over an infinitely long-time period and that people adjust their own consumption and savings today in response to the after-tax incomes they expect to flow to themselves and their heirs in the indefinite future. In this model, additional deficits today require higher taxes in the future, therefore, consumers fully offset increased fiscal deficits with increased personal savings, thereby eliminating any effect of deficits on GDP or GNP. However, there is little empirical support for this extreme proposition and a number of objections may be made to it, e.g., imperfect capital markets, less than full employment states, etc. (Artis, 1987, p. 765).

Some economists have pointed out other reasons as well. For example, the public expenditure side of the budget may also have an effect upon the distribution of incomes. Musgrave (1986, pp. 71-3) assumed that if the pre-tax income distribution was Pareto efficient, then the post-budget income distribution would remain unchanged if the government provided an optimal output of public goods (the REH seems to support his view: 'The choice to finance government expenditure does not affect the consumption of any household nor does it affect capital formation'). The Pareto optimum effectively accepts whatever distribution of income arises out of the free market system and then constructs the 'first best' situation from it. However, Samuelson (1959: I, Chs 31, 32) disputed this proposition and pointed out that relative factor prices and final consumption prices can change following the introduction of the fiscal budget, which would result in a change in the income distribution.

Is fiscal policy, therefore, an unreliable macroeconomic tool, with small and sometimes negative effects on output? Although it is likely to partly crowd out some components of private expenditure, even in the best circumstances, there is little reason to doubt that it can help the economy return to full employment. The REH and direct 'crowding-out' warn us that no tax cut or spending increase will increase aggregate demand but there is little question that temporary spending or sustained income tax cuts will do so. On the other hand, whilst fiscal expansion affects capital accumulation and output (adversely in the case of full employment), it should not be synonymous with steady increases in the debt to GDP ratio, thus highlighting one of the difficulties associated with fiscal expansion (Blanchard, 1987, p. 730).

EMPIRICAL EVIDENCE

Given the above considerations, it should not be surprising to find that the empirical evidence on the Twin Deficit Hypothesis (TDH) (i.e., the link between fiscal and external deficit)[2] and the REH is mixed. This section will outline the state of the debate on empirical grounds.

Evans (1985, 1986, 1987a, 1987b and 1988) found no empirical link between fiscal deficits and domestic interest rates, exchange rates or external balances for any of the major economies. He stated that, 'the facts in over a century of US history support that large deficits have never been associated with high interest rates. Even the post-war periods separately offer no support for a positive association between deficits and interest rates' (Evans, 1985, p. 86).

According to Evans, this places the burden of proof on those who would reject the REH. Findley and Parker (1992) concluded that 'changes in non-defence spending have no significant effect on the one-year interest rate, though increases in defence expenditure do'. Wray (1995, p.17) argued that 'interest payments have increased much faster than government spending' (per cent of GDP, in every OECD country) and concluded that 'orthodox policy recommendations could lead a country like Italy onto a path of ever larger deficits, rising debt-to-GDP ratios, and rising interest payments as a per cent of GDP' (Wray, 1995, p. 23) (see also data provided by UNCTAD, 1993,p. 75).

Researchers have investigated the degree of validity of both views (i.e., REH and TDH) using various models and methods for the US experience (Feldstein, 1982; Berheim, 1987; Sachs and Roubini, 1987; Ebrill and Evans, 1988; Barro, 1989; Miller and Russek, 1989; Abell, 1990; Enders and Lee, 1990; Dewald and Ulan, 1990; Rosensweig and Tallman, 1991). Johnson (1986) concluded that fiscal policy was an important determinant of the current account in Canada. Ahmed (1986, 1987) examined the UK data over two centuries and found evidence linking public expenditure and the external balances, particularly for temporary fiscal shocks.

Roubini (1988) put forward evidence in favour of the TDH when he estimated reduced-form equations for the current account of 18 countries in an effort to address Ferldstein's puzzle that, 'domestic savings-investment correlations are too high, given high international capital mobility'. Roubini pointed out that, in assessing the correlation between domestic savings and investment, one must take account of the fiscal balance since, in the absence of the Ricardian equivalence, the fiscal balance affects private savings independently of the path of domestic investment. He found that, for 11 out of 18 countries, both the fiscal deficit and the level of domestic investment significantly influenced the current account.

Andersen (1990) pushed Roubini's (1988) analysis a step further and argued that the position of the economy, relative to its level of potential, was an important determinant of the strength of the twin deficits linkage. Andersen also used a longer sample period (1960-89) and made use of error-correction models to capture the dynamics of the current account. Although the results vary somewhat across the 16 countries studied, he found that, on average, an increase in the government deficit by 1 per cent of GNP increased the external deficit by 0.4-0.6 per cent of GNP, depending on the methodology used.

Andersen's results accord well with those of Helliwell (1990), who presented the simulation results of fiscal shocks from a variety of multi-country structural models. He found that, on average, an increase in the fiscal deficit was accompanied by an increase in the external deficit, that is, it was approximately half as large. Thus, a consensus seems to be emerging that the degree of Ricardian equivalence is neither zero nor unity, but lies somewhere between the two. The TDH also appears to have some empirical support.

Knight and Masson (1988) investigated the TDH and REH for the USA, Germany and Japan using an empirical version of a model developed by Frenkel and Razin (1987).[3] In their model, government bonds are treated as if some fraction of their outstanding stock is regarded as net wealth by the private sector. An estimation of the model over the 1961-83 period reveals that, although full Ricardian equivalence does not hold, a substantial fraction, perhaps as much as one-half, of any increase in public sector savings is likely to be offset by induced declines in private savings at unchanged real interest rates.[4]

The impression that one gets from reading the literature is that both the TDH and the REH have some validity, and that a link exists between fiscal and external deficits, although the relationship is surely less than one-to-one. Whether fiscal deficits are associated with higher/lower trade deficits or higher interest rates does not appear to have been resolved in the economic literature. Mainstream arguments seem to have been seriously challenged by both the empirical evidence and the reality. In practical terms, this means that the TDH is operative but perhaps only loosely or very loosely; consequently, there may be circumstances in which the correlation between the two deficits is nonexistent, or even perverse, depending on the nature of the underlying shock. In a review of the empirical literature, Barth, Iden and Russek (1984, pp. 79-95) warned that all the results were sensitive to the time period examined, the measurement of the deficit or debt variable, and the choice of dependent and independent variables.

Several empirical questions arise from the various studies that have been reviewed. First, the very essence of the TDH is that it involves more than one country. Thus, a fiscal shock in one country can only influence that particular country's trade balance if it also influences the trade balance of at least one other country. Several authors have tested the TDH and/or the REH for more than one country; however, they have generally chosen not to recognise these cross-country interdependencies in their tests. This is a serious mistake as ignoring the fiscal shocks in a trading partner country, when testing the TDH for the home country, may risk a biased test, since finding evidence favouring the TDH argument in one country requires that the trade balance of the other country moves independently of its domestic determinants, including fiscal shocks. Therefore, it would seem worthwhile investigating the importance of this issue for established results.

Second, it would be of interest to know whether empirical support for the TDH in the 1990s is different from that in the 1970s and the 1980s, since the economic context and political environment (i.e., political and social considerations) are very different.

Third, examining the estimated intermediate linkages between fiscal deficits and trade deficits may, in some cases, be helpful in explaining the lack of direct evidence of such a link.

FISCAL POLICY AND BUDGET

Fiscal or budgetary policy refers to changes in government income or expenditure that is designed to affect the level of activity in the economy as a whole. Sometimes, the prime aim of such a policy has been to maintain a high level of employment without inflation, given that the two may not be compatible. This is often referred to as a stabilisation policy. The budget is generally seen as a powerful instrument for achieving certain aims, namely,

1. high levels of employment;
2. a high level of investment;
3. a reduction in inflation; and
4. a better distribution of income.

However, if the budget is to be an economic stabiliser it must be large enough to have a stabilising influence, and the larger the budget relative to the total economic activity of the community the stronger this influence can be. Governments have tended to try and reduce the growth of government expenditure as a ratio of GDP in recent years, and the large growth in the size of budgets has been a favourable factor.

The subject of fiscal policy in the period following Keynes's *General Theory* concerns the impact of public expenditure and taxation on aggregate demand. More recently, attention has been paid by post-Keynesians to the relationship between the budget and aggregate supply. The structure of government expenditure and taxation has also had an impact that has been studied at the microeconomic level in terms of the effects on individual firms, households and markets. In addition, it is obvious that government expenditure and taxation have an effect on both production and distribution. Musgrave (1959, p. 5) drew a distinction between the three branches of the fiscal budget:

1. the 'allocative' branch (or function), which is concerned with the efficient allocation of resources, both inside and outside the public sector;
2. the 'stabilisation' branch, which focuses attention on the use of taxation, government expenditure and the national debt for short-run demand management of the economy; and
3. the 'distribution' branch, which uses the instruments of fiscal policy to reallocate incomes between individuals in society.

The approach of Brown and Jackson (1990, pp. 48-9) is more static and has added the 'regulation' branch to the above three branches.

Government expenditure may be classified into two main components: expenditure on goods and services, and transfer payments. The former may be divided into current and capital expenditure, and the latter into current and capital transfer payments. Theoretically, this division may correspond to the economic distinction between 'using up' and 'adding to stock' (Peston, 1987, pp. 283-4).

Turning to taxation, the most straightforward classification is direct and indirect taxes. The former, comprising income and capital taxes, may be divided into taxes levied on firms and taxes levied on households. Property taxes can also be included in this category. Indirect taxes include purchase taxes, sales taxes and VAT.

Given the above background, the central macroeconomic propositions are the following ones. An increase in government spending raises aggregate demand. Also, the process depends on tax cuts raising disposable income and private spending. To the extent that taxes are a function of income and expenditure, they influence the size of the multiplier: the larger the marginal tax rates, the smaller the income or expenditure effects, and the lower the value of the multiplier (Peston, 1987, p. 284).

Transfer payments, although they are classified as government spending, work via their effect on disposable income and private expenditure. Some transfer payments may be endogenous (e.g., unemployment benefits) while other social security payments vary inversely with income (Peston, 1987, p. 284).

Because aggregate demand is an increasing function of government expenditure and a decreasing function of taxation, these instruments may be used to manipulate it. If aggregate demand is forecast to be low compared with aggregate supply, and is not expected to adjust automatically and quickly, a combination of government expenditure increases and tax cuts may be used to improve the position. A reversal of the instruments will deal with excessive aggregate demand (Peston, 1987, p. 284).

The government's budgetary position may be defined as the difference between tax revenues and expenditures. Since the various forms of spending and taxation have different effects on aggregate demand, the results of fiscal policy cannot be inferred simply from an examination of the budgetary position. Rather, it is necessary to look in detail at the budget to ascertain the net impact of fiscal action. Budgetary deficits directly affect both the level of aggregate demand and its compositions and, by influencing the amount of national savings and investment, they also influence, but to a lesser extent, the growth rate of real income in the longer run. In general, effects of larger or smaller budget deficits come about through changes in government expenditures and/or tax revenues (Peston, 1987, p. 284).

Following the IS-LM analysis, some support the view that as larger fiscal deficits lead to higher interest rates at any level of GDP, they reduce the share of GDP devoted to investment and increase the share devoted to consumption and government spending. To the extent that investment is crowded out by higher interest rates, future capital stock is smaller, thus future real incomes and consumption are reduced (Perry, 1987, p. 764). The deficits can be estimated as percentages of GDP, and the ratio will depend on the prevailing ratio of national savings to GDP and on the desired ratio of foreign investment or disinvestment to GDP. Thus, deficits can be used to alter the ratio of national savings and investment to GDP.

The difference between public revenues and expenditures indicates the government's budgetary position. Starting from an initial position of budget balance, a surplus may result from an increase in private spending or a reduction in government spending. While the former causes national income and tax payments to rise, the latter causes national income to fall (it may also cause tax payments to fall, but by less than the fall in government spending). By inference, the budget surplus or deficit must be examined in relation to the level of national income (Perry, 1987, p. 762).

It is also important to look at the relationship between fiscal policy and other forms of macroeconomic intervention, and to place budgetary policy in an international context. The expansionary effect of an increase in public spending (especially if it is tax financed) will depend on the government's propensity to import compared with the private sector's, as will the change in the balance of payments or the exchange rate. Possibly, the effectiveness of an increase in government expenditure depends on whether the exchange rate is fixed or variable, as well as the degree to which capital is mobile internationally. Fiscal policy is most effective, at least in the short term, with a fixed exchange rate and highly sensitive international capital flows (Peston, 1987, pp. 284-5).

THE RECENT GLOBAL FISCAL ENVIRONMENT

The majority of macroeconomic policies and models suggest that empirical relations among the key macroeconomic variables are related to, and influenced by, fiscal policies. The world economy is often subject to large changes in fiscal policies. Until the mid-1970s, governments tended not to run deficits (OECD, *National Accounts*, various years); but since the early 1980s, a lot of criticism has been directed against Keynesian economic policies, which were seen as the intellectual basis that provided the green light for governments to intervene excessively and to run budget deficits. 'New Right' macroeconomics and Monetarism were against government intervention in the economy, and attempted to limit the scope of state activity by denying any possibility of alleviating unemployment by means of aggregate demand management. The large size of the government sector was argued to be detrimental to the growth prospects of the economy and directly responsible for inflation. Privatisation of state activities was hailed as the modern miracle 'antidote' to various economic 'ills'. Legislation was often employed by governments in order to decrease the public expenditure and, especially, the social welfare payments.

In the 1980s, the dimensions of economic policies pursued by a number of governments of developed economies (and especially in the UK), were largely dictated by the intellectual force of such arguments: large-scale privatisations, the abandonment of the commitment to full employment, the reduction of public sector employment, substantial reforms in industrial relations legislation and a number of other similar measures were presented as a means of reducing the frontiers of the state (Hadjimatheou, 1994, p. 322).

During the last 25 years, the continuing growth of government spending, without a corresponding increase in tax revenues, along with efforts to finance government deficits, has shifted the emphasis of policy towards financial control and away from government expenditure planning. At least during the last two decades, economic turbulence seems to have seriously affected attitudes towards government expenditure and, as a result of the recent economic recession, many governments have been forced to reduce public expenditure. The tendency by governments to accept the principle of a more limited role of the state has had the effect of arresting the growth of government expenditure as a ratio of GDP. The recent global economic recession has had important implications for adjustment policies which governments have followed in order to maintain a 'reasonable balance' between economic growth and social development. Looking at the OECD data (*National Accounts*: Vol. II, various years), it is noticeable that many countries have reduced their education and health budgets, and there has clearly been a considerable reduction in the rate of growth of expenditure on education and health services in relation to GDP. Barr (1992, p. 795) points out that, despite the new ideology, neither the Thatcher (and the Major) nor the Reagan administrations actually succeeded in 'rolling back the boundaries of the Welfare State'.

Since the beginning of the 1980s, national fiscal policies have exhibited large divergences and all the major countries (the USA, the UK, Germany, France and Japan) have followed a relatively contractionary course. Fiscal policy tightened in Europe over the same period and this was, in general, the trend in the 1980s and the 1990s. Differences in public spending vary widely between countries. It is noticeable that in most countries the rise in public spending continued until the early 1980s; but in the last two decades, public expenditures levelled off or started to decline as a share of GDP while slow economic growth added new burdens on the budget.

For most countries, the last two decades have been characterised by an increase in the share of public debt in GDP, as well as periods of important increases in real interest rates, two factors which contribute to increasing the debt payment. At present, fiscal policy in Europe is still tight, providing no economic stimulus to growth and higher levels of employment. Looking at the data in IMF (*World Economic Outlook*, various years) high and volatile real rates of interest, large fluctuations in real exchange rates and significant variations in private sector spending are also noticeable. These policies, which were undertaken by the major economies, affected the rest of the world.

The co-movements of GDP growth rates and the main fiscal variables (government expenditure and tax revenue) reflected the outcomes of macroeconomic policies as well as unexpected shocks (i.e., the oil crises in 1973 and 1979). Changes in the main fiscal variables and the induced changes in GDP were associated with corresponding adjustments of private sector spending, namely, consumption and investment.

GOVERNMENT SPENDING IN THE EC/EU COUNTRIES

The measurement of government activity, public expenditure and taxation is essential to most policy analysis. Attention frequently focuses upon the relative size of the government sector and the amount of taxation raised, as well as upon the trends of different kinds of government expenditure and taxation relative to GDP. International public expenditure comparisons in the EC area are made difficult by both the different sizes of the various countries' public sectors and the diversity of government priorities in the economy. At an aggregate level of public expenditure trends, inter-country differences do not appear to have declined significantly through time, however, there are deficiencies in the available data. The discussion has had to rely on an incomplete data base. The three main types of government expenditure, namely government spending on defence, government spending on social expenditure, and government spending on economic services for EC Countries, over the period 1970-2000, are discussed below.

Government Spending on Defence

All the EC Countries experienced higher levels of government expenditure on defence relative to GDP in the mid-1970s than in the mid-1980s and the 1990s. The rates of government expenditure on defence vary from one Member Country to another. Italy (2.16 per cent) and Denmark (2.37 per cent) had the lowest rates in the mid-1970s, and Greece and the UK the highest. Italy (2.03 per cent), Spain (2.06 per cent) and Denmark (2.07 per cent) experienced the lowest rates in the mid-1980s and Greece (6.11 per cent) and the UK (4.97 per cent) the highest. The picture remains the same in the 1990s: Greece (5.98 per cent) and the UK (3.91 per cent) had the highest rates and Denmark (1.95 per cent), Spain (1.90 per cent) and Italy (1.74 per cent) had the lowest. The other EC Countries experienced rates of over 2 per cent in the 1990s. In the EC/EU area, on average, the rates of government spending on defence fell from 3.71 per cent in the mid-1970s to 3.21 per cent and 2.94 per cent in the mid-1980s and the 1990s respectively. Although these changes seem to be in accordance with the tight fiscal policies pursued by almost all the EC Governments since the 1980s, other important factors, e.g., the end of the Cold War, must also be taken into account (OECD, *National Accounts*, various years).

Government Spending on Social Expenditure

Almost all the EC/EU Countries experienced higher levels of government spending on social expenditure in the mid-1980s than in the 1990s (Denmark and Spain were the only exceptions). The rates of government spending on social expenditure vary from one Member State to another. The Netherlands (54.77 per cent), France (37.09 per cent), Belgium (35.66 per cent) and Denmark (33.63 per cent) experienced the highest rates in the mid-1980s and Greece (8.52 per cent) experienced the lowest. Similarly, in the 1990s, the Netherlands (52.18 per cent), France (36.39 per cent), Denmark (34.49 per cent) and Belgium (32.83 per cent) experienced the highest rates while Greece (8.32 per cent) experienced the lowest. The other EC Countries experienced rates of over 21 per cent in the 1990s.

In the EC area, the rates of government spending on social expenditure increased from 25.27 per cent (on average) in the mid-1970s to 30.22 per cent in the mid-1980s and fell to 28.98 per cent in the 1990s. These changes are in accordance with the tight fiscal policies pursued by almost all the EC Governments since the 1980s. The tendency by governments to accept the principle of a more limited role of the state has had the effect of arresting the growth of social expenditure as a ratio of GDP (OECD, *National Accounts*, various years).

Government Spending on Economic Services

Almost all the EC/EU Countries experienced higher levels of government expenditure on economic services (agricultural activities, fuel and energy, mining and manufacturing, transport, communication, etc.) in the mid-1980s than in the 1990s (Germany is the only exception). The rates of government expenditure on economic services vary from one Member State to another. Portugal (10.38 per cent) and Belgium (7.51 per cent) experienced the highest rates in the mid-1980s and Greece (below 1 per cent) experienced the lowest. In the 1990s, Portugal (10.38 per cent) and Germany (6.00 per cent) experienced the highest rates and Greece (again below 1 per cent) the lowest. The other EC/EU Countries experienced rates of over 3 per cent in the 1990s. In the EC/EU area, on average, the rates of government spending on economic services increased from 5.89 per cent in the mid-1970s to 7.88 per cent in the mid-1980s and fell slightly to 7.39 per cent in the 1990s. Again, these changes are in accordance with the tight fiscal policies pursued by almost all the EC/EU Governments since the 1980s (OECD, *National Accounts*, various years).

The tendency by governments to accept the principle of a more limited role of the state during the last two decades or so has arrested the growth of government expenditure as a ratio of GDP and damaged long-term growth prospects (R&D, human resources, etc.). Therefore, tight fiscal policies seem to apply to all components of public expenditure (or total government outlays) in the EC/EU area.

THE EC/EU COUNTRIES' TAX REVENUES

Most discussions about government policy are based on the presumption that taxation is important. Therefore, it is important to look at, and measure, changes in tax revenues since these changes have multiple economic effects on the economy.

This section examines long-term changes in the relative size (per cent of GDP) of direct taxation and contributions, indirect taxation and aggregate taxation, and presents estimates of these taxes as a proportion of GDP at constant prices for EC/EU Countries over the period 1970-2000. The direct-indirect distinction may be misleading because it depends in part on who ultimately pays the tax. A further problem is that detailed definitions (of income, for example) are likely to vary from country to country.

The Case of Direct Taxation and Contributions (DTC)

Most EC Countries experienced higher ratios (per cent of GDP) of direct taxation and contributions in the mid-1980s than in the mid-1970s (the UK and Luxembourg are the only exceptions). The rates of tax revenues of direct taxation and contributions vary from one EC/EU Country to another. Luxembourg (33.29 per cent) and the Netherlands (32.02 per cent) had the highest rates in the mid-1970s, and Portugal (11.55 per cent), Greece (13.95 per cent) and Spain (14.90 per cent) had the lowest. The other countries experienced rates which varied from between almost 19 per cent to almost 30 per cent. Belgium (35.71 per cent), the Netherlands (33.36 per cent) and Luxembourg (31.64 per cent) experienced the highest rates in the mid-1980s while Portugal (17.86 per cent) and Greece (17.20 per cent), again, experienced the lowest. The other countries experienced rates which varied from more than 20 per cent to around 31 per cent.

During the 1990s, the Netherlands (36.06 per cent) and Belgium (32.89 per cent) experienced the highest rates while Portugal (17.71 per cent) and Greece (18.01 per cent) experienced the lowest. The other EC/EU Member Countries experienced rates which varied from between almost 19 per cent to almost 30 per cent. Six countries (the UK, Germany, Denmark, Belgium, Ireland and Portugal) experienced lower rates of direct taxation and contributions in the 1990s than in the mid-1980s while five countries (France, the Netherlands, Italy, Spain and Greece) experienced higher rates in the 1990s than in the mid-1980s. In the EC/EU area, the rates of direct taxation and contributions increased from 23.44 per cent (on average) in the mid-1970s to 26.22 per cent in the mid-1980s and fell slightly to 25.66 per cent in the 1990s. These changes may reflect, more or less, the fiscal policies pursued by the different governments of the EC Countries during different time periods (OECD, *National Accounts*, various years).

The Case of Indirect Taxation (INT)

Most (seven) EC Countries experienced higher ratios (per cent of GDP) of indirect taxation in the mid-1980s than in the mid-1970s. The rates of tax revenues of indirect taxation vary from one country to another. Ireland (19.09 per cent) and Greece (17.38 per cent) had the highest rates in the mid-1970s and Spain (6.97 per cent) the lowest. The other EC Countries experienced rates which varied from between 10 per cent to almost 16 per cent. Denmark (19.24 per cent) and Ireland (17.22 per cent) experienced the highest rates in the mid-1980s and Italy (9.06 per cent) the lowest. The other countries experienced rates which varied from more than 10 per cent to around 17 per cent. There were no significant changes in the 1990s: Greece (18.38 per cent) and Denmark (16.36 per cent) experienced the highest rates, and Italy (10.73 per cent) and Spain (10.36 per cent) the lowest. The other countries experienced rates that varied from around 12 per cent to around 15 per cent. Six countries (the UK, France, Denmark, Ireland, Luxembourg and Portugal) experienced lower rates of indirect taxation in the 1990s than in the mid-1980s, and the other six countries (Germany, the Netherlands, Belgium, Italy, Spain and Greece) experienced higher rates in the 1990s than in the mid-1980s. In the EC/EU area, the rates of indirect taxation increased slightly from 13.17 per cent (on average) in the mid-1970s to 14.16 per cent in the mid-1980s and fell slightly to 13.77 per cent in the 1990s. Again, these changes may present, more or less, the economic policies (and especially the price policies) pursued by the different governments of the EC/EU Countries during different time periods (OECD, *National Accounts*, various years).

The Case of Aggregate Taxation (T)

All the EC Countries experienced higher ratios (per cent of GDP) of aggregate taxation in the mid-1980s than in the mid-1970s (Italy is the only exception). The rates of tax revenues of aggregate taxation vary from one country to another. Luxembourg (46.54 per cent) and the Netherlands (42.1 per cent) had the highest rates in the mid-1970s while Portugal (22.59 per cent) and Spain (21.88 per cent) had the lowest. The other Member Countries experienced rates which varied from more than 31 per cent to almost 42 per cent. Denmark (50.46 per cent) and Belgium (47.91 per cent) experienced the highest rates in the mid-1980s and Spain (30.53 per cent) the lowest. The other countries experienced rates that varied from more than 33 per cent to around 47 per cent. There were no significant changes in the 1990s: the Netherlands (49.28 per cent) experienced the highest rate and Portugal (31.80 per cent) the lowest. The other countries experienced rates that varied from between almost 36 per cent to almost 46 per cent. Six countries (the UK, Germany, Denmark, Belgium, Ireland and Portugal) experienced lower rates of aggregate taxation in the 1990s than in the mid-1980s and five countries (France, the Netherlands, Italy, Spain and Greece) experienced higher rates in the 1990s than in the mid-1980s. In the EC/EU area, the rates of aggregate taxation increased from 36.62 per cent in the mid-1970s to 40.39 per cent in the mid-1980s, but decreased slightly to 39.44 per cent in the 1990s (OECD, *National Accounts*, various years).

Obviously, the magnitude of the change of each component of aggregate taxation varies between countries. Indeed, the ratios of direct taxation and contributions are higher than those of indirect taxation in the mid-1970s, and only in the case of Greece and Ireland did indirect taxation contribute more than direct taxation and contributions to the total tax revenues of these two countries. The ratios of direct taxation and contributions are higher than those of indirect taxation in the mid-1980s for all the EC Countries. In the case of Greece, the share of indirect taxation (per cent of GDP at constant prices) is again higher than that of direct taxation and contributions in the 1990s. These changes may reflect, more or less, the fiscal policies pursued by the different governments of the EC/EU Member Countries during different time periods. Although more government revenues from taxation are needed, it is noticeable that, in most EC/EU Member States, tax revenues levelled off or started to decline, as a share of GDP, from 1991 and onwards. Therefore, most Member States seem neither to try to modify their tax structures nor to fight against tax evasion and the black economy effectively.

BUDGETARY TRENDS IN THE COMMUNITY

Most EC/EU Member States entered the 1990s with budgetary positions recording high deficits. Consequently, the budgetary position of the EC/EU Countries seems to be a worrying phenomenon. Some argue that it is the growth of government expenditure that results in high deficits with adverse implications for confidence and economic growth, while others suggest that governments should achieve higher levels of activity. In Member States, where interest payments constitute a significant budgetary item and where the debt ratio is high and increasing (Belgium, Italy and Greece), decisive efforts need to be undertaken in order to reduce budget deficits. In the other Member Countries, their fiscal consolidation is under way. The large fiscal imbalances led to increases in debt ratios in the Community/Union and it was previously projected that, during the 1990s, the gross public debt ratio would increase by close to 18 percentage points to about 75 per cent of the

Community's (Union's) GDP. Significant increases were expected to be registered by all Member States, except Ireland.

In particular, interest payments were expected to exceed 10 per cent of GDP for Belgium and Italy, while in the case of Greece they were forecast to rise to almost 20 per cent of GDP by the mid-1990s. Expressed as a percentage of budget revenues, interest payments correspond to an even larger share of government resources. Several other Member States, where the debt ratio is lower, have also experienced increases in the share of interest payments in terms of GDP since 1991 (CEC, *European Economy*, various years). In the 1994 European Commission's forecast, only Belgium, Ireland, Italy and the Netherlands were expected to record a decline in the ratio of interest payments to GDP in 1995. In recognition of this, virtually all Member States undertook fiscal adjustment efforts, which formed the basis of the neoclassical/neoliberal convergence programmes.

Although high public debts were recognised by virtually all the Member States, halting the rise in the debt ratio and reversing these trends require appropriate state economic policies extending over a multi-annual horizon. Budgetary policy can make an important contribution to employment and growth, and can help through reorienting tax receipts and expenditure functions towards supporting government and private investment and other spending conducive to steady-state economic growth. At the same time, and where necessary, Member States must aim at modifying their tax structures. Laramie and Mair (1996, p. 20) argue:

> Stabilisation need no longer depend on the use of orthodox 'Keynesian' policies of running budget deficits during recessions and surpluses during periods of recovery. Stabilisation objectives can be achieved within given volumes of public revenue and expenditure by altering the structure of taxation (emphasis added).

In certain Member States, significant improvements in tax administration (for example, more effective fight against tax evasion, simplification of the tax system, etc.) are essential conditions for increasing fiscal revenues and promoting budgetary adjustment.

At the present time, a reduction in public expenditure is likely to reduce income and economic activity, thereby discouraging investments. Lower investments at the present time would mean less productive capacity in the future and more difficulties in achieving economic growth and higher levels of employment. High unemployment in the EU area is a strong sign that the Member States do not fully use the means at their disposal. Besides, action may be directed towards removing the imbalances between private savings and investments, and easing the balance of payments constraints.

As far as the efficacy of fiscal action is concerned, there seems little doubt that in the present circumstances an increase in government spending will lead to an increase in output (or GDP), both directly in the short term, and then indirectly, through the operation of the multiplier on personal consumption and the effects of higher activity in increasing investment. The seriousness of the present economic recession is a strong reminder that the capitalist system is disturbed by business cycles, that markets are imperfect, and that the unique powers of the government can be put to good and proper economic use. Therefore, macroeconomic policy considerations should include the following:

1. the efficiency and effectiveness (i.e., the quality) of public sector spending and taxation should be maximised;
2. sound government finances/investments;
3. aggregate demand management; and
4. inflation must be kept under control.

In other words, an appropriate macroeconomic policy package should pay particular attention to a faster, non-inflationary growth of domestic demand. An expansionary fiscal policy during a recession may have little or no impact on the price level and investment and, therefore, no crowding-out 'problem' will occur.

Some people support the view that public debt is a serious problem. Actually they talk about the concept of budget deficit being defined in terms of a trend, rather than full employment level of activity. The irony is that the consequence of failing to take expansionary action now is likely to be the perpetuation of the level of public sector deficits arising from the current recession. It is only likely that these deficits will get back to lower levels once a higher level of economic activity is achieved. Governments have a range of different instruments for achieving these objectives, and the main stimulus must come from fiscal policy. Clearly, different governments behave in different ways in terms of their policies, but the great problem is to secure general agreement that government action can, and should, be taken in order to increase GDP, and to reduce unemployment and public debt (as scientific and political prejudice seems to be a serious problem).

CONCLUSIONS

Public expenditure has increased massively during the twentieth century. Given the widespread misconceptions about the size of public expenditure relative to GDP and the effectiveness of fiscal policy, the details must be studied with great care. All methods of paying for government expenditure themselves produce problems for government policy. An appropriate public finance policy for the EU would require one to take into consideration the following factors:

1. the structure of the tax receipts of EU Governments;
2. the budget stances of the Member States; and
3. the intergovernmental relations between the EU Member States.

Ironically, there have been claims from sections of the political and academic right that major cuts in levels of taxation can be effected without any loss of revenue. It is difficult, however, to know whether to take such propositions seriously or simply to regard them as elaborate cover for a political strategy. Faced by the difficult realities of budgetary stress, more revenue from lower taxes is an implausible story.

NOTES

1. Not enough evidence exists to show that resource crowding-out has occurred in the UK, and the empirical results clearly indicate that complete crowding-out does not occur (Bisham, 1975; Ball, Burns and Miller, 1975; Evans and Riley, 1975; Laury, Lewis and Ormerod, 1978; Gillies, 1978; Thirlwall, 1978; Lewis and Ormerod, 1979; Taylor, 1979; Hadjimatheou and Skouras, 1979; NIESR, 1981; Fetherston and Godley, 1981; Arestis and Karakitsos, 1982).
2. The higher (lower) the level of fiscal deficit, the more (less) it contributes to trade (or external) deficit, i.e., a strong/weak link between fiscal and external deficit.
3. Frenkel and Razin (1987) developed an income-expenditure model of the inter-dependent world economy by focusing on the short-term and long-term effects of fiscal policies on domestic output and private sector spending as well as on foreign output and foreign spending under either a fixed or flexible exchange rate regime.
4. See also the contributions of Cunningham and Vilasuso, 1994; and Fazzari, 1994; in the *Journal of Post Keynesian Economics*, **17** (2), Winter 1994-95.

7. EC/EU Problems and Government

The world is characterised by a large and persistent degree of economic inequality and social disparity at both the individual level and at the level of the nation or region. These differences are present, especially at the regional level, even after controlling for various explanatory factors, like educational levels and the capital/labour ratio. This chapter is not intended to be an encyclopaedic look at these problems but rather to show their persistent nature and discuss policy recommendations that may lead to their reduction.

We note that while entry into the European Union does indeed increase trade (Breedon and Pétursson, 2006), it is not at all clear that the terms of trade are such that regional disparities are bound to disappear. In fact, regional policies of the EU have not been able to arrest regional decline and the adoption of neoliberal 'market-friendly' policies have not contributed substantially to eliminating these disparities. We know that globalisation and integration distribute gains and losses unevenly and that those that gain do not always compensate those that lose (Stiglitz, 2006), but this problem may be exacerbated leading to persistent skill mismatching at the regional level. Hence, trade may result in divergence between and within countries (Ghose, 2004). Of course, regional polices evolve over time within nation states and the fundamental tension between 'have' and 'have not' areas is a political one that leads to slow (or very slow) progress on such issues. However, in the absence of such policies and government intervention, further European integration may be halted or slowed and there can be further problems when fiscal coordination does not occur within the EU.

This chapter begins with a section describing the main theories of regional development, frames the regional problem in the context of the European Union, and evaluates European regional policies. The following sections discuss other economic and social problems that are of concern to the government (e.g., unemployment, slowdown in GDP growth, etc.). We conclude with a special reference to Japan and the USA and a comparison between them and the EU.

THE REGIONAL PROBLEM IN THE EC/EU

Theoretical Perspectives to Regional Development

There are two basic views to regional development found in the literature: the neoclassical approach, and the Post-Keynesian/radical/institutional analysis which has as its starting point the theory of *cumulative causation* (Myrdal, 1957) and was developed and elaborated on by Kaldor (1971, 1978) and Cowling (1987, 1990).

Neoclassical approach

According to neoclassical economic theory, the long-run tendency is an equalisation of returns to each factor of production. This equilibrium condition is characterised by full employment of all resources. Imbalances that exist occur in the short run and thus unemployment may occur due to random unforeseeable events or because of imperfect information such as when market participants speculate that by holding resources off the market system today, they will get a better return tomorrow. This failure of prices and quantities to adjust to their equilibrium values is temporary unless it is the result of imprudent government policies. For example, hysteresis may occur because of the existence of generous unemployment compensation.

In this view, the geographical dimension implies that each region tends to specialise in the production for which it holds a comparative advantage. Underdeveloped regions, according to neoclassical analysis, face low demand for labour and, thus, low wages are provided. The solution to this is outbound migration of labour out of depressed region(s) in search of high wages elsewhere and inward movement of firms attracted by the low cost of labour. These concurrent movements would continue until wages are equalised across regions in the face of full employment provided wage flexibility and full factor mobility are allowed (Sawyer, 1989, pp. 420-21). At the same time, trade can actually *replace* factor mobility with respect to prices based on the internal mobility of resources. Since neoclassical economists believe in marginal substitution between different factor inputs in response to relative prices, resources are viewed as moving in response to price signals, with resources moving into areas of high rewards and away from areas of low rewards (Sawyer, 1989, p. 451).

Post-Keynesian/radical/institutional analysis

The theory of cumulative causation, on the other hand, is based on the concept of geographic dualism, applicable to nations and regions within and across nations, which can account for 'the persistence of spatial differences in a wide variety of development indices including per capita income, rates of growth of industrialisation and trade, employment growth rates and levels of unemployment' (Myrdal, 1957, p. 38).

Myrdal argued that, in the context of development, economic and social forces produce tendencies towards disequilibrium rather than equilibrium in contrast to neoclassical economics. More importantly, these tendencies are persistent resulting in an imbalance in regional resource use. Myrdal (1957, p. 26) argued 'the play of forces in the market normally tends to increase rather than decrease the inequalities between regions'. Trade, capital, labour are all attracted to favoured areas – in what Myrdal (1957, pp. 26-7) describes as 'the power of attraction of a centre'. Thus, unemployment that is seen traditionally as structural in nature due to generous unemployment subsidies is often geographic in nature, resulting from spatial mismatch of skills rather than the unwarranted largesse of the state (Webster, 2005).

Myrdal argued that this geographic 'dualism' resulted not only in the persistence of underdevelopment in the backward regions but also slowed development of the entire economy. Economic and social forces create through a self-reinforcing mechanism a disequilibrium situation that leads to cumulative expansion in the favoured region at the expense of other regions, which become comparatively worse off, and retards their future development. Through a multiplier-accelerator mechanism, Myrdal (1957) envisioned a system that produced increasing returns in the favoured region.

In a mirror image of the periphery, the centre experiences increased demand that spurs investment and increases incomes and demand further, causing subsequent rounds of investment, ad infinitum (Myrdal, 1957, p. 27, p. 38). Supply and demand interact with one another to create cumulative movements that distance various areas from achieving spatial equilibrium. For example, increased wealth allows for public investment in education, health, infrastructure, communications, transport, etc. that can lead to further competitive advantages for the expanding region over the lagging ones. This cumulative process results from an initial push or pull of factors to various regions through what might have been an initial random shock but which now has resulted in path dependency. Hence, regions may become competitive though not due to their own accord but rather simply because of luck, even though structural rationales for the initial conditions are somewhat more convincing (Darity and Davis, 2005).

Kaldor (1978a) attempted to explain the divergence of different regions by focusing on the movement of the 'efficiency wages' (i.e., the index of money wages divided by the index of productivity) in one region relative to other regions. Applying Verdoorn's Law, this results from the relative movement of money wages and productivity. If this relationship moves in favour of an area it will gain in competitiveness and vice versa. Higher productivity growth rates spur higher output growth rates and, as a result, differences in productivity growth tend to exceed the rate of employment growth. In Kaldor's (1978a, p. 148) own words:

> [E]fficiency wages will tend to fall in regions (and in particular industries of regions) where productivity rises faster than the average. It is for this reason that relatively fast growing areas tend to acquire a cumulative competitive advantage over a relatively slow growing area; 'efficiency wages' will, in the natural course of events, tend to fall in the former, relatively to the latter – even when they tend to rise in both areas in absolute terms. . . It is through this mechanism that the process of 'cumulative causation' works; just because the induced changes in wages increases are not sufficient to offset the differences in productivity increases, the comparative costs of production in fast growing areas tend to fall in time relatively to those in slow growing areas; and thereby enhance the competitive advantage of the former at the expense of the latter. . . So, the principle of cumulative causation leads to the concentration of industrial development in a number of successful regions. This principle – which explains the unequal regional incidence of industrial development by endogenous factors resulting from the process of historical development itself rather than by exogenous differences in 'resource endowment' – is an essential one for the understanding of the diverse trends of development as between different regions.

Cowling (1987, 1990) argued that that economic inequalities attributed to cumulative causation resulted in social and political inequalities. Being rich not only means that a region has more to spend but it also tends to result in greater political and cultural power as well.

Furthermore, cumulative causation may lead to industrial concentration. Centripetalism arises from the interaction of firms and markets and 'relates to the tendency for higher level activities and occupations to gravitate to the centre – to be lost to the regions; to be lost to the periphery' (Cowling, 1990, p. 15). Furthermore, Cowling (1990, p. 15) argues:

> Strategic decisions with major implications for local, regional and national communities are being made outside those communities. This is the reason that has led to the loss of a substantial degree of local, regional and national autonomy. The same centralising forces imply a transfer of resources to the centre, which reduces the capacity of the periphery to sustain its own economic, political and cultural development on which future self-determination is based. . . Centripetal economic tendencies become centripetal political and cultural tendencies and the community enters a vicious circle of relative decline.

The central area is more economically advanced and has a higher income level than the periphery. The prosperous/successful regions (i.e., 'centre') always have economic power over the unsuccessful/depressed regions (i.e., 'periphery').[1] This major economic advantage may lead to ownership of production in the periphery by the centre. Furthermore, in concert with the increased economic power, political and cultural power of the centre may be imposed on the periphery. Therefore, we might think of the division between the centre (core) and the periphery as being one in which the core is economically and technically advanced over the periphery and, as a result, it is able to exercise political and cultural domination over the periphery. Indeed, we can think of globalisation itself as embodying such traits and thus economic power translates into other forms of power through commodification (Lysandrou, 2005). Thus, we use cumulative causation to explain the unequal (or uneven) regional incidence of industrial development by endogenous factors resulting from path dependency rather than by 'exogenous differences in *resource endowment*' (Kaldor, 1978a, p. 148).

Modern capitalist economies are characterised by imperfect, rather than perfect, competition. As such, the market usually has no equilibrating tendencies, since there are forces of cumulative causation at work, both at the level of the firm and at the level of the region. Regional problems are result from spatial economic imbalance – geographical disparities of material well-being and rates of growth of income and employment within a nation, or between different areas and/or different nations. Less developed areas are typified by underutilisation of resources and slow growth of such resources when compared with other regions (Sawyer, 1992b, p. 69). The trouble with the neoclassical analysis is that, in a world of static comparative advantage, free trade favours the rich and the strong (whether firms or regions). Also, full employment is not a usual outcome from the operation of markets. Therefore, the allocation and reallocation of resources (and, especially, the creation of them) between sectors, between industries, between regions and between countries cannot be explained successfully by neoclassical equilibrium analysis.

Lastly, the cumulative causation argument relies on some degree of increasing returns to scale. In contrast, a great deal of the neoclassical analysis rests on the rejection of any assumption of increasing returns to scale, and the technical possibilities, the economic structures and the social and political environment are not taken into account.

It may be noted that cumulative causation is thus far more in concert with the conception of trade found in the 'New Trade Theory' of Grossman and Helpman (1990), and Krugman (1991), and the notion of unbalanced growth found in 'New Growth Theory' of Romer (1986), Lucas (1985, 1988) and Azariadis and Drazen (1990).

Regional Disparities and Problems in the EC/EU

Employment and income may have greater fluctuations in some regions than in others. Rural areas, for example, are still heavily dependent on agriculture and thus are subject to the vagrancies of climate in determining their incomes, which tend to be lower than urban areas, especially in less developed countries. Areas that are heavily dependent on only one or two industries may also suffer wider swings in employment levels since the fortunes of those regions conform to that of the industries on which they depend.

Agriculture has been declining as a source of EC/EU GDP, dropping from 5.1 per cent in 1974 to only 2.9 per cent in the 1990s. Over the same time period, agricultural employment as a share of the workforce declined from 11.7 per cent to 6.5 per cent. This drop has occurred across all EC/EU countries and has resulted from technological changes and productivity improvements that have reduced dramatically the need for agricultural labour. Indeed, the biggest drops have been found in the Southern Countries of the European Community, where labour productivity in agriculture is lower (OECD, *Historical Statistics 1960-1990*).

Regional problems tend to go hand in hand with structural problems, although various structural problems and changes in the socioeconomic environment have affected most (if not all) regions in the EU. Yet, the structural changes undertaken over the past two decades in the various Member States have not led to a reduction in regional disparities.

Rural areas, for example, continue to suffer from a lack of adequate infrastructure and social services due, in part, to their lower incomes that would be able to fund such projects and past agglomeration effects. They also suffer from high levels of unemployment, a lack of available job opportunities and lower than average earnings. Depressed regions also suffer from social ills that are unrelated to employment. Many regions are paying the price of unsustainable industrial production in their areas that have spoiled their environments. Other regions cannot maintain the infrastructure they have now in place, yet alone update and expand it. In many depressed areas, transportation systems are inferior to those in growing regions and housing, health care standards, and educational standards tends to be of lower quality.

Disparities in regional growth manifest themselves either as disparities in the levels of GDP or in per capita GDP. Disparities in levels of GDP are measured here in terms of Purchasing Power Standards (PPS).[2] While some regions have improved during the 1980s under this indicator, overall regional disparities have failed to decline. Indeed, disparities across the EU population are considerable with 20 per cent of the EU population living in regions where the per capita GDP fell below 75 per cent of the Community average, and interregional disparities in the EU were at least twice that of the USA (Commission of the European Community, 1991c; CEC, various years). To further the point, per capita GDP in the top ten regions in the 1990s was more than three times greater than that of the bottom ten regions (CEC, various years).

Therefore, there is no tendency towards convergence in the regional per capita PPS (or GDP) in the EC/EU area. There is still a wide chasm between Community Countries that has failed to narrow even with higher growth rates recorded by most of the less-wealthy countries. PPS trends over the 1980s are not showing a convergence towards the EC average principally due to Ireland, Spain, Portugal and Greece. Within the EC/EU Countries, regional disparities (and/or inequalities) are tending to widen rather than converge. Only 40 per cent of regions in 1990 had a per capita GDP that was closer to the Community average than it had been in 1980 (CEC, 1991c). Ben-David (1992) also confirms increasing levels of income disparity in the EC/EU.

Several disparities between various EU Member States, regions, and sectors, and between urban and rural areas are hidden by indicators that are often used to measure living standards. Northern Europe, which is more industrialised, has also better infrastructure and is richer with a higher living standard than in Southern Europe. Thus, the regional distribution of resources as well as social services is highly uneven (Eurostat, *Population and Social Conditions 1990-97*; *Europe in Figures*, 1992).

Regional Policies in the EC/EU

Government economic policies attempt to address regional development by stimulating investment in the following:

1. new production techniques aimed at productivity improvements at the expense of employment; and
2. new activities usually belonging to sectors with high technology products and advanced producer services (Lipietz, 1986; Scott, 1988; Sabel, 1989; Hirst and Zeitlin, 1989).

Moreover, regional policy somewhat influences how economic activity is distributed. Although the various EC countries have great diversity in terms of national and regional conditions, their policies have been similar due to the dominant development paradigm that existed. Indeed, regional policy has some influence on the regional distribution of economic activity. Despite the great diversity of national and regional conditions within the EC Countries, similar experiences exist in terms of both the types of policies undertaken and their results. This uniformity of experience has been shaped by the dominant paradigm of development that lasted from the end of World War II until the mid-1970s (Albrechts et al., 1989, pp. 6-7).

The United Kingdom, for example, attended to reduce spatial socio-economic imbalance and disparities in employment opportunities and economic performance between the economic disadvantaged North and

West and the comparatively advantaged South and Midlands. Through redirection of investment and redistribution of economic activities and jobs, the policies of Britain were mirrored in Italy and Germany. Italy provides the highest levels of fiscal transfer (per cent of GDP) in order to support its weaker regions, due to greater diversity in regional income. According to MacKay (1994, p. 576), for Italy and Germany,

> [L]ow income tends to go with trade deficits . . . [and] fiscal transfers [tend to go] to regions with trade problems. . . The region that fails to develop or loses its export base automatically receives a degree of protection from the tax and welfare system. Standards in [various] declining areas are protected by [the redistribution of] income and by [the maintenance of a certain] level of public services [while] low-income regions usually enjoy fiscal gains (they pay less in taxes than they receive in services and benefits) [with] high-income regions providing the support.[3]

At the same time, France aims at introducing new technology in order to spur productivity growth. Growth coalitions and development agencies (as they operate in France) play their own important role and try to encourage local development (Clout, 1987b, pp. 171-9). Besides, regional development planning is an important component of French planning, and Greece has attempted to replicate this by means of a 'pilot programme' that has not been wholly 'French' in either its theory or its practice.

The Greek authorities themselves usually bear ultimate responsibility for plans and their implementation (Carter, 1987, pp. 427-9). The problem of regional disequilibrium in Greece is bigger than in any other European Country. Regional development has been directed towards integrated growth of the less-developed areas of the country. The Greek Government has attempted to eliminate obstacles that hinder a balanced growth among the regions of the country, and this effort is directed both at furthering the development of immediately productive activities and at securing the formation of the required fixed social capital in the various areas. Greece, with the entry of Portugal and Spain in 1986, adds to regional inequality (and implies larger transfers between different parts, if inequality is to be contained). Hence, the presence of countries that are significant laggards is one reason for hesitancy among many in the EU towards expansion.[4] Integration seems to take a notably different form, since the EC/EU usually gives freer play to market forces.

Table 7.1 presents the different types of regional incentives of the EC Countries and Sweden relative to the role of the state, in the 1960s and 1970s. Grants, as opposed to loans (which are of secondary importance), are the principal mechanism to stimulate regional development. As can be seen in this table, seven of the 13 countries covered utilise fiscal aids with the majority of these being in the form of tax concessions as opposed to accelerated depreciation allowances. Labour-related subsidies are present in about half the countries (Allen and Yuill, 1989, p. 119).

Table 7.1 Main Regional Incentives: Distribution by Country and Incentive Type

COUNTRY	INCENTIVE
BELGIUM	Interest subsidy
	Capital grant
DENMARK	Investment grant
	Municipality soft loan
FRANCE	Regional policy grant
	Regional employment grant
	Local business tax concessions
GERMANY	Investment allowance
	Investment grant
	Special depreciation allowance
	Regional soft loan
IRELAND	Standard capital grant
	Selective assistance
ITALY	Capital grant
	National fund scheme
	Social security concession
	Tax concession
LUXEMBOURG	Capital grant/Interest subsidy
	Tax concession
	Equipment loan
NETHERLANDS	Investment premium
UNITED KINGDOM	Regional development grant
	Regional selective assistance
GREECE	Investment grant
	Interest rate subsidy
	Increased depreciation allowance
	Tax allowance
PORTUGAL	Financial assistance
	Tax concessions
SPAIN	Regional investment grant
	Official credit priority
SWEDEN	Location loan/grant
	Employment grant

Sources: OECD, *Restructuring the Regions: Analysis, Policy Model and Prognosis*, Paris, 1986; and D. Yuill and K. Allen, *European Regional Incentives*, European Policies Research Centre, Glasgow, 1987.

The incentives that have been offered have trended towards

> [G]rants and away from soft loans. [Moreover, where such loans have been maintained] . . . the trend has been towards interest-related subsidies rather than providing both subsidies and loans. A further trend has seen a move away from regionally-targeted tax concessions and, indeed, this trend has been significant in recent years. Finally, and as already mentioned, there has been a growing interest in labour-related subsidies. (Allen and Yuill, 1989, pp. 119-20)

Each incentive type of policy has its own advantages and disadvantages, but traditional policies have failed to lessen disparities between regions and cannot be considered successful in terms of substantially increasing regional development. Thus, regional policy during the 1980s and 1990s shifted to emphasise the following five priority objectives (CEC, 1991):

> *OBJECTIVE* 1: to promote the development and structural adjustment of under-developed regions, i.e., regions whose economy is largely dependent on agriculture and which have high unemployment, relatively low levels of income, and a poorly-developed infrastructure (roads, railways, social services, etc.).
> *OBJECTIVE* 2: to redevelop regions, border regions or areas within regions seriously affected by the decline of industry (i.e., coal, iron and steel, textiles and shipbuilding).
> *OBJECTIVES* 3 & 4: to combat long-term unemployment (unemployed persons aged over 25 in particular) as well as to facilitate the integration of young people into working life.
> *OBJECTIVES* 5a & 5b: to adapt production processing and marketing structures in agriculture and forestry, and to promote the development of rural areas.

Of these objectives, only 1, 2, and 5b are of a specifically regional nature; the other objectives are relevant to laggard regions but do not have a specific identifying criterion for regional assistance. Objective 1 covers EC regions with per capita GDP that is less than 75 per cent of the Community average. These peripheral regions have relatively little industry (i.e., the whole of Greece, Northern Ireland in the UK, the Italian Mezzogiorno, Corsica, Portugal, about 70 per cent of Spain, and the French overseas departments). Around 21.5 per cent of the population of the EC lives in these regions, and the development priorities include the modernisation of communications and telecommunications infrastructure, R&D, vocational training, business services, etc.

Objective 2 covers 60 regions or areas within regions in nine different Member States with a total of 48 million inhabitants. The priority in these regions is given to employment and the quality of the environment, the promotion of new activities, the redevelopment of industrial sites and the renovation of buildings, economic restructuring and the improvement of the region's image, training, R&D, forging closer links between universities and industry, etc.

Finally, objective 5b covers 56 regions or areas within regions in Spain, France, Italy and Germany with a total of 15 million inhabitants, according to the number of persons working in agriculture, their level of socio-economic development assessed on the basis of per capita GDP, etc.

An Evaluation of Regional Policies

In the past four decades, regional policies were often considered as minor complements (an 'epidermic touch') of standard national macroeconomic policies and were limited to the selective promotion of activities (usually the promotion of R&D) in lagging regions. Traditionally, regional policies attempted to influence the spatial distribution of economic activity by retarding growth and development in high growth regions and/or increasing production in underdeveloped regions using a variety of financial incentives for the private sector. In addition, high levels of government spending on infrastructure (often at the level of 'megaproject' designed to benefit politicians by emphasising the size of the project) or attempts to reduce regulatory burdens would be coupled in an attempt to sway businesses to relocate. The majority of OECD countries (and all EC countries) engaged in such policies beginning in the 1960s. At the same time, the EC/EU attempts to reallocate market areas and redistribute production in favour of the most efficient and best-situated firms and industries. This implies geographic specialisation and a concentration of production, a process more likely to benefit the core ('the power of attraction of a centre') than the periphery of the Community (Myrdal, 1957, pp. 26-7).

Regional issues for the EC tend to be concentrated in the South. Indeed, Italy, Portugal and Spain all suffer from severe income and unemployment disparities (the existence of backward agricultural regions characterised by low productivity, heavy emigration and low participation rates). In contrast, the UK and Belgium have fairly uniform regional income levels but widely divergent unemployment rates due to the concentration and emphasis of basic industries in certain regions, which have been unable to compete as effectively since being opened up to competition. In France and Greece, the presence of one hypertrophied capital region monopolises each country's activities. In Germany, regional problems seem less serious than elsewhere in Europe. In general, the regional problem is exacerbated as one moves away from the centre of Europe (Clout, 1987a, pp. 24-37). In fact, the emergence and persistence of various regional problems can be traced to 'the process of [economic] development' – and within this, to shifts in technology, R&D and the pattern of demand (Kaldor, 1978a, p. 148).

All EC countries have moved from agriculture towards industrial and tertiary activities (Clout, 1987a, pp. 32-3). This has been as a result of technological change and improved productivity, which has led to a large reduction in the need for agricultural labour, thereby 'exacerbating the effects of shifting demand' (Kaldor, 1978a, pp. 144-6). In regions where agriculture has been predominant, the industrial and tertiary sectors were seen as not providing sufficient employment opportunities; this is at least in part due to the lack of resources and human capital as well as under-developed infrastructure that constitute unfavourable factors of industrial growth in these regions.

Hence, there is a strong tendency for the market's 'centripetal' forces (Cowling, 1987, 1990) to display cumulative causation (Myrdal, 1957), and for higher-level activities to gravitate towards the centre. Underutilisation and slow growth of resources in such less-developed regions do not aid matters (Sawyer, 1992b, p. 69). Intervention by regional and local authorities can generate some benefits by distributing resources in favour of the losers (whether firms or regions). More importantly, government investment in regions and rural areas is also required to support and develop indigenous resources, firms and industries; to add to the sum total of investment capital, training, R&D, technical development and services available; to create or enhance the opportunities for regional and local economic development and restructuring; and to improve social welfare.

Since the 1950s, regional policies have tended to be state-sponsored and centralised in a manner that fails to allow for regional differentiation. By treating all regions as identical through the use of state subsidies, grants, loans and tax relief (financial incentives), little has been achieved in terms of economic restructuring or transformation of the socio-economic base. This is akin to giving someone a fish as opposed to teaching him how to fish, as the proverb goes. However, many of the problems stem from a regional focus on one particular industry or activity, which makes it difficult to find a useful and effective way of dealing with short-term and, especially, long-term problems.

Geographical concentration of industry turns industrial problems into regional problems. The types of labour most in demand elsewhere may migrate, leaving a less adaptable work force in the region. The development of public services and other facilities may also lag behind that in other regions which, in turn, may discourage the influx of new investment. Some of these regional problems may be temporary and would ordinarily be corrected over the course of a normal business cycle. However, if the industry has left the region as the result of a cyclical downturn, it is not necessarily going to return so readily in its aftermath, especially if the previously trained workforce has already migrated. Tax incentives and credit policies may have a useful role to play. They are offered to firms going to specified areas or development regions; however, these generally have rather less immediate and less sharply focused effects than those that can be achieved by direct fiscal expenditure. This is why there have been calls for government to reduce regional disparities through its own spending and procurement policies. It may also, at times, be preferable to employ direct investment subsidies and/or public capital improvement programmes (Allen and Yuill, 1989, pp. 119-20).

In some cases it is useful, in order to increase a region's industrial attraction, to develop its infrastructure in advance of the need, or to select it as the site for public enterprises. In the case of Southern Italy, which lags behind in social capital, services and innovation, Italian planners counted heavily on government investment in the 'impulse sectors' to generate the private investment needed to attain employment and output targets. This may distinguish the 'market failure' Anglo-Saxon analysis (UK and USA) from the 'developmentalist' policy (France and Italy).

From the 1980s and onwards, dissatisfaction arose in part from the gap between the needs of the problem regions and that which policies could achieve. In general, policies were top-down in implementation and did not lead to increased decision-making in the region or the enhancement of indigenous development, which may have led to self-sustained growth from within the area. Rather, the start-up of new small businesses distorted the occupational structure towards lower-skilled workers, leaving those with technical, professional and managerial skills to seek jobs in more advanced and prosperous regions (Moore and Rhodes, 1987, p. 116).

Another policy problem is that too much attention was paid to the geographical distribution of manufacturers, which have been in decline or growing relatively slowly, and too little was given to service industries. While manufacturing has traditionally been the focus of regional growth, services and inter-sectorial regional linkages are increasing in importance (Moore and Rhodes, 1987, p. 116; Martinelli, 1989, pp. 20-21). High technology is often considered as a panacea for industrial policies and adopted as a 'fashion instrument', but technological complexes usually prove insufficient in themselves to solve the broader problems of regional development and innovation.

The supply-oriented regional policy of the EC in the 1980s and 1990s was confined to generalities. The role of the state, the different instruments, and the kinds of different strategies (i.e., industrial strategies, regional development, rejuvenation and strategic repositioning) have not been thoroughly specified. Besides, each Member Country has its own specific problems and these problems cannot be solved by appeals to general principles. Instead, each EU Member State needs to adopt different national purpose strategies, different priorities, and different types of developmental framework. However, these policies must be coordinated within the EU in order to be effective. It would not do to have every country attempt to be the top provider of computers (for example).

Moreover, 'the Community Budget remains below 1% of Community GDP, provides no automatic response to regional decline [and] has no strong redistributional role between richer and poorer parts of Europe' (MacKay, 1994, p. 572). MacKay (1994, p. 578) goes on to argue:

> It is not strongly redistributive, it is not highly sensitive, it does not act as a built-in stabiliser.[5] The Structural Funds[6] and the Community Budget do not provide anything which remotely resembles built-in stabilisers. At the moment, the Community Budget has at best a weak redistributive effect. MacDougall (1977) estimates that with a Community Budget of the order of 2-2.5% of GDP it would be possible to reduce inequalities of regional *per capita* income by 10%, while a budget of 5-7% of GDP would achieve a reduction of 40% in inequalities. [Therefore,] Community expenditure would have to be strongly redistributive and highly sensitive to cyclical changes in economic fortune.

Market forces left to themselves will not eliminate regional inequalities and disparities. A much larger fiscal budget, a more proactive fiscal policy and fiscal redistribution within countries are necessary to protect weaker regions against cyclical effects (MacKay, 1991, 1994). Automatic fiscal stabilisers are a Keynesian response to a weakness of market systems and, without fiscal transfers, cumulative forces of decline may be set in motion.[7] Within the EU, real compensation and redistributive fiscal policies are required.

A key question for the EU is whether economic integration leads to reduction of regional income inequalities and other regional disparities. In fact, the political drive to unite Europe has placed too little emphasis on regional disparity, and 'efforts to encourage convergence are in effect attempts to impose uniformity of economic performance. Attempts to create a unified Europe have not addressed the question of budgetary transfers adequately. Fiscal transfers have an economic as well as a political role' (MacKay, 1994, p. 584).

To hold the whole European Community together, economic gains must be widely distributed but, in the long run, problems of political will are also important and may frustrate attempts at fiscal transfer. Designing budgetary actions and policies that are politically acceptable and also reduce spatial disparities within the European Union is a challenging and very difficult task.

THE UNEMPLOYMENT PROBLEM IN THE EC/EU

Theoretical Perspectives to Unemployment

The following two major economic paradigms related to unemployment are briefly presented: the neoclassical and the Keynesian/Post-Keynesian view.

Neoclassical approach

Price flexibility is fundamental to the neoclassical economic analysis of full employment of resources including labour. By assuming that the labour market clears and that wage adjustment and labour mobility are present in both the short and long run, deviations from full employment are temporary and usually the result of governmental interference in the functioning of the labour market through schemes such as unemployment insurance that serve to undermine the wage adjustment and labour mobility process. However, even in the presence of such market imperfections, the economic system tends to eliminate involuntary unemployment through price level changes, although this may take longer in the case of price controls on labour (such as the minimum wage). Indeed, many neoclassical theorists go further and argue that markets are in (or near) equilibrium and consequently recorded unemployment is virtually always voluntary unemployment. This leads to a conception of a trade-off between inflation and unemployment (Davies, 1985, p. 13). Even at the regional level, wage flexibility clears the labour market in the short run and inter-regional movements of labour and capital allow for a long-run resetting of equilibrium.

Keynesian/Post-Keynesian approach

Keynesians and Post-Keynesians argue that employment is a function of the level of effective demand and that market forces do not generate full employment when left to themselves. Post-Keynesians, in particular, emphasise the role of 'sticky' prices and wages, especially downward wage rigidity in explaining why there are asymmetries in terms of how labour reacts to changes in the offered wage. At the same time, reductions in wages necessitate the lowering of effective demand which may lead to a vicious cycle: as wages are cut, the ability of workers to pay for the goods is cut as well; this leads to reductions in demand which translates into a further lowering of prices and subsequent demands for greater wage cuts in response. In order to achieve higher levels of employment and vibrant economic performance, it is necessary for governments to use aggregate demand management policies to ensure the smooth running of the capitalist system. Thus, government policies play a role in the promotion of full employment, even in the long run, when supply-side considerations are also important and may themselves be influenced by demand.

Discussion of the Problem

Unemployment has been a persistent problem in most EC countries over the past two decades and, although it has been trending downward since the mid-1990s, the percentage of recorded unemployment in the EU is still between two and three times what it was 30 years previously. This is in sharp contrast to the results in the United States which had most recently driven unemployment down to levels not seen since the 1960s. Indeed, since the late 1990s, around 20 million persons in the European Union have been unemployed each year (OECD, various years).

Unemployment is always on the minds of those who have lost their jobs and presents a thorny political problem, affecting 8.4 per cent of the labour force. More problematically, long-term unemployed may leave the labour force, masking the true unemployment rate. Labour market participation in Europe was just a shade over 51 per cent, one of the lowest rates in the world. Although unemployment rates differ widely among Member States, all suffer from similar profiles in youth and long-term unemployment. In the 1990s, Luxembourg had the lowest rate of unemployment (1.7 per cent) and Spain (16.1 per cent) and Ireland (15.6 per cent) the highest. The rates in the other EU Member States vary between 4.5 per cent and 10 per cent. The 'regional dimension' of the unemployment problem demonstrates even greater disparities, ranging from a low of 1.5 per cent to a high of 29 per cent (CEC, various years). As a result, the overall employment figures serve to understate the geographic dimension of the problem. These disparities have only been widened due to globalisation and the resultant restructuring of the economy. Since the economic landscape of laggard regions is often dominated by an over-reliance on a single industry or small group of related industries, the changing of comparative advantage through globalisation can wreak devastating consequences on such regions or cause a boom period due to increased trade for those areas that hold onto that advantage. For example, during the first half of the 1980s, regional disparities widened due to the changing landscape of manufacturing. In the second half of the 1980s, the trend reversed. While technological change has reduced demand for unskilled labour, this has meant that the long-term unemployed are disproportionately in this category. This has been especially problematic in the poorer traditionally agrarian regions of the Community, which have seen widespread unemployment and poor job growth (CEC, various years).

Clearly, high unemployment tends to be concentrated in regions where traditional industries are in decline. Globalisation and European integration have coincided with rapid decline in manufacturing employment, which has traditionally been the provider of 'good jobs' for blue-collar workers. Similar to the USA, which saw a decline in manufacturing employing from 22.1 per cent to 18.0 per cent during the 1980s, EC manufacturing employment dropped from 27.5 per cent to 23.2 per cent, an absolute fall of almost 5.5 million jobs. Of the former EC(12) Countries, only Portugal and Greece avoided a fall in manufacturing employment as producers sought refuge in low-wage areas. The UK experienced the most extreme cut in employment, with a 16 per cent reduction in manufacturing employment during that decade (more than two million jobs lost). This loss in manufacturing jobs has been coupled with a worsening balance of trade in manufacturing and a rise in unemployment.

This decline has only continued, while service sector employment has rapidly increased. However, such employment is often without the benefits and wages that typified manufacturing jobs and is often part-time in nature or requires non-traditional working hours. These structural changes are amplified at the regional level, resulting in greater regional disparity.

Labour force growth tended to outpace employment growth until the mid-1990s in almost every EC and OECD country, resulting in rising unemployment. Although this has been somewhat mitigated since that time, the reduction in unemployment has been gradual and nowhere near as dramatic as that seen in the North American economies of Canada and the United States. Recorded unemployment has become more concentrated among men and has remained disturbingly high in the EU, with many countries continuing to report unemployment rates in excess of 10 per cent. Ireland and Spain have had the sharpest relative increases in the EU.

As noted, a more disturbing picture of EC's comparative record emerges when Japan and the USA are chosen as the reference points. Indeed, the rate of unemployment in Japan has remained very low, averaging around 2.5 per cent throughout the 1980s and even though it is currently mired in what can only be described as a depression, unemployment in Japan at 4.1 per cent as of August 2006 is a little over half the 8 per cent recorded in the EU.

Government spending on labour market programmes tended to fall in the 1990s from the levels of the mid-1980s, despite rising unemployment. Denmark was one country that bucked this trend, increasing its relative spending on such programmes from 5 per cent of public expenditure in 1985 to more than 6.5 per cent in the 1990s (OECD, *Employment Outlook*, various years). Most of this spending came in the form of subsidies and grants with some governments using grants to encourage firms to allocate more resources to training. Also, structural unemployment occurs when there is a disconnect between an economy's ability to adapt to change and the external pressures that drive the requirement to change. In a world of new technologies, globalisation and international competition, adaptation is the key to success. Labour market programmes must take a long-term view instead of using short-term remedies that only provide a 'Band-Aid solution'. Thus, macroeconomic policy should work in concert with labour market policy to foster faster non-inflationary growth of aggregate demand.

Some OECD (and EU) countries began to take this approach by the mid-1990s but, still, most EC/EU governments have not made this a priority (for example, see OECD, *The OECD Jobs Study: Facts, Analysis, Strategies*, 1994c, p. 31 and p. 44).

OTHER ECONOMIC PROBLEMS IN THE EC/EU

Slowdown in GDP Growth

As GDP growth has slowed down in the EC/EU and regional disparities have increased due to the uneven pace of the growth that has occurred over the past three decades, the EC/EU has found itself lagging behind the growth rates in Japan (at least through the mid-1990s) and the USA. This is so despite the fact that European structural adjustments and expanding regional integration ought to have created a growth spurt if neoclassical economic arguments are to be believed. We turn now to explore some of the reasons for this.

Declining Government Capital Formation

Gross capital formation and capital outlays by governments as a percentage of total government outlays fell in all but one of the EC countries from the mid-1970s to the mid-1980s, with Portugal being the sole exception.[8] These rates also became much more divergent. While in the mid-1970s, the rate of gross capital formation and capital outlays ranged from a high in Portugal of 12.9 per cent of total government outlays to a low of 10.5 per cent in France, they ranged from a high of 19.7 per cent in Portugal in the mid-1980s to a low of 5.3 per cent in Denmark, with most of the countries falling in the 6 per cent to 10 per cent range. The 1990s saw the range further drop with France expending 10.3 per cent and Denmark just 4.2 per cent, and average gross capital formation and capital outlays in the EU falling from 11.4 per cent in the mid-1970s to 9.8 per cent by the mid-1990s, down to 8.4 per cent in the 1990s. The desire for government to retreat from activist policy has spread across the OECD in line with the adoption of the neoliberal Washington consensus.

A comparison with the USA and Japan proves useful. While both experienced drops in the rate of gross capital formation and capital outlays as a percentage of total government outlays from the mid-1970s to the mid-1980s, this trend had reversed itself by 1990. Japan, in particular, has made industrial policy a national priority recording much higher rates of gross capital formation and capital outlays than either the USA or the EC (OECD,

National Accounts, various years). This large-scale public investment has been done in concert with industry to allocate investments based on long-term planning.

From 1960 to 1986, the Japanese government made public investments at a level of twice that of other Western economies and, even despite cuts on government expenditure in the mid-1980s, the Japanese have continued to significantly outpace their economic rivals (OECD, *Economic Outlook*, various years). Indeed, Japan's emphasis on investment as opposed to consumption by government makes its policy quite divergent from the normal OECD pattern.[9]

Indeed, while the Japanese State has limited purchases of goods and services to roughly half the rate of other major economies, state investment in Japan has remained at far higher levels than its industrial rivals. Sweden and Denmark have some of the higher levels of social transfers as well as government consumption, while the UK, the USA and Japan have far lower levels of transfer payments.

Industrial Policies in Europe and International Competition

Industrial policy remains a controversial topic. We can discern two main theoretical views with regard to industrial development. The *traditional* view of international differences in growth rates, based on the neoclassical assumption that all countries have access to the same technology and the rate of change of technology, contends that 'all countries should converge to the same level of development' (Solow, 1956). Consequently, less-advanced countries will catch up with the leading ones through a faster rate of technological progress.

On the other hand, 'industrial strategy' theorists building on the work of Myrdal (1957) and Kaldor (1966) argue that countries tend to follow their own national growth paths and build their own technological capabilities, usually with divergent growth paths and little tendency for convergence in income or productivity levels. Hence, growth and development take place in a context of 'cumulative causation' (that is, a number of factors influence the cumulative mechanisms). On the other hand, 'endogenous growth' theorists of the so-called 'New Growth' school (Romer, 1986; Lucas, 1985, 1988) have focused on the possibilities of divergent growth paths between different countries (the national accumulation of knowledge and technology is basically *endogenous*, and countries try to build their own technological capabilities).

Since the 1960s, state interventions have tended to be microeconomic in nature with industrial policy being only a minor complement to national macroeconomic policies. Governments have looked at the problem at an industry level as opposed to a national or regional level, and have sought to correct market imperfections and provide protections to industrial sectors that are politically or strategically important. The traditional argument for state intervention to industry has been the 'market failure' rational and tends to emphasise the promotion of R&D and selective promotion of certain industries:

1. promote new industries and high technology;
2. help old ones to restructure; and
3. keep declining sectors alive in order to save jobs and avoid social and political tensions (Price, 1981, p. 18).[10]

Of course, promotion of one sector is denigration of all others as such economic policies favour the one sector at the others' expense. Still, while governments have thus far not recognised this duality, they have come to recognise that their actions have a major influence on the development and performance of industry through the promotion of structural adjustment and the provision of *accelerators* (i.e., education, training, R&D, innovation, business services, etc.) in the context of industrial policy for improved industrial competitiveness. State aids to industry (which are by definition loans, subsidies and other special financial benefits to specific firms and industries) show the EC/EU Governments' support to local industry as well as their policy orientation.

Different governments have different orientations and policy priorities. Government support of small and medium-sized firms and enterprises is a defining characteristic of the policies of the Netherlands and Belgium. Greece and Ireland attempt to promote exports and regional aid, while Spain emphasizes firm-specific and sector-specific support and Italy attempts to spread its aid to specific regions of the country.

While private R&D expenditure has exceeded public R&D spending in most of the OECD Countries (Eurostat, 1992; Eurostat, various issues), most governments attempt to leverage this expenditure by sponsoring research activities in high-risk ventures; by offering inducements to companies that engage in R&D investment; or by directly and indirectly subsidizing innovation. Yet, despite these activities, the EC/EU devotes just over 2 per cent of its GDP to R&D, while the USA and Japan (around 2.8 per cent) expend far greater amounts. R&D expenditure also varies widely among the various countries and regions of the EU, ranging from 2.9 per cent of GDP in Germany to less than 1 per cent in Greece, Spain, Ireland and Portugal. Interestingly, however, these variations become even more glaring when one examines the source of R&D expenditure. A majority of R&D expenditure in Greece (69 per cent) and Portugal (66 per cent), both of which have some of the lowest R&D expenditures when one considers both industry and government together, is provided by government. At the other end of the scale is Belgium with only 28 per cent of its spending being provided by government and Germany, whose government provides just 36 per cent of R&D expenditure. This latter example is particularly interesting given that Germany has also the highest percentage of R&D expenditure in the EU when one considers both industrial and government support for such activities.

When one examines R&D expenditure at the regional level, we find that there is considerable regional variation, such that it is estimated that the technology gap between the most and the least advanced regions is on the order of 1 to 100, seven times greater than the highest differences between individual Member States (Eurostat, 1992; Eurostat, various issues). Also, EC/EU governments finance roughly 47 per cent of the R&D undertaken in their territories, a figure comparable to that of the USA but considerably lower than in Japan, where more than three quarters of all research is funded by industry.

Manufacturing in Europe continues to play a major role in the world economy, contributing more than a third (34.4 per cent) of gross value-added, ranking it second to Japan and ahead of the USA. Since 1974, the value-added in manufacturing as a percentage of GDP has slowed, while, since 1983, industry production has grown at an average rate of 4 per cent per year, although this figure has been declining over the years. This rate of growth is lower than that in the USA and Japan, and industrial employment fell beginning in 1974 and only began to stabilise towards the end of the 1980s. This is in contrast to the USA which experienced a rapid expansion in the mid-1980s and relative stability for the rest of the decade.

Japan tended to do better than the EC and the USA during the same period (OECD, *Historical Statistics 1960-1990,* 1992). Over the past three decades, annual productivity growth averaged 5.5 per cent in Japan, 3.4 per cent in the EC, and 3.2 per cent in the USA. With industrial output growing at a similar pace to that of productivity, an industrial 'shake-out' similar to that seen in the USA and Europe in the early 1980s has been forestalled. Available data show that the rate of growth in industrial production tended to decline during the 1980s and the 1990s. This decline was higher in the EC than in the USA and Japan (Eurostat, various issues).

All the above factors clearly illustrate the importance of the increasing *openness* of national economies to international competition along with changes in technology. Therefore, nations must actively trade if they are to be prosperous and successful. R&D and human capital expenditure must become the focal points for procuring significant advantages in national competitiveness. There is no doubt that the degree of openness of EC/EU economies to imports and exports has steadily increased. Indeed, statistics published by OECD and the EU show how rapidly exports and imports (per cent of GDP) have grown over time for EC/EU Member States.

The Commission of the EC/EU usually argues that in order to maintain 'an international ability to compete', advanced economies must become internationally competitive and to specialise in higher technology industrial sectors, as a response to increasing competition, especially from newly industrialising countries and China in low technology products. It considers that Japan and the USA are 'continually pushing ahead with specialisation in the high-tech industries' (EC, 1988, p. 129), and that 'the relatively low level of productivity achieved by European countries in the high-tech industries goes a long way towards explaining their weak performance in international trade' (EC, 1988, p. 25) in a number of sectors. Furthermore, 'completion of the internal market . . . is likely to give a fresh boost to these new advanced technology industries and, through a cumulative process, revive European competitiveness' (EC, 1988, p. 115).

However, scientists (such as Hughes, 1992, 1993) argue that a shift into high technology sectors is neither necessary nor sufficient for improved performance, since there is no apparent relationship between technological specialisation and trade performance. For example, Japan, Germany and Italy, with the best overall trade performance in the 1980s, had their best performance in high, medium and low technology products respectively, whereas the UK and the USA, with a relatively poor overall performance, had their best performance in high technology sectors (Hughes, 1992, p. 175). Moreover, Hughes argues that:

> Both EC economies and the USA had problems with respect to R&D and to skill with respect to Japan. . . [Therefore,] competitiveness is determined by a variety of factors in ways that vary across countries. (Hughes, 1993, p. 156) The determinants of overall patterns of competitiveness are clearly more complex than a simple interpretation of [neoclassical] theories of trade would imply and depend on [many] other factors than innovation. (Hughes, 1992, p. 181)

Overall, disparities at the regional level in unemployment rates or per capital income tend to persist over long periods of time and these disparities create harmful economic, social and political effects. Thus, unregulated market forces not only cannot solve the social and economic problems that are created at the regional level, but, in fact, create these problems in the first instance. Furthermore, market forces do not generate full employment, despite protestations to the contrary from neoclassical economists. The current emphasis on balanced budgets, control of inflation, and industrial/ labour market reforms to reduce unemployment as part of the neoliberal 'Washington consensus' is more likely to deter rather than ensure successful operation (that is involving low unemployment rates, sustainable economic growth, and reduction of regional disparities and poverty) of the European single market and currency.

CONCLUSIONS

This chapter has sought to exhibit some of the various problems in the EC area, due mostly to inefficiencies of the current market structure that prevail in the various economies; to explain the issues surrounding these problems; and, finally, to look at the role of the state in addressing these problems. The key point is that imperfections and inflexibilities are always present in market economies and no matter how much we might wish to assume them away, their persistence causes a divergence from the neoclassical ideal. At the same time, it is clear that traditional polices of industrial support may not be available under globalisation wherein countries are obliged to reduce subsidies and support for selective industrial policy. On the other hand, negative incentives for industries that are undesirable and broad-based initiatives such as support for infrastructure or R&D, which are designed to increase international competitiveness across sectors are more adaptable to the global landscape. In particular, economic policies designed to encourage diversification and/or global repositioning of industries by providing such infrastructural needs within stagnant regions would be beneficial. Otherwise, regional disparities (e.g., in unemployment rates or per capita incomes) will continue to persist with their harmful social, economic and political effects left intact.

Neoclassical and New Right policies, on the other hand, tend to increase social inequalities and regional disparities. The *invisible hand* does not promote balanced regional growth; indeed, the creation of winners and losers in the global marketplace causes, through a process of cumulative causation, these very same regional imbalances. The policy prescriptions of neoclassical economics and the New Right would lead to the abandonment of vast territories and create further social and political divisiveness.

On the other hand, active Keynesian policies can strengthen the link between aggregate demand growth and sustainable regional development. A 'modern' state must aid the meeting of social needs, future requirements, and long-term or strategic objectives. The Developmental State, which is organised and concerned with the promotion of economic and social development, particularly industrial development, can offer realistic policy solutions. However, while the tools available to such a state have been constrained by global agreements, the same policies can be implemented, as we will see in the case of East Asian tigers, through the use of selective *dis*incentives to promote industries that are more conducive to a high standard of living.

NOTES

1. In Neo-Innisian terminology, these are referred to as the heartland and the hinterland. The centre and the periphery concept can be applied at a number of levels, of which the regional and national will be the two discussed here.
2. Calculations are based on an exchange rate that is the purchasing power parity. This rate uses the prices of a selection of comparable products and it thus takes account of the real purchasing power of a currency. The amounts obtained using this rate are called Purchasing Power Standards.
3. Madjd-Sadjadi (1996) makes the same argument with regard to Canada.
4. See also: CEC (1987), *Third Periodic Report from the Commission on the Social and Economic Situation and Development of the Community*; CEC (1991), *Fourth Periodic Report on the Social and Economic Situation and Development of the Regions of the Community*; and J. Delors (1989), *Regional Implications of Economic and Monetary Integration*.
5. The built-in stabilisers, which are two groups of automatic fiscal adjustments, are taxes (in particular income taxes) and government transfer payments.
6. The three Structural Funds are Regional, Social and Agricultural Guidance.
7. Using only government transfers seems to be a partial and unsuccessful economic and political response to regional disparities and to the weakness of market systems, because the market forces (due to 'cumulative causation') will keep perpetuating regional inequalities and disparities. Consequently, a 'kind' Welfare State should always provide fiscal transfer payments to weaker or poorer regions without offering effective solutions to their developmental problems. Madjd-Sadjadi (1996) argues that these transfers act as a form of 'insurance' that reduces instability. Active demand-oriented disparity-reducing policies and a Developmental State are also necessary if substantial regional development is to be achieved.
8. The share of capital formation and capital outlays of general government to total government outlays either at current or at constant prices (it will not make any important difference) can be obtained, because:

$$\sigma_{ct} = [(KF/deflator)/(GE/deflator)].100 = (KF/GE).100 = \sigma_{cur}$$

9. When considering the lower levels of government consumption in Japan, many economists often choose to exclude defence spending due to the constitutional limitations bequeathed by the USA occupation. Therefore, allowing for defence closes the gap in government consumption. But if we assume that some government investment goes on defence, then this should in theory widen the gulf between Japan and others who have no formal limit on defence spending. In addition, there are some problems with the USA data because part of their public investment is included under public consumption. Taking this out will lower the USA data, which will also close the gap in government consumption.
10. Recently, the 'New Right' theorists (and, especially, the Austrian approach) strongly support the view that, by keeping resources locked up in declining sectors, industrial policy reduces national income below what it would have been in its absence and society bears an additional burden.

8. The Experience of Japan, South Korea and Taiwan in Retrospect

Most students of economics (if they have even been taught the history of economic thought) would be led to believe that economic theory prior to Adam Smith can be summarised in the works of five major figures: Plato (who discusses division of labour and sees commercial activity as a corrupting influence on the military and government in his *Republic*); Aristotle (who first distinguished between use value and exchange value); Thomas Aquinus (who develops the theory of the 'just' price as the initial precursor to the labour theory of value); Thomas Mun (a mercantilist who in *England's Treasure by Foreign [sic] Trade* argues that a favourable balance of payments and strong manufacturing base is the key to financial prosperity); and Quesnay (a physiocrat and precursor to Smith who showed in his *Tableau Economique* how agriculture increased wealth).

This extreme Western reading of the study of economic wealth ignores the fact that until the late 1500s, China was by far the wealthiest nation on the planet. Certainly, great economic heights could not have been achieved without a fundamental understanding of the economic process. This process was continued and expanded throughout the region through the Chinese Diaspora. The first part of this chapter explores Chinese economic thought until the modern era. The second part deals with the mass emigration of the Chinese across the breadth of Southeast Asia. The third parts deals with the concept of the developmental state as a model of political economy in Asia. The following three parts see how this model was applied in Japan, South Korea and Taiwan. The final part wraps up the chapter.

THREE SCHOOLS OF CHINESE ECONOMIC THOUGHT

There are three great 'schools' that can be extracted from Chinese economic thought, two of which have proven dominant in the context of Chinese economic development. The first is the Legalist tradition, which was imported quite readily by the Koreans and Chinese and stresses the linkages between state and society. The second is the Taoist tradition that is more in line with contemporary Libertarian philosophy epitomised by Chuang Tzu who is echoed in Adam Smith's description of the invisible hand when he says, 'allow all things to take their natural course; and admit no personal or selfish consideration: – do this and the world will be governed'. Ssu-ma Ch'ien similarly argues the market system is self-regulating (Hozumi, 1940; Spengler, 1964). However, these voices, which were heard by the common people who undertook an entrepreneurial spirit, were rarely heeded by the government of the day. Indeed, such sentiments could spell rebellion in the countryside and so the Taoist element in economic thought was neglected in the formulation of economic policy in China.

Instead, legalism with its pro-state approach and Confucianism with its decidedly mixed-state approach were the prevalent philosophies that came to dominate East Asian doctrine, and which were subsequently exported to Japan and Korea. That doesn't mean that the Taoist legacy was for naught. Indeed, it can probably be said that without the tempering influence of the Taoist school and its associated preference for free markets, the governments of Korea and Japan created somewhat of a disdain for unbridled capitalism and, instead, fostered a form of economy best thought of as corporatism. In neglecting the traditional role of the state as both ruler and caregiver, and focusing more on the former role than the latter, successive Japanese and Korean governments delinked the importance of reciprocity in such a relationship and so cultivated what was altogether too strong of an influence in regard to the influence of big businesses as seen in the *zaibatsu* and *keritsu* that have come to define the landscape of Japanese and Korean industry. On the other hand, Taiwan, Hong Kong and Singapore having had the Taoist traditions tempered their autocratic tendencies with a 'governing the market' approach that emphasised the role of small and medium-sized businesses over large-scale industrial giants. For this reason, even when the Kuomintang lost power in Taiwan and the autocratic state was sharply curtailed, society was not left rudderless.

We do not want it taken to mean that Taoism was absent completely from South Korea or Japan. Taoism has been present in the Hermit Kingdom and the Land of the Rising Sun for at least the past 1400 years. However, in neither case were serious inroads made by Taoist philosophy. Indeed, it was more commonly practiced as folk religion in Korea (Kim, 1988, p. 203) and Japan.

In the next section, we will discuss some of the important concepts of microeconomics and macroeconomics, which originated in China, not the West, as is commonly believed.

CONCEPTS OF MICROECONOMICS

Microeconomics is the foundation for all economic inquiry. Indeed, an understanding of the process of how transactions are completed is essential for management of efficient allocation of resources in a society. Several concepts in microeconomic theory are found in early Chinese writings. Instead of presenting a chronological history, we have chosen to discuss these on a conceptual basis. The major reason for this is that many of the writers who discuss economic concepts are reporting on the application of economic theory as opposed to writing economic theory. As such, an understanding of these processes often predates the written record and clouds the chronological history of economic thought in East Asia.

Microeconomic theory begins with the concept of supply and demand. Xun Kuang in the third century BC provides the earliest conception of a demand curve in Chinese thought. He differentiates the desire for something from the ability to acquire it. He notes that scarcity limits our ability to acquire everything and, consequently, one must prioritise in order to fulfil one's desires.

The Art of War by Sun Tzu written in the fourth century BC expresses other aspects of the concept. The concept of diminishing marginal utility and the notion that marginal utility must equal marginal cost for there to be a maximisation of gain is discussed in terms of military battle: 'When you do battle, even if you are winning, if you continue for a long time it will dull your forces and blunt your edge' (Sun Tzu, 1988, p. 57). A commentator to this, Jia Lin, writing during the Tang Dynasty (618-906) continues this point: 'Even if you prevail over others in battle, if you go on too long there will be no profit' (Sun Tzu, 1988, p. 57). The importance of using *The Art of War* cannot be underestimated. Although theoretically dealing with warfare, the book is really about maximising gain in all arenas, and it is today considered more of a book of philosophy than a tacticians' guide to warfare.

Also, the concept of transportation costs and increasing marginal costs to transportation are elaborated on by Sun Tzu although it is the commentator Du Mu's writing in the ninth century AD who more clearly makes the point: 'When provisions go for three hundred miles, the country is out a year's supplies; when provisions go for four hundred miles, the country is out two years' supplies' (Sun Tzu, 1988, p. 60). The notion that increases in demand will push up prices and supply are also given by Sun Tzu who warns that prices near an encampment inevitably rise.

The Book of Guan Zi, written during the Warring States period (475-221 BC), developed a concept of equilibrium price and natural price. He notes that price movements fluctuate during the seasons because of fluctuations in supply, and although many might want to maintain the same price for a given commodity it is inherently unnecessary to do so. All prices, Guan Zi maintained, would eventually correct to a 'natural' price in the long run. He continues his discussion with a brilliant exposition of price discrimination: 'The wealthy families [should] be charged a heavy rent for the material used, but the poor families [should] be charged a small rent' (Hu, 1984, p. 34).

In *The Book of Mo Zi*, a commentator writing in the Warring States period noted the difference between value in exchange from value in use with this passage: 'A straw sandal used as a medium to buy something else is a straw sandal no more' (Hu, 1984, p. 10). It is indeed a coincidence of history that Aristotle used the same commodity to make his distinction between use and exchange value.

Mencius, in a conversation with Chen Xiang during the fourth century BC, noted that division of labour increased the quantity of goods supplied because each specialist could concentrate on that job for which they were most suited. It was only through exchange that all needs in society could be met.

In *The Treatise on Salt and Iron* in 81 BC, Sang Hongyang argues for the nationalisation of iron and salt production on the grounds that the larger the unit of production the more efficient and lower the cost of production. Additionally, the price of salt would not be subject to competition. Thus, a government monopoly could increase profits by maintaining a price above that which would exist in a perfectly competitive market. This is precisely the argument for a 'natural monopoly' given by Adam Smith in *The Wealth of Nations*.

What would later be called Gresham's Law, the notion that 'bad money drives out good money', would first find its voice in Jia Yi in the second century BC. He argued that there was an incentive to adulterate coinage unless the government guaranteed the weight and content of the metals in coins.

A price support mechanism was suggested in the fifth century BC by Fan Li and implemented by Sang Hongyang in 110 BC. He argued that the price of grain had to be regulated so that it traded within a band. If the price went 'too high', he argued for government to enter into the market and supply grain. If it went 'too low', the government would purchase grain. In so doing, he understood the fundamentals of supply and demand: increases in supply bring down prices while increases in demand increase prices. The band was set in such a way that only exceptional circumstances could trigger intervention. Normal trading activity was always within the band and the government, in directly interacting with the market and refusing to institute direct price controls, helped to ensure that a black market did not occur.

CONCEPTS OF MACROECONOMICS

Just as no well-established economy can exist without a fundamental understanding of microeconomic laws, it is inconceivable that the whole of China could be prosperous without an understanding of aggregate supply and demand. Public works projects to control flooding had to be undertaken, invaders had to be kept at bay, and the populace had to be kept contented. An ancient Cantonese saying that 'the mountains are high and the Emperor is far away' gives us an insight into macroeconomic behaviour in China. Certainly, taxation of far-off lands had to be at a lower rate than those closer to the central government. Indeed, this concept of equal sacrifice first finds expression in 'The Tribute System of Yu' written in the fourth or fifth century BC. Higher quality land was assessed a higher rate but factors such as the distance between the central government and the tributary state as well as the relative wealth of that state caused a differential assessment across similarly graded land.

Fu Xuan gave a similar system of taxation based on ability to pay during the third century, and Wang Yuan introduced a modern graduated income tax system for firms during the seventeenth century. In order to convince people to reveal their income, and thus be subject to higher marginal taxes, larger marginal tax rates carried with them greater privileges and rights than those accorded to individuals who paid at a lower marginal tax rate due to their limited income.

Also, during the Eastern Han Dynasty (25-220), Emperor Wang Mang formulated a government loan policy which shares some characteristics of modern stock ownership. The government would give zero-interest loans to individuals for noncommercial uses but would receive 10 per cent of the profits generated from the use of a loan for a commercial purpose. Profits were revenues net of production costs but wage payments were not included in production costs. As such, there would be little incentive to increase wages without a corresponding increase in production. Additionally, there was no incentive to hire your friends to hide corporate profits because all wages were included in this calculation. Certainly, this method would have created incentives for the state to make favourable and market-friendly business conditions because such regulations would have the result of increasing returns to the government. In fact, one can think of this tax as a pure income tax in that it did not discriminate between the workers and the self-employed. As there were no direct taxes on workers, the wage bill ended up being the primary method of calculating tributes. As well, there was an incentive to save your own capital because the government tribute was only given when a loan was taken from the government.

In the *Analects of Confucius*, written during the fifth century, the first conception of the overburdens of taxation appears in a Chinese text. In fact,

Confucius admonishes his students that a government cannot be wealthy when its people are poor and the government cannot be poor when the people are wealthy. High tax revenue can only come from high production and high production only comes when individuals are allowed to keep most of their production. In a sense this idea has been reformulated in the late 1970s as the Laffer Curve where Professor Laffer (formerly of the University of Southern California) argued that a 100 per cent tax rate and a 0 per cent tax rate yielded exactly the same amount of revenue, zero.

There are several books which discuss what causes a rising price level (described as a rise in the monetary cost of all commodities by the ancient Chinese). *The Book of Guan Zi* (described earlier) argues that the price of goods is proportional to the quantity of money in circulation. This has been called the 'Quantity Theory of Money' and forms the basis for modern Monetarism. Another aspect of this book is its emphasis on spending money to increase demand. During times of commercial contraction, Guan Zi argues that the government should spend money to stimulate demand for goods and services. He argues that each individual's income forms the basis for his or her consumption. This is precisely the same argument given by John Maynard Keynes. The interesting thing about this text is that it also preaches the concept of saving during expansionary times. The purchase of government goods and services, according to this ancient scholar, should not be undertaken except to keep individuals busy. This countercyclical theory is much more robust than similar passages quoted in the Bible (such as saving for the seven years of lean from the seven years of plenty) because this is a responsibility of the state to protect the public as opposed to an admonishment of individuals to save for economic downturns on their own. Also, it fundamentally underscores an understanding of the business cycle and the role that government can play in stimulating aggregate demand.

Finally, let us look at the works of Hung Liang-Chi who published his essay on population five years before Thomas Malthus' famous treatise on population. An understanding of the exponential rate of population growth was well-known in China which had reached a population by that time of nearly 400 million. Besides, Xu Guangqi, writing in his *Complete Treatise on Agriculture* on the eve of the ascension of the Manchu Dynasty, had observed that the population tended to double every two generations and that only warfare seemed to be able to contain it. But Hung Liang-Chi found that this increase in population was not met by equal increases in farm land, which grew at a much slower rate of expansion. He argued that the limits of land would eventually cause a decline in population and that the slowing of population growth could only occur because of natural calamity (such as disease or drought) or by government control (such as reducing immigration or increasing emigration). He also argued that reducing tax burdens and reclaiming land could alleviate the problems of population growth. In the near term, his concern was more for the rising jobless rate associated with the population rise as opposed to running out of food (Silberman, 1960). It is this idea of movement of peoples from the Middle Kingdom which sets the stage for the great Chinese Diaspora.

THE GREAT DIASPORA

Then suddenly, there was no more great economic insight. The seventeenth century saw the rise of the Manchu Dynasty and the gradual collapse of China as a world power. Increasing poverty and a government, which no longer seemed founded on Confucian values of care for the populace, caused an international migration from the homeland. Of course, Chinese traders had always sought opportunities beyond the Middle Kingdom but there was no movement *en masse* to Nanyang (the Chinese term for Southeast Asia). As millions of Chinese poured across borders throughout Southeast Asia after 1644 (the succession of the Manchu Dynasty), they set up shops and began working with the only advantage they had over the native elements: *guanxi*. Guanxi means connections, relationships, the ability to call on their fellow Chinese, a distinct advantage in business; but their insular nature and distrust of the native populace would be a key reason why Rama VI, king of Siam, would call them 'the Jews of the East'.

This designation was meant to be an insult and it carried with it the connotations which have followed hated groups throughout history. The Chinese were seen as greedy, willing to do anything for a dollar, owing allegiance to only their own and not to their newfound lands. But these labels served more to turn Chinese away from their adopted lands than it served to cause them to interact and accept the cultures with which they were coming into contact.

Nowhere is this Chinese insularity hated more than in Indonesia where 3 per cent of the population is Chinese and they control 70 per cent of the wealth. In Thailand, they control over half the assets in the country with less than 10 per cent of the population. In Malaysia, they are one-third of the population but control 80 per cent of the assets, and more than 90 per cent of all scientists and engineers in that country are of Chinese descent (Kotlin, 1992, p. 180).

How did they do it? There are several explanations. First is education. Confucian values had always placed a high importance on learning and the new emigrants maintained this with a passion. They enrolled their children in local schools and preached hard work as the means to success. Imbued with this passion for learning, when local officials sought to limit admissions of ethnic Chinese, they responded by going overseas to American and British universities. Besides, Chinese educational patterns were not the typical ones stressed by other groups: education in the sciences and engineering were their two most favoured subjects (with business and economics following closely behind). During the late 1980s, more than 25 per cent of all American doctorates in electrical engineering were being awarded to foreign students of Chinese heritage.

The second key characteristic is an acceptance to learn new ideas from others. The goal was always to take the best from each society that they visited and make these aspects distinctively Chinese. Thus, they donned Western dress and adopted English as the language of commercial trade even though they continued their Chinese cultural practices and use of the language within the home and in dealing with other Chinese.

Never entirely suited to any one land, the Chinese can also be called the 'gypsies' of the East. Wherever they have gone, they have seen persecution and contempt from local societies. As such, they have always been willing and able to move onward. Even in mainland China, the repression felt from their native government has caused a mass exodus from the Middle Kingdom for many years. Mainland China has, on different occasions, attempted to recall these individuals from abroad. In 1712, the Manchu government ordered all Chinese to return home. This had the direct effect of reducing emigration by those who were contemplating it because it limited their freedom to return home to maintain the gravesites of their ancestors. But despite reducing the flow of Chinese emigrants, it did not have a measurable impact on those who had already left. Few accepted the ultimatum; yet, the vast majority still retained the traditional Chinese Confucian values and identity.

During rioting in Southeast Asia against Chinese merchants in the early to mid-1960s, Mao's government offered to take back any Chinese who wished to return to the homeland. Once again, few accepted the offer. At the same time, Mao's government moved under Premier Zhao En-Lai to strip overseas Chinese who carried another passport of their citizenship rights by making dual citizenship illegal. In 1980, a further tightening of the regulations, nominally designed to ensure that China's population would not dramatically expand, stripped descendants of overseas Chinese of the right to reimmigrate back to China.

Other countries would take action as well. The *Chinese Exclusionary Act of 1872* was the first restriction on immigration passed by the United States. It was a challenge to this law, brought before the Supreme Court in the 1890s, which first established the principle of citizenship by virtue of birth within the borders of the United States.

The third ingredient had already been alluded to: small credit associations known as *huis* and often organised under the term 'family association' are found in virtually every city in which Chinese gather. Nominally, they are social clubs which assist individuals with the same family name. In reality, they are the breeding grounds of *guanxi*. With local banks refusing to loan money to Chinese, the Chinese were forced to assist themselves and this reliance on the group has served to reinforce traditional Chinese group identification.

One key fact remains: the Chinese, no matter where they are, are always Chinese. They constantly search for, and strive to return to, their roots. Most of the foreign nationals in Hong Kong are of Chinese descent, and the illegal trade between China and Taiwan has grown to such proportions that the port city of Kiaoshung had to be declared 'offshore' in order to reduce the substantial indirect trade with the mainland through Hong Kong (Sung, 1984).[1]

THE DEVELOPMENTAL STATE

Although this discussion can explain much about the expansion of the economy prior to the 1700s, it does little to aid us in understanding modern processes. By the sixteenth century, the Europeans began their colonial conquests and had begun to nibble away at Chinese influence and power. First was the taking of the port city of Malacca (in what is now Malaysia) by Portugal in 1511. This provided a way station where ships bound for China could restock their supplies and regroup. This was especially useful during typhoon seasons because there was a dry port where one could dock and wait for clearer weather. Then came the ceding of Macao to Portugal in 1557. This was the only time in Chinese history that a piece of Chinese sovereign territory was handed over voluntarily by the central government. It was a reward to the Portuguese for aiding the Middle Kingdom in its fight against pirates on the high seas (although there is evidence that it was the Portuguese themselves who were the pirates!). This seemingly insignificant rock would have a profound impact on Western-Chinese relations because, for the first time, trading rights between ordinary Chinese and western agents could be carried on without interference from, or tribute paid to, the central government.

At this time, it may be well to remember the reason why Columbus first sailed towards the West. He sought a new passage to China and all of the wealth that the Chinese could confer. Europeans, newly emerged from the Dark Ages and entering into the Renaissance, could scarcely wait to trade with the great power in the East. Unfortunately, for Europe, there was little that China wanted except vast sums of gold and silver for their incense and silk.

The Spanish took control of the Philippines in 1564, and even Japan was beginning to open up to the West with its Christian missionaries and desire for trade. But in 1637, Japanese Christians attacked the Tokugawa shogunate in the Shimbara Rebellion. Citing 'unacceptable foreign influence', Japan would turn inward by 1640 and banned all but a small Dutch settlement in Nagasaki from the Empire of the Sun. The following year, the Dutch effectively kicked out the Portuguese from Malacca and took Jakarta and the East Indies as well.

The British were relative latecomers to the area as their foray into the region through Penang (in what is now Malaysia) began in the late eighteenth century. Later, in 1819, they would add Singapore and, by 1824, would challenge the Dutch by displacing them from the Malay Peninsula and Burma (which they made a protectorate in 1858 and annexed to India in 1885).

Still, the British lacked the one thing they really wanted: an expansion of trade with China. Heavy imports of Chinese tea with no reciprocity of exports to China meant a rapid decline in the terms of trade. In order to satisfy Chinese desires, they began to look for products which would appeal to the locals. Opium provided an answer. China responded by an all-out attack on the trade, seizing British ships when inspections of them discovered the dreaded cargo. The British responded by attacking China, an unthinkable act for any but the Royal Navy. China was easily defeated and the first of the 'unequal treaties' came into being with the absolute ceding 'for all time' of Hong Kong and Kowloon to Britain, as well as trade access to the all-important cities of Guangdong (Canton) and Shanghai being granted as well.

America was interested in establishing trade of its own with Asia and, by 1853, Admiral Matthew Perry was sent to reestablish Western links with Japan. It soon became apparent that the Japanese could no longer dictate the terms of their contact with the West any better than could China. By 1858, trade and foreign residency had resumed.

France was next and, by the turn of the century, had Laos, Vietnam and Cambodia under its wings. Japan was the final entrant in the race for colonies and in separate attacks on China (in 1894-95) and Russia (in 1904-05) took Korea and Taiwan from China and the Sakhalin islands from Russia.

All of this diminishment of power caused a rebellion in China. The Boxer Rebellion in which Chinese citizenry took arms against the foreign quarter in Beijing showed the degree to which the central government had weakened. Unable to halt the assault on the foreigners, the government of Beijing was embarrassed as five principal colonial agents (Japan, Britain, the United States, Germany and Russia) repelled the attackers and then turned the bill for the fighting and damages over to the central government for collection. What's more, the already heavily indebted government was in no condition to resist the Republican Revolution of 1911 and the boy emperor abdicated with very little blood being shed. But the new Republic of China was still incapable of preserving Chinese territorial interests. Mongolia was ceded to Russia just two years later, and Japan began an all-out war on China in 1931 reaching the height of indignity to China, as Japan placed the former Emperor of China on the throne of the puppet state of Manchukuo in 1934.

Beginning in the late 1920s, China was internally divided as well. The Communists sapped the strength of the Republican forces throughout this period. In 1935, the Kumingtang had struck hard at their Communist foes and the forces of Mao Zedong retreated to the North on what would be known as The Long March. The Japanese drove a wedge between the two forces, effectively splitting them with the Communists in the North and the Nationalists in the South. The Communists employed guerilla tactics against the Japanese while the Nationalists retreated from virtually every advance. After retreating from Beijing to Nanjing, they were evicted by Japanese forces in 1937 and forced to relocate to the inland city of Chungjing. The Japanese were brutal in slaying hundreds of thousands of defenceless Chinese men, women and children while the Republican guard sought to save its strength for the coming inevitable fight with the Communist forces.

In late 1941 and early 1942, in a blitzkrieg effort not unlike that seen in the European theatre of operations by the Germans, Japan took control of much of Southeast Asia including the British ports of Singapore and Hong Kong as well as their holdings in Malaysia, the Portuguese port of Macao, the American colony of the Philippines, French Indochina, the Dutch East Indies, and the only independent country in the region, Siam, now Thailand. Their Greater East Asian Co-prosperity Sphere was built upon the idea that Japanese manufacturers would secure raw materials from these regions including much needed oil and rubber.[2]

Following the defeat of Japanese forces in 1945, and the exile of the Nationalist government to Taiwan in 1949, Asia was in tatters. Indeed, its economies were stagnant; rampant famine was the rule not the exception. The dismantling of colonial empires over the next 15 years would see the establishment of newly independent states: in the Philippines in 1946; North and South Korea in 1948; Burma in 1948; Indonesia in 1949; Cambodia in 1953; Laos in 1953; Vietnam in 1954; Malaysia in 1957; Singapore in 1959 although it was part of Malaysia from 1963 to 1965; and Brunei in 1984.

The American occupation of Japan from 1945 to 1952 brought with it a rebuilding of the nation with a republican form of government. It is hard to say if it was truly a democracy, however. Allegiance to the emperor was displaced following Emperor Hirohito's renunciation of godhood in 1945. It was replaced with allegiance to the state and to the *keritsu*. To understand this displacement, it is necessary to understand Eastern culture. Rudyard Kipling once wrote, 'East is East and West is West and never the "twain" shall meet'. But they have met and have changed each other. Still, there are several aspects of Eastern culture which are totally foreign to western eyes. First is the importance of the group over the individual. The group helps the individual and the individual owes allegiance to the group for this assistance. In Asia, truly, the whole body (in economic and political terms) is greater than the sum of its parts. Second, within each group there is a hierarchical structure which is semi-paternalistic. Workers are subservient to managers just as subjects were subservient to the Emperor. However, this paternalistic pattern manifests itself only within certain spheres. In Japan, for example, wives defer to husbands in terms of work and external status but wives are seen as the master of the home, taking control of the education of the children and receiving the pay directly from the company, passing only a small allowance on to the *salaried-man* husband. There is an obligation that is given for power to be exercised. Power is conferred on elders, on the emperor, and on husbands only to the extent that they take the needs of their subjects into consideration. Due to this familial-like tie of obligation which finds its roots in Confucian teachings, blind obedience is the rule not the exception. Finally, there is an emphasis on consensual decision-making mechanisms. Power is not typically demonstrated through force but through gaining the confidence of the subjects. This is typified by the following quote from *The Art of War:* 'The general rule for use of the military is that it is better to keep a nation intact than to destroy it. . . Therefore, those who win every battle are not really skilful – those who render others' armies helpless without fighting are the best of all' (Sun Tzu, 1988, pp. 66-7).

With the displacement of the Emperor, the people looked elsewhere for an organisation to take care of them. In Japan, they found it in the *keritsu.*[3] We see a similar pattern of behaviour in Korea, where it is loyalty to the *chaebol*, and in Hong Kong, where it is loyalty to the *hong* (ironically these were British trading companies until the recent Sinofication of the territory as the crown colony prepared for its recent reunification with the mainland).

Governments throughout the region have employed the principles of Confucianism to establish a model, which is known as the 'developmental state' model. This is not to say that Confucianism is a sufficient or even a necessary condition to ensure industrial take-off. Indeed, there are aspects of Confucianism that can be seen as stifling of innovation, especially its emphasis on formal scholarly education as opposed to practicum. Still, once the necessary preconditions for industrial take-off were set in place, Confucianism's guiding principles assisted East Asian in achieving success. Yet, for those entities not privy to Confucian values, these policies can be replicated. Each of the New Industrialised Countries (as well as Japan) in East Asia can trace their successes to five key elements:

1. widespread and large investments on the 'modern factors of growth and competitiveness', and an equitable distribution of income;

2. selective incentives using the price mechanism (very similar to the theory developed in China on how to ensure that prices trade within a predetermined band in the fifth century BC) to foster development of public and private infrastructure as well as the rationalisation of industries so as to take advantage of Akamatsu's (1961) 'flying geese model';
3. an insulated, well-paid and highly educated bureaucracy which can determine policies without external pressures;
4. the establishment of a domestically-controlled, production-oriented industrial and financial sector; and
5. an investment-based, as opposed to a consumption-based, economic system.[4]

As long as these five rules were followed, economic growth continued on an upward trajectory. Those states that have failed to implement these policies (such as the Philippines) have seen anaemic growth when compared to their neighbours. Those states that have only partially practiced these policies (such as Indonesia, which lacks an insulated bureaucracy) have seen some growth spurts but also have seen calamity in the recent 'Asian contagion'. Other states which practiced these policies for a time (such as South Korea and Japan) have allowed their bureaucracies to become too entangled with their private sectors, resulting in capture by these private entitles. This can be traced to 1984 in South Korea where several of the *chaebol* were declared 'insolvent' despite being able to pay their debts when they refused to provide pay-offs to the government. One of those casualties was the Hanbo Group (which build the Seoul subway system) whose past chairman is suing in a California court for a return of his assets. Thus, while we agree with Alice Amsden that South Korea's success was principally due to getting the 'right' relative prices 'wrong', we see the non-insularity of the bureaucracy as being a very critical factor as to why the Korean miracle was sidetracked. We now turn our attention to the specific countries in question, and discuss how they link up with the concept of an East Asian theory.

JAPAN

Unique among the East Asian countries, Japan not only had a Confucian legacy imported from China but also incorporated its own theory. Writing in the early seventeenth century, and paralleling and preceding Physiocratic ideas about agriculture serving as the basis of all wealth-production, Kumazawa Banzan argued that opulence of some led to poverty for others (McMullen, 1999, pp. 239-49). He was also one of the first scholars to note a connection between ecological devastation and economic prosperity. He derided the use of specie as a medium of exchange, although his analysis was more of a moral statement than an economic one. Yet, his argument rings true more from a developmental state viewpoint in that he argued against importation of luxuries and focused instead on basic needs.

Arai Hakuseki (Honjo, 1940) parallels more closely the philosophy of the mercantilists in his liking of specie. But this late seventeenth and early eighteenth century philosopher differs from them in arguing for an insulated state. Although deriding the loss of specie on foreign imports, he did not propose to make it up with exports. Instead, he was the consummate autarkist, arguing for the elimination of foreign trade in line with Banzan, except in the case of medicine, which he happened to believe was a stopgap measure to be used only until Japan could be self-sufficient in that as well (Honjo, 1939).

Yet, recurrent throughout Tokugawa economic thought in Japan was the concept of the feudal system as epitomised by the Samurai. This was derided by some scholars as late as the nineteenth century who tried to turn back the clock to a day when the business interests were not so powerful, and desires for government monopolies to ensure traditional social order are seen in such works as the *Chirizukadan*, the *Rikenron*, and the *Shumaken Josho* all of which promote the idea of transferring rights of commercial interests to the state in the manner of lending money and the rice trade (Honjo, 1938, pp. 26-7). At the same time, we see additional government intervention in the marketplace in the form of taxation, government monopolies and confiscatory schemes all with the aim of maintaining the predominant social order. Yet, it was the forced opening to the West by Matthew Perry that reversed these trends and sent Japan down the road of foreign trade; so, we see the opening of Japan against its prevalent economic doctrine being forced to adapt to an influence not of its own making.

Furthermore, the persistence in belief that foreigners should not mould one's economic destiny is precisely the rationale behind the expansionary doctrine culminating in the Greater East Asia Co-Prosperity Sphere that permeates Japanese economic thought in the early 1940s. Liberal economics carried with it the dangerous ideas of individual liberty that lay at the cornerstone of democratic reform. This concept of universal application of economic law ran counter to the notion of Japanese 'exceptionalism' that took hold in the first part of the twentieth century. Indeed, when the Japanese began to look at the great empires and how they developed, they saw one overriding theme: the development of dynamic competitive advantage through government manipulation of the marketplace. As a result, having seen how empire can be built and extended, the Japanese undertook a policy that can only be described as Listian.

Indeed, the concept of dynamic competitive advantage came to Japan via Oshima Sadamasu who, in 1889, published his translation of List's *National System of Political Economy*. The Listian argument is simple to understand and conceptualise: the neoclassical paradigm is fundamentally based on a static argument wherein each produces according to their own comparative advantage. Nevertheless, if one specialises in one's own comparative advantage, one can never leave that advantage behind in a systematic process. Therefore, the poorer countries that lack manufacturing will, too often, fail to achieve anything more. Indeed, the classic argument of Portugal making port (a type of wine) and England making cloth is fundamentally at the heart of Listian economics as cloth is a manufactured good while port is an agricultural good; consequently, while Portugal is made relatively better off in the short run, in the long run it is condemned to poverty relative to England. This creates a rationale for state intervention in the marketplace to alter the comparative (or competitive) advantage of nations in a systematic fashion (Morris-Suzuki, 1989, pp. 59-65).

More to the point, Oshima argues that protectionism not only benefited industry but also agricultural interests because the benefits that accompanied industrial growth would add to the benefit of agricultural interests through their consumption patterns. Indeed, it was free trade, not protectionism, that was guided by short-term interests. What was to be pursued was the development of productive processes that were the basis of all real wealth creation as opposed to the false hope of cheap consumption by relying on the expertise of others (Sugiyama, 1994, pp. 102-4).

The Great Depression put to the test what can only be described as proto-Keynesian ideas from Japanese Finance Minister Korekiyo Takahashi, who ordered Japan off the gold standard and instituted contemporaneous monetary and fiscal expansion. As a result, the Japanese experience during the Great Depression was shorter-lived and their recovery much more stable and sustained than that of any of the other industrial powers. Takahashi realised that a deflationary spiral, if left unchecked, would cause the economy to spiral out of control causing the depression. By simultaneously depreciating the yen, providing liquidity to the market through easy credit and stimulating the economy through deficit financing, Takahashi did exactly the opposite of the prescription of the neoclassical economists who argued for fiscal 'responsibility' through balanced budgets. Yet, the 'Japanese Keynes' was assassinated on 26 February 1936 in an attempted coup of the government.

From 1937 until the end of the Second World War, the military took over and the Japanese economic engine began to serve that imperial force. Yet, the lessons learned from these experiences were to come back in the post-war period through the innovative work of trade theorist Akamatsu, whose 'flying geese' model of industrialisation showed how development patterns in East Asia resembled 'flying geese': as countries developed they would lose their weaker industries to neighbouring countries and a cascade effect would occur so that each of the countries in the industrialisation order would shift up the path of industrialisation when the leading country (Japan) made its entry into the next stage. Similarly, Kiyoshi Kojima (1978) noted that this product cycle theory was fundamentally based on work from neoclassical economics itself through the Heckscher-Ohlin and Stolper-Samuelson models of trade formation. Ricardian analysis is fundamentally static but the very nature of acting on one's comparative advantage alters the fundamental balance of natural resources in a society. Some goods deplete resources, thus altering the balance in favour of other industries. Others enhance them, causing a process of cumulative causation to occur, wherein the engine of growth reinforces itself. At the same time, rising reliance on labour inputs will cause increases in wages that will undermine competitiveness in labour-intensive industries and result in a shift towards capital-intensive ones as well as an expansion of domestic desires for consumption goods. This shift, if guided by government industrial policy, can result in allowing countries to initiate market-friendly policies that will enable the country to better take advantage of these changes by casting off relatively wage-poor industries to neighbouring countries instead of seeking to maintain employment levels in these less-desirable economic sectors.

As discussed by Yamazawa (1990, p. 20), the Japanese process of development could be traced from primary to light industrial to heavy manufacturing through a process by which Japan altered its competitive advantage as it moved from one stage to another, importing goods that were contrary to its competitive advantage and exporting according to its competitive advantage at each stage, except during the transition phases when competitive advantage was altered through import substitution policies. Moving from one stage to another required the coordination of investment decisions (Keynes, 1936) so as to achieve industrial objectives. Since capital accumulation and development of higher competencies of factors of production are required to advance the economy, and these skills and capital need to be directed into areas which are not immediately ripe for profits, the state has a role in directing financial, social and human capital investment into new areas. At each stage of development, products were identified for imitation or by requiring the settlement of branch plant facilities that will produce the good onshore. Initially, exportation of goods occurred at the low end of the market. As local industry began to achieve technical competence in the production of the good and began to make improvements in product quality that went beyond the original product, Japan stopped competing solely on price and started to compete on quality. However, Yamazawa (1990, p. 232) warns that the flying geese model cannot be replicated *ad infinitum*. While Japan could throw off its lesser industries to those in lower stages of development, eventually countries at the lowest ends of development will find that there is no one left to whom they can toss off their defunct industries.

While this might seem like a giant Ponzi scheme with the last player left holding the bag, these processes may actually prove beneficial as we move to a new model of development incorporating the best features of the developmental state with an understanding that no general theory can ever be used at all times and places (Hodgson, 2001). By understanding the historical specificity of each argument, we can see the solution to this lies in the last country standing being one of sufficient population that it can incorporate all types of good production within its mix. Meanwhile, inevitably, wages will rise in this and in all countries and cause a general rise in the relative price of such goods, reversing the trend of hundreds of years towards decline in the relative price of unskilled labour. This will eventually cause the rise of all boats promised by economics for years.

Another potential difficulty is that import substitution policies cannot always be achieved effectively when attempting to build world-class heavy industry. The fact is that some countries are simply too small to be able to sustain cost-effective import substitution policies unless they are part of a larger free trade region of similarly positioned countries at early stages of development. However, such regions can serve only the interest of import substitution because trade most benefits countries that are at different stages of development. Besides, coordination among countries to select appropriate industries needs to occur; but such international coordination is notoriously difficult to achieve as, for nationalistic reasons, each country might wish to have its own automobile, shipping and chemical industries. Furthermore, development of products at the international level often reflects the tastes of developed nations and would be considered luxuries at the level of the developing country. Both of these reasons may lead to a collapse of the sustainability of these import substitution policies (Roxborough, 1979, pp. 34-5).

Always throughout this process was the notion that free trade was an inevitable consequence for countries that were leading in terms of economic development. One did not need to alter the comparative advantage once one was in a position of superiority. Hence, industrial policy, as instituted by MITI, was really guided by the principle of acquiescing to the market as opposed to actively opposing it. Western observers, beginning with Johnson (1982), often saw it as a model for the US, although it is really a mechanism to play catch up instead of maintaining a lead. This is because East Asian industrialisation was often about learning through imitation, not innovation. Planning is often the antithesis of innovation. And innovation policy is fundamentally different from industrial policy in that while one can actively dissuade certain activities by picking 'losers' for elimination, merely throwing a lot of capital at a problem does not automatically lead to a solution. The education system that worked so well in creating workers obedient and bonded to the nation and corporation did not fare so well in realigning priorities for new invention.

The collapse of the Japanese model can best be thought of as a situation where the Japanese actually started to believe the rhetoric claimed in the West for the model. As Japan moved from imitation-driven growth to innovation-driven growth, the model started to buckle. It is quite easy to run a race where someone is in front of you. Just as in racing one can 'draft' the car in front, Japan was not a leading industrial power until the 1980s. Instead, it was a second-tier economy partaking of the 'flying geese' model by taking on industries that were slowly losing their competitive advantage in the West. But it failed to properly move towards policies that were broad-based instead of sector-specific. Indeed, altering this policy can become difficult if the bureaucracy is penetrated too deeply by economic interests (Porter, 1990; Johnson, 1985). Of course, one could argue that the reason for Japan's growth wasn't industrial policy at all. With such a large savings pool, Japan was going to succeed with virtually any policy and the reason for the reduction in growth has more to do with declines in that savings pool than anything else. Still, as we will see in the next chapters, governments can have a role in creating that pool of savings in the first place.

We believe that one of the main reasons for the Japanese inability to sustain the 'miracle economy' was that they had imported the Confucian and, to a lesser extent, the Legalist traditions from China, but not the Taoist. As such, they lacked the tradition that was most compatible with the western idealised form found in capitalism. The concept of *laissez-faire* was, though well known to the Japanese, somewhat foreign to their philosophical outlook. Their economy was based instead, like the Korean one we will discuss in the next section, on an interrelationship between big business and government instead of one based on entrepreneurial small businesses. This is the fundamental difference between the economies of Taiwan, Singapore and Hong Kong and that of South Korea and Japan. It is also this difference which best explains why South Korea became embroiled in the problems of the 1997 meltdown known as the East Asian Crisis (and Japan had been a laggard since the late 1980s) while Taiwan reacted almost as if the crisis never occurred, and Hong Kong and Singapore were hit predominantly because of their status as entrepots (in the case of Hong Kong, too, due in part to the handover to China that occurred in the same year). Indeed, the uniqueness of the Chinese element to political economy is not one made only in hindsight:

> It is even more difficult, especially for an economist, to analyse the importance to East Asian success of the culture of the region. . . But it does seem significant

that East Asia, that is the *countries with a Chinese-based culture, and only those countries*, achieved a consistently higher growth rate than any other region, and without the benefits and costs of profitable raw-material exports. (Papanek, 1988, pp. 75-6; emphasis added)

SOUTH KOREA

Much of what was said about Japan can also be said about South Korea with the exception of the development of its own theory. South Korea inherited from China the Confucian traditions that also found their way to Japan. The founding of the Chosun Dynasty in 1392 was based on neo-Confucian ideals imported from China, and its position as a satellite kingdom under the influence of China was great until the early twentieth century when Japan annexed the nation, ending the Chosun Dynasty in 1910.[5] Under Japanese rule, infrastructure projects boomed as Korea was brought into a trading regime from a largely autarkic existence. Railroad lines were built that traversed the country; telegraph lines dotted the landscape; and ports for Japanese ships were completed. Furthermore, the Japanese laid the foundations for industrial society thorough the development of heavy industry and mining. It was a transformation that was resisted by the Koreans: 'Colonial administrators remarked that what could be done with economic incentives in Taiwan required coercion in Korea' (Cummings, 1987, p. 54). Indeed, much of that resistance came from nationalist elements that were cultivated by the Japanese university system itself, which undertook to educate the best and brightest of the Korean students, and the fairly benign policies towards such movements by Governor-General Saito in the 1920s, following the crackdown on the nationalistic March First Movement in 1919 (Borthwick, 1992, p. 193, p. 197). These policies were later reversed in the mid-1930s, however, with the imposition of Japanese as the only language of instruction and Shintoism as the new national religion (Borthwick, 1992, pp. 199-200).

Indeed, these nationalistic reactions and clampdowns by the Japanese authorities made for the imposition of far greater control over South Korea than was seen in Taiwan. Ironically, as a result, the approach of the developmental state in the aftermath of Korean independence following the Second World War was one that was more in line with Japanese economic thought than Taiwan ever had. For example, the Korean *chaebols* were created along the same lines as the Japanese *keiretsu*, both of which are descendants of the Japanese *zaibatsu*, interlocking large conglomerates that were intimately intertwined with the Japanese government in setting industrial policy.

The *zaibatsu* were characterised by interlocking directorates that would find the same persons sitting on the boards of several different companies, all of which traded with one another more as a cartel than as separate entities. In each case the *zaibatsu* would be linked to a bank, which would advance credit at below market rates, and the conglomerate would work together to achieve joint goals and reduce competitive pressures. However, the primary difference between *zaibatsu* and the progeny was that control was linked to a single family through a holding company and had interlocking directories in the former case but not the latter. Interlocking directories were outlawed during the Allied occupation of Japan and the *zaibatsu*'s stock ownership was divested to the general populace. However, difficulties in achieving financing and an inability to market products successfully led to the development of the *chaebols* in Korea and the *keiretsu* in Japan.

These entities are a series of independent companies linked together through cross-shareholding in which each company owns shares of other members of the *chaebol* or *keiretsu*. This joint share ownership makes them more interdependent than other companies, and joint financing is often achieved by the appeal to the common bank that heads the *keiretsu* (the lone exception is the Toyota Group, which lacks a banking entity), although not the *chaebol*, which typically lacks such a banking company. In addition, joint ventures are common and often organised through a trading company that is part of the group. Typically, intragroup competition is kept at a minimum, while there is sometimes intense competition between *keiretsu* or *chaebols*. As time progressed, more and more shares wound up in the hands of other corporations so that companies could work towards long-term profitability goals instead of achieving quarterly targets. This had the effect of making these companies impervious to potential takeovers because no one could purchase enough shares to achieve a controlling interest on the open market. This trend has been partially reversed in recent years due to difficulties of the Japanese economy in the late 1980s and the restructuring of Korean industry following the 1997 economic crisis.

One key difference is that, with the exception of Samsung (founded in 1938) and Kia (founded in 1944), the Korean *chaebols* all were founded after the Japanese occupation ended. Another difference is that the Korean industrialisation takes place in the context of the Korean War, which has never officially ended. This has meant that far more expenditure on GDP was required for national defence than the constitutionally limited amounts in Japan. Whereas Japan chose to move to heavy industry as the result of industrial upgrading, the zeal undertaken by the Koreans was driven not just by desire but also the perceived national need to advance development in the face of a potential military threat. Korea has also suffered more from a roller-coaster ride in GDP, often accelerating but also plunging deep into recession, such as that which occurred in 1980, where its GDP dropped by 6 per cent in one year (Cummings, 1987, p. 79).

TAIWAN

Taiwan shares with Korea linkages as a colony of Japan, and its obsession with industrialisation includes a military component with the threat of war with mainland China always on its mind. Like both Japan and South Korea, for much of the post-World War II period, Taiwan exhibited a strong one-party state structure. Indeed, what is generally true of all three countries as well as the city-states of Singapore and Hong Kong is that competitive elections have either not come at all or have come only in the last decade or so to these countries. Although all have, at least nominally, democratic structures, they lack the Western democratic tradition. This is not to be thought of as a precursor to success but it does point out that taking a long-term view may be somewhat more easily undertaken in what Cummings (1987, p. 71) calls 'Bureaucratic-Authoritarian Industrialising Regimes' that are 'ubiquitous in economy and society: penetrating, comprehensive, highly articulated and relatively autonomous of particular groups and classes'.

Yet, unlike South Korea and Japan, both of which were dramatically hurt by the East Asian financial meltdown of 1997, Taiwan shares with Hong Kong and Singapore a remarkable resiliency. Hong Kong, of course, was hampered by its coincident handover to China but, still, it has performed far better than could ever be projected at the time. However, whereas Hong Kong and Singapore are entrepot city-states, Taiwan is a small but diverse country that is self-sufficient in some agricultural produce, and which has a population that is about twice the combined size of the two city-states and half the size of South Korea.

Taiwan was colonised by Japan in 1895 and thus was under the Japanese thumb for about 50 years until the conclusion of the Second World War. It enjoyed only a relatively brief period of semi-autonomy however, when the Nationalist Government of China took refuge there following their defeat in the Chinese Civil War in 1949. Going from being a onetime distant province to the seat of a government-in-exile led to another *de facto* colonisation, this time by other Chinese.

Likewise, Taiwan was transformed from a backward agrarian economy into a developing industrialising one by the Japanese imperial forces. In this way, Taiwan moved from the periphery to the semi-periphery, acting as conduits between the core and the periphery and as enforcers to align the interests of the periphery with that of the core (Kindleberger, 1951). Ironically, at the time that Japan's imperialism was in ascendancy, those of Western states had begun their decline. As such, a new liberalism was sweeping over the West that saw self-determination as a rallying cry. Yet, Japan's late entry into World War I on the side of the Allies saw it capture the remnants of German imperial holdings in East Asia and validated its presence as a colonial power. As in South Korea, the Japanese developed the railroads in Taiwan that would deliver agricultural produce from the centre of the island to the ports. Unlike South Korea, Japan proceeded with land reform in Taiwan, and the Taiwanese population was much less militant towards the occupation forces. Besides, Taiwanese industries were developed to act as a processing station for raw materials from China and Southeast Asia and the transformation of these materials into semi-finished goods (Lin, 1973).

The return of Taiwan to China was, however, not accomplished in a manner that would allow an indigenous Taiwanese government to take advantage of these changes. One key difference is that the ruling party in Taiwan was not a product of that colonisation process. The Kuomintang that came to rule Taiwan from the mainland had been China's ruling party from the 1911 revolution by Sun Yat-Sen to the end of the Chinese Civil War in 1949. A second period of land reform occurred with the establishment of the Nationalist presence on the island. In addition, along with the military officers fleeing from the mainland, a large number of professionals from the burgeoning middle class of China made it to Taiwan. This influx of immigration created dynamism that did not take hold in either South Korea or Japan. Both countries were drawn into the sphere of influence of the free world's superpower, the United States. Ironically, the development strategy was spurred on by the United States and economic planning was actively encouraged. However, this support from the United States was more for the purposes of ensuring social order and acting as a bulwark against the 'threat' of Communism than out of any belief that it contributed to economic growth (Cummings, 1987, pp. 70-73).

Moreover, the Taiwanese failed to have the *zaibatsu/keiretsu/chaebol* structure found in Japan and South Korea, except for entities affiliated directly with the Taiwanese State. Indeed, it was state-run enterprise, not private enterprise, that grew to a large size in the island nation owing in no small part to the paranoia that existed among the Kuomintang government officials who feared economic power being concentrated in the hands of native Taiwanese. Yet, despite this or perhaps because of it, small and medium-sized enterprises became nimble participants in the international market, accounting for over half of all exports, a figure far higher than that of similarly sized enterprises in either South Korea or Japan (Chen, 2004, p. 71). In addition, corporations were far less beholden to a diet of taking on debt, relying instead on the generation of internal capital to fund expansion. This is in keeping with the small size of these enterprises and, thus, the concept of 'too big to fail' that reigns over the economic restructuring of

South Korea and Japan never took hold in Formosa. Indeed, the principles espoused by South Korea and Japan to allow capitalists free reign of the economy are in sharp contrast to Sun Yat-Sen's practices as implemented in Taiwan.

Sunist policies still differed from orthodox Marxism in a way that generally facilitated private sector industrial development, but only set constraints on some private sectors and regulated industries, either directly or indirectly, related to national defence or monopolistic and large-scale industries like banking, railroad and aviation. Sun Yat-Sen firmly believed once those industries were operated by private individuals, they could easily manipulate the quantity and price of production to cause economic disorder (Chen, 2004, p. 74).

Indeed, it is clear that the philosophical orientation of Sun Yat-Sen is far more compatible with the reorientation of the developmental state that we are espousing in this text. The danger is concentration of power, and the government must act as a power-neutralising force so that the forces of capital and labour as well as producers and consumers can be brought back into balance.

Another striking comparison is that agriculture has been more world competitive in Taiwan than in either South Korea or in Japan. Part of this has to do with the land reform undertaken by both the Japanese and Nationalist Governments. While rice growing is really a source of national pride in Japan and considered attached to its cultural traditions, for Taiwan, it was a source of significant export revenue up until the 1960s. In addition, despite dropping from more than half of all export earnings in the early 1960s to the single digits in terms of percentage of foreign exchange earnings today, and the mass exodus of workers from the rural agrarian base to the industrial centres, agricultural production has continued to expand with both rice and sugarcane yields increasing significantly up for the first 40 years of post-war industrialisation (Wu, 1988, pp. 186-90).

Another key difference is that Taiwan has not been so preoccupied with the development of manufacturing processes that require global markets to achieve profitability. For example, while both South Korea and Japan concentrated on developing an automobile industry, Taiwan allowed its nascent industry to stumble along without much government assistance. Taiwan realised its pathway was in technological and not capital-intensive development of industries, and so did not pursue the same trajectory that South Korea and Japan did. This can be seen in the development of the Taiwanese hard drive and semiconductor industries, both of which have achieved phenomenal success (Wang, 2004).

A salient feature of all five East Asian economies is the expansion of education, especially at the secondary and tertiary levels. In the Taiwanese case, as late as the early 1950s, fewer than 15 per cent of all students who attended primary school graduated from high school and less than 1 per cent received tertiary education. By the 1990s, virtually all students received at least a high school education and more than a quarter were earning a tertiary degree (Chen, 2004, p. 47).

A final difference between South Korea and Japan on the one hand and Taiwan, Singapore and Hong Kong on the other is structural. The companies in the Chinese societies tend to be far less financially leveraged, far less capital-intensive, and those firms that do participate on the stock exchanges find their shares in the hands of the public at large as opposed to other corporations, large institutional shareholders or a small group of investors. We now turn our attention to the two city-states, Singapore and Hong Kong, which, many observers argue, are two extremes on the spectrum of the developmental state.

NOTES

1. Since 1978, China has attempted through its 'open door' policy to establish direct links with Taiwan in the hope of reintegrating it with the mainland. Taiwan initially responded with the 'three No's:' no discussing, no bargaining, no compromising. It has since weakened this policy based on the thriving illegal trade. Beijing and Taipei officials have met since then to discuss such topics as hijacking (with an agreement to return hijackers to their native country, usually mainland China) and the safety of Taiwanese businessmen who are on the mainland (with Taipei assisting mainland authorities in carrying out investigations of crimes committed against Taiwanese).
2. It has been argued that the Japanese incursion into Southeast Asia was a response to America's refusal to engage in trade with them in rubber products. The Japanese government's supplies had dwindled to only six months worth of rubber by late 1941. This argument, while convincing as to why the Japanese attacked when they did, is not entirely convincing as to its corollary that Japan would not have attacked had America assisted it in the provision of rubber. Japanese external ambition during the twentieth century must be seen as a desire to create a colonial empire, and it is doubtful that Japanese ambitions would have been contained had trade continued past Roosevelt's ban in 1937, following the Rape of Nanjing.
3. Note that there is a dark side to this emphasis on group dynamics. We see this in the United States with gang affiliations, in Hong Kong and China with its *triads* (also referred to as *tongs*) and in Japan with the *Yakuza*. The key difference is the lack of truly consensual policies in these crime organisations with their emphasis on what the *Yakuza* call *Mimbo*, the (not-so-gentle) art of 'persuasion'. This darker side can be seen with the rampant corruption in Hong Kong prior to the establishment of the Internal Commission Against Corruption in the mid-1970s and the recent gangland killings which have turned the sleepy city of Macao into one of Asia's most dangerous cities.

4. For alternative rationales for their successes, see Simone and Feraru (1995), and World Bank (1993).
5. Its status as a satellite and tributary state to China meant that industrial development was stagnated for much of this period. One neo-Confucian scholar, Chong Tojon, attempted to build an agrarian state through a tax policy that punished industry, and a land reform campaign to redistribute land to the peasantry (Palais, 1996, pp. 27-9). Similarly, trade with Japan was actively discouraged as was trade with China except for the payments of tribute (Palais, 1996, p. 31). Indeed, the only scholar of note to write on economic matters was seventeenth century writer Yu Hyongwon who wrote extensively about inflation cycles and developed a theory of currency (Palais, 1996).

9. A Tale of Two City-States: Singapore and Hong Kong

The Newly Industrialised Countries' 'East Asian Miracle' is not a case of 'letting the free market work' but a case of state-driven industrialisation based on the selective use of investment incentives and disincentives, what might be properly called 'capital manipulation'. These economic policies were initiated in order to ensure 'growth with equity' and have succeeded in producing rapid industrial growth without the severe economic disparities found in either the less-developed countries or in the industrialisation period of the advanced industrial countries. But neither neoclassical theories of development (which promote growth) nor Marxist theories of development (which promote equity) are capable of explaining this success.

Economic debate on development policy has traditionally centred on the opening up of trade. According to classical liberal economic theory, through the elimination of protectionist measures, countries would be able to specialise in those production areas in which they held a comparative advantage. This would lead to allocative efficiency and a growth path leading to industrial take-off. Of course, there would still be a need for regulation by the government to prevent the formation of monopolies and to ensure that exploitation of those unable to make decisions for themselves (such as children) would not occur. But, in general, the state was supposed to retreat from active interference in the market and, instead, establish laws compatible with the functioning of the free market. Commons (1957) argues that such laws not only are designed to prevent the coercive or discriminatory taking of property or liberty but even value.

Overall, neoclassical trade models tended to ignore capital flows, and articles like Samuelson (1948) reinforced the view by showing that factor prices could be equalised with trade. More recently, the 'New International Economics' has emphasised the market structure aspects of international industrial organisation. Studies such as that of Helpman (1992) were geared towards showing that, in the face of differences in international factor prices, multinational firms can arise. Vernon (1966), on the other hand, emphasised how foreign investment comes only after products achieve a degree of maturity in their product cycle, building on the work of Kaname Akamatsu (1961) discussed in the previous chapter.

However, Marxist theorists such as Lenin (1939a, p. 22) (and later the neo-Marxist dependency theorists) argued that, under capitalism, both uneven development and income disparities are 'fundamental and inevitable conditions and premises of this mode of production'. To Lenin, the export of capital occurred because of unequal returns between host country and recipient. It was the potential for profit which drew capital to them, and which beat back the inevitable 'declining rate of profit':

> In these backward countries profits are usually high, for capital is scarce, the price of land is relatively low, wages are low [and] raw materials are cheap. The possibility of exporting capital is created by the fact that numerous backward countries have been drawn into international capitalist intercourse. . . [Actually,] the necessity for exporting capital arises from the fact that in a few countries capitalism has become 'over-ripe' and [owing to the backward state of agriculture and the impoverished state of the masses] capital cannot find 'profitable' investment. (Lenin, 1939a, p. 22)

However, the results of a Marxian analysis seem totally at variance with the facts. Very little capital was ever repatriated back to the host countries and most of the gains from international investment have accrued to the recipient countries in the case of East Asia. One notable exception is Stephen Hymer (1976) who notes that capital transfers across national boundaries have more to do with the reaction of firms to trade barriers promulgated by the receiving countries than factor exploitation.

Recently, non-Marxists have continued this analysis too. Neoclassical economist Richard Caves (1970), for example, argues that direct investment leads to product differentiation. He also notes the positive and negative sides of international investment in that the firm may hasten technology transfer but may encourage oligopolistic market behaviour as opposed to competitive behaviour. This will result in more advertising for products than would otherwise be the case and a reduction in the number of firms competing in the marketplace through mergers and acquisitions.

Firms may use intra-corporate markets to bypass the traditional market whenever transaction costs of using markets are high. This command-and-control aspect aids in the reduction of uncertainty in unstable economies and allows for the accumulation of capital in areas that lack capital in their locality through direct foreign investment.

Transaction costs analysis places emphasis on the role of institutions in economic development. However, it does not go far enough. If institutions matter, then actions should be taken to create a supportive institutional environment for their maintenance and growth. Institutional economists advocate such an evolutionary view. Weber (1958) argues that capitalism is a force that can only succeed when the habits and proclivities resonating with it are nurtured in a population. The role of the state is more than maintaining a competitive environment. It is about engineering policies that support the development of national-based firms and moving comparative advantage in an appropriate direction. Doryan (1993) argues that market and state must not work at cross purposes, and the state can effectively play a role in assisting private enterprise in industrial restructuring, by providing public services that can create a competitive advantage for the nation's businesses and by building institutions that can assist firms in becoming more technically innovative and productive. This is particularly true for countries with very small capital bases. As they are more influenced by the fluctuations of the market, they must move to reduce their exposure to these risks through the manipulation of capital flows in both direction and magnitude.

THE IMPORTANCE OF CAPITAL MANIPULATION

In the following section of the chapter, we concentrate our efforts on Singapore. We will examine the restrictions on, and incentives for, capital mobility in the context of the city-state, noting that it has far more in common with the creation of dynamic comparative advantage (Southard, 1931; Plummer, 1934; Phelps, 1936; Veblen, 1939) through industrial policy (Hamilton, 1928; List, 1977) than on the conducting of trade on the basis of the current comparative advantage of nations *à la* Heckscher-Ohlin-Samuelson (H-O-S) theory of international trade. Indeed, we argue that the neoclassical model, despite its refinements of the original Ricardian analysis to allow for transportation costs, mobility of factors of production and scale economies, still retains its fundamentally static nature that makes it of little use for the implementation of public policy. These controls on capital mobility can take any of four basic forms:

1. restrictions on capital flows into the country (particularly foreign investment limits);
2. restrictions on capital flows going out of the country (e.g., forced savings and exchange controls);
3. incentives for capital flows to enter the country (like tax exceptions or abatements); and
4. incentives for capital flows to exit the country (such as foreign aid credits).

In a seminal article, Harry Johnson (1965b) showed absolute restrictions on capital flows entering the country are designed to appeal to a country's sense of nationalism. However, when these restrictions are on an industry-by-industry basis, there are several possible reasons for their existence:

1. national security;
2. exploitation of the terms of trade; and
3. discouragement of investment in the sector.

National security arguments come predominantly from the viewpoint that a country's first responsibility is the security of its borders. While we would not disagree with this, it is an often-overused point. Indeed, when the industry is not genuinely necessary for securing the borders of the country, the result can be a decrease in national security through the destruction of a country's economic base: 'Development of industries without regard to market considerations or comparative advantage can weaken a society economically' (Gilpin, 1987, p. 47).

Exploitation of the terms of trade is based on the conception of goods as 'strategic' in that demand for them is not price-sensitive and there exists no easily available substitute in the targeted country. This is not the same thing as military goods because consumer goods might very well fit this definition while military goods might not. Indeed, buttons, toys,combs, breakfast food, tractors, wheat or clothing might be strategic goods while military goods are not 'obviously, self-evidently or necessarily more strategic . . . than so-called civilian items' (Baldwin, 1985, p. 216). When a country has market power in a strategic good, it can extract a 'rent' similar to that charged by a monopoly or, if the country is a monophony with respect to a good which is not price-sensitive with respect to supply, the country can exploit this with import protection.

Discouragement of foreign investment in a sector may be designed to destroy comparative advantage in an industry in which the state no longer deems necessary. Mason (1978a, p. 129), on the other hand, argues that this is done because it is felt that 'needed technologies can be acquired on competitive terms and that local firms can meet national needs equally as well as foreign firms could in these industries. One might call this selective nationalism'. We argue that this may not be the case: by making a sector wholly unattractive to investment, the country serves to 'freeze' it in regard to its existing base of technology. In so doing, the relative prices in that industry *vis-à-vis* the rest of the industries in the country rise, ensuring the destruction of comparative advantage. In general, countries do not admit to this type of activity for political reasons, although it could be argued that the promotion of certain investment areas (such as is done in Singapore) amounts to the discouragement of other areas.

Absolute restrictions on capital flows exiting the country are designed to stem capital flight (Williamson and Lessard, 1987). However, when citizens are forced to save a portion of their funds (and thus are unable to use a portion of their funds for their own use, such as is the case with Singapore's Central Provident Fund), it serves also to dampen economic fluctuations, and aid in industrial policy by allowing the government to make selective investments and engage in 'state capitalism'. Another form of selective restriction is the discouragement of repatriation of profits, which ensures that the gains from investments are realised in the country.

The dampening of economic fluctuation occurs because forced savings represents a drain on the fiscal resources available for consumption. A 20 per cent drop in consumption patterns in the face of a 50 per cent required savings allocation will result in only a 10 per cent drop in effect on the entire economy. Additionally, the government can alter the required savings rate as a counter-cyclical device to encourage or retard spending growth.

Selective investments by the government sector can be used to establish 'backward linkages' with the rest of the economy. By investing in multinational firms, the government can encourage them to invest in the country and to cooperate with other local firms. When the financial sector of an economy is underdeveloped, this mechanism can often prove superior to the capital market. Banks may be incapable of making proper decisions in the early states of development because they are equally starved for capital and often emphasise cash flow over prudent long-term investment. Even when the sector is developed, the guarantee of deposit insurance (which acts as an incentive for individuals to place their money in banks without regard to the underlying financial fundamentals of the bank) can cause financial disaster if there is inadequate government oversight to prevent banks from taking egregious risks with their depositors' money (witness the collapse of the many savings and loans schemes in the United States).

Selective investments might also take the form of short-term bond stakes designed to generate quick profits and hedge against risk. It is crucial that the government act in a responsible and safe manner with the forced savings lest it be subjected to widespread criticism for mismanagement of funds. Building a competent and incorruptible civil service, by promoting and hiring based on merit, is therefore a major need in development (World Bank, 1993, pp. 174-80).

Absolute incentives for foreign investment are designed to attract multinational corporations to come to the host country (Glade, 1987). However, selective incentives towards specified sectors of the local economy are also designed to increase the country's comparative advantage in the designated areas.

Absolute incentives for foreign investment attract multinationals to a country by either bribing them through tax abatements or by punishing them with high tariffs if they refuse to produce in the country. Through export credits and other tools, foreign investors are given incentives to behave in the manner that the government desires. However, when these investment incentives are absolute, they serve to generate enormous costs to the government with little reward in return. The firms that migrate tend to be those that can exploit the current comparative advantages, not the ones the country is trying to foster.

Selective incentives towards specific industrial sectors serve to shift the comparative advantages of countries to the next product cycle by changing the balance of the relative prices in a country towards that of the favoured industry. By enticing foreign investment, countries are able to 'capture' capital from foreign governments and transfer it to themselves. After the initial investment, these ventures begin to finance expansion with retained earnings. Thus, for the developing country, the multinational corporation is a source of both foreign investment and domestic investment. One possible exception to this would be if the accumulation of capital from the multinational firm displaced local capital formation in the aggregate; however, this does not seem to be the case for Singapore.

Incentives for capital to exit a country in the form of aid credits are designed to improve the economy of the receiving country so that it can purchase additional exports from the host country. Selective incentives (such as providing aid to a particular industry or to a particular country) allow a country to manipulate the comparative advantage of other nations to their own advantage.

The case for foreign aid is supported by the aftermath of the Marshall Plan. By improving the economic status of another country, it is possible to improve its position so both countries can enjoy the benefits of multilateral free trade. It was the money left behind by Great Britain after independence, as opposed to direct foreign investment, which was the key 'jump-starter' for Singapore (although direct foreign investment would later play the central role in 'manufacturing the Singaporean miracle') as it was for many other East Asian countries which benefited from foreign aid in the wake of the Japanese defeat in World War II. The receiving country distributes the funds given to it unless it has an industrial policy, in which case aid gets diffused across several industries and comparative advantage likely stays static.

Selective incentives take this process one step further. Instead of merely allowing the receiving country to act in the way it desires, a selective incentive helps to ensure the aid is channelled into a particular industry or region. In so doing, the sending country is able to manipulate the relative comparative advantages it enjoys *vis-à-vis* the receiving country, and allows the sending country to ensure a market for its products which it might not otherwise have had.

However, in order for the country which is sending these industries elsewhere to continue to develop, it must only engage in this activity after it has successfully added to its technological base and developed its human and social capital to take advantage of the next stage of product-cycle industrialisation. It also must ensure that its citizens receive the benefits from this industrialisation in an equitable manner so that the society does not become internally fragmented. Growth without equity inevitably leads to revolution, an ungovernable social welfare system or a polarisation of society, which is demoralising to the populace and is inimical to future growth.

In order to develop a technological base and ensure wage equity over a reasonable range, an economically proactive government must phase out some of its low-wage, low-technology industries in favour of high-wage, high-technology industries, which would benefit its citizenry. This is especially important to Singapore because of the rapid rate of development that it is attempting to maintain. The large scale presence of low-wage, low-technology industries serves to discourage the pursuit of education and eventually causes an increase in unemployment and crime when the industry reaches its limits.

Another problem is that these industries tend to congregate in specific areas. One policy is thus to diffuse these industries throughout the country in order to achieve political stability. As communism and communalism have their roots in the disparity of wages from one region to another, if low-wage industries are concentrated in one area, it is more likely that these movements will take form.

Carrying this argument further, a newly industrialising country should try to phase out its own low-wage, low-skill industries by 'exporting' them to its developing neighbours, thereby securing interregional political stability by creating linkages between them. This, in turn, sets in motion growth in those countries receiving these industries that will advance them to the next stage of development.

This is also beneficial to the receiving country. By ensuring that the aid is concentrated in one industry, the sending country might speed up the development of comparative advantage in the receiving country even if the receiving country does not have an industrial policy of its own.

Coupled with the desire to concentrate aid in some selected industries is the desire to disperse aid to as many geographical regions as possible. However, as shown by Myrdal (1957), the natural tendency of the market is to send capital into a concentrated area. This tends to create inflationary pressures (coupled with growth) in the favoured region while creating deflation (coupled with stagnation) in the unfavoured ones. In the process, the unfavoured areas are deserted while individuals flock to the favoured ones. Such a situation can cause economic refugees to flood into an already overcrowded area, causing crime and increasing pollution. By engaging in counter-cyclical policy, it is possible to negate, or at least partially offset, these pressures.

SINGAPORE

In many ways, Singapore is a free port with few restrictions on foreign capital involvement; but it is considerably restrictive when it comes to its own citizens. For example, Singapore has the world's highest savings rate not because of free market incentives or a natural disposition of its people to save; instead, its Central Provident Fund (CPF) is a 'forced savings' plan that ensures savings rates closely parallel government dictate.

CPF was founded in 1958 during Singapore's period of home rule. It was designed to create a domestic investment pool to allow Singapore to transform itself from colony to independent entity. Under British rule, there were four basic sectors in the Singaporean economy: plantations (occupying 38 per cent of the economy), the British military base at Sembawang (occupying a similar percentage of the economy), industry (occupying 15 per cent of the economy) and commerce. Home rule would lead to a decline in the military presence, and industrialisation required a movement from an agricultural base to an industrial one.

The people of Singapore were typically very poor (with 70 per cent of the population earning less than $100 per year, and per capita income hovering around $200 per person). In order to get them to transfer from an agricultural base to an industrial one, infrastructure projects would have to be undertaken and public housing would have to be built to replace the shantytowns. But from where was the money going to come? The answer was a government-run investment scheme. Therefore, the CPF was devised to allow Singaporeans to save. Each Singaporean contributed 15 per cent of his salary to the scheme. A promise of a 7 per cent return on investment was given for every dollar contributed and the proceeds from the fund could be borrowed for purchasing housing, medical treatment and furthering education (drawing down the fund only occurred at retirement). When individuals used CPF funds to buy housing they received a preferential rate for the purchase. Soon everyone was contributing to the plan. This created a pool of revenue which then was used to pay contractors to build housing. The contractors would hire local workers to build the housing, increasing aggregate demand and stimulating additional contributions to CPF. When the houses were completed, individuals could borrow from the fund and occupy the houses. Additional funds were given for infrastructure or were invested to generate the promised 7 per cent return on investment. Looking at this from the standpoint of theory, the CPF performs four functions that impact the distribution of capital in the country.

First, it serves to increase the government's control of capital. As funds go to the central government, it provides a convenient 'tax' that is not reported and, by expanding the asset base, it allows the government a greater degree of borrowing power. This borrowing comes at a heavy price: with the promise of payouts far in excess of contributions and the tax exempt nature of the system, deposits into the CPF are taken at a higher cost than direct borrowing. Some authors, like Deutsch and Zowell (1988), suggest the taxation of the CPF as a remedy to ensure that each individual's contribution reflects after-tax income. Nevertheless, this may be a solution to a non-problem. Through heavy promotion, the government promises the citizens of Singapore a share of the national 'pie'. This has resulted in a greater percentage of citizens owning stock in Singapore than any other nation, a quasi-Communist accomplishment for a capitalist country in that each receives a share of the profits generated from CPF investments.

Another aspect of the CPF is that the payments into it are mandatory. As this is not a market instrument, it is unclear whether the government could raise these funds from the populace at the promised interest rates without requiring the contributions. The funds from the CPF have been given to five investment corporations: the Jurong Town Corporation, the Singaporean Government Investment Corporation (SGIC), the Port Authority, Temasek Holdings and Sembawang Corporation. The Jurong Town Corporation used funds for the building of housing and the development of infrastructure. The Port Authority upgraded Singapore's military ports for commercial purposes (the subway and airport were funded through bond measures, not CPF). Sembawang Corporation used the funds to convert the military base to industrial use. Temasek Holdings is the leading venture capital firm in the City-State and has at least some holdings in virtually all publicly traded companies. The Port Authority and Sembawang were later privatised and Temasek bought many of the shares. SGIC directs Singapore's considerable overseas investments.

As shown by Harry Johnson (1965b), these nationalist overtures can actually increase the productivity of the populace by solving the principal-agent problem. Workers begin feeling that they are part owners of the companies for which they work and so are more likely to act in a socially desirable fashion. Further, tax exemption is a noticeable feature of many government bond programmes. Those with high wages receive higher after-tax rates of return as these funds are not taxed. However, these individuals are also the ones who are most likely to be able to fund these programmes due to their wealth. Because of a declining marginal utility for savings, paying higher returns to those who contribute more may be a good idea.

The most important feature of such a programme is its mandatory nature that ensures that the supply of capital is constant over a long period of time and reshapes the distribution of income. The more the government takes at the source the less the disparity in income after taxes. But this has helped Singapore avoid the terrible income inequalities that have plagued much of the developing world.

Second, with the increased financial support, the government is able to pool the resources of its people to gain international leverage. It is able to borrow an increased amount from the IMF and gains a favourable bargaining position in terms of key inputs such as oil and heavy capital equipment as well as in terms of intergovernmental lobbying for MFN status.

Third, it allows the government to engage in profitable ventures. In the case of Singapore, the government builds housing and then sells it to the population for a marginal profit. As 87 per cent of all Singaporeans live in these government-built projects, the government exerts a great deal of control over the housing market (*Government of Singapore*, 1993, p. 210). The population is enticed to buy from the government because it allows them to purchase housing at a discount if, and only if, they use their forced savings account. This simply transfers the wealth from one government account to another, reducing an individual's claim on future benefits in realisation of the current housing benefit. After purchasing the property, the individual is forced to pay property tax, which increases the share of government wealth once again and thereby contributes to another profitable cycle. The plan has created a nation of homeowners (more than 80 per cent own their units), which, in turn, has led to a population that takes pride in these homes and creates support for the government.

This has created an unevenly distributed housing price system which has driven up the cost of non-government offered housing to astronomical levels. This has, in turn, led to a steady increase in the price of housing offered by the government in an effort to eliminate this differential. After five years, individuals are allowed to sell their homes, which allow them to realise a healthy profit. With the availability of new housing (since 1989 there has been a booking system which effectively ensures that allocation is based on a lottery that promotes the requests of married couples over single individuals), there should be a thriving rental market. But by offering rentals at a price below the market-equilibrating rate (in order to ensure that no one is homeless), the government discourages the ownership of rental properties, enabling its monopoly on the building trade to continue.

Finally, forced savings serve as both a financial weapon and a social tool. As a financial weapon it allows the government to manipulate the land and asset markets. The forced savings generate interest returns that become the benchmark for competition in regular financial markets. Since interest rate policy can control inflation, the government can indirectly regulate the banking sector and force high rates or low rates.

As a social tool, it makes the people subservient to the government since they fear that their savings might be misused, or worse, simply confiscated; consequently, they become captive audiences for government policies. This tends to reduce personal protest in anticipation of a government payoff in return for silence and has had the effect of reducing senseless litigation such as that found in the United States; but it may also serve to make it harder for challenges to the existing regime to be heard.

Forced savings is the creation of a pseudo-financial market that has given Singapore the highest savings rate in the world. The CPF has allowed people to borrow against their savings, but also requires them to pay back these loans with interest. Money borrowed, therefore, becomes money made by the CPF. The citizen is, knowingly or unknowingly, borrowing from his future. This has the effect of acting as an incentive to boost productivity.

The purchase of housing, however, only applies to the physical structure and not to the land on which it sits. In Singapore, all land belongs to the government. Foreign investors must lease space from the government. This creates the opportunity for the government to give incentives to desired industries.

The government can also try to influence capital movement through its control of organised labour. The government-controlled National Trade Union Congress (NTUC) organises a quarter of the nation's labour force. A government minister is appointed to oversee the labour unions and state bureaucrats run it (Lim, 1983, p. 757). Initially, Singapore emphasised low-wage low-skill jobs (e.g., in the textile industry) as the government gambled on the existing supply of cheap labour and tax incentives, and contributed to this by suppressing wage increases to rates below domestic inflation. This caused chronic and persistent labour shortages. In 1979, using the National Wages Council's power to regulate wages, it attempted to increase the wage level in the country to drive out these low-wage industries and replace them with high-wage industries. Over the next two years, massive restructuring of the economy occurred and, as a result, Singapore entered a brief recession. Emerging in 1981 after scrapping the 'high-wage' policy, Singapore finally achieved rapid increases in the standard of living of its citizens, which match the country's spectacular rise in production.

The goal of Singapore's chief planner, Dr Goh Keng Swee, was to get foreign investors to bring technology to an industry that the government would then subsidise and train its own people in. The people were, in turn, forced to save and were not allowed to consume what they had produced. The plan called for increased technology, increased domestic production, and increased productivity but not increased consumption. The savings were used to invest in quasi-governmental industries run by foreign-trained civilians. These managers were paid based not on traditional wage schemes but on a bonus system which gave them incentives to compete, innovate and increase production.

Furthermore, Singapore has a policy of managing its exchange rate. The regulatory board, the Monetary Authority of Singapore (MAS), has a strategy to stabilise the local currency market by limiting the local money supply and through laws pertaining to investment financing. By limiting monetary demand for the local currency, the MAS can hold a monopoly on it. Therefore, it can ensure the market does not proceed on a speculative rise or fall that is not based on underlying fundamentals. As the only major influencing agent in the market, it can, to a large extent, sway the market in the direction it wishes. By raising investment in foreign currency, the MAS plays the 'dirty float' and influences investment flows.

If the MAS wishes to hold fewer Japanese yen and more US dollars it can encourage Japanese bidders, thus causing an appreciation of the local dollar versus the Japanese yen. The MAS then takes the Japanese yen, which it has just received, and exchanges them for US dollars. In such a way, the financial instrument can be used to manipulate the exchange rate. It can also be used as a weapon to influence the currencies of fragile economies, like the Philippine peso and the Malaysian ringgit or the Indonesian rupiah. For example, in 1993, capital began to move from Singapore to Malaysia based on a strengthening ringgit and a high interest rate differential. The MAS took action to bring the exchange rates back to a 'reasonable' trading zone (from the point of view of Singapore).

Control can also be by the creation of an incentive mechanism. For example, the government might take the lead in investing in a 'flagship' project. If this venture proves 'profitable' (which it always does due to the ability to internally manipulate bookkeeping as well as the premium which the Singapore government places on competence of its managerial elite), the government subsidiary will go public to raise more funds.

Moreover, this can encourage entrepreneurs to enter the field in hopes of benefiting from economies of scope. This strategy can create its own demand through a process of 'cumulative causation'. This process creates a 'bubble economy' that occurs when demand is driven to the point that speculators vastly outnumber investors in a market, such as that which happened in the late 1980s and early 1990s in the Japanese housing market. If this happens, the government can enact new regulations on growth or lower dividends, causing a 'soft landing' (so that the price level does not decline rapidly, causing a depression in the property market) because of the heavy government involvement in the economy. All of this is done with the people's money, but there are no complaints because the ordering of the market through forced savings brings wealth, jobs and infrastructure.

Government invests in corporations through bonds as well as direct investments. More than 50 per cent of all secured construction projects have some government support, mostly through the securities short-term bond market. The government must approve all construction within the Central Business District (CBD) through the Urban Renewal Agency (URA), and lending is only forthcoming if there has been a process of active bidding in the design and production phases so that costs can be kept under control. In exchange for approval, it often demands the ability to invest in the projects as the government is the only 'guaranteed' source of credit. This investment has been used as a counter-cyclical measure when other industries are depressed.

In the area of foreign aid, the emphasis is, once again, on selective incentives. Using a 'joint venture' approach, the government purchases part of a foreign corporation, and then endows it with the technology and expertise to make it successful. An example of this approach is the Chinese Investment Project in which the government leased an up to 400 sq. km area within and around the town of Suzhou, 100 miles north of Shanghai.

Other example is the purchase in the mid-1990s of 40 per cent of Royal Cambodian Airlines by the 70 per cent government-owned and operated Singapore Airlines. However, not all ventures emanate solely from the government. Singapore supports private enterprise activities too. Although Singapore's government-owned Asia-Pacific Brewery received some government funding for its recent joint venture, Vietnam Brewery Limited undertaken with the Vietnamese brewery and the Ho Chi Minh City People's Committee Second Foodstuffs Company are projects that were undertaken without government interference or initiative. Government involvement is limited to the stake that has been put in, so that Singapore is acting as an ordinary shareholder showing confidence in the decisions that the free enterprise has already made. Such ventures have become so successful that Singapore is now the seventh largest investor in Vietnam and the largest among the Association of South-East Asian Nations (ASEAN).

In so doing, the government achieves two goals at once: expansion of the development of surrounding countries while controlling the changes of comparative advantage in those countries. Recent government activities, such as the Johar 'growth triangle' continue this trend. By increasing trade dependency with Singapore (and by implication, reducing trade dependency between the developing country and the advanced industrial countries), the developing country is able to link itself to Singapore's success and ensure political stability: if these countries are doing well, they are not as likely to look with envy towards Singapore. Vietnam, for example, is now asking to be allowed to pool its resources with ASEAN in the areas of defence and security, in an effort to pave the road to future membership in the association. Such activities for an island nation that spends a considerable portion of its government budget on national defence is obviously seen in a positive light because it reduces the possibility of armed conflict.

The discouragement of investment in areas that are non-desirous is found in the actions Singapore has taken in the textile and clothing sectors. As noted by Pangestu and Hasni (1991, p. 191), Singapore has experienced a 'substantial decline in textile production due to its declining comparative advantage in such production and a shift in its industrialisation policy'. What is unspoken is that Singapore has deliberately engaged in a policy of streamlining the industry to enable it to become the fashion hub of the region, instead of a labour hub. It has attempted to destroy its low wage base by raising wages, and has discouraged investment in the industry except in those sectors that cater to the high end of the market (and thus afford a high wage to the workers) (Pereira, 1993, p. 209). The result is that, as journalist Philippe Regnier (1987, p. 90) puts it, 'textile mills, owned by seventy two companies, are due to disappear progressively as part of the process of delocalisation into Malaysia and Thailand'.

More than 80 per cent of all investment in Singapore comes from abroad and more than 3 000 companies are investors in the country (Sesser, 1993, p. 26). To ensure that the funds continue to roll in, the government acts to control dissidents who might desire to nationalise a company's hard-won gains. It is for this basic reason that the Communist party is outlawed in Singapore. Pragmatic approaches to economic management, coupled with the high competence and incorruptibility noted earlier, ensure that the leadership does not act in a rapacious fashion. This has led to a high degree of support for the government: it may act in a paternalistic fashion but the people have accepted this because they see the process as fair.

However, the need for competent and incorruptible civil servants in the management of these funds cannot be overstated. One of the reasons why this capital manipulation has worked in Singapore and has failed in the Philippines (which restricted profit outflows in the 1970s and 1980s) was because of the honesty of the civil service: just as in Hong Kong with its Independent Commission Against Corruption (ICAC), the Singaporean Government with its Corrupt Practice Investigation Bureau (CPIB) goes to great lengths to ensure the integrity of its officials by checking assets against income and disciplines those who accepts the smallest of bribes.

It is also clear that these attitudes can only be engendered through reward as well as punishment. Singapore has the highest paid civil service in the area, offering its government employees compensation directly in line with (and often exceeding) the private sector. This is in sharp contrast to China, which, in the province of Anhui in 1994, caught more than 300 000 provincial government officials (or 20 per cent of all public servants!) in the embezzlement of nearly one billion Chinese Yuan. The temptation to do wrong is greatly increased when the opportunities for profit are numerous and the discrepancy between private and public compensation is large.

Singapore's zeal for fairness is best exemplified by the trial of five individuals associated with announcing the official economic growth flash estimates for the entire economy and the sectoral breakdowns for the second quarter of 1993, a few days prior to their official release. The publication of these estimates constituted a violation of the Official Secrets Act on the grounds that this gave unfair advantage to the readers of the *Business Times* over other members of the community. The defendants were later found guilty and were fined thousands of dollars for their actions (with one of them receiving a suspended jail sentence).

The government has moved quickly to develop the infrastructure and educational resources of an advanced society and has 'built shells of factories on speculation, so that arriving companies wouldn't have to spend time planning a new building from the ground up'. It creates science parks to encourage high-tech ventures and helps fund innovative programmes. When companies leave, Singapore does not simply abandon the workers or buildings. For example, Sembawang's conversion in 1979 to a commercial shipyard from a British military base was completed without any layoffs or interruption of work (Sesser, 1993, p. 27).

Singapore has also tried to pave the way for regional integration. Along with Malaysia, Indonesia and Thailand, Singapore formed a growth triangle as a subgroup of ASEAN. This triangle started in 1991, after the economies of the above countries agreed that there should be a unified economy to battle the outflow of investment spending by the western powers. Outflows are defined as the taking out of previous investment or the cancellation or reduction of promised investment. Singapore always seeks a mixture of investment from different countries, and worries about becoming too dependent on any one country either for investment or trading purposes.

This is a vision of a new society. With income inequality continuing to increase in the world and with the call for more, not less, restrictions on the mobility of labour, it is increasingly becoming clear that the economic mission of government is one of how to get capital (and therefore jobs) to move to where the people are. Governments cannot issue decrees and believe in an inward-looking Marxian approach if they hope to succeed. Singapore does not, however, wish to allow the corporate entities to change the structure and composition of their societies as these organisations search the globe for new profit opportunities. As such, Singapore is encouraging regional dialogue. To do otherwise would reduce labour power to the lowest common denominator in the world. As Benjamin Disraeli once said, 'Individuals may form communities but it is institutions alone that can create a nation' (quoted by Lorenzo Berardinetti in *Hansard*, Legislative Assembly of Ontario, 3 June 2004). If countries allow corporations to dictate the activities which their citizens will undertake, they will have ceded control over their territory and have ceased to be sovereign. Instead, they must unite through regional and, ultimately, global organisations to ensure a social contract exist between labour and capital. Corporations, with plants and stockholders in every corner of the globe, are increasingly tied to no one nation. Singapore's success is in recognising this change: government power is not diminished by the increase in the power of the multinational but it is refocused. Singapore and other countries could help create an alternative vision to a north-dominated 'New World Order' if, and only if, they are willing to think beyond their own borders and establish connections with their neighbours. Only with such assurances could 'economic miracles' be translated into high standards of living for the populace at large.

This is not to say that there are no problems and dissent in Singapore as the government has been slow to act on calls for democratic reform. Human rights, as defined in American terms, are not a major priority. But even so, Singapore defies the assessment that political and economic freedom is necessarily supportive of one another. Indeed, Singapore has come a long way in the last 40 years. The country has achieved spectacular success in the war against poverty (partly from outlawing destitution but mostly from well-planned industrial policy). It has an excellent infrastructure, a clean environment and is relatively free of the crime that plagues most urban centres. This City-State has achieved all of these without the benefit of large natural endowments and despite a large military budget. Eastern Europe and the Soviet Union could learn much from this quasi-Communist country: by mixing public leadership with private initiative, Singapore is on its way to creating a 'classless' high-income society.

HONG KONG

Hong Kong is often portrayed as the mirror opposite of Singapore in the literature. According to Milton Friedman, Hong Kong is successful because of its embracement of free market policies. Paul Krugman views Hong Kong's success as an example to Singapore that private enterprise, properly liberated from state directive, can achieve equal, if not greater success than government-run initiatives. Even a prominent economist at the Chinese University of Hong Kong, Sung Yun-Wing (1989, p. 155), has stated, 'the Hong Kong government has largely confined itself to limited functions' in sharp contrast, he claims, to the interventionist activities of South Korea, Taiwan and Singapore. On the other side of the debate, Robert Wade (1990, p. 299) notes that if Hong Kong is not an example of free market superiority, the East Asian miracle would have to be seen in an entirely different light. He goes on to argue that the conception 'that Hong Kong is close to a free market economy is misleading' (Wade, 1990, p. 332). Reconciling these seemingly irreconcilable positions is the purpose of this section.

Hong Kong is not exclusively a free market success story. While it is true that the former crown colony and current Special Administrative Region is a free port with low taxes and seeming non-intervention (or, in the words of former financial secretary Philip Haddon-Cave, 'positive non-interventionism'), it is equally true that there are several other factors contributing to Hong Kong's success story.

First are the obvious, and not so obvious, unique characteristics, which serve to boost Hong Kong's productive growth. There is the stream of labour and capital from Guangdong province in China, which has continued unabated for most of this period. This importation of population and capital (especially capital from Shanghai, which had been the commercial centre of China for nearly two centuries) contributes greatly to the early growth of the crown colony because of two important reasons: first, increases in the physical numbers of individuals naturally raise growth rates by stimulating aggregate demand; and second, the age structure of immigrants leads to an influx into the labour market, boosting aggregate supply to a larger extent than domestic increases in population and keeping the lid on wages that would threaten to derail the experiment of exportation on a labour-intensive basis based on the exploitation of low-wage labour. Indeed, Hong Kong's reluctance to introduce statutory minimum wages as late as the 1980s was coupled with a minimally effective unionised sector, which meant that, in the absence of such countervailing union power, 'positive non-interventionism' meant positive support for industry over labour, given the inability of the market to design effective employment standards (Hong, 1982). Indeed, it is a testament to the importance of this labour supply that Hong Kong's growth only began in earnest after the conclusion of the Chinese Civil War, even though all of the factors deemed responsible for the success of Hong Kong from a free market perspective were already in place well before that time.

A second factor is Hong Kong's role as the conduit for the illegal trade between Taiwan and China. As long as Taiwan's Government prohibited direct trade, Hong Kong was seen as a convenient indirect method of trading with the motherland for many expatriate Chinese.

Another aspect is the cheap importation of food, and the provision of energy and power from China. This allowed Hong Kong to move quickly from an agricultural base to an industrial one. Food in East Asia is often purchased live, which limits the transportation of these goods. Without cheap imports, Hong Kong would have to devote a higher percentage of its workforce and land to agriculture, which typically offers lower returns to labour.

A fourth key consideration is Hong Kong's location, which lies at the juncture between several trading nations. This, coupled with Hong Kong's efficient port system and well-developed financial institutions (inherited from the major trading companies known as the Hongs), led to the colony's rapid development as an 'entrepôt' and financial centre for Southeast Asia. As Asia developed, these services became relatively more important, so the initial endowment in these areas contributed dramatically to the growth rate (in fact, Singapore enjoys no such advantages and has drawn much hostility from its neighbours, especially the Malaysians, who kicked them out of the Malay Federation in 1963).

Another problem for the neoclassical free market vision of Hong Kong is that the pro-market basis of the economy was well set prior to the Second World War. It was only after the Chinese Civil War, however, that Hong Kong's economic growth took off. In the aftermath of World War II, Hong Kong, as part of the British Empire, was committed to the Sterling Area. The conclusion of World War II, however, created a serious balance of payments problem for Great Britain. Much of Great Britain's industrial base had been destroyed, and the need to rebuild led to large-scale importation of materials from the United States. This set off a balance of payments crisis in 1947.

Britain used its colonial base to generate needed exports to the United States to provide dollars for the purchase of American commodities for the homeland. Hong Kong, lacking any natural resources, turned to its labour force that was swelling with refugees from the Chinese Civil War. In fact, cheap labour provided a potential industrial base and the immediate need to export led to an export-oriented industrialisation, not an import-substitution industrialisation (ISI) strategy (except as noted below). The closing of China to the West also promoted this process because many entrepreneurs moved from there and reestablished themselves in Hong Kong, bringing their skills to the forefront and enabling Hong Kong to develop as an alternative source for Chinese manufactures.

The government aided this process through a system of rationing, which allocated raw materials to those industries most capable of exporting goods (Birch, 1974), has been active in trade promotion activities, and also seeks to create public-private partnerships for improving technology (Fong, 1988, p. 226 and p. 231). Land usage, always controlled by the crown through its lease system, was juggled so that the most favourable leases would go to the industrial areas. This was extended after the 1954 floods to the housing market, so that inexpensive government housing could be constructed and the population could be granted a place to live. By 1972, Governor General MacLehose extended planned intervention in the housing sector to ensure adequate supplies of accommodation and reduce the political tension that bubbled over in the riots of 1967. Indeed by 1968, there were over 400 000 squatters and 'over 3 million people living in less than thirteen square miles of built-up land' (MacPherson and Chan, 1997, p. 4).

A government committed to social order cannot safely ignore such large numbers. Similarly, the government has made large-scale investments in public hospitals and education, including up to the tertiary level. Also, the government began its push for mass transit beginning with buses and later culminating in the Kowloon-Canton Railway and the Municipal Transit Railway whereby all transit led to the central business district. The Imperial Preference System allowed Hong Kong to develop further its industry by granting it preferential status for its exports to Britain (thus, at least within the British Empire, some import substitution occurred, allowing Britain to conserve precious dollar reserves). Indeed, Choi (1994) argues that this was critical to the success of the Hong Kong textile industry.

Besides, Great Britain left a competent and insulated (from the domestic population) civil service. The rule of law led to an enforcement mechanism for contracts, and Great Britain's obsession with security issues led to the establishment of the Independent Commission Against Corruption (ICAC) during the 1970s when Triad involvement and bribery threatened to infiltrate the civil service. Shortly thereafter, the Organised Crime and Triad Bureau was established to reduce the criminal element and drive it offshore. But although triads still exist in Hong Kong, there was a diminishment in their activities because these elements were forced back onto the mainland and to neighbouring Macao, a Portuguese protectorate.

At the same time, Hong Kong could provide serious questions for the developmental state. Its policy of 'positive non-interventionism' clearly places it well below the interventionism practiced in the other Asian tigers and in Japan. It emphasises not sector-specific but broad-based development policy. But this general development policy still had sector-specific effects. Furthermore, its proximity to China and exclusive access to that market for so long enabled it to apparently pursue a policy of *laissez-faire*. However, Hong Kong really pursued a policy of accommodation for the burgeoning entrepreneurial sector by retarding the freedom of labour to organise; provided important transportation, education, medical and housing services; and regulated the flow of the labour market through various policies related to refugees from China.

PART III

Modern Policy

10. The Developmental State View

It is now time to move beyond East Asia and discuss what has come to be known as the Developmental State in a broader context. Is it, as Wierda (1999) has argued, something that emanated solely out of the local context and that is incapable of transplantation to other venues? Of course, a similar charge has been levelled against Western neoclassical economics (Blaut, 1993), and we have explained that the indigenous elements of East Asian economic theory allowed for the development of a parallel but divergent capitalism that was better able to survive in the East Asian institutional matrix.

However, the problem is whether the fact that the Developmental State came into being owing to an established economic tradition that differed in critical ways from the Western model requires that historical specificity and institutional matrix to survive at all. We are not arguing for general theory, knowing very well that one of the essential problems in all of social science and economics in particular is, in fact, historical specificity (Hodgson, 2001). Similarly, culture and institutions must play a role in whatever system of governance and economics that is devised. Still, there may be 'essential elements' that can be transplanted elsewhere once the relevant institutional matrix in other lands is considered. Of course, it would require adaptation in the new surroundings rather than mere displacement of existing methods without proper regard for existing traditions and cultures. After all, the Veblenian dichotomy should be noted, because the nature of institutions to honour tradition can be stagnating, and the trick is to find the proper combination of techniques so that technological advancement can be achieved despite the needs to adhere to tradition.

In this chapter, we seek to elaborate on the theoretical framework of the Developmental State and examine the concept, while remaining mindful that the *nature* of the Developmental State can only be examined using the relevant theoretical framework. In addition, we will examine the role of the Developmental State and its changing condition that arises from present economic and social problems.

In recent years, economists have sought to minimise the role of the state in the contemporary Japanese economy (e.g., Reading, 1993) so as to support the neoliberal *laissez-faire* perspective. Although, '[t]he main thrust of the analysis which pictures Japan as the *epitome* of a liberal free market has come from the USA, this interpretation is also popular among Japanese commentators' (Eccleston, 1989, p. 89). Most of these attempts (such as, Reading, 1993) have narrowly focused on industrial policy in attempting to argue that the Japanese experience actually demonstrates that government intervention is unnecessary for rapid economic growth (and is, in fact, usually inimical to it). However, nurturing infant industries (or aborting those that are undesirable for one reason or another) and easing the suffering caused by industrial decline is only one aspect of economic policy-making and the entire array of government management activities also need to be considered.

In this vein, the Japanese state should be seen as both a planner and an investor. Japan has never experienced a *laissez-faire* stage of economic development and 'its recent history has been marked by more cooperative relations between the government and private business' (Eccleston, 1989, pp. 91-2). Clearly, even with less direct state expenditure, there is still a determination to promote a more orderly adjustment than the market would produce if left to itself and the Japanese state has been 'an *active* participant rather than a *passive* umpire' (Eccleston, 1989, p. 122). Of course, such interventionism is not a uniquely Japanese phenomenon. As shown in the earlier chapters, they figure prominently in the Chinese diaspora economies and South Korea as well. Indeed, from a Listian perspective, it might be considered that most of the countries that experienced a Rostowian 'take-off' had large-scale government intervention: Alexander Hamilton with the Manufacturers policy in the United States; Sir John A. MacDonald and the building of Canadian identity through industrialisation in Canada; and List's native Germany with its *Zollverein* that was used to consolidate and advance the German industry through a internal customs union but not unilateral free trade. Indeed, as we have noted in the previous chapter, even the City-State of Hong Kong was not entirely a free market-oriented success story.

Finally, we need to ask in what sense is the Japanese government *less* interventionist than other Western governments? Quantitative measures are ambiguous as Japanese public investment is the highest in the OECD; but Japan spends a much smaller percentage of GDP on public administration, defence, health care or housing than the average OECD country and it actually has a greater percentage of GDP produced by the private sector than most OECD countries. Therefore, any argument about interventionism must address Japan's high rates of saving and investment (per cent of GDP) while answering the obvious question of how these high levels have been maintained during the last four decades or so.

JAPAN AND NICS: A NEW EXPERIENCE

Japan and the NICs offer an alternative model for development. Although Japan, for example, was never a command economy, its industrial policy represents a government/private partnership characterised by bargaining and compromises (Nester, 1991, p. 29). This resulted in the identification of certain targeted export-oriented strategic industries that were nurtured through a *dynamic* mixture of cooperation and competition, even though declining industries were granted protection (Nester, 1990, pp. 167-70; 1991, p. 29). This dynamism produced thorough and efficient industrial policies and prosperity for various industrial sectors (Nester, 1991, p. 29).

The Japanese government spurred R&D and innovation in industries that were 'thought to be vital for the rapid growth of productivity and per capita incomes' (Singh, 1979, pp. 202-24). At the same time, 'as Japan's productive capacity expanded sharply, expenditures on the [total] output it generated necessarily increased; among the components of aggregate demand, investment and exports played key roles in the rapid expansion' (Ito, 1992, p. 50).

Maddison (1965) believes growth was 'the result of the success of the Japanese development polices rather than the cause of this success' and argues that these policies were effective for the following reasons:

1. government commitment to the promotion of industrialisation;
2. government efforts to transfer and develop a technology suitable to the Japanese conditions (the role of R&D, innovation and human resource development is very important); and
3. a high savings and investments ratio and a relatively high rate of growth.

The Japanese government and the private sector have been mutually intertwined for many years. Household savings, which has been roughly 75 per cent higher in Japan than in the West since the end of the Second World War, have been transferred into investments in both the public and private sectors through a series of initiatives directed by the state. The Japanese Post Office, which oversees roughly a quarter of all Japanese household savings and is scheduled to be privatised in October 2007, was, for many years, a principal source of funds for the Fiscal Investment and Loan Programme (FILP). FILP lent money at below-market interest rates to various public agencies, which then lent funds to private firms, ensuring a steady stream of low-cost capital to these entities. It was only due to fiscal reform by the Ministry of Finance in 2001 that this programme was fundamentally altered to allow Postal Savings and Public Pension funds to be directly invested in financial markets, with FILP instead raising its funds through the bond market (Japanese Ministry of Finance, 2001).

Although Japan's household savings have proven to be a robust source of capital for corporate Japan, since 1975 government bonds have also become a major mechanism to raise financial capital (Eccleston, 1989, p. 99; Ito, 1992, pp. 120-21). Japan's government has encouraged savings through the allowance of tax-free accounts and by regulation of these government bonds, which attract a negotiated yield (Ito, 1992, pp. 120-21). These policies have allowed for rapid and sustainable capital accumulation and, similar to the NICs, Japan has been able to sustain high investment rates for many years. Thus, the government policy to encourage savings (see Table 10.1) and discourage consumption, has meant that Japan's GDP has been represented by a greater proportion of investment spending than in the EC or the USA. Indeed, it is only in the past recessionary environment in Japan that the government has sought fit to attempt to reverse this course to spur consumption spending. However, habit and tradition, as well as fear caused by the loss of the traditional lifetime employment system employed by companies for the past two generations, have hampered efforts by the government to alter this behaviour.

Table 10.1 Average Gross Saving (% of GDP) in the EC, USA and Japan: 1960-90

Country	1960-67	1968-73	1974-79	1980-90
EC average	24.7	25.5	22.6	20.5
USA	19.9	19.6	19.8	16.3
Japan	33.6	38.5	32.8	32.1

Source: OECD, *Historical Statistics 1960-1990*, Paris, 1992b.

Cowling (1989) and other experts on the Japanese production system, argue that the Ministry of International Trade and Industry (MITI) helped to spur supply-side improvements in the economy. Hashimoto and Raisian (1985), and Mincer and Higuchi (1988) observed high levels of investments in human capital in the Japanese industry. The R&D agencies and public corporations of Japan's technology policy 'stress the priority of knowledge-intensive industries to Japan's industrial economy and future' (Best, 1990, p. 202). However, by the end of the twentieth century, MITI was no longer the powerhouse that it was once in Japan and its duties were incorporated into the newly created Ministry of Economy, Trade and Industry (METI).

Strategic competition by Japanese firms on the basis of price, quality, technology and innovation, has led them to play a leading role in the world economy. These organisations are continuously adapting to new challenges that are creating new productive services by teamwork and experience through an inter-firm relationship that can be both cooperative and market-oriented. No longer requiring the government to manage these relationships, Japanese firms have succeeded because the strategy – culture – productive organisation (through the elimination of wasteful practices and 'right-on-time automation') is a basic principle for them (Best, 1990, p. 138, p. 166).

Companies in South Korea, Taiwan, Hong Kong and Singapore have successfully imitated this success, and the NICs' governments (with the exception of Hong Kong) have achieved high growth rates through export-oriented industrialisation strategies by establishing government organs to direct outward-oriented economic development; by amassing capital for producer goods (such as iron or coal); and in fostering import-substitution industries. Besides, these governments have pursued macro-level policies designed to influence private decisions, economic sectors, whole industries, and individual enterprises within industries in ways that these governments deem desirable (comprehensive state intervention which has loomed large in the economic restructuring of recent years). Each of these NICs, similar to Japan, have had governments play a role not simply in financing research and development but in directing and coordinating the efforts of private industry in this matter. This is accomplished by financing high-risk R&D projects where there is a divergence between public and private costs and benefits as well as by assigning resources to certain firms in an effort to reduce internal competition and enhance international competitiveness. The exception of Hong Kong in all of this is worth noting. Hong Kong's success has been predominantly the result of being an entrepôt for China (which has embraced these policies as well) and due to its business-friendly political climate, which has emphasised universal subsidisation through infrastructure rather than a 'picking winners or losers' mechanism.

Moreover, in the case of South Korea, Kang (1989) argues that industrial development occurred for the following reasons:

1. export orientation: large expansion of exports;
2. government economic planning: overall planning of infrastructure development, social development, research, financial planning and external relations planning (thoroughness of planning);
3. technology acquisition from abroad (industrial know-how); and
4. the high-technology push into electronics (as well as construction, steel and automobiles).

Thus, the Korean State has acted as a planner with R&D supported by the government to facilitate the importation of foreign technology and allow for its adoption and adaptation into Korean manufacturing. Educational and training programmes have similarly developed the necessary human capital.

Greater coordination of investment between the government and private sectors in addition to reductions in internal competition have given greater incentives for worker training with Japan leading the way among OECD countries in this regard. Germany and France have, since the early 1980s, had similar pushes to increase worker aptitudes. This is in sharp contrast to the USA, where formal training is minimised (Lynch, 1991).

As we have seen, Japan and the Asian NICs have generated a blended capitalism, combining this with a state-industry relationship that emphasises their co-dependence and symbiotic relationship. This point is in contrast to certain notions that neoclassical economics has recommended for growth and development (i.e., trade liberalisation, private enterprise, and a restricted economic role for the state) (Singh, 1995, p. 9).

THE DEVELOPMENTAL STATE

The Developmental State literature (e.g., Dore, 1986; Amsden, 1989; Best, 1990; Wade, 1990; Papandreou, 1991; Cowling, 1990, 1992; Sawyer, 1990, 1992, 1994; Singh, 1993, 1994, 1995; Chang, 2002, 2003) argues for the widespread and intensive use of government policy (and, in particular, government industrial policy) to purposefully guide the market economy.

The successful developmental experience of Japan, South Korea and Taiwan provides a strong argument for adopting an industrial strategy of market guidance. Indeed, what distinguishes the NICs' industrial policies (or, better, strategies) from those of many other developed and developing countries is these states' ability to use both 'carrots' (for example, incentives and subsidies to private enterprises) and 'sticks' (various punishments) in a purposive attempt to influence firm behaviour (Singh, 1995, p. 10). These NICs have had 'greater autonomy' than in many other countries (Amsden, 1989; Wade, 1990; Fishlow, 1991) in developing national goals through a system of public-private cooperation in which the state develops these goals and then works with the private sector to carry these goals out.

This is quite different than the system in place in many other countries where the goals of the state are subordinated or even equated to those of private interests (e.g., the bureaucratic authoritarian regimes of countries in South America, India and Mexico). Much of this has occurred because of strong authoritarian pressures. Even in Japan, where there have been conflicts among various interest groups within its political system and more deeply rooted competitiveness among industries, 'extensive economic and political agreements have been as important to Japan's economic dynamism as competition' (Nester, 1991, p. 57). Indeed, until Japan entered the protracted economic crisis in the 1990s from which it is only now emerging, mainstream opposition parties often voted with the government and had a say in most policies. But the recent breakdown in political unity seems to have sparked at least part of the difficulties Japan currently faces in the economic realm.

Relative state autonomy from dominant classes and interest groups as well as a dominant state technocracy, which is well-educated, well-trained and efficient, are hallmarks of the NICs. Furthermore, it is the government's commitment to economic development and growth which is crucial to the success story of the Asian tigers. Thus, we might define the *nature* of the Developmental State by the following features:

1. a relatively strong state;
2. an effective and productive state;
3. a state which is not influenced by interest groups; and
4. a strategic state.

The Developmental State occupies the middle ground between strong states that utilise the military as the basis for their power and weak states that have been captured by the private sector and interest groups (Myrdal, 1968). Its relative position is a reflection of and/or depends on the relative strength of the existing political forces (i.e., social classes, interest groups, local governments, trade unions, etc.).

Three desirable notions and/or 'key elements' (discussed further below) are of great importance in analysing the concept of the Developmental State:

1. the role of the market and the state;
2. emphasis on government investments; and
3. strategic planning aspects.

Market – State and the Developmental State

Market and state have been seen as essentially in opposition in most Anglo-American economic analysis. However, the fundamental problem is that neoclassical analysis is left with theoretical inconsistencies: the development of free-market capitalism is seen as promoting perfect competition. Hence, according to this argument, there is no mechanism by which monopoly or oligopoly can arise out of perfect competition.

At the same time, the perfect competition concept is a fairy tale based on a theoretical flaw: firms may increase output indefinitely without affecting price due to a perfectly elastic demand curve, while monopolies, which face downward-sloping demand curves, will cause reductions in price even with minor changes in production. But the differing analysis of monopoly and perfect competition is even more egregious, because it involves assuming two logically incompatible things at once. Marshallian theory assumes that firms are 'atomistic' – which means that they don't consider what other firms might do in response to their own actions. This is described as having a 'conjectural variation' of zero in the language of neoclassical economics. As a result, if one firm changes its output, the other firms will not respond strategically to this change – in contrast to the Cournot-Nash game theory approach, where it is assumed that firms will respond strategically. Hence, if one firm increases its output by one unit, industry output will increase by one – there will not be offsetting changes by other firms in direct response.

This is all well and good, but it is incompatible with the argument that each firm faces a horizontal demand curve when at the same time the market demand curve slopes downwards. If the market demand curve slopes downward, then a one-unit increase in output causes a fall in price, no matter how small this might be. So, the demand curve for the individual firm has exactly the same slope. The only way around this is to assume that perfectly competitive firms are too small to perceive the change, while the monopoly is big enough to notice. This is often how the alleged anomaly is explained to students, but it is logically incoherent too. Aside from the twist that a small observer is not supposed to see a small change that a huge observer can perceive, it rests the outcome of perfect competition on the notion of bounded rationality. Indeed, perfect competition assumes limitless rationality. The irony then is that a theory that preaches rationality is, at its core, fundamentally irrational. Yet, neoclassical economics continues to be taught and practiced by Western policy-makers and the logical implications of this model are completely ignored (see Keen, 2002, 2007).

This framework limits policy discussion on matters like monopoly, oligopoly and restrictive practices, 'which are not generally fundamental to the pace of industrial development' (Sawyer, 1992b, pp. 54-6). Besides, this theory ignores important elements of the real world such as competition through new products, strategic planning and uncertainty.

Within the market failure view of Anglo-American industrial economics there is a sharp division between state and industry, and their roles are quite different (Sawyer, 1992b, p. 54). The role of government is seen to be one of control and regulation rather than of aiding industrial development and of creating new opportunities for private business, which would not otherwise exist (Sawyer, 1992b, pp. 56-7).

Moreover, the New Right schools (mainly, the Austrian and monetarist approaches) support the view that government action almost always limits the effectiveness of markets, while the market failure analysis suggests that governments should, and do, restrain and correct the operations of the market. In complete contrast, the Developmental State analysis suggests a developmental role for the government which involves the active promotion of industrial development, with the state setting the general developmental framework within which firms operate and seeking to aid firms to fulfil the developmental strategy (Sawyer, 1992a, p. 8).

However, Japan and the NICs have been the antithesis to *laissez-faire*. The state in these economies has played a vigorous role, guided the market towards planned structural changes, and followed a highly active industrial policy (Singh, 1995, p. 9). The Developmental State of these countries has been absolutely different from the state-'night watchman' (according to the Austrian approach) and the state-'Leviathan' (according to the monetarist view), and has had nothing to do with the interaction of politicians, voters and bureaucrats which, according to the Public Choice analysis, produces a bureaucratic state with significant weaknesses. These views (i.e., the New Right approaches) suggest cuts in public spending on infrastructure, R&D, education, training, innovation, etc. in the name of fiscal prudence and widening individual choices (which actually damage the long-term growth prospects of any economy) and consequently preclude any discussion about the range of government economic policies which may prove useful in the encouragement of industrial development.

Indeed, while orthodoxy argues that market and state are essentially in opposition to one another, the Developmental State perspective is one that stresses harmony and cooperation with the state adopting an entrepreneurial role and actively promoting industrial development, either in its promotion of private firms or in its own industrial operations, and creating opportunities that would not otherwise exist (Sawyer, 1992b, pp. 54-7).

In this manner, Japan supported and promoted high-technology sectors with high capital intensiveness in an effort to alter competitive advantage. Without such intervention, the electronics and car manufacturing industries, which form the basis of the Japanese economy today, would have been unsustainable, as the comparative costs of production would have precluded such investment. The short-term perspective of marginal analysis, which lacks a proper conception of time, would have concluded that the high cost side of these industries (expenditure on human resource development, R&D, technology, innovation, etc.) would have dominated any (potential) indirect and intangible benefits. This is especially true in an environment where uncertainty rules the unfettered marketplace; but it is decidedly false when the government reduces uncertainty by funding R&D, which is otherwise inhibited by a significant divergence between private and social returns and by long-term and uncertain pay-offs. Thus, while from a short-term static perspective, investment in such industries is not a 'rational' developmental policy, from a long-term perspective, one can see that these are precisely the industries in which Japan would be capable of competing strategically on new grounds (on the basis of rapid technological progress, fast labour productivity, product quality or innovation). Moreover, public spending (on the modern factors of industrial competency and competitiveness) financed projects whose development costs are very large or risky and the difference between private and social returns could lead firms to under-invest.

Therefore, the experience of Japan and NICs provides a strong argument against *laissez-faire* and in favour of government involvement for guiding the market. In the case of all these countries, the governments have played a positive enabling role in the economy and, indeed, there is

> a degree of complementarily between the market system and an active state. The complementarily arises from the government setting the [developmental and comprehensive] framework within which firms operate, and seeking to aid firms to fulfil the developmental strategy. The potential complementarily between them implies that the state adopts an entrepreneurial role and is thereby able to create opportunities which would not otherwise exist. If successful, the operation of the state enhances the operation of markets. Moreover, a variety of relationships between firms themselves and between firms and the government can be involved, with substantial differences emerging as between different economies. (Sawyer, 1992b, p. 57)

Emphasis on Government Investment

Economic growth requires that investments actually take place. Investment goods (and capital equipment) are of great importance and are intimately involved with variations in output (generally arising from fluctuations in demand) and in the labour employed (Sawyer, 1989, p. 379). The growth of output depends on the growth of demand which provides opportunities for the growth of supply (which may not be forthcoming). The importance of demand over supply does not mean that supply is unimportant, but rather that where there is sufficient effective demand supply generally follows. On the other hand, there is no automatic process by which supply is translated into demand. Say's Law simply does not hold: you may build it but they might not come.

Without continuous investment, economies not only have their potential for growth curtailed, they can also end up in a situation where they are actually shrinking due to a reduction in production capacity. On the other hand, where there is sufficiently high demand, investment will generally follow in search of profits. So long as that investment, on balance, exceeds the depreciation of the capital stock, there is a general expansion of capacity and, by extension, potential growth. At the same time, investment spending itself is a component of demand, that being the demand for capital goods.

Gross investment has to take place in order for technical change (either new products or processes) can be brought into effect. The Kaldorian view is relevant here: 'It is the "technical dynamism" of the economy [...] which is responsible, in a capitalist economy, both for making the rate of capital accumulation and the rate of growth of [total] production relatively small or relatively large' (Kaldor, 1978a, p. 37).

Kaldor sought to express some of these ideas in the form of a technical progress function (Kaldor and Mirrless, 1962; Kaldor, 1978a) and concluded 'technical progress is infused into the economic system through the creation of new equipment, which depends on current [...] investment expenditure'. Technical progress influences the volume of investments and opens up new and more profitable opportunities for expansion. The dependence of profits on investments arises from the Kaldorian theory of income distribution. Kalecki (1933, pp. 42-6) argues the level of investment determines total profit (under certain Kaleckian assumptions), and the logical link between the variables of investment, profits and national income operates in the following direction:

$$\text{Investment} \rightarrow \text{Profits} \rightarrow \text{Profit margin} \rightarrow \text{National Income}$$

Both present and future profitability depend upon technical progress, and the rate of technical change can influence both economic growth and capacity utilisation. But the implementation of technical progress requires expenditure on investment. Faster technical change requires more and better new capital equipment for its implementation and relies on a higher rate of investment spending. The growth of the capital stock depends on investment expenditure, which depends on profit and growth expectations, etc.

Also, the stimulus of aggregate demand from technical change can arise through two routes. The first is the introduction of new products, which can stimulate consumer demand; and the second is through investment spending (Sawyer, 1989, pp. 392-3). A faster rate of growth of demand will stimulate a faster rate of technical change; but on the other hand, the cost-reduction aspect of technical change may retard growth in aggregate demand.

Investment expenditure has been given a central role in most Post-Keynesian macroeconomic analysis and models, and is seen as 'the engine of growth'. Investment spending is influenced by a multitude of economic factors which assume varying degrees of importance in different situations; hence, different models emphasise different factors as determining the rate of investment. Our argument is based on the multiplier principle and on investment helping also the supply side. In other words, the size of the change in output depends on the amount of investment. As $\Delta K = I$ and for the government sector $\Delta K_g = I_g$, it is possible to examine the magnitude of the impact of gross capital formation of general government (GCF) and of corporate/quasi-corporate enterprises (QCF) or total gross capital formation (TGCF) on GDP growth.[1] What is particularly of importance here is the contribution of capital formation to the process of GDP growth.

Strategic Planning Aspects

Without strategic planning, the Developmental State model loses its *raison d'être*. While mainstream economic analysis has no place for strategic planning, because cases for market intervention arise solely from market imperfections, Developmental State action seeks to alter static comparative advantage as part of a dynamic process of strategic management of the economy. In sharp contrast, the neoclassical view is one dictated by short-run, often highly partial, considerations and short-term measures that are often in contradiction to long-term strategic objectives. As Cowling (1990, p. 12) argues:

> The market could not be relied on since, within the market, there are vicious and virtuous circles of cumulative causation. This short-termism does not give proper attention to longer-term considerations and crowds out long-term issues. So, fundamental changes, involving leaps in product, process or structure will not be handled well.

Hence, the government can look ahead of the market to draw up long-term parameters of a developmental intervention which does not deny the importance of the market system operating within this overall strategy. In its developmental part, the state takes a leading and proactive role, and the market works within the long-term parameters set by government at various levels, e.g., local, regional and national (Cowling, 1990, p. 32). Market and state are intertwined and the resultant economic system exists only because of the institutional context in which it resides. Property rights are a social construct, modifiable by institutions, and changes in those institutions will result in different economic outcomes (Schmid, 1987, pp. 23-4). Equally important, historic patterns reinforce one another so that institutions are the product of their environment (Hodgson, 1999, 2001, 2006) and strategic planning must occur in that context.

Cowling (1990, pp. 12-15) supports the view that a coherent, national strategic planning system is required for any efficient economic system that seeks to address three important problems: transnationalism, short-termism of the market and centripetalism. The operation of unfettered market forces generates uneven development since the forces of cumulative causation (Myrdal, 1957) and centripetalism (Cowling, 1987, 1990) are involved in the operation of the market and sustain, exacerbate and perpetuate inequalities and disparities between regions and nations. These strong forces and the three central tendencies (mentioned above) within modern market economies cause detrimental conditions in less successful firms, regions and nations. Consequently, national/community planning is required if efficiency in the allocation and utilisation of national/community resources is to be achieved (Cowling, 1990, p. 15). Additionally, the Developmental State should be concerned with offsetting regional disparities and the lack of machinery and capital equipment, training, education and social services. Public support is forthcoming for productive activities at both national and local levels, for the promotion of research, technical development and innovation, and for skill development and training.

Improvements and increases in infrastructure, capital equipment and R&D do not occur overnight. Regional restructuring, similarly, is a long-term goal. Neither is likely to be accomplished by firms bent on beating last quarter's economic estimates. Instead, it is the role of government to take a long-term perspective. Central to that perspective is a commitment to a comprehensive strategic plan that will not be abandoned for the expediency of winning the next election. Government investments in technological and capital equipment, and in improving, renewing and extending physical, business and social infrastructure, will increase the productive capacity of an economy. Government investment in regions and rural areas adds to the sum total of investment capital, skills, technical development and services available and to the opportunities for local development and social welfare.

The enhancement of decentralised activity should be considered here in terms of the expansion of economic strategies by local authorities. Local economic restructuring is related to the following (Martin, 1989, p. 41):

1. the need to support and/or develop indigenous resources, firms and industries;
2. the growth of concern with the quality and quantity of employment through training, education and workplace experience programmes;
3. an increasing direct involvement of local authorities with local industry and trade unions; and
4. the desire of many local authorities to increase democratic control over work and the economy.

A thorough development strategy rests on a complete knowledge of the resources and needs of regions (particularly of those which provide the locations for such a strategy) with the development of local resources as its first priority. The formulation and execution of such planning by public and developmental agencies and local actors within regions allows concrete linkages between industrial and regional policies. Also, the Developmental State successfully contributes to long-term supply-side initiatives aimed at establishing 'growth poles' (in order to offset the 'power of attraction of the centre') and, consequently, at restructuring or promoting the activities of particular firms, sectors and regions, especially those where resources are inefficiently utilised. This state action increases overall national growth by increasing the efficient use of such resources.

A government might adopt a growth pole strategy since potential growth and further development can be stimulated by government intervention. A growth pole policy creates greater external economies, and economies of scale accrue as a result of investment, mainly in R&D, by the government sector and by firms or industries (the larger and more powerful the growth centre, *ceteris paribus*, the greater the external economies). The existence of these external economies makes the poles/centres more attractive for new industrial development, and creates conditions and opportunities conducive to faster growth of existing and incoming industry.

Perroux (1968, 1988) made considerable use of the concept of external economies as a vehicle for spreading the possibilities of growth into many sectors, and stressed the vital role of propulsive industries in growth pole theory. The benefits of a growth pole are felt in surrounding regions/areas: the maximum utilisation of investment; exploitation of external economies; an improvement in the range of services likely to be available to people and to industry; spatial diversification of economic activity; and, the ability to adjust to future structural changes and cyclical downswings.

Such a thorough strategy is a long-term solution. However, if one talks about 'a polycentric system of intervention with a diversified innovation and restructuring strategy for regions' (Martin, 1989, p. 41), then such a strategy must emphasise science parks, information, technology complexes, research, technical education and training. The promotion of technology transfer from public sector education bodies to private enterprises is also of great importance, especially for those industries characterised by small firms, each of which is too small to undertake their own research and development. Technology resource centres and public sector bodies can provide access to high-technology plants that are normally beyond the reach of smaller firms. Cowling (1990, pp. 19-20) suggests that:

> (A proactive developmental state will also) give priority to those industries, both old and new, which appear viable and indeed strategically important in a long-term perspective, but which are vulnerable in the short or medium term without significant intervention. Such industries have to be provided with the resources and commitment to allow them to grow and mature, so that in the longer term the degree of intervention can be progressively reduced and the focus switched to other industries which have emerged as new priorities.

The Developmental State, whether it decides to select sectors and firms for government attention and support (a process often described as 'picking winners') or it decides to target sectors for shrinking (a 'picking losers' strategy), must always endeavour to create a developmental environment that allows winners to emerge. A *qualitative turn* is required and needed: instead of placing emphasis on consumption spending and transfer payments only, the state should also consider government investments (especially on the 'accelerators' of industrial competency and growth) as very important. In other words, governments should rely heavily on government investments which are production-increasing and productivity-increasing expenditures, especially when those investments can positively affect multiple sectors.

Lastly, in the European context, this new and modern approach offers a framework for the long-term evolution of a strategy for European industry and the European economy. Policy initiatives would appear to be necessary on the international-national-local interplay. The first of these is necessary because of the international focus of strategically important activities. National-level policy initiatives are also important because the detailed characteristics of socio-economic norms are nationally based. Finally, the idea behind regional or local initiatives is to improve the capacity to supply goods and services by exploiting existing, or dynamically creating new, competitive advantages (Albrechts et al., 1989, pp. 5-8).

ASSESSING THE DEVELOPMENTAL STATE MODEL

The development pathways of Japan, South Korea, Taiwan, Hong Kong, Singapore and, recently, Malaysia have been characterised by a partnership between government and private business that uses strategic planning to promote the private sector. 'The intimacy of the Developmental State with the private sector and the intensity of its involvement in the market provide directional thrust to the operation of the market mechanism' (Johnson, 1981, pp. 9-10; quoted in Leftwich, 1995, p. 403).

Indeed, it is a process of careful guidance towards long-term economic transformation that creates the fertile conditions so that endogenous growth can take hold. Industry accepts its role in the process and there is significant government intervention without direct ownership of the productive assets. The private sector owns most of the assets but government provides the physical, social and human capital infrastructure to allow those assets to be utilised effectively and efficiently in the global marketplace.

However, this 'developmental orientation' has a pragmatic, rather than an ideological, basis and thus strategic plans of Developmental States differ from both the well-known 'five-year plans' of the Soviet-type command economies and from the 'regulatory orientation' of typical liberal-democratic states. The Developmental State also engages more in what might be termed 'strategic oversight' of industry by gaining consensus through consultation and cooperation. Economic coordination and development in these states is managed by specific institutions whose main task it is to organise the critical interactions between state and industry. These have been the 'core centres' or 'pilot agencies' (to use Johnson's term) of strategic economic direction (Johnson, 1982, p. 26; quoted in Leftwich, 1995, p. 412).

A fundamental characteristic of the Developmental State is having a strategic industrial policy organised around government directives that are broad-based in scope and leave the operational details to the individual firms. Incentives and punishments are used to shape future development and endogenous competency and the entire process is founded upon a model of good and eclectic steersmanship (i.e., state capacity). In addition, such states 'concentrate considerable power, authority, autonomy and competence in the central political and bureaucratic institutions of the state, notably their [determined developmental elites, or] economic bureaucracies' (Leftwich, 1995, p. 420).

Compared to other regimes, Developmental States have numerically small but tightly organised bureaucratic structures that are insulated from corruption due to a highly selective, meritocratic recruitment system that provides long-term rewards and excellent remuneration for career service. This serves to further enhance the solidarity and corporate identity of the bureaucratic elites, and ensures that the government service recruits and retains a highly capable and professional pool of managerial talent. The size of the bureaucratic apparatus helped to consolidate the elite position and authority of the bureaucrats in society and achieve 'equilibrium between accountability and autonomy' (Onis, 1991, p. 124).

Thus, bureaucratic autonomy and close public-private cooperation have been hallmarks of the East Asian Developmental State, and have ensured that the policies of these states are comprehensive, competently derived, and well-received by industry. Without the essential elements of autonomy and cooperation, the Developmental State will likely fail as state elites would quickly fall prey to rent-seeking behaviour carried out by firms. Besides, corruption, which is kept to a minimum in such states, would threaten the viability of any model of government-led development.

Moreover, the corporatist nature of the Developmental State model has been predicated on specific politico-institutional arrangements that allow for cooperation between state and private power to a degree that is difficult to reconcile with the pluralistic standards of 'Western' democracy. Indeed, the stability of government and the limited opposition party success in most of these countries prior to the 1990s suggest there might be a great deal of truth that citizens in these countries will take economic prosperity over political pluralism, at least as long as the government is delivering the goods, so to speak. However, Developmental States can follow this sort of action with governments which have the legitimacy and support, and understand the importance of determination, commitment, seriousness and motivation.

It needs to be pointed out that the strategic partnership between public and private sectors is not a symmetric process. The bureaucrats exercised an extraordinary degree of control over the financial systems in many of these countries and conglomerate dependence on bank finance tended to elicit compliance with strategic industrial policy. The case of Hong Kong, once again, proves to be somewhat different from the others. Financial power generally resides in a limited number of large banks as opposed to being with the state. However, the Hong Kong Special Administrative Region (HKSAR) has exclusive control over land, which allows it to raise extensive revenues without heavy taxation. This control, derived from the policy of land leasing as opposed to sale, allows the HKSAR to act in a somewhat Keynesian fashion to stabilise the property sector through control of land releases and thus assist conglomerates indirectly by ensuring the continued prosperity of the property sector.

Developmental States have generally been successful in their attempts to raise both the quantity and quality of industrial investment. Rather than succumb to short-term goals, these states have focused on increasing growth, productivity and exports by adhering to their strategic long-term economic plans. Because of their insulated and professional civil services, the NICs and Japan have had more technically proficient development plans and have utilised both 'sticks' and 'carrots' to influence industries' decision-making (Leftwich, 1995, p. 412). 'Weak' states, in sharp contrast, have a dearth of economically desirable institutions and an excess of politically motivated and economically harmful policy actions.

The Developmental State allows its bureaucracy to take the initiative and operate effectively, ensuring 'greater autonomy' than in other countries (Amsden, 1989; Wade, 1990; Fishlow, 1991; Onis, 1991). This allows for the government to develop national goals and then translate these goals into effective policy action, as opposed to having the state serve private interests (e.g., India, Mexico, Caribbean states and the bureaucratic authoritarian regimes of some countries in South America). However,

> [T]he pattern of MITI's (or its South Korean and Taiwanese counterparts') involvement in the economy was consistent with both the economic logic of selective industrial policy [. . .] and the logic of finding an equilibrium between 'bureaucratic autonomy and effectiveness', on the one hand, and 'bureaucratic power and accountability', on the other (i.e., correspondence between 'state autonomy' and 'state capacity'). (Onis, 1991, p. 115)

This public-private partnership in the process of policy-making as well as the 'unusual degrees of bureaucratic autonomy' (Onis, 1991, p. 114, p. 119) are features of both the 'authoritarian' and 'democratic' forms of the East Asian Developmental State that allow for the formation and execution of strategic economic policy. The concept of the opposition checking the government à la Westminster model of governance is not part of the equation. Instead, coalition government tends to be the rule even when there has been a dominant party in many of these countries. Minor parties are at the table helping to shape policy and do not actively oppose it. Political cooperation allows for stability in the planning process and reduces the uncertainty that long-term objectives will last only until the next election. This contrasts sharply with the experience in many countries where vibrant rivalries between political parties have sometimes devolved into armed conflict. In Cantonese China, the focus is on business for 'the mountains are high and the Emperor is far away'. However, the war over spoils seems to consume the passions of socio-political actors or groups in some countries.

The autonomy of the state has also ensured that special interest groups do not dominate the economic or political landscape. State autonomy and power were consolidated before national or foreign capital and interests became influential, and during a time when private economic interests were generally politically weak (if not insignificant) relative to state power (Leftwich, 1995, pp. 416-17). Nonetheless, private interests *predate* the establishment of political entities in most less-developed and developing countries as well as a number of developed nations. There are difficulties with taking the model wholesale and adapting it to different contexts.

The bureaucracy is insulated from private special interests by the central political executives in these states. Indeed, one reason for the problems of Japan's economic system in the late 1980s and the 1990s was the marked increase in the number of corruption scandals. Whereas the Shipbuilding Scandal of 1954 and the Lockheed Scandal of 1976 proved that Japan was not immune to corruption, it was not until the Recruit Scandal of 1988-89 and subsequent scandals such as the Kyôwa Affair of 1991, the Sagawa Kyûbin Scandal of 1991-93, the Kanemaru Shin tax evasion scandal of 1993, the Genecon Corruption Scandal of 1993, and a series of scandals involving the Japanese bureaucracy from 1996 to 1998 that corruption apparently became the rule as opposed to the exception. It is perhaps not coincidence that it was also during the early 1990s that Japan's economy entered into a protracted recession.

Of course, politicians must legitimate and ratify decisions of bureaucrats. But when the civil service is competent and is given both responsibility and authority, it tends to rise to the occasion. Certainly, the ability of the Developmental State to deal with both civil society and particular local and foreign interests highlights the need for state capability in shaping mutually advantageous economic relationships (Onis, 1991, p. 115).

Thus, Developmental States are distinguished by the character of their developmental elites and the relative autonomy of these executive elites, as well as the state institutions which they oversee (even though the form and extent of relative autonomy has varied). However, the specific nature of this 'embedded autonomy',

> [Should] be seen as the product of a historical conjuncture of domestic and international factors. It is an autonomy embedded in the concrete set of social ties which bind state and society and provide institutional channels for the

continuous negotiation and re-negotiation of goals and policies. (Steinberg, 1989, p. 74; quoted in Onis, 1991, p. 123)

Still, 'relative autonomy' is only a necessary but not sufficient element in the Developmental State's success. It also requires a strong commitment to industrial development and high economic growth. When such states have turned from commodity production to focusing on service provision, this has undermined growth patterns. Ironically, given the supposed focus of Communist parties on the betterment of the working class, one of the fears of China's Communist Party is that Hong Kong's Democratic Party under Martin Lee Chu-Ming might acquire sufficient influence to institute social welfare mechanisms that would retard Hong Kong's growth.

Of course, the key consideration is whether the East Asian development paradigm can be adopted in other less-developed and developing countries. Neoclassical economists, used to generalise their models, believe that history doesn't matter and culture matters even less, whereas, in fact, these two factors matter a great deal in determining how an economy works (Towse, 2003; Hodgson, 2001, 2004). We can see that, while there are lessons that can be gleaned from the successful East Asian development experience, one cannot adopt it wholesale into other societies as it developed based on specific historical and cultural circumstances that allowed it to flourish. To do otherwise would be to impose an Asiacentric perspective that would be just as fallacious as the Eurocentric one imposed by the West on its former colonies (Blaut, 1993).

Even in the East Asian context, the Developmental State faces challenges from liberal 'western'-type political systems that have emerged in the region. Whether the two can co-exist will depend on the ability of each paradigm to adapt to the presence of the other. This is likely to continue to be a central problem for comparative political economy during the next decade(s). Of course, this dynamic requirement for change is one that has always been present in all institutions: the question of how the Developmental State will address the Veblenian dichotomy is one that will go a long way to prove if the system is sustainable. Globalisation has already started to constrain the ability of such states to use specific industries for subsidisation ('carrots'). However, can these states live with having to rely on general infrastructure improvements and negative reinforcements ('sticks') to deal with laggard industries? Although we believe this is possible, indeed necessary, to ensure survival of the model in the context of the neoliberal Washington consensus and increased globalisation, only a positive response to that question will ensure the continued relevance of the Developmental State model.

Of course, there are still important lessons that can be gleaned from the model and its performance over the past half-century. If they are to achieve any meaningful results, states must learn to think strategically and utilise long-term approaches to development as opposed to fabricated and often partial solutions based on short-term requirements for success at the polls. Modern states must also develop competent and insulated civil services to formulate these strategic plans and implement them so that corruption and rent-seeking behaviour are kept to a minimum. The challenge is to devise forms of strategic industrial policy which are consistent with the norms of democratic accountability and, perhaps, with more limited concentration of state and private power than has been the case in the East Asian context.

A final lesson that emerges from this new experience is that the transfer of specific Developmental State policies and strategies to new environments will be self-defeating in the absence of the politico-institutional conditions required for their effective implementation. In drawing on the comparative literature, it is thus the main purpose of this chapter to elaborate on elements of the 'desirable' developmental intervention based on developmentally-driven political purposes and institutional structures. These notions form the subject matter of the following section.

DEVELOPMENTAL POLICY CONSIDERATIONS

Based on the above notions and taking the main modern economic problems into account, the following considerations can be outlined.

The Role of Aggregate Demand

Economic growth is governed by the growth of aggregate demand which, in turn, determines total output growth and job creation. Therefore, aggregate demand management policies are necessary for GDP growth, higher levels of employment and good economic performance. On the other hand, supply-side considerations are also important and may be influenced by aggregate demand. Besides, aggregate demand must be sufficient enough to stimulate production and a higher rate of capacity utilisation and must lead to a rising efficiency of production (the efficiency and effectiveness of government sector spending and taxation is a requisite and must be maximised). Indeed, active policies are important and can strengthen the links between aggregate demand growth and capacity utilisation. In other words, appropriate policies designed to sustain the level of demand would be required if higher levels of capacity utilisation are to be expected. However, countries cannot rely solely on export-driven growth as they may also need to develop platforms of production for domestic needs and internal requirements. An appropriate macroeconomic policy should focus on the following:

1. faster, non-inflationary growth of domestic demand (i.e., aggregate demand management); and
2. sound public finances/investments (especially on R&D and skills).

In the same vein, Sawyer (1994, pp. 10-14) points out the following five considerations as being important for the achievement of full employment:

1. adequate aggregate demand for full employment;
2. the absence of inflationary pressures at or near full employment;
3. the ability to compete in new technology sectors (the role of imports and exports and the growth of exports);
4. the social and political environment; and
5. the relationship between the financial and the productive sectors.

Accelerators of Growth

Although many (economic and non-economic) factors influence investment decisions, investment is the fundamental independent variable of the system. But not all investment is the same. Indeed, investment on the accelerators of growth is a prerequisite for prosperity. Throwing additional investment into areas of industrial decline will do nothing more than delay that decline; it is not the basis for successful industrial policy. More importantly, investment that can be utilised in multiple industries can act as an accelerator of growth because of its multiple positive effects. The key role of investment rests on the independence of capital accumulation as the driving force of the process of economic growth. Capital accumulation is central to technical progress and adds to both demand and capacity, i.e., it 'provides the incentives and the means of further expansion' (Kaldor, 1966).

Improvements in production result from a combination of innovation, R&D and invention. In addition, the relation between technological progress and improvements in human capital is very strong. Investment in human capital takes many different forms, including expenditure on health services and facilities, on-the-job and institutional training and re-training, formally organised education, study programmes, etc. Human capital investments can overcome many of the characteristics of the labour force that act as impediments to greater productivity. Improvements in human capital can considerably increase the productivity and earnings of labour and may be preconditions for the introduction of more advanced technology applied to production.

Training may be either general or specific in nature. Training provided by the state, which is more broadly applicable to multiple industries, is more likely to increase growth than narrowly focused training that is specific to a particular process or industry. Ensuring that structural unemployment is kept at a minimum by making the workforce adaptable is a key consideration that must be addressed. Since individual industries are likely to produce only specific training for fear of losing employees to competitors, the provision of such a 'public good' goes a long way to enhancing the well-being of the society. Besides, the amount of resources devoted to investments in human capital is an allocative problem (which has also political characteristics) that each country has to solve by itself; but there are many potential benefits of investment in human resources in the widest sense.

Industry as the Engine of Growth

The expansion of industry represents a net addition to the effective use of resources and, therefore, to the overall growth of the system. The growth of industry and, as a result, overall economic growth are led by the growth of demand for industrial products which, in turn, leads to the growth of output and efficiency gains, both in industry and in the economy as a whole. But on the other hand, supply-side factors (i.e., R&D, learning, technical change, capital accumulation and mechanisation, etc.) are also important for further industrial development, competitiveness and economic growth. Indeed, the supply considerations may themselves be influenced by demand, may induce further growth of demand, and so on.

A proactive government needs a strategic view of national development and must provide a range of support mechanisms to those sectors deemed to have a key role to play in the future (Sawyer, 1992a, p. 8). Industrial strategy should be an important part of state policy-making and will be determined by the capacity and competence of the state to undertake a developmental role across key specific industries. This is clearly a process of industrial targeting, properly involving nurturing or restructuring or repositioning (or any combination of this sort of action) of prioritised sectors, which leads to product differentiation. In fact, strategic industrial policy targets and centres around strategic sectors, which can be expected to fuel future economic growth. It may also target certain existing industries for decline and foster retraining of such workers so as to make them available for positions in more favoured sectors. By recognising differentiation of sectors and industries, policy can address the problems that are rooted in the growth of these sectors and industries, and thus become effective.

Moreover, the role of various industrial sectors in the process of regional growth is complex and depends (to a large extent) on the location decisions of industries and their competitive performance. Hence, structural factors may play some role in determining a region's economic performance. Some of the strategic aims that are necessary for a restructuring-oriented regional policy are the following (Martin, 1989, p. 37):

1. the development of a new local economy based on high-technology industrial sectors and innovatory activities, R&D, science parks and technology transfer centres;
2. the modernisation of existing mature industries and firms through the application of new production technologies and new product development so as to raise efficiency and competitiveness;
3. the upgrading of skills and technical qualifications of the labour force through various workplace-experience programmes, reskilling, education and training; and
4. the improvement and/or extension of physical infrastructure (e.g., roads, utilities), business infrastructure (e.g., telecommunications, IT, advisory services) and social infrastructure (e.g., educational, cultural and leisure facilities).

DEVELOPMENT WITH DECENTRALISATION AND PARTICIPATION

We must consider the concept of decentralisation too because globalisation has been accompanied by cries for localisation: the nation-state is being torn at from both ends. Local governments, being closer to the people they serve, may be better able to carry out the duties of serving the public. Such a policy of devolution can lead to more flexible, innovative and creative administration. Consequently, the efficiency of a central government could be increased by decentralised governance. In addition, decentralisation can facilitate coordinated planning between the various government agencies and/or departments and make plans more relevant to local needs. This is why it is widely regarded as a necessary condition for economic, social and political development. At the same time, it must be ensured that localities act cooperatively to solve regional problems as opposed to competitively in a policy prescription that may allow companies to pit one government against another. Hence, such devolution must occur with certain ground rules that prevent bidding wars to begin for corporate headquarters. After all, if one firm is subsidised, this is equivalent to providing a net tax on everyone else since existing firms are forced to pay the shortfall in taxes granted to the subsidised firm.

The localised state is a controversial topic; but whatever its ideological foundation or level of intervention, the contemporary state must localise its governmental apparatus (due to the demand for decentralisation to regions). Liberalism argues a normative case for political democracy at the local level on the basis of a political model of man. Neoclassical economics predicts behaviour under specified conditions on the basis of an economic model of man, while providing some analytical confirmation of some of the positivist elements in liberal theory. Marxists are concerned with social movements in addition to collective interests within specific historical circumstances. According to Smith (1985, pp. 47-52), the following facts may result from decentralisation:

1. Decentralisation to regional and/or local levels allows officials to disaggregate and tailor development plans and programmes to the needs of heterogeneous regions and groups. Indeed, democratic decentralisation is an effective way of meeting local needs and can result in a variety of policies as there is an imbalance of resources and requirements between levels of government. Decentralised structures may be favoured because they promote diversity in public policies and may allow better political and administrative 'penetration' of national government policies into rural areas.
2. Decentralisation may lead to the development of greater administrative capability among local governments and private institutions in the regions. So, local government's role can be supportive and facilitative through environmental improvement and local infrastructure, and by increasing and improving the provision of public goods and social services at local levels (i.e., local development and regional growth). It can generate additional resources, encourage more efficient use of existing resources and give local authorities the opportunity to improve and expand the infrastructure in regional and rural areas (i.e., the developmental role of regional/local authorities).
3. Local government can identify and even define service requirements and deliver, plan or regulate public services. By reducing diseconomies of scale, decentralisation can increase the number of public goods and services, and the efficiency with which they are delivered, at a lower cost. Besides, the main sources of revenue available to local and regional governments are taxes, charges, grants and loans. Nevertheless, tax decentralisation (its concept and measurement) is not straightforward, as it involves sub-national controls over all aspects of tax policy. This does not imply a rejection of a useful role for active local participation in the administration of social policies to assist the poor (i.e., welfare policies); to promote regional and industrial development; and, to improve R&D, innovation, etc.
4. Decentralisation can increase popular participation in development and planning, and may also allow greater representation for various social and political groups and unions in development policy decision-making that could lead to greater equity in the allocation of public resources and investments. If political decision-making is decentralised among sub-national units, each unit may tailor its tax and service package to the

> preferences of its citizens. Efficiency and social welfare are therefore likely to be maximised under highly decentralised political structures. Decentralised government structures require political choices, and the governance values might justify whether the political decision-making process is centralised or decentralised, i.e., to what extent/degree. Decentralisation is desirable since, by devolving real decision-making to local levels of administration, higher levels of interest and participation in local government result. It also provides for greater flexibility and speed of decision-making, because regional/local development requires such flexibility.

There is clearly a strong link between decentralisation and participation, which must be considered as a requisite for high quality public policies (given that high centralisation and inefficiency often go together). Indeed, participation in the design and execution of work can improve efficiency. Uphoff and Esman (1984, p. 13) define participation as: 'before-the-act involvement in the choices and efforts producing benefits'.

Moreover, participation in policy decision-making can take many forms, and democratic participation requires a decline in the power of central administration. The Developmental State argument must be concerned with fuelling politico-institutional changes in order to facilitate the emergence of developmental paths in a decentralised way.[2] This pays particular regard to the enhancement of democracy in at least two dimensions. First, it argues that participation by local authorities and other 'social partners' can improve the organisation of production. It contributes to a less inequitable income distribution amongst its goals, to substantial regional development, to more efficient economic and social development, etc. and, consequently, social efficiency could be intimately bound up with democratic participation (i.e., the active involvement of all the social partners). Second, a more open style of government restrains the power of small groups who have access to government decision-making and allows local governments (or authorities), trade unions and other social forces to be fully involved in the evaluation and implementation of proposals.

CONCLUSION

This chapter has briefly presented the successful developmental paths of Japan and NICs, and special emphasis has been placed on the role of state investments. Government projects usually encompass a large number of targets (e.g., employment levels, labour training, etc.) or multi-dimensional targets, and a large number of important activities can only be administered by governments. Hence, governments can contribute to economic growth and development by increasing both production-increasing and productivity-increasing investment expenditures; by curtailing policies and practices that create inefficiencies; and by pursuing appropriate fiscal policies as well as specific policies in specific areas (such as, industrial strategies/policies, regional policies, etc.).

The Developmental State, based on *qualitative* government intervention, clearly plays a key role. Although demand management policies are clearly necessary for growth and good economic performance, the Developmental State can improve the longer-run supply potential of any economy and can play an active role in it.

NOTES

1. In Karagiannis (1996), the contribution of GCF and QCF, or TGCF, to the process of growth of the EC countries, the USA and Japan, over the period 1970-95 was tested (the discussion, however, had to rely on an imperfect and incomplete data base). The author provided comparable results for a number of EC countries, the USA and Japan, which confirm our previous notions.
2. The Japanese state tried to create 'winners' and thereby it was (to a large extent) a centralised and powerful state. On the other hand, the Korean state was (more or less) not so democratic. In comparison, Singapore epitomised the small state preoccupation with infrastructure and avoiding 'losers' and thus used powerful disincentives to alter comparative advantage against sectors that were not in favour. However, this has been undertaken through consultation rather than directive and with a desire to let market forces, rather than central dictate, be the determinant of those sectors that would become the eventual 'winners'.

11. The Developmental State and the EC/EU

Various EC/EU governments have instituted national, industrial and regional polices in an effort to address inequalities and disparities in their respective nations. These problems, which vary considerably from country to country, have cost European nations over $10 billion per year since the late 1980s on grants and 'soft' loans to firms alone. Although this is less than 1 per cent of the Community GDP, it is still a considerable sum, and the intractability of the situation suggests that these problems will not disappear in short course. Besides, a wide variety of other incentives such as accelerated depreciation allowances, tax concessions and employment subsidies are offered. These difficulties tend to be most prevalent in the periphery of the continent, and this has created tensions among various Member States in regard to EU expansion (*European Economy*, July 1989).

Growth, which has been uneven and generally weak since the collapse of Breton Woods in 1973, has also been divergent across the EC/EU (and OECD) countries. There are several elements, both internal and external, that do not bode well for the prospects for additional development and growth. Besides, political and social characteristics (or barriers) are of great importance in how these elements can combine into an effective national policy. Some elements, internal and external, may have had some negative influence on the prospects for additional development and growth. One, of course, is that Europe has broken down many of its internal barriers to trade so that the benefits that neoclassical economics sees from trade have already been gained. This is ironic since the economic performance of Europe during this time of integration has been lacklustre while economic disparities have widened when compared with many of its trading partners.

Indeed, while the 'invisible' hand of the free market exacerbates natural disadvantages, inequalities and disparities, the 'visible' hand of the state can act not only as a corrector of these but, more importantly, as a capable corporate agent that can improve industrial development, competency and competitiveness. Thus, a high quality of state intervention and, especially, developmentalist policies are needed.

GENERAL CONSIDERATIONS

1. Traditional regional and industrial policies attempt to improve on existing strengths by taking competitive and profitable industries ('winners') and 'investing in their success'. This is done by using the state to reallocate capital and labour towards successful regions and firms if the industry undertakes some policy that the state deems important (e.g., investing in a particular region). It may also entail elimination of market failures so as to streamline and improve market efficiency. On the other hand, the Developmental State seeks to improve the general operation of the market and 'create success' where it is lacking. Since market forces tend to move low-growth regions further away from spatial equilibrium, due to the forces of cumulative causation, the Developmental State attempts to offset these self-perpetuating disparities and the lack of human and material resources by reshaping the industrial landscape and taking a leading developmental role in the economy. Table 11.1 allows us to contrast the *orthodox*/mainstream and the Developmental State views to regional development.

Table 11.1 Two Opposite Policies to Regional and Industrial Development

	Characteristics of Market-Based Policies	Characteristics of Developmental State Policies
Theoretical framework	• Neoclassical theory • Small state sector • Free enterprise culture • Deregulation, privatisation	• Post-Keynesianism • High quality state Intervention • Supply potential and Strategies • Growth poles
Causes of disparities		
1. General	• Inefficiency in problem regions due to market rigidities	• Demand-based explanations incorporating the principle of cumulative causation
2. Specific	• Lack of entrepreneurial 'culture' • Excessive government intervention	• Structural weaknesses • Low investment • Drain of financial capital to prosperous regions • Inadequate government participation in regional growth

Table 11.1 Cont'd

Policy	• Micro-policy options • Reactive policies (correction of market failure/imperfections) • Minimal public expenditure • Financial incentives to overcome market failure • Low tax • Selective assistance • Regulatory role of the state • Deregulation of regional markets • 'Close' integration with the world economy	• Comprehensive policies • Proactive policies • Aggregate demand management • Planned investments in infrastructure and modern factors of development • Expenditure injections on regional and local growth • Industrial strategy • Decentralisation and Participation • 'Managed' or 'strategic' integration with the world economy

Source: Karagiannis, 1996.

2. Traditional regional and industrial policies have failed to reduce regional disparities and have been partially successful in boosting industry. With an emphasis on using financial incentives/schemes and working at the edges of the market system, these policies have been unsuccessful for the following reasons:

   (a) inadequate demand management and/or limited supply-side policies;
   (b) general and specific regional and industrial problems (which differ from one country to another);
   (c) general and specific micro-problems (such as new technologies and equipment, profitability, employment, uncertainty, etc.);
   (d) centripetal market forces;
   (e) short-term policy decision-making; and
   (f) strong competition (mainly international competition).

Traditional incentive policies (and automatic stabilisers) may contribute to some industries' commercial viability but do not get at the root of the problems. By offering financial support to existing firms to undertake policies that create jobs without having a strategic plan sets up an undesirable situation where firms use the system so as to attract funds for marginal projects and refuse to undertake additional investments to make these jobs a long-term reality. Such funds are frequently given to firms that are from outside the region. But these firms often fail to source supplies from local industry and sometimes even import skilled labour so that, while certain jobs are created, little is done to alleviate the unemployment of individuals in the locality. At best, these financial schemes are the equivalent of 'providing a man with a fish without teaching him to fish'. Instead of simply engaging in 'job creation', special emphasis needs to be placed on planned investments in research, technology complexes, education/technical education, training and re-training, work-place experience programmes and information, which are both production-increasing and productivity-increasing expenditures. Furthermore, investments can stimulate indigenous regional growth in less-developed areas (i.e., the multiple effects of investment injections on local development).

3. Traditional market failure measures (i.e., regulatory change or taxes or subsidies) cannot easily correct the technical inefficiencies and failures to adequately develop and use new products and processes that often occur, especially since the nature and causes of these failures are usually unclear. Instead, cooperation between firms and between firms and the state, which is a characteristic of the Developmental State, can assist in ensuring that a competitive lead will occur by allowing for cooperative problem-solving at a time of rapid technological change (Best, 1990, p. 16). By giving priority to key sectors, which are viable and strategically important in a long-term perspective but may be vulnerable in the short and medium-term if state intervention is not forthcoming, a proactive Developmental State can provide these sectors with the resources and commitment to allow them to grow and mature. Obviously, this requires Developmental State action to ensure the appropriate 'developmental environment' so that these targeted sectors can become competitive and efficient.

Moreover, the New Competition literature emphasises the relevance of relationships between firms (as well as between firms and the state). General equilibrium analysis supports situations of perfect competition and, consequently, long-term relationships appear as rigidities in the sense that prices may not immediately respond to variations in demand and supply, and demand and supply are not coordinated solely by price variations (Hodgson, 1988). But technical inefficiencies and failures to develop and use new products and processes often occur. Pressure for inter-firm cooperation and coordination across phases in the production chain comes, in part, from problems such as rapid technological changes, a lack of innovation, inadequate (or a lack of) R&D, etc. (Best, 1990, p. 16).

The New Competition analysis suggests that cooperation, rather than competition, among small firms may be necessary in order to '. . . shape the rules of the market game and complementary investment strategies' (Best, 1990, p. 17). For example, the NICs' economies that are able to generate more effective long-term-oriented cooperative arrangements regarding technological and organisational learning and investments (in human and physical assets) have outperformed countries that rely on classic free market mechanisms.

4. By first defining development goals (both in the aggregate and by sectors and regions) and then coordinating development programmes (by sectors and regions) in order to fulfil these goals, the Developmental State analysis is closely linked to the concept and policy of 'growth poles'. State policies (as part of an overall economic strategy), designed to invest wisely in infrastructure and encourage the establishment of new dynamic industries, might have a better prospect of stimulating economic expansion. When looking at the broad picture, it is also easier to identify which factors are missing (such as skilled labour training or R&D). The object is to attract centres, sectors and specific industries that are capable of growing successfully and that can capitalise on the natural advantages of depressed areas. As a result, this allows for indigenous growth and rejuvenation.
5. Governments need to realise that industrial planning (dynamic industrial complex planning and comprehensive urban-regional development planning) is a necessary component to ensure the best use of natural resources, land, manpower, industry and commercial potential. Thus, by focusing on government investments on the accelerators of development and growth at the national and regional/local levels, the Developmental State is intimately involved in picking short- and, especially, long-term developmental paths and plans for the future.

Orthodox economic analysis focuses on short-term decision-making. State interventions are dictated by partial equilibrium analysis that does not recognise the interconnectedness of various factors. However, this is especially problematic because orthodox economic analysis itself has, through the concept of the Second Best, identified that attempts to solve imperfections in the market on a partial basis may actually leave the overall economy in a worse position than when it started. In sharp contrast, Developmental State analysis (and the New Competition view) is based on strategic actions to achieve endogenous competency, growth and competitiveness, and can successfully contribute to long-run supply-side initiatives that can promote particular firms, sectors and regions (longer-run structural reforms instead of short-run measures). Strategic refers to '. . . long-term market-shaping activities in contrast with market-reacting responses' (Best, 1990, p. 11). A Developmental State takes a leading role in the industrial economy with the market system continuing to play a substantial, indeed crucial, part, but working within the parameters set by government at various levels (local, regional and national) (Cowling, 1990, p. 16).

In order to combat cumulative causation (Myrdal, 1957) and the three central tendencies within modern market economies (transnationalism, short-termism of the market and centripetalism), strategic planning is necessary. Indeed, a coherent national strategic planning system, where economic, social, political and cultural forces and linkages as well as the capacity of local, regional and other (economic and social) organisations to handle their responsibilities are taken into consideration, is 'an essential element of any efficient economic system' (Cowling, 1990, p. 15).

EXPERIENCES IN THE EC AREA

The need for the state to play a role in development has been well known, both in theory and in practice, since the writings of Alexander Hamilton and Friedrich List. But it has only been in the post-war era that governments have intervened in such a manner as to become major participants in their national economies. Their primary task was the maintenance of conditions that facilitate steady growth and full (or almost full) employment, and their secondary one the promotion of industrial development and balance in the economy. Still, with a large number of governments facing the crucial task of creating basic economic and social infrastructure (ranging from roads, schools and hospitals to plant, machinery and capital equipment), there has been a spate of interest in development theory which was expected to guide the attempts of states to foster development.

Dore (1986) classifies state interventions in the economy as follows:

1. *Regulation* of individual transactions for market efficiency;
2. *Regulation* of production and trade to prevent imperfect competition;
3. *Intervention* to promote economic growth in two sub-categories:
   (a) state actions taken wholly with regard to the domestic economy (Dore, 1986, calls this 'domestic developmentalism'); and
   (b) state actions taken explicitly to promote the competitiveness of the nation in the global economy (in a similar way, Dore, 1986, labels this 'competitive developmentalism); and
4. 'Pork barrel' *intervention* – the use of government power to promote particular sectional interests for personal and electoral advantages.

As noted earlier, industrial and regional policies have often been minor complements of national economic policies. Regional policies, designed to influence the geographical distribution of economic activity (either by encouraging expansion in depressed regions through financial inducements to the private sector in addition to correction of micro-imperfections or by a differentially high rate of public expenditure to improve the infrastructure), have been used for five decades; therefore, some lessons can be learned from this experience. Countries that embrace the 'market-failure Anglo-Saxon' tradition versus the 'comprehensive-developmentalist' tradition reproduce the above distinction on regional, industrial, and full employment policies. In the following sub-sections, we discuss some examples of development in the post-war era.

British Regional and Industrial Policies

In the post-war era, although more so from the 1950s through the 1970s, British regional policy has aimed at reducing regional disparities in job creation and unemployment and providing a greater geographic dispersion of industry. This has been triggered by concerns about Britain's growth performance (as regional policy has been seen as a way to achieve a faster national growth rate) and the problems of excessive growth in the Greater London area (Armstrong and Taylor, 1985, pp. 174-8). Public expenditure on regional and industrial aid in the form of loans, grants, tax incentives and subsidies, has largely been directed at encouraging capital investment by firms in assisted areas based on the assumption that such investments would generate jobs.

Selective government intervention has attempted to improve industrial performance. Besides, there was some restructuring of 'sun-set' industries (e.g., textiles) and much of this occurred during the 1950s and 1960s (e.g., the nationalisation of steel and shipbuilding industries). Unemployment patterns in the UK have been dominated by problems of old industries; thus, these economic policies were concentrated on creating new manufacturing opportunities. By the late 1960s, the regional policy framework comprised the following four major elements:

1. employment subsidies;
2. automatic subsidies for investment spending in assisted areas;
3. discretionary financial assistance; and
4. controls on location decisions.

Growth pole policy in the 1960s concentrated special public investment (using direct or indirect incentives) in parts of regions that had the most favourable prospects for self-sustained growth and that were best located to generate activity over a large area. In 1966, this policy was abandoned in favour of broad development areas, and regional policy aimed at raising economic activity in three categories of assisted areas: intermediate areas, development areas and special development areas. The first two categories were based on levels of unemployment, while the third one was based not only on current unemployment but also on anticipated future unemployment due to regional dependency on the declining industries of shipbuilding and coal (*Industrial Development Act*, 1966).

During this time, governments directly pursued restructuring efforts in British manufacturing as international competition increased and important industries such as steel-making were experiencing new difficulties. Falling employment in many key industries increased the North-South gap in terms of employment (CSO, *Abstract of Regional Statistics*, 1974; CSO, *Regional Trends*, various years); however, the operation of other economic policies undermined the effectiveness of regional policy (Armstrong and Taylor, 1985; Wood, 1987; Bowers, 1991).

In the 1970s, the Regional Development Grant and Regional Selective Assistance were used to help firms maintain profitability and employment as well as create new employment (*Local Employment Act*, 1972; *Industry Act*, 1972; *Industry Act*, 1975). The government's intention was 'to continue and develop the financial and other incentives now available for the location of new industry and the expansion of existing industry in the assisted areas' (House of Commons, *Parliamentary Debates*, Vol. 872, session 1974, cols. 347-8).

That decade also saw the reduction of employment in many industries, a retrenchment that accelerated following the oil crisis of 1973, and rising unemployment, with all its consequences, became politically untenable. The nationalisation programme of Labour Governments not only transferred ownership to the public sector but also changed the industrial structure. As a result, the privatisation programme that began in 1979 allowed the privatised companies to make *de facto* industrial policy. This resulted in changes that were not always in the national interest, with a considerable number of jobs lost, especially in heavily depressed areas. In addition, the Conservative Government, led by Thatcher, placed a higher value on private ownership than competition in determining economic performance.

From the 1970s and the late 1980s, regional policy expenditure declined dramatically, from 0.5 per cent of GDP in 1970 to 0.3 per cent of GDP by the early 1980s and 0.13 per cent of GDP by the late 1980s (*Regional Studies Association*, 1983, p. 15; *Economic Trends*, various), a figure which has little changed since then. Real total public expenditure in 1975-76 was double (or more) that of the year 1972-73 but fell significantly in 1978-79 and 1979-80 (CSO, *Regional Trends*, various years). Scotland and Wales experienced declining shares of manufacturing investment over the period 1971-82, but the share of Northern England fell even faster than either of them. There was an increased share of capital expenditure on economic services, at least until the public expenditure cuts of 1980-82, but there is no evidence of increased shares of public spending on human capital. With housing and community development, total UK expenditure (at current prices) fell from £2.1 billion to £0.5 billion between 1980 and 1982 (CSO, *Regional Trends*, various years). Regional policy has been further downgraded since 1979.[1]

Since 1979, most industrial policies in the UK have presupposed that state intervention is solely for the purpose of promoting price competition (Best, 1990, p. 46). Market failure, in this regard, may be corrected by limited regulation in order to address market imperfections through limited regulatory schemes, and the main thrust of British industrial policy has been for the government to adopt a regulatory, rather than developmental, role with particular emphasis on competition policy.

Following Dore's classification, British policies come under headings 1 and 2, although there are also elements that could be placed under headings 3 and 4. These have particularly arisen from Labour governments; a number of policies pursued during the 1960s and 1970s by Labour governments involve a more developmental role for the state. But the timid nature and brief life of those policies (e.g., the National Plan of 1965-66 and the industrial strategy of 1975-79), along with the hostile academic response, indicate the dominance of market failure analysis (Sawyer, 1992b, p. 57). In addition, training and training schemes have been reactive, rather than proactive, in nature, being dictated by the pressure of unemployment and lack of qualified manpower. Strategic planning simply didn't occur.

There has also been little emphasis on government investments on the modern factors of growth and competitiveness. British governments spent relatively little on regional infrastructure and other accelerators of growth and development. In contrast, the Developmental State view suggests much more government spending on infrastructure and accelerators rather than direct payments to firms. The accelerators of growth should be considered as a complete package of development tools. Improvements in production result from a sophisticated combination of new technologies, innovation and R&D, and investment in human resource development can spur the labour force to greater productivity.

In brief, the 'market failure' tradition has been dominant in most British regional and industrial policies, with only occasional elements of active developmental policy to be found when Labour governments were in power; but still those governments did not achieve desirable industrial performance, significant regional restructuring or competitiveness.

German Regional and Industrial Policies

The German State is the most decentralised system in Europe with its federal constitution reflecting 'the relatively weak sense of central identity in the country as a whole' (Littlechild, 1982, p. 155). The principle aim of German domestic economic policy is to improve social services and let an unfettered market economy, based on open and free competition, act as the guiding force behind economic development. Although in the 1960s the government encouraged mergers to create large industrial enterprises in automobiles, oil and gas, shipbuilding, chemical and electrical engineering, and electric power (*Statistisches Bundesamt*, 1971), since 1973, Germany has focused on anti-trust policy seeking to encourage competition.

At the same time, 'there has been a strong sense of responsibility at all levels of government, and there have often been *implicit* regional policy considerations in the pattern of government expenditure and commitment to a uniform standard of living in all parts of the country' (Blacksell, 1987, p. 250). State involvement has occurred in regional aid policy; in subsidising coal production; in promoting certain high-tech sectors; and in occasionally providing adjustment assistance (for example, in the case of Volkswagen in 1974). However, the state will not provide assistance to rescue a company from failure, although the private banking system may do so.

Since the mid-1970s German regional policy has been hampered by a lack of national coordination. Although in 1975 attempts were made to coordinate regional policies with those of the Federal Government (Mellor, 1978), by the 1980s, the various *Länder* (equivalent to states or provinces) emphasised their own development plans while the Federal Government began to retreat from regional policy, questioning its effectiveness and citing the strict division of responsibilities under the German constitution.

The 1980s saw a period of 'reorganisation' and 'rationalisation' in all major sectors of manufacturing, which produced only short-term efficiency improvements. One major result was a reduction in the need for manpower. Although some other sectors, notably services, are expanding, they are not growing fast enough to compensate; as a result, unemployment has been an increasingly serious problem (Riquet, 1976; Blacksell, 1987, pp. 245-6). *Statistisches Bundesamt* (various years) presents employment in the major sectors of the German economy by *Länd*, illustrates the seriousness of unemployment, and shows how it has developed since the early 1970s.

In contrast, a Developmental State would use government policy in a widespread and intensive fashion to purposefully guide the market economy. The state would develop national goals and then with government-private cooperation see these goals translated into operational activity. Rather than focusing largely on supporting the existing market mechanism, as has been done in Germany, a Developmental State would fashion the market after its own needs and goals. Thus, there exists a high degree of complementarity between the market mechanism and an active state that does not require the usurpation of private property. Whereas German state policies presuppose the market as it currently exists and are, to use Amsden's words, 'market-conforming', an active Developmental State seeks to create opportunities that would not otherwise exist and therefore takes an approach that Amsden (1989) calls 'market-augmenting'.

The lack of coordination between the Federal Government and local governments as well as the adoption of short-term perspectives rather than strategic planning in economic decision-making have precluded discussion of the range of government strategies and policies that may prove useful in the encouragement of industrial growth and rejuvenation. This strategic *planning* (which is different from *intervention*) involves,

> conscious attempts by the government of a country – usually with the [effective] participation of other collective bodies – to coordinate public policies more rationally in order to reach more fully and rapidly the desirable ends for future development which are determined by the political process as it evolves. (Myrdal, 1960, p. 15)

Since Germany has failed to take a proactive role and has actually cut expenditure in the name of fiscal 'prudence' in such key areas as education, research, technological improvement, etc. over the past two decades or so, the country's long-term growth prospects may have been harmed. There is a significant body of empirical research which suggests that the main factor in determining the distribution of new high-technology industries among nations is the location of government investment in higher education and R&D as opposed to the granting of economic incentives (e.g., Giese and Nipper, 1984; Amsden, 1989; DeLong and Summers, 1991; Amable, 1992; Munnell, 1992; Archibugi, 1993; Dowrick, 1993; Boyer and Caroli, 1995; Amable and Petit, 1996). At the same time, such investment expenditure that has occurred has happened outside the context of long-term economic, industrial and investment planning and without comprehensive government policies aimed to address strategic issues of importance to the successful development of the German economy.

Germany's economic policies have followed orthodox prescriptions that seek to reduce the functions of the state to those of regulation and restriction. As a result, German policies are losing momentum and effectiveness (e.g., socio-economic problems, regional inequalities, 'Eurosclerosis'). However, Germany can effectively reverse this situation by taking cues from the New Competition approach and by adopting a developmental role for the state that would embrace a comprehensive and supportive role that differs from 'standard' policy-making.

French Regional and Industrial Policies

France, on the other hand, has developed a series of National Plans to foster economic development. These plans created close links between industry and the public sector and various French governments have been extensively involved in the running of many sectors of the economy, including gas, coal, oil refining, steel, motor cars, electronics, chemicals, nuclear energy, telecommunications, transport, computers and insurance. Clearly, French governments have been more proactive than the British or German ones in adopting growth pole/developmentalist policies as a counterweight to the attraction of Paris. These growth pole policies were strengthened in various aspects during the 1960s and 1970s in order to allow for the movement of selected industrial plans and the relocation of manufacturing and tertiary jobs. Still, growth poles were always strongly subordinate to Paris and few really attracted significant decision-making functions (Clout, 1987b, p. 179). Indeed, if success is measured by results, only a limited number of key factories were moved from Paris to the provinces (Brunet and Sallois, 1986).

During the 1960s, a movement was underfoot to relieve the pressures of rising productivity in agriculture, which was transforming the agrarian way of life in many areas and contributing to urbanisation. At the same time, global competition was contributing to a decline in certain old mainline manufacturing industries. For this important reason, the French government gave numerous grants to the countryside and areas with declining industries to attract employment from offices, higher education and research activities. By the 1970s, financial aid for tertiary development had been extended to all areas that qualified for industrial grants including the growth poles and many other provincial cities. The government negotiated with banking and insurance firms to relocate their offices and talked extensively about the desirability to move research, administrative and management functions to the countryside. Still, even while the national economy shifted from the secondary to the tertiary sector, many large private firms and international corporations preferred to stay in Paris or its surrounding areas (Clout, 1987b, p. 181). In the wake of increasing international competition, traditional industries, such as textiles, shoes and clothing simply could not compete, while even newer industries such as steel, coal, car manufacturing and oil refining went into decline. Jobs continued to be lost and, without thorough proactive strategic planning for the spatial concentration of industries, there were few agglomeration economies. Instead, industries remained spatially fragmented, poorly managed and overstaffed, and financially uncompetitive and inefficient.

During the 1960s and 1970s, France often used government investment plans to foster economic development. These plans presented a consistent economic framework that allowed individual firms to make investment and other decisions and assisted in making expectations somewhat self-fulfilling with the expectation of high growth being translated into higher levels of investment, which allow growth to occur. In general, successive French governments provided assistance to industries on a highly selective basis based on the desire to grow national champions in certain strategic, high-technology, large industries. This assistance consisted of direct government investment, subsidies and protection from foreign competition.

By the 1980s, the national government began a decentralisation process allowing local authorities and regions to have a greater say in the 'National Champions' policies and make these key industries more efficient through managerial restructuring, the closing of surplus capacity and decreasing labour redundancies. Urban and rural planning, job creation and relocation, and the improvement of services were paid for by the central government and made available to both manufacturing and service firms; but the spatial grading of assistance varied for the two sectors (Brunet and Sallois, 1986). Despite all these activities, Paris continued to grow in both population and service employment and most high-level operations remained in or near Paris (Clout, 1987b, p. 192).

Much of this inability to diversify the base of operations is owing to the significant agglomeration economies that Paris enjoyed. As the leading metropolitan area in France and with its centralised location in the county, it naturally formed a locus point for further growth. Instead of developing a consistent policy that allowed for concentration of specific industries in certain areas, French policy focused on the aggregate. In other words, while key strategic industries were identified on a national basis, there was no corresponding regional or spatial policy that could allocate these industries. Therefore, industrial development remained fractured and many companies preferred to maintain their offices in areas where they were guaranteed close proximity to suppliers and customers. Faced with the growing employment crisis of the early 1980s, extra sources of finance were made available from the government to improve industrial sites in special development areas, ensure a rapid insertion of young people into the labour force and focus retraining of existing workers for new employment in modern industries or the tertiary sector.

Yet, all of this was done without much regard to the growing openness of the French economy to international competition and the 'national ability to compete on international grounds' (as the New Competition argument suggests) was never taken seriously into account. This resulted in a focus on 'domestic developmentalism' (to use Dore's phrase) as part of an inward-oriented growth and development policy.

The main point is that French governments did not really work on the 'shaping of markets' to provide new profitable opportunities that would not otherwise have existed. Instead, their focus appears to be more emphasising a decentralisation of the economy that would avoid spatial concentration of economic resources in important industries. To the extent that it worked, this actually corresponded to a decline in competitiveness. However, private decision-makers largely ignored this aspect of policy by maintaining and even increasing their concentration in and around Paris. This, of course, created other problems because it made other regions far too dependent on existing and declining industries and agriculture. Retraining efforts have too often focused on the near-term consequences of unemployment instead of attempting to develop training in a strategic manner that would match job skills in a region with job creation for that region.

Also, French governments have placed too much emphasis on the use of incentives and financial schemes that redirected marginal activities of firms to the hinterland, which made them vulnerable during economic downturns. Instead, France should have focused on the accelerators of development and growth, which would allow these depressed areas to catch up and become competitive in their own right. Indeed, the accelerators of development and growth must be considered as a thorough and necessary package of 'useful tools' for the promotion of outward-oriented economic growth, since these accelerators seem to be the main factors in determining the distribution among economies of new technology sectors. But in the face of growing unemployment, and the social and political pressure that this implies, strategic planning at the national level never went to the next step: to allocate these goals within a regional framework.

Less-developed regions and relatively depressed locations in France have seen slow growth of economic resources (e.g., education, skills, machinery, capital equipment, etc.) as a result of existing underutilisation of these same resources. After all, there is little incentive to increase resources when there is underutilised/unutilised capacity and labour in an area. This has also been exacerbated by the gravitation of higher level activities to Paris ('the power of attraction of the centre'). State investments in regions and rural areas should be designed to achieve the following:

1. add to the sum total of investment capital, technical development, training, current research, innovation and services available;
2. support and develop indigenous resources, firms and industries; and
3. add to the opportunities for regional/local growth, restructuring and social welfare.

In brief, the National Champions policy followed by French governments has reached its limit, since it has neither achieved a 'better distribution' of industry nor reduced regional disparities. This occurred because these firms did not improve their 'ability to compete on international grounds', thereby facing difficulties or operating unsuccessfully outside the national territory.

Moreover, French policy resulted in a spatial mismatch due to an inability to develop a regional strategy to allocate industries in a balanced and efficient manner.

Italian Regional and Industrial Policies

Since World War II, Italy has practiced a policy of regional planning and supportive government intervention within the context of a free market (King, 1987, p. 129). Regional planning has been focused on encouraging new factories to open and expand in the South to combat continuing high levels of out-migration and a decline in traditional industrial and agricultural employment. To the extent that the South has developed, it has been a dependent development, relying heavily on multinational capital and the North (King, 1977, pp. 87-102). This has resulted in an unbalanced spatial intensity as well as a high concentration within a narrow group of sectors, with 73 per cent of the jobs created by 1980 being accounted for by the chemical, metallurgical and mechanical branches, mostly in large, capital-intensive units (ISTAT, various issues). This large capital intensiveness of industry has done little to alleviate the problems of unemployment and disparities, and its focus on resource extraction is inherently unsustainable in the long-run. On the other hand, small and more labour-intensive firms in traditional industrial branches, such as food processing, wood products and textiles, have received only limited support (Giannola, 1982, pp. 67-92). Also, Southern growth has resulted, since 1957, mostly because of planned investments by state firms along with capital infusions from Northern Italy or abroad (King, 1987, p. 149; ISTAT, various issues). Little has been done, however, in the way of indigenous development.

In the 1970s, left-wing governments in various regions began to assert power in four areas: administrative organisation; social services; economic development; and planning matters (King, 1987, p. 160). However, Italy is a unitary, not a federal state, although the division is not as clear cut since the Italian constitution spells out a certain degree of autonomy for certain regions, like Sicily. The constitution further recognises administrative and legislative functions within these regions (Ziblatt, 2006).[2] This resulted in a certain degree of antagonism between the central administration and the regions, with consequences for the autonomy of regional policy-making and the financial independence of the regions. Consequently, the financial and bureaucratic structures of the central government have been reproduced at the regional level (Freddi, 1980, pp. 383-98). Moreover, the deep crisis in its national economic planning has provided no framework of priorities for action in the regions. Behind all else lies the objective of using development policy (which appeared to be a response to political pressure) as a means of recruiting political support for the ruling party, i.e., the Christian Democrats (Wade, 1979; Allum, 1980).

Italy (and especially its North-Central part) had a different experience. In general, Italian industrial policy has acted as a buffer against global crises and the compensation for structural characteristics of the domestic industrial and financial system. North-Central Italy (as distinct from the industrial North and the agricultural South of Italy) is based on groups of small entrepreneurial firms pursuing a strategy of continuous innovation and flexible production methods (Best, 1990, p. 87). A large number of cooperative institutions (mainly quasi-public development agencies) within North-Central Italy serve as functional equivalents to managerial hierarchy and contribute to the development of the industrial district as a collective entrepreneur. Even though North-Central Italy is led by internationally competitive, independent small firms, there has been a variety of forms of cooperation between firms, and between firms and government, which appear to have been economically successful. Inter-firm cooperation and an administrative governmental structure (that does not base decision-making authorities on ownership) are very important. Cooperation in the provision of services with substantial economies of scale has helped small industries maintain their independence in production.[3] North-Central Italy (as well as Japan) offers a new approach to the promotion of small and medium-size firms: both depend upon a combination of cooperation and competition, and both approaches seek to develop sector strategies and to promote innovation and R&D which will encourage firms to learn to cooperate (specialisation by activity) (Best, 1990, p. 118).

In the case of Italy, the government has adopted some elements of a developmental role. The Italian policies can be placed under headings 3 and 4 (identified by Dore, 1986). But the antagonistic relations between central administration and local governments (especially in the 1970s) have caused a deep crisis resulting in uncoordinated national and regional planning. This creates severe difficulties that limit the success of strategic planning of any sort since such planning involves 'conscious attempts by the government of a country – usually with the participation of other collective bodies – to coordinate public policies' (Myrdal, 1960, p. 15). As a result, there exists the possibility of intra-regional competition that serves to sap the resources of the regions and transfer them to firms that are able to cause the regions to bid against one another. This also hinders the national government's ability to develop goals and strategies and dynamically alter Italy's comparative advantage in a prudent and constructive manner. Consequently, the central government cannot provide a consistent developmental framework for action to firms and, especially, to regions. In contrast, the Developmental State literature suggests both the central administration and local governments have a significant and strategic role to play, because they can enhance the operation of the market system and create opportunities which would not otherwise have existed. This will only occur if they work together rather than against one another.

Centripetal market forces have generated uneven development between the North and the South of Italy, and cumulative causation has exacerbated regional disparities over time. The continued reliance of the South on resource extraction industries is a direct result of the inflow of financial capital from the North, which seeks to keep the South in the role of supplier rather than potential competitor. Since such resources tend to be priced by international markets rather than allowing for the creation of a certain degree of market power, the South is placed at a relative disadvantage to the North in the terms of trade. Besides, the lack of indigenous capital formation means that development tends to work for the benefit of the capital-sending region. In contrast, the Developmental State is concerned with offsetting such regional disparities and the lack of human and material resources, and attempts to generate the conditions for sustainable local growth. As planned investment in R&D and human resource development improves, renews and increases the productive capacity and competitiveness of an economy, investment flows will be undertaken based on the presence of economic opportunity for sustained growth in the locality rather than merely to acquire a financial inducement for a marginal operation.

The convergence of economic and political functions in the Italian State, along with an inability to form stable long-term governments at the national level (although for the first 50 years of its post-War existence, a coalition led by the Christian Democrats was in power for 44 of those 50 years) has had disastrous effects in the economic sphere. Given that the efficacy of 'pork barrel' intervention is questionable (even though the tenure of a Prime Minister was just 18 months in the post-War period to 1995), successive governments have attempted to use the state's power to promote particular interests for both personal and electoral advantage. This is in contrast to the Developmental State view, which sees strategic and developmental goals as serving a 'national purpose' as opposed to ones that are reducible to various political pressures and private interests. Indeed, it is the 'pork barrel' nature of various Italian economic policies along with an inability to adhere to thorough long-term planning because of the instability of various coalition governments that have resulted in the inability of the state to replicate the success of the North-Central region in other areas of the country.

Greek Regional and Industrial Policies

Greece has generally emphasised the need to improve infrastructure in its regional policies. This was done to ensure that local populations are able to find employment without having to migrate to greater Athens or overseas. Thus, regions developed around growth centres that would provide medical, social and cultural facilities for the populations in the area. Linkages to the outside world were developed through the improvement of transportation and communication networks as well as banking facilities. Power and water supplies have been improved; so, the populace has the basic infrastructure necessary to carry out business, and educational facilities have sprung up to ensure stability of the population (*Statistical Yearbook of Greece*, various issues).

From the 1960s until about 1980, Greece pursued an active regional development policy through the use of grants, tax concessions and low interest rates, and with the objective of steering private investment spending into regional incentive schemes to lessen the burdens of over-population on Greater Athens. However, none of these policies were undertaken as a legal framework for government policy-making. Instead, they tended to be *ad hoc* in nature and were carried out either on the basis of social equity or economic efficiency based on specific needs and political pressures (Carter, 1987, p. 429).

In the 1980s, in the aftermath of Greece accession to the EC, the Greek Government found itself in a better position to financially boost investment and development in the economy. In order to accelerate decentralisation, promote regional socio-economic development and encourage greater co-ordination in government administration, the character of regional assistance changed. Instead of merely looking at regional development in the context of infrastructure, greater importance was given to technological and other factors for financing technical centres, as well as industrial and agricultural cooperatives. Investments were geared towards increased production and applied research, and to projects that made use of new technology (Carter, 1987, p. 430). Government grants ranged from 10 per cent to 50 per cent of a project's cost, depending on its location and a combination of pre-determined socio-economic and commercial standards. For the purpose of investment policy, the country was divided into four zones (no grants were available in zone A; zones B, C and D – the undeveloped frontier area – got grants ranging from 10 per cent to 25 per cent, 15 per cent to 40 per cent, and 20 per cent to 50 per cent of project investment costs respectively). The government also decentralised the process to encourage greater local and regional participation, and the central administration now had to work hand in hand with the local officials instead of dictating policy to them. Hence, since 1981, Greece has moved closer to a developmentalist approach to regional policy.

Recently, during the period 1996-2004, the Greek Socialist Government pursued Developmental State-type policies: planned large-scale investments in infrastructure and the accelerators of development and competitiveness;

technically proficient planning; and comprehensive regional and industrial strategies and policies. But since 2004, the new Conservative Government has been pursuing neoliberal policies with undesirable social and economic consequences (e.g., deterioration of the country's economic performance). Some also argue that this is a return to similar policies pursued before 1981, where perfect competition was seen as bringing benefits to Greek consumers and state intervention was limited to the elimination of market imperfections as well as the provision of public goods.

On balance, however, the policies pursued have been a varying mixture of the four types of policies identified by Dore (1986). But 'pork barrel' politics have been a problem for Greek governments because state policies often relate to satisfaction of strong and influential private interests. Indeed, one of the major shortcomings of modern Greek political economy has been the substitution of personal and electoral interests in place of the national interest. Such parochial undertakings have had the direct effect of making politicians look good but harming the economy.

Greek economic policy has also suffered from a lack of strategic vision. Instead, it emphasises a short-term perspective to alleviate social concerns of a temporary nature as opposed to dealing with structural problems. In addition, there are limited attempts to correct technical inefficiencies, and R&D expenditure in Greece is very low resulting in failures to develop and use new products and processes. But this limited R&D expenditure is often squandered by harmful inter-firm competition (rather than cooperation), so that specialisation by activity fails to occur. The lack of strategic vision also means that sector-based development strategies that promote innovation, skills and R&D have failed to materialise because there has been a lack of coordination across phases in the production chain. As a result, Greece has never been able to acquire 'the competitive lead that accompanies problem-solving at times of rapid technological change' (Best, 1990, p. 16).

Greek governments have tended to place too much emphasis on financial incentives, which often encourage the establishment of marginal enterprises in depressed areas and result in increased instability in employment levels, in addition to a withering of the general competitiveness of industry in the locality. After all, if one company receives a subsidy, this means that there is less money to go around to other businesses or that the other companies (in some cases, businesses that are in competition with the subsidised company) have to pay higher taxes. This leads to the perversity of incentive schemes wherein more successful firms are taxed to help laggards that are incapable of maturing into profitable enterprises.

Besides, the Greek governments have not emphasised the importance of government investments on the modern factors of growth and development (e.g., R&D, on-the-job and institutional training and re-training, innovation, etc.). Consequently, instead of improving production capacity and local competitiveness, the result has been the opposite: Athens has received the bulk of investment spending whereas the less-developed locales in Greece have suffered from underutilisation of resources and inadequate resource growth. To alleviate these issues, government investments in regions and rural areas should be designed to achieve the following:

1. add to the sum total of investment capital, current research, R&D, technical development, training, innovation and services available;
2. support and develop indigenous resources, firms and industries; and
3. enhance opportunities for local growth, restructuring, rejuvenation and repositioning, as well as social welfare.

In order to combat the forces of cumulative causation and centripetalism that have served to sustain and perpetuate inequalities and disparities across regions in Greece, a strategic planning approach, rather than a short-term approach based on political expediency, is necessary (Cowling, 1990). Such a radical approach can provide the essential requirements for a supply-side strategy that would solve deeper structural problems.

An Overall Evaluation

Overall, most regional and industrial policies in the EC/EU area have been based on market failure analysis, and most government interventions have taken the form of *ad hoc* responses to pressing problems. Evidently, the policies pursued by European governments have failed to achieve a 'better balance' in the geographic distribution of industry and have led to increases, rather than reductions, in regional disparities. The forces of cumulative causation have operated at both the level of the firm and the aggregate level of a region or nation breeding success and failure.

Moreover, while politicians will score political points by having a large international corporation open a plant in an area, the resultant siphoning of funds from local enterprises can result in an actual reduction in jobs overall. However, few recognise this because the international corporation provides a good number of jobs whereas the losses are triggered by the closing or reductions in labour of only a few persons in each of hundreds of firms. On balance, employment may be reduced but this is 'unseen' by the media and politicians and could be even dismissed as characteristic of the standard movement of the business cycle. Voters ought to be wondering how it is that large megaprojects that generate a number of jobs keep appearing in their areas but the overall unemployment rate may remain stubbornly high. The answer is that it is the politicisation of regional policies that do the most harm to society.

Since the 1980s, the shift to 'less' state did not work as intended. 'One difficulty in the reform process has been that the advocates of reforms have assumed that "one size fits all" and that any [EU] government could be improved by the institutionalisation of their preferred new pattern' (Peters, 1996, pp. 17-18). Besides, the current orthodox perspective (the 'third way' since the late 1990s) that has focused on monetary policy over fiscal policy, on low inflation rather than unemployment, and on labour market 'reforms' over industrial policies has only exacerbated these problems. At least in the economic field, it can be seen as a retreat from any notion of developmental intervention (which had, to some extent, informed industrial policies before).

Existing economic difficulties, and fiscal pressures in particular, are making governments more prepared to tackle difficult institutional issues than would be the case in more normal times. At the same time, the current conditions in European economies may increase the potential advantages of pursuing governed-market policies, thereby bringing seriously the 'nation-state back to business'. As the pressures for increased liberalisation grow, the policy problem of operationalising an appropriate role for the state in European economies intensifies. But in the absence of rational and realistic foundations, those who seek to use mainstream theoretical premises are led to adopt a dismal view of government's active involvement, beyond some minimalist level, and suggest state action being neutral, rather than active or sensitive to any 'special cases'.

In Europe, therefore, it seems inevitable that the leading and supportive 'visible hand' of the entrepreneurial type of state must extend its strategy and scope beyond the World Bank's prescriptive box, since proactive state policy and its associated multiplier effects can be used to 'crowd in' private spending and promote sustained economic growth, endogenous competency and competitiveness. European governments must be proactive and require firms to invest in new production facilities, skills training and upgrading, and critical kinds of science and technology initiatives. There will probably be less room for financial incentives, protection and nurturing of firms, and specific subsidisation in the future. Still, government can act as a catalyst for growth through expenditure on R&D, education and infrastructure, and by ensuring that these direct incentives are compatible with the strategic industries they seek to foster.

Clearly, governments have placed too much faith in the ability of private firms to stimulate industrial growth, competency and regeneration, forgetting that the pursuit of profit is the sole goal of such companies. Unless goals and interests are properly aligned, there cannot be a meeting of the two, and this misalignment has translated into polarisation rather than balanced regional growth. However, markets need competent and appropriate governments to work at all, given that the state is fundamental to social and economic development as a partner, catalyst and facilitator. What is more important is that government be efficient, facilitative and appropriate to its circumstances rather than merely 'small'. Therefore, what really matters is not the 'extent' of government intervention but the 'quality' of such intervention.

Moreover, research suggests countries that do best in the global arena are those which can manage change and use their institutional arrangements to protect their national economies from international vagaries and disorder (e.g., Tyson, 1992; Singh, 1995; Boyer and Drache, 1996; Chang, 1998; Karagiannis, 2002 – among others).[4] Contrary to the current orthodoxy, developmentally-driven institutional structures and political purposes may better be achieved by an active state (as a capable corporate agent) which approximates the Developmental State model (ideally, but not necessarily, the 'Western democratic' type). This might be the best viable development policy option left for European nations.

ELEMENTS OF DEVELOPMENTAL INTERVENTION

The experiences of Europe and East Asia point to the key fact that the state plays an important role in shaping the social and economic milieu under which we all operate. If it does so in a developmental way, it can actively and adequately contribute to development, whereas if it cedes this role to the 'free' market, it will find that its economy will be shaped by 'external' forces that may unleash a system that is not representative of the type of society in which its citizens wish to live.

There are actually four different roles that the state needs to achieve through its budget: allocation, stabilisation, distribution and development and, in fulfilling the fourth of these tasks, it can generate structural change that would allow it to have a greater pie to allocate, distribute and stabilise. Still, the view that the state is the 'main engine' of economic development, structural change and the process of policy reform, inevitably raises the important issue of state capability and capacity (Ahrens, 1997, p. 114). As Evans (1992, p. 141) argues: 'the consistent pursuit of any policies, whether they are aimed at "getting prices right" or implanting local industry, requires the enduring institutionalisation of a complex set of political machinery'.

In the new millennium, therefore, the role of government in adapting to and managing change is crucial, even though this role is constrained in its possible actions due to the pressures of globalisation and other forces. It might be necessary to 'refine' the role of government to achieve objectives using alternative methods, since the Developmental State is about outcomes and results rather than processes. Therefore, by taking into consideration the importance of institutions as well as the environment and incentives they create, governments can use a range of instruments to utilise the 'creative dynamics' of the market forces while, at the same time, guiding them. In addition to international competition, it is the organisational design of, and the incentives within, the government and the institutions linking the public and private sectors (i.e., the institutional environment) that are crucial to the developmental consequences of state policies. In fact, effective economic policies not only require credible commitment but crucially depend on the administrative, technical, and political capacity and efficiency of policy-makers (Ahrens, 1997, pp. 115-17). Indeed, different kinds of state structures create different capacities for action. 'Structures define the range of roles that the state is capable of playing. Outcomes depend both on whether the roles fit the context and on how well they are executed' (Evans, 1995, p. 11).

The outline of the above argument could be essentially recapitulated in four points (Ahrens, 1997, p. 118):

1. the ability to [both] craft and adopt specifically tailored institutional structures is as important to effective governance as the formulation of policies;
2. effective governance structures and hence developmental outcomes depend on the roles that policy-makers pursue as well as the general character of state structure;
3. while the initiation of politico-economic reforms may be facilitated by discretionary authority of government, political institutions and elites that insulate policy-making from distributive claims of interest groups, their consolidation requires stabilised expectations regarding a new set of incentive structures as well as the confidence that these cannot be discretionarily altered; and
4. policies need to match institutions and vice versa.

What will modern interventionism be like in the twenty-first century? At the very moment when post-World War II institutions are being reassessed and partially reformed under the pressures of international competition, anti-Keynesian political programmes, liberalisation and deregulation, modern interventionist and radical analysis holds that the state remains the most powerful institution to channel and tame the power of markets. As the goal now is to make government action better through *reinvention*, the nature of government involvement has changed (and is likely to change further). Even though prediction of any kind has risks, there are some characteristics of 'modern' developmental intervention (which European governments should pay particular attention to in the next century) compared to the 'old' one.

First, modern developmental intervention needs to be socially sensitive and egalitarian in Europe, which requires governments to maintain adequate social services and promote the well-being of citizens. Only by meeting the real, basic needs of a wide spectrum of the population will any development strategy succeed. More than this, however, the implementation of social programmes has broad potential implications in terms of the whole set of goals of national development. For example, there is wide agreement that well-planned social programmes are important components of successful economic growth. Consequently, while proficient social programmes can be important causal components of economic growth, economic growth can also be a foundation for the expansion of social programmes (MacEwan, 1999, pp. 176-7).

Whether or not the expansion of social programmes enhances economic growth and has an impact on overall productivity depends on the way social programmes are constructed and on the particular social programmes that are emphasised. On the other hand, it is useful to recognise – and practice would suggest that it is not as obvious as it seems – that the expansion of social programmes may not necessarily lead to economic growth or other desirable ends. They might instead simply act as redistributors of wealth and, if implemented too widely, may create disincentives to undertake risk or to higher productivity.

Therefore, spending on education, health, and public transportation have a more beneficial effect on future economic progress than provisions of unemployment insurance and welfare (although the later two have important safety net features). Indeed, even the best shaped social programmes (in terms of achieving a more productive workforce) are likely to have limited impact on economic growth, skills or national competitiveness if the overall development strategy fails to incorporate growth-generating policies and competency-inducing plans. It does little good to provide training for jobs that may never materialise. The macroeconomic framework is one set of such policies, and the means to shape the private sector activity are another (MacEwan, 1999, p. 195).

Second, there should be increased focus on improving relations between the governments and private sectors in the European Union. Governments might seek to ensure the evolution of institutional frameworks characterised by integrated and dynamic public and private sector partnerships with the capacity to capitalise on strategic and tactical alliances. Rather than seeing each other as antagonistic, government and industry should focus on ways that they can cooperate to achieve mutually satisfactory results. In fact, the public and private sectors can cooperate in a range of different arrangements, each contributing what it does best and both participating in the financial returns within the context of socially defined agendas. When government sets the agenda and the returns, it can enhance the operation of markets and create opportunities that would not otherwise exist.

Third, strategic state intervention is necessary. Traditional government bureaucracies need to emphasise forward thinking that will survive changes in government instead of ceding this responsibility to the politicians under the guise that it is a 'political' decision (Hughes, 1998, p. 149). The notion of strategic intervention is one that takes the long-term view rather than the short-term 'win the next election' approach, which is often associated with government.

Markets are complex dynamic structures that must be shaped, moulded and regulated. While there are systemic arguments for relying on the creative dynamics of the market forces to play a centrally important role in modern economies, there are also parallel arguments for imposing on these market forces coherent strategies, within which they are allowed to operate. Hence, strategic planning could be seen as promoting 'national purpose goals' in European economies, and the mandate of 'a European-type' Developmental State should contain the following goals:

1. to provide a sense of overall direction to the overall evolution of the local economy;
2. to manage effectively the dynamic mixture of inward and outward orientation; and
3. to channel capital into those sectors identified as priorities.

The essence of strategy is to achieve results. The role of strategy is to try to specify what the results should be and to set out how achievements aggregate into the overall purpose ('national purpose' in the case of Japan and NICs). Strategic planning gives direction and purpose to government organisations; without strategy, state policy-making is subject to temporary concerns. In fact, it is the planning process not the plan itself which is more important, and the use of long-term parameters allows the public institutions from top management down to develop a shared vision for the future.

Although the nature of planning is all important, it must not get involved with the operational detail. The market system may carry out the operational details of industry better than central planners. Indeed, government should provide the goals and priorities and set the ground rules but let the market system carry out the details. Planning should be strategic, proficient and proactive rather than passive; selective rather than comprehensive; but wherever possible based on broad consensus (Cowling, 1990, pp. 16-17).

Fourth, accountability between the administration of government and the political system is critical. An accountability system would be required by European governments, since the two forms of accountability, political and managerial, are tightly related (even though this link has often been problematic). 'The system of accountability is what ties the administrative part of government with the political part and ultimately to the public itself' (Hughes, 1998, p. 225).

In the traditional, bureaucratic public administration there is some form of accountability which seeks to avoid errors than achieve outcomes (but also leads to inefficiency). This form of accountability relies upon the formal links provided through hierarchy (Hughes, 1998, p. 233). Hence, improving accountability should be a specific aim of the move towards developmental intervention. Effective institutions of political authority in EU countries would then be responsible for the effective execution of strategic plans and monitoring the progress of these plans as well as for their own performance. In fact,

> [I]nstitutions can formalise the commitment to such [developmental strategies], and their structure, procedures and personnel can act to ensure that such commitments cannot easily be reversed, but they are simply ratifying plans already established. The history of planning [in several European states] shows how fragile was the commitment, despite the creation of many new institutions, [and the lack of teeth of these institutions was obvious]. With clear goals, and a determination to pursue them, institutions with teeth should be forthcoming. (Cowling, 1990, p. 23)

State effectiveness depends on the coherence of state policies, which requires state autonomy. Otherwise, the state is beholden to 'pork barrel' policies and influential interests. European governments should eliminate external pressure on appointments and political patronage, so as to be more effective, and increase the degree of 'relative insulation' or 'autonomy' from surrounding social and political pressure (Wade, 1990, p. 375).

Fifth, various capacity-building programmes and public sector reforms have often been introduced without systematic and disciplined diagnoses of institutional capacities. This results in wasted investment, inadequate levels of skill and competence, ineffectiveness and performance shortcomings. The economic success in Japan and the Asian NICs required both competent technostructures and developmental elites in economic and social planning. Therefore, government should acquire the best and brightest to generate a strategic vision by paying competitive salaries and providing opportunities for advancement. After all,

> the executive technostructures must be in a position to recruit from among the best and the brightest people of outstanding talent based on meritocratic criteria. Once the central bureaucracy acquires a reputation for attracting the most competent and talented, the system can develop a momentum of its own. It continues to attract such people (even at lower salaries than the private sector) because selection is based on meritocracy. Its personnel can be motivated by the belief that what they are doing promotes the national development and welfare. This sense of 'national mission' can motivate the executive technostructure to use its powers in line with 'national purpose' goals. The more the government intends to intervene and to play a leading role, the more important are professionalism, motivation, authority, staffing and the responsibilities of the central core. (Wade, 1990, p. 371)

Hence, capacity building and competence are important strategic goals that determine the extent and pace of changes within institutions and public sectors in European nations. Institution-building measures to develop fiscal, managerial and intellectual resources should be a part of state efficiency initiatives as opposed to simply attempting to reduce the size and scope of government. Investments in human resource development (i.e., high quality and timely education, training, and the continuous development of scientific manpower and expertise) will modernise governments and lead to more effective state action.

Sixth, any such thorough state intervention requires more efficient use of resources. Hence, programmes that most assist the attainment of strategic objectives need to take priority. Infrastructure needs and development of intellectual and social capital, as opposed to unnecessary and non-essential government spending, need to be emphasised. Government may not need to spend more public funds; it must just make more efficient use of its limited resources by redistributing wisely existing/available funds from unnecessary consumption and transfer payments to government investment.

Moreover, with the advent of modern information technology, the need for a highly centralised public administration with paper as the focal point of communicating became obsolete. With the computer, electronic mail, the internet, satellite transmission and fax machines, new communication tools are widely used. This might lead to reductions in clerical staffing levels and/or dislocations in the work force of public organisations and institutions. However, these reductions and dislocations may be inevitable but should be based on 'rational', efficient and effective human resource management and planning. For instance, less employees (but well-educated and well-trained) may replace those civil servants who retire or resign. Such a decision and policy action is expected to bring about twofold benefits: it will improve skills, expertise, efficiency, competence and operations quality, especially when combined with better utilisation of modern technology; and it will release resources for higher levels of government investment (which will improve the environment for more productive activities to take place within European economies).

CONCLUSIONS

It is clear from the preceding survey of regional and industrial policies in a number of EC countries that each government's ability to pursue supply-side policies has faced specific limitations (for example, on the use of state subsidies); therefore, both demand management and supply-side policies are necessary.

The development of regional and industrial policy in the EU has been the subject of a number of conflicting forces. It was argued above that there are different traditions among the Member Countries, although the Treaty of Rome and the Single European Act tend to support more the Anglo-Saxon anti-trust approach. In complete contrast, the Developmental State and the New Competition views clearly suggest a more interventionist approach.

It also needs to be mentioned that a description of the objectives of a single government at a given moment of time would be difficult enough; long-term developmental plans are needed. Although the EU is essentially an economic Community, its political dimension should also be taken into account since, in many cases, the underlying political aims may be opposed to the explicit economic goals. In the long run, political will should not be an obstacle for each individual Member Country nor for the EU as a whole.

NOTES

1. See: 1a. Office of the Minister for Science, *Report of the Committee on the Management and Control of Research and Development* [Zuckerman Report], 1961, London, HMSO; and CSO, *Research and Development Expenditure*, 1973, London, HMSO;
   1b. Department of Trade and Industry, *The Machine Tool Industry. Report of the Machine Tool Expert Committee*, 1971, p. 76, London, HMSO;
   1c. Department of Industry, *Survey of the United Kingdom Aerospace Industry*, 1975, London, HMSO;
   1d. Shipbuilding Industry Board, *Shipbuilding Industry Board 1967-1971*, 1971, London; and Department of Trade and Industry, *British Shipbuilding 1972*, 1973, London, HMSO; and,
   1e. Department of Trade and Industry, *Industrial and Regional Development*, Cmnd 4942, 1972, London, HMSO; Treasury, *An Approach to Industrial Strategy*, Cmnd 6315, 1975, London, HMSO; 'Criteria for Assistance to Industry', Appendix A to Department of Industry, *Industry Act 1972. Annual Report for the Year Ending March 31*, 1976, London, HMSO.
2. The 2001 amendments to the Italian Constitution specify that the regions and the central authority have equal 'dignity'; this recognition of regions as not being necessarily subordinate to the central government is a further step in the development of a nascent Italian federalism.
3. A similar outcome is found in the Mondragon cooperative; the Basque group of independent companies is the second largest worker cooperative in the world.
4. The rapid development of Japan, South Korea and Taiwan, though fostered by Developmental States, occurred by sheltering emerging industries in the early stages from the global economy. Those economies may have pursued policies more in the direction of export promotion than import substitution; however, their domestic markets were protected. Foreign investments were controlled and capital flows limited.

12. The Relevance of the Developmental State Today

So we have come full circle. The lessons of the developmental state remain as vital as they ever were and the lessons of the East Asian meltdown can now be seen in their proper context. The developmental state is decidedly *not* a paradigm to be employed by all nations at all times. Instead, it is a very Listian idea that is to be employed during periods when the nation-state is playing the proverbial 'catch-up' necessary to become a developed nation. At the same time, parts of the developmental state are also necessary for *all* modern governments regardless of their state of development. What we shall do in this chapter is examine which concepts particular to the developmental state are to be employed at which state of development.

The first, and most clear, lesson to be learned is that development is a dynamic process that cannot occur in a vacuum. It must be part of a general programme to lift society and, therefore, needs to touch upon and address all aspects of the nation-state: culturally, politically, socially and economically. It must be a holistic approach that addresses the Veblenian dichotomy: showcasing the fundamental duality of institutions as both ceremonial and productive. To the extent that the institution glorifies the past at the expense of future growth, it serves to retard progress. Yet, it is the very stability of the institutional structure that allows productive change to occur. People are resistant to change and only with the confines of such institutions could technological progress be realised successfully. Thus, the development process draws upon the nation's cultural, political and social traditions to craft an economically successful programme.

There is much to be said, for example, of the harnessing of the so-called 'Protestant work ethic' but equally clear is that this step forward was not unique to the culture: it simply allowed the culture to breathe life into the economy because it was not inimical to growth in that sphere. Similarly, Islamic countries need to address growth from an Islamic standpoint, crafting laws that produce similar results within a cultural context that does not allow for the widespread and wholesale importation of Western ideas. Instead, each concept needs to be taken apart and redefined for the culture in which it will be placed.

As we saw, the Chinese and Japanese did this by appealing not to Western economic traditions but to decidedly Eastern ones. The institutions in East Asia responded to the threat of external economic dominance not by copying the West but by adapting to it, creating a unique system that was concerned with traditional Confucian values such as loyalty to society, family and the nation, as opposed to methodological individualism. In doing so, it insured that growth did not follow the so-called Kuznets Curve wherein economic inequality increased with growth, only to fall again after a point of inflection wherein the inequality becomes inconsistent with that increase in economic activity (Kuznets, 1955). While Western countries grew predominantly by directing gains from economic activity towards the formation of physical capital, only to be caught in later years by the need to expand human and social capital and thus required the broadening of economic activity to all sectors of the nation, those nations that engage in the developmental state have traditionally attempted to expand all three prongs of the economic trident that propels growth. All individuals in society marched as the rising tide raised all ships.

The necessity of such an approach in modern economic development cannot be understated: when the West was rapidly industrialising, there were no other models of economic activity that had successfully created a living standard by which the public could make invidious distinctions. Although it was true that certain members in the same society were now wealthier, it was by no means clear that one could simply move to another location to gain an economic advantage, such as can be done today. One's station in life was more akin to a lock-in and thus the acceptance that some would prosper now so that others might prosper later might have been feasible in the democratic context. However, modern governments face a fundamental tension: those individuals who could most contribute to growth are also those who are most able to leave. As such, power tends to concentrate and the masses do not receive the benefits. Only by trying to reduce tensions which exist when inequality is allowed to breed can a nation overcome such defects and maintain a steady growth pattern.

Each philosophy has its high water points and also the points at which it is plunged into the depths. When the culture becomes resistant to change, when it no longer contributes to the growth of the nation, it must alter but it must also do so in a way that does not destroy its essential character. The Japanese and South Koreans used a decidedly oligopolistic model of growth that ultimately met its demise due to an inability to meet their fundamental societal obligations to full employment. Essentially, the culture was created of loyalty first to the Emperor, later to the nation, and more recently to the corporation, which was cut, however, because of a failure to live by the Confucian ideal of reciprocal responsibility. It was not enough that the workers pledged their loyalty to corporation and nation when the social orderings in society failed to exercise their proper responsibility to the individuals in the society itself.

We see this time and again: Jamaica experienced a period of social and human capital creation but failed to create the necessary outlets for the development of physical capital through the imposition of onerous taxes during the Manley era. Also, it has fundamentally failed in recent years to honour the ultimate commitment to the people: to create a safe environment for such formation by ensuring social order and a sense of justice. Europe has torn down the wall of Communism but failed to replace it with a social safety net that can adequately capture those left behind in the transition. Yet, the economies of Hong Kong, Singapore and Taiwan have, thus far, avoided these traps by balancing the needs of society and the individual through a process that acts as a power-neutralising entity.

Another key lesson applicable to all states at all stages of development is that the state should engage in the formation of social and human capital as well as pave the way for proper capital formation. Neoliberals argue that creating a minimal state should do this. They are the Jeffersonians to the Developmental State's Hamiltons. 'Government is best that governs the least' is their mantra and they view government action with suspicion, if not outright hostility. Their goal is to get the 'prices right', privatise state-run enterprises, balance fiscal budgets, remain neutral on incentives, reduce and/ or eliminate regulatory oversight, conform to international standards in intellectual property rights, and allow firms to act on the basis of world factor prices to properly allocate scarce resources.

It is a recipe that plays out neatly in the elegantly crafted models based on perfect competition, constant returns to scale, diminishing marginal returns to capital and labour, no externalities, all wrapped up with static technology. However, the real world is one based on imperfect competition, externalities galore, increasing returns to scale, increasing marginal returns to both capital and labour (at least over some range of output), and dynamic technology. In other words, orthodox development theory is a fairy tale told to neoclassical economists so that they don't have to deal with the real world.

In recent years, endogenous growth theory has incorporated many of these criticisms, and the result is a movement towards the developmental state argument. As there are significant public goods aspects to private investment in (both) human and social capital formation, and some degree of externalities are found even in physical capital formation, government investment in the underlying infrastructure can yield significant benefits (Todaro, 2000, pp. 100-101). In recognising market failures, the presence of incomplete information, and imperfect capital, labour and product markets, the World Bank (1993) has sought a market-friendly approach to economic development.

We concur that such investments in education, housing, transportation, medical care and child care are an important step in the right direction, but much more needs to be done too. One cannot abandon the use of selective instruments, the traditional developmental state policy of 'picking winners and losers'.

There are also some key considerations that reflect a particular period in industrialisation. The picking of winners and losers through industrial policy depends on the development of the nation. When the country is far behind, it can engage in some forms of infant industry protectionism. However, the drawback to such efforts is that the infant industries sometimes do not grow up, relying on that subsidy for years to come. Instead, a better strategy is to provide broad-based infrastructure and human capital formation support through the public purse. The state becomes the risk-guarantor. Indeed, this is the very core of the developmental state. Just as parents nurture their children, so too does the state nurture the economy, providing capital only when it is absolutely necessary and doing so in a way that augments and reinforces the market mechanism rather than replaces it. The goal is to be 'market-augmenting', not 'market-replacing'.

In addition, a better strategy than the picking of winners is the selection of losers. It is clear that while East Asia did a little of both, it is only because of the high degree of savings that existed in the economy that it could afford to 'pick winners'. Most countries do not have this luxury. Jamaica, for example, is debilitated with a carrying cost of debt equal to more than half of the 30 per cent plus of GDP that the government takes in every year. Just to pay yesterday's bills requires that a considerable amount of current GDP is extracted from the economy, leaving precious little to subsist on. Besides, direct payments are not as effective as tax expenditures, providing tax credits for favoured activities (Okimoto, 1989).

At the same time, the choice of what sectors to emphasise must be made with a clear understanding of the role of the political, social, historical, cultural, philosophical, religious and economic realities and linkages in the broader society as well as an appreciation of the likely reaction of trading partners. One must determine at which stage of development one is and how best to reach the next stage of development. It is in this arena that coordination of investment decisions with various trading partners needs to be made. The goal is to attract capital from 'dying' industries in wealthier, more advanced trading partners and throw off one's own 'dying' industries to those nations further down the trade cycle chain. In addition, it may be better to follow the lead of industry and guide the market towards its natural tendencies as opposed to trying to fashion a policy directly at odds with investment decisions made in the private sector. Governments can influence the development of competitive advantage but not unilaterally create it (Wade, 1990; Porter, 1990).

One does not decide to try to dominate the Internet when one has difficulty providing even basic electrification and phone service. A country does not seek to hang on to labour-intensive industries that offer low pay when moving to the ranks of middle or high-income countries.

At first, one can pick likely infant industries (usually dynamic industries of high potential) and provide through a combination of selective policies and infrastructure development the environment for a successful incubation period; but this period must always be fund- and time-limited and, from the start, the support given must be available to all participants in the nascent industry that provides employment to the nationals of the country. Indeed, by providing positive incentives for firms to contribute to the development and social goals of the government, market and state can work together and thus leverage each other's relative strengths in a process that is market-augmenting, rather than replacing the market.

The governments of East Asia had plans in place to promote and retard growth in specific sectors of the economy. They provided the necessary technical and administrative support and used a variety of tools to increase or reduce opportunities for expansion in various market sectors (Amsden, 1989; Wade, 1990). As highlighted in the section on Singapore, this often took the form of capital manipulation of investment decisions so as to guide companies towards long-term strategies that are not inimical to the interests of the whole country.

To some extent, these entities also coordinated investment activity between various groups within industries. But where Japan and South Korea went wrong was the wholesale and broad-based partnership between certain industrial giants and the nation-state. In so doing, they allowed for developmental capture wherein the needs of the corporations instead of the needs of the nation became paramount. While there are some industries (like aircraft and vehicle production) that benefit immensely from increased concentration of productive capacity, there are many others (like computer software) where such concentration may prove unhealthy because it limits the ability of the corporation to react quickly to changing circumstances. Simultaneously, a culture of competition between entities is always healthy and needs to be a priority from within the nation-state.

One clear lesson, however, is that the state coordination of investment solved the 'animal spirits' dilemma noted by Keynes. All of the East Asian high-growth economies shared a common base of high levels of savings. Government through the building of infrastructure that would otherwise have had to be provided by the private sector translated these savings into productive investment. Where the nation provides the infrastructure it also owns it, and the general twin policies of access and accountability found within the government sector provided an equal playing field for all players, both large and small. Government investment was significantly higher in

Japan and the four tigers than in the developed world or the rest of the developing world. In fact, East Asian public expenditure tended to centre on investment decisions, as opposed to consumption or transfer payments, as a percentage of overall government expenditure. Even for relatively thrifty governments, such as Hong Kong, the share of government expenditure devoted to government investment is much higher than its counterparts among similar high-income economies. Simultaneously, East Asia tends to spend more on research and development on a per capita basis than the rest of the developed world, but most of this is performed by the private sector. The traditional emphasis in the West is to have a large percentage (in some cases exceeding 50 per cent) of research and development being in the hands of the government due to research performed in state-run institutions of higher education, the military and government think tanks. With less spending on infrastructural needs as well as lower payments for workers owing to the development of comprehensive medical care, transportation systems and government-provided or subsidised housing, industry in East Asia can concentrate on improvements in their product line. R&D spending by governments tends to focus on large-scale infrastructure projects, and the model of development that is based upon incremental as opposed to revolutionary changes in product quality means that companies typically take less risk even though they spend more funds on research.

Strategic repositioning based on changes in the global economy occurs regularly and in consultations between state and industry. Government-sponsored research tends to have broad application; but it is up to industry to translate these applications into commercial products. Policy tends to focus on broad initiatives that allow industry to craft responses to changing market circumstances. Thus, Japan was able to enter the car market and move more nimbly than Detroit in response to changes in the market power of OPEC. While Detroit was satisfied with maintaining its lead in so-called 'muscle cars' and moved slowly to embrace fuel efficiency during the first oil shock, Japan responded much faster. The fundamental difference in approach is that, while East Asian firms look at long-term policies, US companies focus on hitting the profit benchmark each quarter. Part of this is, no doubt, the result of a concerted effort among governments in East Asia to control inflation and ensure low interest rates for capital formation.

However, the aspect of cumulative causation cannot be overlooked. The fact is that market forces cause disparities in job creation and growth that are region and sector-specific (Prices and Income Commission, 1969). The goal, therefore, of the developmental state is to smooth out these disparities so that they do not translate into social disorder.

THE PROBLEM OF UNBALANCED GROWTH

The relative weakness of countries to conduct a coherent developmental state policy may be complicated by the presence of unbalanced growth in their economies. Unbalanced growth carries with it several important problems for the economy in the context of globalisation. First, it impacts negatively the tax base of the localities, which are at a disadvantage, and therefore reduces their tax capacity. As a result, localities which wish to generate equivalent amounts of revenue must increase their tax effort.[1] Growth pole policies can create incentives for certain regions to cause higher rates of inflation and others to generate low rates of inflation. However, the reality of increased fiscal pressures on governments at all levels will lead inevitably to a reduction in the national grants to regions which are at the heart of the argument to be put forward later.

Second, politically, one may find it difficult to abandon the notion that regional disparities are a problem (e.g., Brewis, 1969; Richardson, 1979; Armstrong and Taylor, 1993) even though some have argued that little of real consequence has been done about them (Bickerton, 1990) or that the policies to address these issues have failed (Phillips, 1978). Politicians tend to react with political solutions to the economic problem. Thus, we get 'megaprojects' such as Newfoundland's Hibernia oil project, the Bricklin car project in New Brunswick, and the Venture gas field in Nova Scotia, or various policies that run counter to the natural development of industry like the policy implemented in Canada's Newfoundland to try to develop greenhouses which were going to grow cucumbers in the province. Such actions should not surprise us. Megaprojects are politically 'sexier' than more mundane forms of regional policy. They create excellent photo opportunities, provide a concrete and highly visible example of federal and provincial action, and readily employ large numbers of workers. However (as in the above examples), they often have little basis in efficient economic activity.

Third, important regional differences often lead to interregional migration. Such migration has severe consequences in that it is often the young and better skilled who can make this transition, leading to a 'brain drain' from poorer provinces similar to that experienced by Third World countries in addition to creating greater social problems for poorer provinces as they are left with a greater percentage of 'unemployables' than richer provinces.

Fourth, there is an impact on richer provinces. As individuals continue to congregate in more prosperous areas, they demand more services and cause strains on the social and economic systems of the areas experiencing immigration, while similarly providing for the underutilisation of these systems in areas where emigration is occurring (Holland, 1976, pp. 27-8). Costs include greater pollution (Richardson, 1979, pp. 144-5); redistribution payments (Phillips, 1978, p. 23); relocation costs to migrants, including the non-pecuniary costs (Armstrong and Taylor, 1993, pp. 120-21); and the increased time to commute.

Fifth, we have a problem of political power. If individuals emigrate from one region to another, it causes a corresponding change in the political power of the region. The greater the concentration of individuals in an area, the more likely that they will be able to use the governmental structures to 'rig' policies which benefit them. As the individual's desires for political action change relative to where he or she is, the result will be an increase in the relative power of the richer regions over time, both economically and politically. This has had a profound impact on at least one 'have-not' province in Canada, Quebec, in its agitation over the loss of its ability to protect and promote its French culture due to the declination of its political strength. It has also placed strains in the context of China's development resulting in massive displacement of individuals through the so-called 'floating population' of unemployed individuals who try to move from the rural areas to the cities. China has attempted to deal with this issue through a residency permit system but the resulting pressure can ultimately only be dealt with properly through a policy of 'place prosperity'

PLACE PROSPERITY VERSUS PEOPLE PROSPERITY

One of the central questions that must be addressed when one questions the wisdom of unbalanced growth is whether one wishes to emphasise 'place prosperity' or 'people prosperity'. Those who support the former approach argue that labour has only a limited mobility, and that non-economic costs (cultural and social) are high when we force individuals to move, while those who support the latter view argue from the basis of reductive individualism that freedom dictates a decoupling of the individual from society: there are only individual wants and needs not societal ones (Savoie, 1986, p. 20). Those who argue for the latter simply state that people should move to where the jobs are, not the other way around. Yet, the tradition of regional economics is inimical to that notion: 'The mobility of both labour and capital within countries tends to be [over-estimated by] economists in their desire for clear-cut assumptions. . . There is only an imperfect mobility within countries, and there is also some mobility between them' (Kaldor, 1970, p. 338).

This is not a mere question of theoretical debate. It lies at the core of which form of argument the authors will advance. Thomas Courchene (1992), the noted Canadian economist, argues eloquently for 'people prosperity', but acknowledging the political damage that this may cause, also tries to mitigate its impact by balancing the needs of regions and people (Courchene, 1986). Unfortunately, for those theoreticians who continue to advocate for 'people prosperity', politics is a place-dominated venue. Constituencies cannot be offended as electoral strength is diminished, and any party which aspires to be truly national must come to grips with regionalism and the disparities which are entailed by it.

IS THERE A REGIONAL PROBLEM?

Kaldor (1970, p. 339) has noted that natural factor endowments, which have traditionally been the means by which economists have determined that some regions have lagged while others have grown, are not adequate to the task of explaining the differences that are seen:

> The prevailing distribution of real income in the world – the comparative riches or poverty of nations or regions – is largely to be explained not by 'natural' forces but by the unequal incidence of development in industrial activities. . . It is as sensible – or perhaps more sensible – to say that capital accumulation results from economic development as that it is a cause of development. Accumulation is largely financed out of business profits; the growth in demand, in turn, is largely responsible for providing both the inducements to invest capital in industry and also the means of financing it.

With the advent of modern technology, there should be less regional differentiation over time. After all, modern transportation has made such costs far less burdensome than they were in the past. Yet, the modern semi-conductor industry continues to thrive in Silicon Valley; the automobile industry, despite some locational diversification, still has its base in, and around, Detroit; and the computer software industry has grown up largely around Route 128 in Boston, the San Francisco Bay Area and upstate Washington (home of Microsoft). The main reason for these locations is the network externalities and increasing returns to capital.

Myrdal (1957, p. 11) has made the case for how capital deprivation in a region leads ' . . . [T]o a circular and cumulative process, continuously pressing levels downwards, in which one negative factor is, at the same time, both cause and effect of other negative factors'. Regions that are poor and underdeveloped stay this way relative to other areas because no one is willing to pay for the tremendous expenditure of resources necessary to allow them to catch up. This process is not self-equilibrating but can only be brought back into balance by bringing exogenous pressures onto the system. However, when such pressure is used, the result is not a stable equilibrium, for the same forces that took it to the point of imbalance can step in any time there is a shock to the system. In reality, only with a great deal of difficulty can ' . . . [T]he position of rest [be] achieved by policy interferences, planned and applied, with the [clear] intention of stopping the movement. This is, of course, the very opposite of a "natural tendency" towards equilibrium, endogenous to the system' (Myrdal, 1957, p. 13).

Unemployment is one such force which causes continued imbalance. Not only has the general tendency in advanced industrial societies over the past 25 years been towards higher unemployment, but the unemployment differentials in Canada and Europe were far closer 40 years ago than today. Besides, recessions tend to affect poorer regions far more than richer ones (Economic Council of Canada, 1986, p. 104).

Martin (2001) shows that there has been a steady divergence in regional employment growth as well as only weak productivity convergence in the European Union, and that even this convergence stopped in the mid-1980s. Wang and Ge (2004) consider the question of China and find that the booming coastal cities have steadily experienced economic divergence from the rest of the country. Indeed, neoclassical economists, such as Easterlin (1958, p. 325), note that convergence is by no means a foregone conclusion:

> It is by no means certain that convergence of regional income levels is an inevitable outcome of the process of development. For, while migration and trade do appear to exert significant pressure towards convergence, they operate within such a rapidly changing environment that dynamic factors may possibly offset their influence. One may argue, of course, that migration and trade may become progressively more important during growth, as a result, for example, of improvements in transportation, and consequently that the pressures towards convergence will tend increasingly to predominate. But whether this is generally the case cannot be settled on *a priori* grounds.

Indeed, interregional factor movements may exacerbate the process of income divergence, especially in the developing world where growth rates tend to be more divergent across regions and there are more barriers to the movement of unskilled labour. These features can be compounded by regional differentiation in the availability of credit (Losch, 1954; Richardson, 1979; Madjd-Sadjadi, 1996).

Some economists have argued that we should not worry about regional unemployment, only the national rate of unemployment. People should move to where the jobs are. However, the sociological reality is that many individuals cannot move. Political reality is that governments must care about both inflation *and* unemployment in order to achieve macroeconomic stability and a high living standard. Furthermore, many governments care about balancing growth. 'Place prosperity' is very important from a political perspective because voters are distributed in geographic regions. If one area of the country is doing well but another is doing poorly, the representatives in the poorer regions will find increasing pressure to increase income. As the wealthier areas typically have larger populations, they do not feel the impact of the regional redistribution as greatly as the receiving areas. Therefore, the poorer regions are 'bought off' through transfers while the larger group does not feel the pinch.

Once a firm goes under, the result is that those who are thrown out of work have less money to spend in the region. This, in turn, causes additional job losses in the region:

> If there are no other exogenous changes, the community will be less tempting for outside businesses and workers who had contemplated moving in. [However,] As the process gathers momentum, businesses established in the community and workers living there will increasingly find reasons for moving out in order to seek better markets somewhere else. If they do, this will again decrease incomes and demand. It will usually also change the age structure of the local population in an unfavourable direction. (Myrdal, 1957, p. 23)

As hinted at by Myrdal, a crucial problem is that the individuals who move are those best equipped to do so. The result is a brain and skills drain on the locality and increasing financial hardship on those left behind. For this reason, welfare policies exist; however, these policies become strained in times of fiscal crisis. The poor don't contribute to the coffers of political parties. Moreover, world-lending institutions (like the IMF) take a critical eye towards such redistributive measures. But what makes things worse is that these same institutions do not like to see a government take on inflation as a solution to its problems. Governments in fiscal difficulty are required to adopt tight fiscal policies, which serve to force marginalised firms out of business, creating greater difficulties and suffering in the short run. Hence, neoliberal institutions instead disparage the very policies that might be used to alleviate regional disparity. Regional divergence thus continues to march forward, culminating in severe dislocations that have potentially severe social consequences.

Moreover, regional variations are not temporary but persist over time and may even be found not only in growth rates of production but even in inflation (Madjd-Sadjadi, 1996). These small differences actually may hide severe 'hidden' inflation, which is found in the unemployment rates. Under administrated prices, inflationary pressures will hide themselves in terms of quantity constraints. In a similar vein, the Prices and Income Commission (1969, pp. 381-2) has noted, '[S]ince the mobility of goods among regions is apparently much higher than the mobility of . . . labour, the burden of adjustment . . . will be observed primarily as differences in regional rates of unemployment rather than as divergences between regional rates of inflation'. This points to the possible use of monetary policy as a stabilising influence. As discussed earlier, regional variation in credit provision does already occur. Despite this, there has also been little work done on the formation of a mechanism for a monetary-based regional stabilisation policy. One of the few exceptions was the brief discussion by the Economic Council of Canada (1986, p. 106) on one possible use:

> Many economists believe that the ready mobility of monetary capital makes it impossible to achieve regional differentiation in interest rates beyond that [rate] pertaining to normal risk; some maintain, however, that this is not true for mortgage rates. It is also possible that the rationing process known as moral suasion could be applied on a regional basis.

However, it may be that tax policy through preferential credits against income tax will be a better method that will alter the effective after-tax rate of interest without actually interfering with the monetary system itself.

WHAT CAN BE DONE?

The developmental state has basically three weapons at its disposal. The first is 'fiscal federalism', a system in which a national government attempts to alleviate the stresses by transferring gains from richer areas to poorer areas through vertical equalisation to ensure an equitable tax capacity in all areas of the country. The second is government spending designed to inject money and jobs into a struggling economy. The third is a policy of inter-regional trade promotion. The first solution typically causes resentment among the richer regions and encourages economic dependency on behalf of the poorer ones. The second lends itself to pork barrel intervention and political expediency at the expense of 'proper' economic policy. The third is one which is most conducive to the developmental state by binding the heartland and the hinterland into one common national policy of income promotion.

Fiscal Federalism

While fiscal federalism is normally associated with federal states, it can actually be examined any time that localities have a stream of income that they can tap independently of the nation as a whole. Since public goods are often provided out of the public purse, those areas that are relatively more able to attract such dollars can build more infrastructure, creating yet another cycle of cumulative causation. It seeks to address equity considerations at the individual, vertical and horizontal levels as well as the provision of minimum service levels.

The standard assumptions for all of the equity aspects are that there is low consumer mobility and that decentralisation is preferred. Economists have often opposed equity grants by arguing that there is a good deal of consumer mobility.

Tiebout (1956) argues that individuals locate on the basis of the desired public spending level by a locality. Beginning with the dubious assumptions of perfect mobility, no spatial rents, full knowledge, no externalities affecting other communities, and an optimum size criteria by which communities either expand or contract services in a effort to secure residents, Tiebout (1956, p. 424) argues that efficiency (the maximisation of consumer utility) can result just as in the private market: 'For a substantial portion of the collective or public goods, this problem *does have* a conceptual solution. If consumer-voters are fully mobile, the appropriate local governments, whose revenue-expenditure patterns are set, are adopted by the consumer voters.' These assumptions are too unrealistic for proper consideration, however. As Buchanan and Goetz (1972) have shown, the introduction of spatial rents (i.e., the ability to charge a different price based on location) introduces inefficiencies to the Tiebout (1956) model while work by Williams (1966), Brainard and Dolbear Jr. (1967) and Pauly (1970) all reach different conclusions about the nature of efficiency in the face of externalities (that is, costs or benefits imposed on other governments from the activities of one government).

Furthermore, a related problem is that shared functions are the norm, not the exception: health care and welfare may be provided at the one level of government but national regulations also act as a constraint on subnational action. On the other hand, revenue sources are shared (in the taxing of individual and corporate income), creating problems of spill-overs when one level of government attempts to raise taxes.

Decentralisation is beneficial to the extent that local governments can provide more easily social services catering to local needs than can larger authorities; but it is problematic when these localities begin to compete with one another for jobs and public revenue. When other regions begin to court companies within a country to move, they are not engaging in beneficial behaviour from the perspective of the nation but are attempting a 'beg-thy-neighbour' policy which helps them at the expense of the other region. In addition, this competition tends to transfer benefits from the states to the companies or individuals being courted. Tax abatements, favourable loan provisions and special jurisdictional concessions create economic rents for the companies and individuals which would normally accrue to the populace of the province as a whole if no province engaged in such behaviour. The result is a general deterioration of the wealth of some jurisdictions *vis-à-vis* others, just as we would expect in a competitive model. Fiscal federalism is an attempt to combat these problems by addressing individual, vertical and horizontal equity considerations as well as the provision of minimum service levels.

Individual equity is redistribution of monies to account for individual-level differences in income. Programmes like old age security, progressive income taxation, unemployment insurance, programmatic financing and welfare assistance are attempts at the national level to generate individual-level equity. Vertical equity (also known as revenue sharing) is designed to compensate local governments for their limited tax base:

> In a federation, it is unlikely that revenues of each level of government will match expenditures at each level. Few would suggest that [regions] should spend only what they raise from their own revenue sources. Some degree of vertical intergovernmental fiscal imbalance is . . . a reflection of the superior revenue-raising potential of the central government and the fact that the states have jurisdiction in areas where expenditure demands are heavy and increase automatically as the economy expands. (Hunter, 1977, p. 37)

Vertical imbalance may increase when there are limits on the ability of subordinate governments to raise funds and when the federal government begins to intercede in revenue sources traditionally used by subordinate governments. Conflicts between the national and subnational governments resulting in a breakdown of intergovernmental cooperation can contribute to these problems.

The third equity problem in a federal system is horizontal. This accounts for geographic-level differences in income at the individual level. This differs from individual equity, which is given to all regions and is designed to alleviate problems associated with income inequality of individuals in that it is designed to compensate states for having a lower level of per capita income than other states. It differs from vertical equity in that it is designed to provide for the equalisation at the same level (usually at the regional level) of government (to level the playing field) as opposed to equalise the imbalances between different levels of government:

> When federal grants are used to correct for vertical imbalance by compensating the provinces for loss of tax revenues, they will usually be distributed on a 'derivation' or local collection basis. Such distribution will tip the scales heavily in favour of highly industrialised and densely populated provinces. Equalisation grants can be expected to lessen the impact of such a distribution on the less affluent provinces. (Rowell-Sirois Commission, 1940, p. 113)

One argument which partially supports this is that individuals must not be treated differently simply on the basis of where they live: the difference, called the 'fiscal residue', between what individuals pay in taxes and what they receive in services should be equal (Buchanan, 1950).

If the individual is paying out more in taxes than he is receiving (due to the imbalance created by vertical compensation) then some transfers to alleviate this should be forthcoming. A more expansive argument in favour of transfers is that equal treatment should not be based on fiscal residue but equal provision of services. Graham (1963) argues that provinces must have the ability to raise the revenue needed to carry out their functions and that if this revenue is not sufficient, the other provinces in a federation must make up the difference.

However, many economists disagree with this line of reasoning. They counter that areas which are poor are poor because of their limited base of natural resources, and that transferring funds to them only saps the strength of those areas which have more resources. A better way, to these theorists, is to ensure that production is centred in areas of relative prosperity and to discourage the intransigency of individuals who do not wish to move there, by not engaging in wealth or income transfers between regions (Scott, 1950).

The fourth reason for aid is to establish minimum service levels. A common rationale for this is seen in the Rowell-Sirois Commission Report on Canada's regional inequalities, which mandates these transfer payments to compensate the poorer provinces and ensure that they are not forced to raise taxes to levels far in excess of the national average: 'all provincial governments [should] be put in a financial position, by National Adjustment Grants from the Dominion, to supply education and welfare services, equivalent in quality . . . to the national average' (Rowell-Sirois Commission, 1940, p. 83).

These take the form of conditional grants or mandated programmes by which the national government establishes a programme and then gives the subnational governments the wherewithal to fund them but does not limit them from going beyond the minimum federal provisions. Examples of this include the provision of government highway funds, airport funds, national aid to health care and environmental clean-up transfers. These allow the national government great latitude in mandating new social programmes and ensuring that no citizen's ability to enjoy these services falls below a specified federal 'floor'. They have also the effect of limiting flexibility of regional governments, which may wish to 'opt out' of a programme.

Megaprojects and Contracts

Megaprojects often take the role of contracts provided by the national government for the provision of a good or service which can sustain an entire region. As noted earlier, these projects are often politically desirable because it appears that the national government is 'doing something' about regional development. However, these are, in reality, high stake gambles with the future of the region hanging in the balance.

Far more prevalent and important are the handing out of smaller contracts when the national government acts as a procurer of goods and services. In doing so, it bypasses the regional and local authorities and purchases goods and services directly from a private vendor. While this may appear innocuous, it has a grave effect on localities. The expansion of national largesse into an area can make that area dependent on such an infusion of funds. The increase and later retrenchment of such funding can hurt an area when that assistance is withdrawn. This is most evident when a government procures from itself, such as in the establishment of military bases. The end of the Cold War brought with it devastation for those regions which were targeted for base closings, reducing the tax bases for regions that did not properly diversify, and increasing their fiscal responsibilities to deal with the dislocations.

Regional Trade Promotion

The national government also attempts to compel regions to trade among themselves in an effort to use trade promotion as a weapon against regional differentiation. Countries do this with the development of railroads and other transportation linkages to ensure at least a partial national orientation to trade, and the persistence of national subsidies to ensure equal access to goods and services throughout a nation ensures a large proportion of trade is directed towards trade creation within a nation and trade diversion from outside. There is, of course, a natural 'home bias' that one finds in most countries, which is magnified by cultural and linguistic anomalies that present themselves every so often when a manufacturer fails to pay proper heed to them. Although pure urban legends without foundation in fact, apocryphal stories about General Motors foray with Chevy Nova in Mexico, Pepsi-Cola's supposed 'Bite the Wax Tadpole' mistranslation into Chinese, and the cautionary tale of Gerber baby food formula being mistaken as containing actual babies are worth a chuckle when revealed to be the false stories that they are.

Moreover, the need to diversify growth away from simply the growth poles represents a challenge for the developmental state, which seeks to mitigate social displacement. These plans must be developed with a firm understanding of the relative strengths and weaknesses of various regions, and demand management policies need to be designed in such a way so as to unleash the market potential of the area without causing a realignment of incentives that might cause resources to be directed towards uses that can only be sustained by an extended period of protectionism. Still, the mere fact that every developed country subsidises its agricultural sector to some extent or another is evidence of the desire among political entities for some form of regional stabilisation policy. After all, someone must grow the food that we eat. Yet, of the major success stories in East Asia we have studied, none have a vibrant agricultural sector. At the same time, the Caribbean economies are based on agricultural production, primary resource sector extraction and tourism, while the economies of Europe are mixed.

The key is not to embrace agricultural self-sufficiency or a desire for food security. As witnessed by the devastation of the country's agricultural sector in the face of Hurricane Ivan that swept through Jamaica in late 2004, the promise of food security due to trade protectionism is a false one. Similarly, a country should not subsidise a crop merely because others are subsidising them. Instead, it should coordinate a plan for agriculture, just as it plans the economy in the industrial sector, relying upon the natural advantages that home-grown crops have (since imported crops face high transportation costs and varying degrees of perishability). Food security is a non-issue if the people cannot pay for food: 'Opening up the Jamaican milk market to US imports in 1992 may have hurt local dairy farmers but it also meant poor children could get milk more cheaply' (Stiglitz, 2003, p. 5).

The emphasis on the freshness of produce, meat and milk should be harnessed to the advantage of the industry, allowing it to go 'up market' instead of down. With increased competition comes increased need for quality, and the government that engineers a policy crafted towards quality standards in its own food production cannot but improve the living conditions of its people. Similarly, the withdrawal of such subsidies must be accomplished in a systematic fashion so as to allow for the absorption of the surplus population that will inevitably move from rural areas to cities. Unless this is accomplished, social dislocations and disparities will threaten economic success. It is not because of a desire to remain poor that the wooden shoes known as sabots were thrown into the cogs of machines by the Dutch in a display of dissatisfaction with the mechanisation of various industries; this act of sabotage was a reaction to the perceived failure of the economy to deliver jobs to those displaced by technological improvement.

Thus, regional policy must be crafted so as to take advantage of the core attributes of various regions. Developing the agricultural base may mean sacrificing some agricultural diversity in favour of increased food processing done in the region itself, because the quicker that the raw foodstuffs are turned into processed foods the higher the quality will be for those products. The goal should be for vertical integration of the industry, but to do so only in those products which either cannot be procured adequately on the open market or in those products which can effectively compete internationally. Then subsidies for agriculture can be slowly withdrawn. There is no reason for California to be a rice-producing entity; its climate requires the dumping of millions of gallons of water to create man-made rice paddy-fields that are better created by nature.

Similarly, governments must move to allow for and create agricultural cooperatives that can effectively acquire technology and distribute it to its members. Revenue-sharing strategies can insure against the vagaries of uncertainty in the weather, and smaller countries can band together to create a common agricultural policy to distribute this risk-sharing across a broader geographic area. Also, the development of transportation linkages through road and railway development should be accomplished in order to ensure the economic viability of the sector.

Most important is the introduction by government of minimum quality standards and access to education that can implement technology effectively as opposed to relying on government hand-outs from more developed nations that often have ulterior motives to sell to a developing country goods produced by the developed nation itself. One needs only witness the disaster that befell the introduction of heavy farm equipment in some parts of Africa by development agencies that failed to adequately consider the soil conditions and whether the ground could withstand the pressure of the equipment without causing the equipment to sink into the ground, rendering it useless. Similarly, provision of goods without provision of the necessary support materials, such as spare parts and consumable supplies, leads to waste and unemployment. Nothing cripples a manufacturing process more than having a critical machine break down and be unable to restart it because of a shortage of spare parts. Technical knowledge gained from international research can be gleaned and distributed to the sector through the introduction of sector-specific educational programmes that are brought to the region. Agricultural education, for example, must occur in a rural, not an urban, context for it to be meaningful and effective. In some cases, it is necessary to target and nurture specific industries. In other, one can achieve the same results with a different type of selective intervention: research and development of technologies that will assist those industries that are seen as moving the nation-state up the supply chain ladder. This has the additional benefit of assisting also other important industries in terms of possible spin-off technology that the government may be unable to foresee.

FINAL POINTS

By way of summary, the neoclassical approach denies the importance of the state in the promotion of regional and industrial development; argues in favour of a small, deregulated state sector engaged in privatisation; and the development of free enterprise. It seeks to eliminate market rigidities due to allocative inefficiency and to develop the necessary support mechanisms for the free enterprise to flourish, especially through the correction of market failure on a minimally invasive level, low taxation, and the introduction of internationally accepted property rights schemes. Its emphasis on 'free' trade however, is hampered by a desire for 'fair' trade among its proponents.

The developmental state, on the other hand, uses a post-Keynesian neo-institutional approach that emphasises the role of cumulative causation, first mover advantages, rectifying the imbalance between savings and investment and the promotion of growth poles coupled with assistance for lagging areas. Aggregate demand management, infrastructure development, strategic industrial policy and managed trade are all characteristics of this approach to economic development.

In the area of education, these two views also differ. The developmental state recognises that individuals and companies are threatened by uncertainty in the marketplace and have a critical need for not only skill upgrading but also the provision of broad-based skills applicable to many different areas.[2] Education is one area that neoclassical economics also recognise as being underprovided by the free market, and education for governments that adopt free market policies tends towards training at the firm level (that is firm-specific and based on relevancy to particular industries). The developmental state recognises that in an increasingly mobile world, workers simply fail to stay long enough for firms to be able to benefit from such training; hence, actions to broaden this education as part of a comprehensive strategy to raise productivity using a sector-based as opposed to firm-based training is likely to see more success.

As noted in the chapters on East Asia, another critical feature of the developmental state is the provision of a high quality government sector. The devaluation of the state by free market proponents leads to corruption and wastefulness, creating a self-fulfilling prophecy. Instead of often attracting inadequately qualified people to government through inadequate compensation and a lifetime commitment to employment, the government sector needs to emphasise superior skills, benefits and wages, and a priority on performance. If a firm performs poorly, the major impact falls on the individuals of the firm. It is thus in their interest to do well. However, failure of the government to perform adequately its mission leads to failures that are felt economy-wide.

A proper property rights mechanism is central to this mission. Instead of providing the private sector with whatever it *wants*, government needs to be concerned with providing the private sector with what it *needs*. While defining property rights is imperative as a precursor for economic growth (de Soto, 2000), the regime that best protects everyone isn't necessarily the one that business would like most. The interests of the nation are not necessarily best served by ensuring that the interests of General Motors are met. Indeed, the private sector, despite protestations to the contrary, is not interested in the promotion of competition but in its elimination. Monopoly in the pursuit of profit has its own set of inefficiencies that are introduced. However, it is the discipline of competition, not the motive for profit, which provides the theoretical underpinnings for both quality performance and efficiency.

To see this, we only need to examine the debate over whether or not to extend copyright protections that occurred starting in the 1960s and 1970s in the United States. The US first copyright act specified a period of no more than 28 years, which was extended in 1831 to 42 years, and in 1909 went to a maximum of 56 years. Beginning in 1909, copyright protection was only available after registering the copyright, adhering to certain basic and fairly universal standards of informing others of the claim, and required the renewal of such copyright after an initial 28-year grant. This renewal was allowed once for a total of 56 years of protection. No distinction was made based on whether the author was an individual or a corporation. Today, in the name of promoting the interests of intellectual property rights producers, but actually in order to ensure that Mickey Mouse doesn't fall into the public domain, the granting of such rights no longer requires registration, lasts for 95 years (in the case of the corporation) or life of the author plus 70 years, and technical 'defects' in the copyright claim (such as a failure to provide notification of copyright) do not automatically render the claim invalid.

The irony is that the House of Mouse may not enjoy copyright protection for its signature character after all. As noted by Vanpelt (1999), the images of Mickey Mouse created by Walt Disney were introduced to the world in the film 'Mickey Mouse in Plane Crazy' in April 1928, and the copyright of that film was never extended – Mickey Mouse therefore logically entered the public domain on January 1, 1957. Furthermore, proper notice, required by the copyright act prevalent at the time, was never served on Mickey Mouse Club membership materials published in the late 1920s and early 1930s, and technical defects in the copyright notice rendered the copyrights inapplicable in the films that Mickey Mouse originally appeared in. These technical defects were never corrected, meaning that Mickey Mouse may, in fact, be a character open to all.

However, even putting aside the dubious claims of Mickey Mouse as private work, an examination of the claim that such extensions assist in the creative process of creating new intellectual property does not stand up under close scrutiny. Assuming a real interest rate at 2 per cent per annum, the value 56 years from now of a product produced today would be about one third in present dollar terms. Raise that interest rate to 4 per cent and its value declines to one ninth its present dollar value. Extending copyright to 95 years would push the value at an interest of 4 per cent to one fortieth of its present value, while at an interest rate of 2 per cent its value declines to one sixth. This assumes that the sales over a period of 56 or even 95 years from now are still at the same level as they were initially. However, for the most part, they will not be. Instead, they will likely be far less. Such a long-term time horizon doesn't factor into the creation of content that likely sees a useful shelf-life that can be measured in months, or at most a few years, as opposed to decades. Yet, by limiting access to such works through the public domain, the reduction in cost to the consumer through competition or the possibility of derivative work is flatly denied.

Moreover, there is little justification for making copyright uniform for all types of created work. Computer programmes, for example, are almost never sold for more than a few years and the locking up of that intellectual property serves to hamper development efforts as witnessed by the rampant efforts to extend the proof of concept to the even more onerous patent legislation which, thankfully, lasts a mere 17 years. The irony is that of the two forms of protection, patents probably have more useful value to society, given the billions of dollars that are spent on a single drug's research and development. Compare that to the cost of movies, which run at most into the low hundreds of millions of dollars, or recordings or books, which usually are created for only a few thousands.

However, the biggest fallacy is the notion of retroactive extension of copyright protection. No matter what anyone might want to argue, the fact is that Mickey Mouse was created in a copyright regime that would have seen his face enter the public domain in just 28 years without an application to extend copyright and in 56 years with such an application. No alteration in the existing copyright scheme could ever cause the creation in the past of additional content. It can only affect content being created on and going forward. Given that few works will ever see the light of day beyond a few years, at the very least, developing countries should insist on the payment of a nominal fee (even as low as $1) to maintain copyright on works beyond even the initial 28-year period.

In conclusion, the developmental state is the epitome of good governance in society. Mindful of its limitations but steeped in a regard for reducing the fundamental tensions that permeate throughout a society, it tries to develop through rigorous planning a society that is prepared to go to the next level of development. As such, this type of state is a good overseer and facilitates the development path through provision of public goods like infrastructure and by directing savings into productive investments. It guides the market system, steering it but only in such a way as to conform to the inherent underlying advantages that the marketplace has already identified. Ironically, it may best do this not by 'picking winners' but by 'picking losers', destroying static comparative advantage in favour of altering its base so as to create a new competitive advantage.

We titled this book with a provocative question: does globalisation signal the death of the Developmental State model? Our answer, of course, is a resounding 'No'. Yet, globalisation signals the end of an era and the beginning of a new phase for the Developmental State. We are reminded of a famous quote from the Bhagavad Gita, 'Now I am become Death, the destroyer of worlds'. It is only through this process of 'creative destruction', so praised by Schumpeter (1934), that we create a new world. Only by recognising change and the institutional means to address the Veblenian dichotomy can the government fulfil its mandate, for every tax on one activity is a subsidy for all activities and every subsidy for one activity is a tax on all others. Therefore, by utilising creative punitive taxes to destroy one industry, one saves the others. It is an irony and a lesson that must never be forgotten. Finally, we end this book with the realisation that we must conform to the essential truth stated by Choi (1994, pp. 28-9) where he warns practitioners of the Developmental State approach not to replace a 'mystified market' with an equally 'mystified state'. If the free market approach is guilty of distorting reality, the statist-interventionist is at least guilty of painting an incomplete picture. For a realistic understanding of the development process, one has to transcend the market-state dichotomy and to firmly base discussion on the formation and evolution of the national and global socio-economic forces in which the market and state are embedded.

NOTES

1. Tax capacity is defined as the amount of revenue which a region collects relative to other regions if each region applied a uniform Representative Tax System (Advisory Commission on Inter-Governmental Relations, 1983, p. 6). Tax effort is defined as 'the ratio of a [region's] actual tax collections to its tax capacity' (Advisory Commission on Inter-Governmental Relations, 1983, p. 14).
2. Quite often, development policies of many countries have failed to deal with a crucial problem: the mismatch between the demand for certain types of skills and other modern factors of growth (for social and developmental purposes) and the supply of them. Developmental State action, which seeks to take care of the quantitative and qualitative parameters of industrial investment, can fix these mismatches through thorough, technically proficient planning.

Bibliography

Abell, J. D. (1990), 'Twin Deficits During the 1980s: An Empirical Investigation', *Journal of Macroeconomics*, **12** (1), 81-96.

Abouchar, A. (1985), *Project Decision Making in the Public Sector*, Toronto: DC Heath.

Adelman, I. and A. E. Yeldan (1999), 'The End of the Developmental State? A General Equilibrium Investigation on the Sources of the Asian Crisis within a Multi-Region, Inter-temporal CGE Model', Working Paper **888**, Agricultural and Resource Economics and Policy, University of California-Berkeley.

Advisory Commission on Intergovernmental Relations (1983), *1981 Tax Capacity of the Fifty States*, Washington, DC.

Ahmed, S. (1986), 'Temporary and Permanent Government Spending in an Open Economy: Some Evidence for the United Kingdom', *Journal of Monetary Economics*, **17**, 197-224.

______ (1987), 'Government Spending, the Balance of Trade and the Terms of Trade in British History', *Journal of Monetary Economics*, **20**, 195-220.

Ahrens, J. (1997), 'Prospects of Institutional and Policy Reform in India: Toward a Model of the Developmental State', *Asian Development Review*, **15** (1), 111-46.

Akamatsu, K. (1961), 'A Theory of Unbalanced Growth in the World Economy', *Weltwirtschaftliches Archiv*, **86** (2), 196-215.

Akerlof, G. (1970), 'The Market for "Lemons:" Qualitative Uncertainty and the Market Mechanism', *Quarterly Journal of Economics*, **84**, 488-500.

Albelda, R., Gunn, C. and W. Waller (1987a), 'Institutionalist Perspectives on Policy', in R. Albelda, C. Gunn and W. Waller (eds), *Alternatives to Economic Orthodoxy*, pp. 263-5.

______ (eds) (1987b), *Alternatives to Economic Orthodoxy*, Armonk, NY: M. E. Sharpe.

Albo, G. and J. Jenson (1989), 'A Contested Concept: The Relative Autonomy of the State', in W. Clement and G. Williams (eds), *The New Canadian Political Economy*, pp. 180-211.

Albrechts, L., Moulaert, F., Roberts, P. and E. Swyngedouw (1989a), 'New Perspectives for Regional Policy and Development in the 1990s', in L. Albrechts, F. Moulaert, P. Roberts and E. Swyngedouw (eds), *Regional Policy at the Crossroads*, pp. 1-9.

______ (eds) (1989b), *Regional Policy at the Crossroads*, London: J. Kingsley Publishers.

Allen, K., Yuill, D. and J. Bachtler (1989), 'Requirements for an Effective Regional Policy', in L. Albrechts, F. Moulaert, P. Roberts and E. Swyngedouw (eds), *Regional Policy at the Crossroads*, pp. 107-24.

Allum, P. (1980), 'Thirty Years of Southern Policy in Italy', *Political Quarterly*, **52**, 314-23.

Althusser, L. (1973), *Lenin and Philosophy*, London: New Left Books.

Althusser, L. and E. Balibar (1977), *Reading Capital*, London: New Left Books.

Amable, B. and P. Petit (1996), 'New Scale and Scope for Industrial Policies in the 1990s', *International Review of Applied Economics*, **10** (1), 23-41.

Amsden, A. (1989), *Asia's Next Giant*, New York: Oxford University Press.

Anderson, P. W., Arrow, K. J. and D. Pines (eds) (1989), *The Economy as an Evolving Complex System*, Redwood City, CA: Addison-Wesley.

Andic, F. M. and S. B. Jones-Hendrickson (eds) (1981), *Readings in Caribbean Public Sector Economics*, Kingston: ISER.

Archibugi, D. and M. Pianta (1993), 'Patterns of Technological Specialisation and Growth of Innovative Activities in Advanced Countries', in K. S. Hughes (ed.), *European Competitiveness*, pp. 105-32.

Arestis, P. (1992), *The Post-Keynesian Approach to Economics*, Aldershot, UK and Brookfield, USA: Edward Elgar.

Arestis, P. and V. Chick (eds) (1994), *Recent Developments in Post-Keynesian Economics*, Aldershot, UK and Brookfield, USA: Edward Elgar.

Arestis, P. and M. C. Sawyer (eds) (1994), *The Elgar Companion to Radical Political Economy*, Aldershot, UK and Brookfield, USA: Edward Elgar.

______ (eds) (1998), *The Political Economy of Economic Policies*, London: Macmillan.

Armstrong, H. and J. Taylor (1985), *Regional Economics and Policy*, Oxford: Philip Allan.

______ (1993), *Regional Economics and Policy*, 2nd edn, Hemel Hempstead: Harvester Wheatsheaf.

Arthur, B. W. (1989), 'Competing Technologies, Increasing Returns, and Lock-In by Historical Events', *Economic Journal*, **99**, 116-31.

Artis, M. J. (1987), 'Deficit Spending', in J. Eatwell et al. (eds), *The New Palgrave*, Vol. 1, pp. 764-5.

Asimakopoulos, A. and J. Burbidge (1974), 'The Short-Period Incidence of Taxation', *Economic Journal*, **84**, 267-88.

Atkinson, A. B. and J. E. Stiglitz (1980), *Lectures on Public Economics*, New York: McGraw-Hill.

Auerbach, A. J. (1987a), 'Taxation of Income', in J. Eatwell et al. (eds), *The New Palgrave*, Vol. 4, pp. 604-6.

______ (1987b), 'Taxation of Wealth', in J. Eatwell et al. (eds), *The New Palgrave*, Vol. 4, pp. 606-8.

Auerbach, P. (1988), *Competition: The Economics of Industrial Change*, Oxford: Basil Blackwell.

Ayres, R. (1994), 'Development', in P. Arestis and M. C. Sawyer (eds), *The Elgar Companion to Radical Political Economy*, pp. 81-5.

Azariadis, C. and A. Drazen (1990), 'Threshold Externalities in Economic Development', *Quarterly Journal of Economics*, **105**, 501-26.

Bacon, R. and W. Eltis (1978), *Britain's Economic Problem: Too Few Producers*, 2nd edn, London: Macmillan.
Bagchi, A. K. (2000), 'The Past and the Future of the Developmental State', *Journal of World Systems Research*, **6** (2), 398-442.
Bailey, S. J. (1995), *Public Sector Economics*, London: Macmillan.
Baldwin, D. A. (1985), *Economic Statecraft*, Princeton: Princeton University Press.
Baldwin, R. E. (1969), 'The Case Against Infant-Industry Tariff Protection', *Journal of Political Economy*, **77**, 295-305.
Banting, K. (ed.) (1986), *The State and Economic Interests*, Toronto: University of Toronto Press.
Baran, P. and P. M. Sweezy (1973), *Monopoly Capital*, London: Pelican.
Barnet, R. J. and R. E. Müller (1974), *Global Reach: The Power of the Multinational*, New York: Simon and Schuster.
Barr, N. (1987), *The Economics of the Welfare State*, London: Weidenfeld & Nicolson.
Barro, R. J. (1989), 'The Ricardian Approach to Budget Deficits', *Journal of Economic Perspectives*, **3**, 37-54.
Baumol, W. J. (1965), *Welfare Economics and the Theory of the State*, 2nd edn, London: Bell.
Becker, G. S. (1983), 'A Theory of Competition Among Pressure Groups for Political Influence', *Quarterly Journal of Economics*, **3**, 371-400.
Behrman, J. N. (1970), *National Interests and the Multinational Corporation*, Englewood Cliffs, NJ: Prentice-Hall.
Bell, C. (1987), 'Development Economics', in J. Eatwell et al. (eds), *The New Palgrave*, Vol. 1, pp. 818-25.
Bennett, R. J. (ed.) (1990), *Decentralization, Local Governments and Markets*, New York: Oxford University Press.
Berardinetti, L. (2004), *Hansard*, Toronto: Legislative Assembly of Ontario, 3 June.
Berger, P. L. and H.-H. M. Hsiao (eds) (1988), *In Search of an East Asian Development Model*, New Brunswick, NJ: Transaction Books.
Berle, Jr. A. A. (1969), *Power,* New York: Harcourt, Brace and World.
Best, M. H. (1990), *The New Competition,* Cambridge, UK: Polity Press.
Bhagwati, J. (1958), 'Immiserizing Growth: A Geometrical Note', *Review of Economic Studies*, **25** (2), 201-5.
______ (1968), 'Distortions and Immiserizing Growth: A Generalization', *Review of Economic Studies*, **35**, 481-5.
______ (1988), *Protectionism*, Cambridge, MA: MIT Press.
Bhagwati, J. and T. N. Srinivasan (1983), *Lectures on International Trade*, Cambridge, MA: MIT Press.
Bickerton, J. (1990), *Nova Scotia, Ottawa, and the Politics of Regional Development*, Toronto: University of Toronto Press.
Birch, A. (1974), 'The Control of Prices and Commodities in Hong Kong', *Hong Kong Law Journal*, **4** (2), 133-50.
Blackaby, F. T. (ed.) (1978), *British Economic Policy 1960-74*, Cambridge: Cambridge University Press.
Blacksell, M. (1987), 'West Germany', in H. D. Clout (ed.), *Regional Development in Western Europe*, pp. 229-56.

Blanchard, O. J. (1987), 'Crowding Out', in J. Eatwell J. et al. (eds), *The New Palgrave*, Vol. 1, pp. 728-30.

Blaut, J. M. (1993), *The Colonizer's Model of the World: Geographical Diffusionism and Eurocentric History*, New York: Guilford.

Bloch, A. (1991), *The Complete Murphy's Law: A Definitive Collection,* Revised Edition, Los Angeles: Price Stern Sloan.

Bobbio, N. (1987), *Which Socialism? Marxism, Socialism, and Democracy,* Cambridge, UK: Polity Press.

Boltho, A. (ed.) (1982), *The European Economy, Growth and Crisis*, Oxford: Oxford University Press.

Boyer, R. and E. Caroli (1995), 'Production Regimes, Education and Training Systems', in C. Buechtemann (ed.), *Human Capital and Economic Performance*, New York: Sage.

Boyer, R. and D. Drache (eds) (1996), *States Against Markets: The Limits of Globalization*, London: Routledge.

Bozeman, B. and J. D. Straussman (1990), *Public Management Strategies*, San Francisco: Jossey-Bass.

Brainard, W. C. and F. T. Dolbear Jr. (1967), 'The Possibility of Oversupply of Local "Public" Goods: A Critical Note', *Journal of Political Economy*, **75**, February, 86-90.

Breedon, F. and T. G. Petursson (2006), 'Out in the Cold? Iceland's Trade Performance Outside the European Union and European Monetary Union', *Cambridge Journal of Economics*, **30** (5), 723-36.

Brewis, T. N. (1969), *Regional Economic Policies in Canada*, Toronto: Macmillan.

Brittan, S. (1975), 'The Economic Contradictions of Democracy', *British Journal of Political Science*, **5**, 129-59.

______ (1977), *The Economic Consequences of Democracy*, London: Temple Smith.

Brown, C. V. (1983), *Taxation and the Incentive to Work*, 2nd edn, New York: Oxford University Press.

Brown, C. V. and P. Jackson (1990), *Public Sector Economics*, 4th edn, Oxford: Martin Robertson.

Buchanan, J. M. (1950), 'Federalism and Fiscal Equity', *American Economic Review*, **40**, September, 583-99.

______ (1975), *The Limits of Liberty: Between Anarchy and Leviathan*, Chicago: University of Chicago Press.

______ (1986), *Liberty, Market and State: Political Economy in the 1980s*, New York: New York University Press.

Buchanan, J. M. and G. Tullock (1962), *The Calculus of Consent*, Ann Arbor: Michigan University Press.

Buchanan, J. M. and C. J. Goetz (1972), 'Efficiency Limits of Fiscal Mobility: An Assessment of the Tiebout Model', *Journal of Public Economics*, **1**, January, 25-43.

Buchanan, J. M. and R. E. Wagner (eds) (1978), *Fiscal Responsibility in Constitutional Democracy*, Boston: Martinus Nijhoff.

Cagan, P. (1987), 'Monetarism', in J. Eatwell et al. (eds), *The New Palgrave*, Vol. 3, pp. 492-6.

Cameron, D. (ed.) (1986), *The Free Trade Papers*, Toronto: James Lorimer.

Carlton, D. W. (1986), 'The Rigidity of Prices', *American Economic Review*, **76**, September, 637-58.

Carter, F. W. (1987), 'Greece', in H. D. Clout (ed.), *Regional Development in Western Europe*, pp. 419-34.

Cason, T. N. (1995), 'An Experimental Investigation of Seller Incentives in EPA's Emission Trading Auction', *American Economic Review*, **86**, September.

Castells, M. (1980), *The Economic Crisis and American Society*, Princeton: Princeton University Press.

Caves, R. E. (1970), 'Uncertainty, Market Structure and Performance: Galbraith as Conventional Wisdom', in J. Markham and G. Papanek (eds), *Industrial Organization and Economic Development*, pp. 282-302.

Caves, R. E., Johnson, H. G. and P. B. Kenen (eds) (1965), *Trade, Growth and the Balance of Payments: Essays in Honour of Gottfried Haberler*, Chicago: Rand McNally.

Chamley, C. (1987), 'Taxation of Capital', in J. Eatwell J. et al. (eds), *The New Palgrave*, Vol. 4, pp. 598-600.

Chandler, A. D. (1992), 'Organizational Capabilities and the Economic History of the Industrial Enterprise', *Journal of Economic Perspectives*, **6**, Summer, 79-100.

Chang, H-J (1998), 'Globalisation, Transnational Corporations and Economic Development: Can the Developing Countries Pursue Strategic Industrial Policy in a Globalising World Economy?', in D. Baker, G. Epstein and R. Pollin (eds), *Globalisation and Progressive Economic Policy*, Cambridge: Cambridge University Press, pp. 97-116.

______ (2002), *Kicking Away the Ladder: Development Strategy in Historical Perspective*, London: Anthem Books.

______ (2003), 'The Market, the State, and Institutions in Economic Development', in H.-J. Chang (ed.), *Rethinking Development Economics*, London: Anthem Books, pp. 41-60.

Cheema, G. S. and D. A. Rondinelli (eds) (1983), *Decentralization and Development*, USA: Sage Publications.

Chen, H.-R. E. (2004), *The Corporate Economy and the Development of Corporations in Taiwan*, Ph.D. Dissertation, University of Southern California.

Cheung, S. N. (1973), 'The Fable of the Bees: An Economic Investigation', *Journal of Law and Economics*, **16** (1), 11-33.

Chodos, R., Murphy, R. and E. Hamovitch (1993), *Canada and the Global Economy*, Toronto: James Lorimer.

Choi, A. H.-K. (1994), 'Beyond Market and State: A Study of Hong Kong's Industrial Transformation', *Studies in Political Economy*, **45**, Fall, 28-64.

Chowdhury, A. and I. Islam (1993), *The Newly Industrializing Economies of East Asia*, London: Routledge.

Clement, W. (1975), *The Canadian Corporate Elite: An Analysis of Economic Power*, Toronto: McClelland & Stewart.

Clement, W. and G. Williams (eds) (1989), *The New Canadian Political Economy*, Montreal: McGill-Queen's University Press.

Cleveland, H. V. B. and W. H. B. Brittain (1976), *The Great Inflation: A Monetarist View*, Washington, DC: NPA Committee on Changing International Realities.

Clout, H. D. (1987), 'Regional Development in Western Europe', in H. D. Clout (ed.), *Regional Development in Western Europe*, pp. 19-38.

______ (1987), 'France', in H. D. Clout (ed.), *Regional Development in Western Europe*, pp. 165-94.

______ (ed.) (1987), *Regional Development in Western Europe*, 3rd edn, London: D. Fulton Publishers.

Coase, R. (1937), 'The Nature of the Firm', *Economica*, **4**, November, 386-405.

______ (1960), 'The Problem of Social Cost', *Journal of Law and Economics,* **3** (1), 1-44.

______ (1974), 'The Lighthouse in Economics', *Journal of Law and Economics*, **17** (2), 357-76.

Cohen, S. S. and J. Zysman (1987), *Manufacturing Matters: The Myth of the Post-Industrial Economy*, New York: Basic Books.

Cohn, E. (1979), *The Economics of Education*, USA: Ballinger Publishing Company.

Cole, A. H. (ed.) (1928), *Industrial and Commercial Correspondence of Alexander Hamilton, Anticipating His Report on Manufacturing*, Chicago: A.W. Shaw.

Colgate, P. and J. Stroombergen (1993), A *Promise to Pay: New Zealand's Overseas Debt and Country Risk*, Wellington: New Zealand Institute of Economic Research.

Commission on Global Governance (1995), *Our Global Neighbourhood*, London: Oxford University Press.

Commons, J. R. (1957), *Legal Foundations of Capitalism*, Madison: University of Wisconsin Press.

______ (1961), *Institutional Economics*, Madison: University of Wisconsin Press.

Cooper, R. and A. John (1988), 'Coordinating Coordination Failures in Keynesian Models', *Quarterly Journal of Economics*, **103**, August, 441- 63.

Corden, M. W. (1977), *Inflation, Exchange Rates and the World Economy*, Oxford: Clarendon Press.

______ (1984), *The Theory of Protection*, Oxford: Clarendon Press.

Cornwall, J. and W. Maclean (1984), *Economic Recovery for Collective Action*, Toronto: Canadian Institute for Economic Policy.

Courchene, T. J. (1986), 'Avenues of Adjustment: The Transfer System and Regional Disparities', in D. J. Savoie (ed.), *The Canadian Economy: A Regional Perspective*, pp. 25-62.

______ (1992), *Rearrangements: The Courchene Papers*, Oakville, ON: Mosaic Press.

Cowling, K. (1987), 'An Industrial Strategy for Britain: The Nature and Role of Planning', *International Review of Applied Economics*, **1** (1), 1-22.

______ (1990), 'The Strategy Approach to Economic and Industrial Policy', in K. Cowling and R. Sugden (eds), *A New Economic Policy for Britain: Essays on the Development of Industry*, pp. 6-34.

Cowling, K. and R. Sugden (eds) (1990), *A New Economic Policy for Britain: Essays on the Development of Industry*, Manchester: Manchester University Press.

Crane, D. (1980), *A Dictionary of Canadian Economics*, Edmonton: Hurtig.

Creedy, J. (ed.) (1994), *Taxation, Poverty and Income Distribution*, Aldershot, UK and Brookfield, USA: Edward Elgar.

Crispo, J. (ed.) (1986), *Free Trade: The Real Story*, Toronto: Gage.

______ (1986), 'Dispelling the Fears of Free Trade Doomsayers', in D. Cameron (ed.), *The Free Trade Papers*, pp. 195-8.

______ (1987), 'The Case Against the Critics of Free Trade', in P. W. Fox and G. White (eds), *Politics: Canada*, 6th edn, pp. 55-61.

Cullis, J. and P. Jones (1992), *Public Finance and Public Choice: Analytical Perspectives*, New York: McGraw-Hill.

Cummings, B. (1987), 'The Origins and Development of the NE Asian Political Economy: Industrial Sectors, Product Cycles and Political Consequences', in F. Deyo (ed.), *The Political Economy of East Asian Industrialism*, pp. 44-83.

Dalton, H. (1954), *Principles of Public Finance*, London: Routledge & Kegan Paul.

Daly, H. and R. Goodland (1992), 'An Ecological-Economic Assessment of Deregulation of International Commerce under GATT', New York: World Bank.

Darity, W. Jr. and L. S. Davis (2005), 'Growth, Trade and Uneven Development', *Cambridge Journal of Economics*, **29** (1), 141-70.

David, P. A. (1985), 'Clio and the Economics of QWERTY', *American Economic Review*, **76**, 348-59.

Davidson, P. (1991), *Controversies in Post Keynesian Economics*, Aldershot, UK and Brookfield, USA: Edward Elgar.

______ (1994), *Post Keynesian Macroeconomic Theory*, Aldershot, UK and Brookfield, USA: Edward Elgar.

______ (1996), 'The Viability of Keynesian Demand Management in an Open Economy Context', *International Review of Applied Economics*, **10** (1), 91-105.

Day, R. H. (1993a), 'Bounded Rationality and the Coevolution of Market and State', in R. H. Day, G. Elliasson and C. Wihlborg (eds), *The Markets for Innovation, Ownership and Control*, pp. 57-79.

______ (1993b), *Complex Economic Dynamics: An Introduction to Dynamic Systems and Market Mechanisms*, Vol. I, Cambridge, MA: MIT Press.

Day, R. H., Elliasson, G. and C. Wihlborg (eds) (1993), *The Markets for Innovation, Ownership and Control*, Amsterdam: North-Holland.

De Valk, P. and K. H. Wekwete (eds) (1990), *Decentralizing for Participatory Planning*, London: Gower Publishing Company.

Demas, W. G. (1976), 'Planning and the Price Mechanism in the Context of Caribbean Economic Integration', in W. G. Demas (ed.), *Essays on Caribbean Integration and Development*, Kingston: ISER, pp. 22-41.

Deprez, J. (1994), 'Aggregate Supply', in P. Arestis and M. C. Sawyer (eds), *The Elgar Companion to Radical Political Economy*, pp. 10-15.

de Soto, H. (2000), *The Mystery of Capital: Why Capitalism Triumphs in the West and Fails Everywhere Else*, New York: Basic Books.

Deutsch, A. and H. Zowall (1988), *Compulsory Savings and Taxes in Singapore*, Singapore: ASEAN Economic Research Unit.

Dewald, W. G. and M. Ulan (1990), 'The Twin-Deficit Illusion', *Cato Journal*, **9**, 689-707.

Deyo, F. (ed.) (1987), *The Political Economy of East Asian Industrialism*, Ithaca: Cornell University Press.

Dobb, M. (1976), *Theories of Value and Distribution Since Adam Smith*, Cambridge: Cambridge University Press.

Dore, R. (1986), *Flexible Rigidities: Industrial Policy and Structural Adjustment in the Japanese Economy, 1970-80*, London: Athlone Press.

Doryan, E. (1993), 'An Institutional Perspective of Competitiveness and Industrial Restructuring Policies in Developing Countries', *Journal of Economic Issues*, June, 451-8.

Downey, E. H. (1987), 'The Futility of Marginal Utility', in R. Albelda, C. Gunn and W. Waller (eds), *Alternatives to Economic Orthodoxy*, pp. 48-59.

Downs, A. (1957), *An Economic Analysis of Democracy*, New York: Harper & Row.

Doyal, L. (1979), *The Political Economy of Health*, London: Pluto Press.

Dyker, D. (ed.) (1992a), *The European Economy*, London & New York: Longman.

______ (ed.) (1992b), *The National Economies of Europe*, London & New York: Longman.

Easterlin, R. A. (1958), 'Long Term Regional Income Changes: Some Suggested Factors', *Papers and Proceedings of the Regional Science Association*, **4**, January, 313-25.

Easton, D. (1965), *A Framework for Political Analysis*, Englewood Cliffs, NJ: Prentice-Hall.

Eaton, J. and G. M. Grossman (1981), 'Tariffs as Insurance: Optimal Commercial Policy When Domestic Markets are Incomplete', *Working Paper* **797**, National Bureau of Economic Research.

Ebrill, L. P. and O. Evans (1988), 'Ricardian Equivalence and National Saving in the United States', *IMF Working Paper* **WP/88/96**, Washington, DC: International Monetary Fund.

Eccleston, B. (1989), *State and Society in Post-War Japan*, Cambridge: Polity Press.

Economic Council of Canada (1986), 'Towards Regionally Differentiated Stabilisation Policy', in D. J. Savoie (ed.), *The Canadian Economy: A Regional Perspective*, pp. 104-31.

Economist (1994), 'Slicing the Cake', 5 November, 13-14.

Eichner, A. H. (1980), *The Megacorp and Oligopoly: Micro Foundations of Macro Dynamics*, White Plains, NY: M. E. Sharpe.

Enders, W. and L. Bong-Soo (1990), 'Current Account and Budget Deficits: Twins or Distant Cousins?', *Review of Economics and Statistics*, **72**, 373-81.

Eshag, E. (1987), 'Fiscal and Monetary Policies in Developing Countries', in J. Eatwell et al. (eds), *The New Palgrave*, Vol. 2, pp. 363-5.

Ethier, W. J. (1986), 'The Multinational Firm', *Quarterly Journal of Economics*, **101**, November, 805-33.

EUROSTAT (1992), *Europe in Figures*, 3rd edn, Luxembourg.

Evans, P. (1985), 'Do Large Deficits Produce High Interest Rates?', *American Economic Review*, **75**, 68-87.

______ (1986), 'Is the Dollar High because of Large Budget Deficits?', *Journal of Monetary Economics*, **18**, 227-49.

______ (1987a), 'Do Budget Deficits Raise Nominal Interest Rates? Evidence from Six Countries', *Journal of Monetary Economics*, **20**, 281-300.

______ (1987b), 'Interest Rates and Expected Future Budget Deficits in the United States', *Journal of Political Economy*, **95**, 34-58.

______ (1988), 'Are Consumers Ricardian? Evidence for the United States', *Journal of Political Economy*, **96**, 983-1004.

Evans, P. (1992), 'The State as Problem and Solution: Predation, Embedded Autonomy and Structural Change', in S. Haggard and R. R. Kaufman (eds), *The Politics of Economic Adjustment*, Princeton: Princeton University Press, pp. 139-81.

______ (1995), *Embedded Autonomy: States and Industrial Transformation*, Princeton: Princeton University Press.

Evans, P., Rueschemeyer, D. and T. Skockpol (eds) (1985), *Bringing the State Back In*, Cambridge: Cambridge University Press.

Ewener, J. (1995), 'Budget Zen: Sound of One Invisible Hand Clapping', *Toronto Star*, 6 March, p. A15.

Fazi, E. and N. Salvadori (1981), 'The Existence of a Two-Class Economy in a General Cambridge Model of Growth and Distribution', *Cambridge Journal of Economics*, **9**, 155-64.

Feldstein, M. (1982), 'Government Deficits and Aggregate Demand', *Journal of Monetary Economics*, **9**, 1-20.

Feldstein, P. J. (1979), *Health Care Economics*, Chichester, UK: John Wiley & Sons.

Foley, D. (1978), 'State Expenditure from a Marxist Perspective', *Journal of Public Policy*, **9**.

Fong, P. E. (1988), 'The Distinctive Features of Two City-States' Development: Hong Kong and Singapore', in P. L. Berger and H.-H. M. Hsiao (eds), *In Search of an East Asian Development Model*, pp. 220-38.

Fox, P. W. and G. White (eds) (1987), *Politics: Canada*, 6th edn, Toronto: McGraw-Hill Ryerson.

Frenkel, J. A. (ed.) (1988), *International Aspects of Fiscal Policies*, Chicago: Chicago University Press.

Frenkel, J. A. and A. Razin (1987), *Fiscal Policies and the World Economy*, Cambridge: MIT Press.

Friedman, M. (1953), *Essays in Positive Economics*, Chicago: University of Chicago Press.

Frum, D. (1995), 'Radio Discussion Concerning the Ontario Election', on CBC Radio's Ontario Report, Morning of 9 June.

Galbraith, J. K. (1952), A *Theory of Price Control*, Cambridge: Harvard University Press.

______ (1967), T*he New Industrial State*, Boston: Houghton Mifflin.

______ (1973), E*conomics and the Public Purpose*, Boston: Houghton Mifflin.

______ (1983), T*he Anatomy of Power*, Boston: Houghton Mifflin.

Galtung, J. (1986), 'A Structural Theory of Imperialism', in J. Vasquez (ed.), *Classics of International Relations*, Englewood Cliffs, NJ: Prentice-Hall, pp. 265-73.

Ghose, A. K. (2004), 'Global Inequality and International Trade', *Cambridge Journal* of Economics, **28** (2), 229-52.

Giannola, A. (1982), 'The Industrialisation, Dualism and Economic Dependence of the Mezzogiorno in the 1980s', *Banco di Roma Review of Economic Conditions in Italy*, **36**, 67-92.

Giddens, A. (1995), 'Government's Last Gasp: Is Capitalism Causing the Withering of the State?', *The National Times*, November/December, pp. 42-44.

Gilpin, R. (1975), *US Power and the Multinational Corporation: The Political Economy of Foreign Direct Investment*, New York: Basic Books.

______ (1987), *The Political Economy of International Relations*, Princeton: Princeton University Press.

Glade, W. P. (1987), 'Multinationals and the Third World', *Journal of Economic Issues*, **4**, December, 1889-1914.

Gordon, M. S. (1963), *The Economics of Welfare Policies*, Columbia: Columbia University Press.

Gough, I. (1979), *The Political Economy of the Welfare State*, London: Macmillan.

Government of Singapore (1993), *Singapore 1993*.

Graham, J. F. (1963), *Fiscal Adjustment and Economic Development*, Toronto: University of Toronto Press.

Grimwade, N. (1989), *International Trade: New Patterns of Trade, Production and Investment*, London: Routledge.

Grossman, G. M. and E. Helpman (1990), 'Comparative Advantage and Long-Run Growth', *American Economic Review*, **80**, 796-815.

Grossman, G. M. (ed.) (1992), *Imperfect Competition and International Trade*, Cambridge, MA: MIT Press.

Hadjimatheou, G. (1994), 'Public Expenditure', in P. Arestis and M. C. Sawyer (eds), *The Elgar Companion to Radical Political Economy*, Aldershot, UK and Brookfield, USA: Edward Elgar, pp. 319-23.

Hadjimatheou, G. and A. Tackie (1992), 'Modelling Public Expenditure', *International Review of Applied Economics*, **6** (1), 62-95.

Hagen, E. (1958), 'An Economic Justification for Protectionism', *Quarterly Journal of Economics*, **62** (4), 496-514.

Hahn, F. (1982), 'Reflections on the Invisible Hand', *Lloyds Bank Review*, **144**, 1-21.

Hamilton, A. (1928), 'Report on the Subject of Manufactures', in A. H. Cole (ed.), *Industrial and Commercial Correspondence of Alexander Hamilton, Anticipating his Report on Manufacturing*, pp. 247-320.

Hayek, F. A. (1944), *The Road to Serfdom*, London: Routledge & Kegan Paul.

______ (1973), 'Economic Freedom and Representative Democracy', *Occasional Paper No.* **39**, London: Institute of Economic Affairs.

______ (1976), *Denationalisation of Money*, London: Institute of Economic Affairs.

______ (1988), *The Fatal Conceit*, Chicago: University of Chicago Press.

Haynes, J. (1996), *Third World Politics*, Oxford: Blackwell.

Heald, D. (1983), *Public Expenditure*, Oxford: Martin Robertson.

Heckscher, E. (1919), 'The Effect of Foreign Trade on the Distribution of Income', *Ekonomisk Tidskrift*, 497-512.

Helliwell, J. F. (1987), 'Fiscal Policy and the External Deficit: Siblings but not Twins', *Working Paper No.* **3313**, Cambridge, MA: NBER.

Helpman, E. (1992), 'Multinational Corporations and Trade Structure', in G. M. Grossman (ed.), *Imperfect Competition and International Trade*, pp. 285-302.

Helpman, E. and P. R. Krugman (1985), *Market Structure and Foreign Trade*, Cambridge, MA: MIT Press.

Herber, B. P. (1975), *Modern Public Finance*, 3rd edn, New York: Richard D. Irwin.

Hewlett, S. A. (1993), *Child Neglect in Rich Nations*, New York: UNICEF.

Higgins, B. and D. J. Savoie (eds) (1988), *Regional Economic Development*, London: Unwin Hyman.

Hillard, J. V. (1994), 'Aggregate Demand', in P. Arestis and M. C. Sawyer (eds), *The Elgar Companion to Radical Political Economy*, pp. 5-10.

Hirschman, A. O. (1958), *The Strategy of Economic Development*, New Haven: Yale University Press.

Hitchner, D. G. and C. Levine (1981), *Comparative Government and Politics*, 2nd edn, New York: Harper & Row Publishers.

Hodgson, G. (1988), *Economics and Institutions: A Manifesto for a Modern Institutional Economics*, Oxford: Polity Press.

______ (1999), *Evolution and Institutions*, Cheltenham, UK and Northampton, MA, USA: Edward Elgar.

______ (2001), *How Economics Forgot History: The Problem of Historical Specificity in the Social Sciences*, London: Routledge.

______ (2006), *Economics in the Shadows of Darwin and Marx*, Cheltenham, UK and Northampton, MA, USA: Edward Elgar.

Holland, S. (1976), *Capital versus the Regions*, London: Macmillan.

Hong, N. S. (1982), 'From "Voluntarism" to "Intervention by Discretion": The Changing Stance of Labour Administration in Hong Kong', *Hong Kong Journal of Public Administration*, **4** (1), 31-50.

Honjo, E. (1938), 'A Survey of Economic Thought in the Closing Days of the Tokugawa Era', *Kyoto University Economic Review*, **13** (2), 21-39.

______ (1939), 'Economic Thought in the Early Period of the Tokugawa Era', *Kyoto University Economic Review*, **14** (4), 1-17.

______ (1940), 'Economic Thought in the Middle Period of the Tokugawa Era', *Kyoto University Economic Review*, **15** (2), 1-33.

Horsman, M. and A. Marshall (1994), *After the Nation-State*, London: Harper Collins.

Howlett, M. and M. Ramesh (1992), *The Political Economy of Canada: An Introduction*, Toronto: McClelland and Stewart.

Hozumi, F. (1940), 'Ssu-Ma Chien's Economic Outlook', *Kyoto University Economic Review*, **15** (1), 17-29.

Hu, J. (1984), *Chinese Economic Thought Before the Seventeenth Century*, Beijing: Foreign Language Press.

Hughes, K. S. (1992), 'Technology and International Competitiveness', *International Review of Applied Economics*, **6** (2), 166-83.

______ (1993), 'The Role of Technology, Competition and Skill in European Competitiveness', in K. S. Hughes (ed.), *European Competitiveness*, pp. 133-57.

______ (ed.) (1993), *European Competitiveness*, Cambridge: Cambridge University Press.

Hughes, O. E. (1998), *Public Management and Administration*, 2nd edn, London: Macmillan.

Hume, D. (1951), *Theory of Politics*, Edinburgh: Thomas Nelson.

Hunter, J. S. H. (1977), *Federalism and Fiscal Balance: A Comparative Study*, Canberra: Australian National University.

Hymer, S. H. (1976), *The International Operations of National Firms: A Study of Direct Foreign Investment*, Cambridge, MA: MIT Press.

Innis, H. A. (1956), *The Fur Trade in Canada: An Introduction to Canadian Economic History*, Toronto: University of Toronto Press.

Ito, T. (1992), *The Japanese Economy*, Cambridge, MA: MIT Press.

Jackson, P. (1982), *The Political Economy of Bureaucracy*, Deddington: Philip Allan.

James, S. and C. Nobes (1978), *The Economics of Taxation*, Oxford: Philip Allan.

Jessop, B. (1982), *The Capitalist State*, Oxford: Martin Robertson.

Jessop, R. (1977), 'Recent Theories of the State', *Cambridge Journal of Economics*, **1**.

______ (1987), 'Economic Theory of the State', in J. Eatwell et al. (eds), *The New Palgrave*, Vol. 2, pp. 75-7.

Johnson, A. F., McBride, S. and P. J. Smith (eds) (1994), *Continuities and Discontinuities: The Political Economy of Social Welfare and Labour Market Policy in Canada*, Toronto: University of Toronto Press.

Johnson, C. (1982), *MITI and the Japanese Miracle: The Growth of Industrial Policy, 1925-1975*, Stanford: Stanford University Press.

______ (1985), 'Political Institutions and Economic Performance: The Government-Business Relationship in Japan, South Korea and Taiwan', in R. A. Scalapino, S. Sato and J. Wanandi (eds), *Asian Economic Development – Present and Future*, pp. 63-89.

Johnson, D. (1986), 'Consumption, Permanent Income and Financial Wealth in Canada: Empirical Evidence on the Intertemporal Approach to the Current Account', *Canadian Journal of Economics*, **19**, 189-206.

Johnson, H. G. (1953), 'Optimum Tariffs and Retaliation', *Review of Economic Studies*, **21**, 142-53.

______ (1958), *International Trade and Economic Growth*, London: Allen & Unwin.

______ (1962), 'International Liquidity-Problems and Plans', *Malaysian Economic Review*, **7** (1), 1-19.

______ (1965a), 'Optimal Trade Intervention in the Presence of Domestic Distortions', in R. Caves, H. G. Johnson and P. B. Kenen (eds), *Trade, Growth and the Balance of Payments: Essays in Honour of Gottfried Haberler*, Chicago: Rand McNally, pp. 3-34.

______ (1965b), 'A Theoretical Model of Nationalism in New and Developing States', *Political Science Quarterly*, **80**, June, 169-85.

______ (1967), 'The Possibility of Income Losses from Increased Efficiency or Factor Accumulation in the Presence of Tariffs', *Economic Journal*, **77** (1), 151-4.

______ (1971), *Aspects of the Theory of Tariffs*, Cambridge, MA: Harvard University Press.

Johnson, N. (1987), *The Welfare State in Transition*, Hemel Hempstead, Harvester Wheatsheaf.

Jones, R. W. and J. P. Neary (1984), 'The Positive Theory of International Trade,' in R. W. Jones and P. B Kenen (eds), *Handbook of International Economics: International Trade*, Vol. 1, pp. 1-62.

Jones, R. W. and P. B. Kenen (eds) (1984), *Handbook of International Economics: International Trade*, Vol. 1, Amsterdam: North-Holland.
Jones, R. W. (1989), 'Protectionism and the Optimal Tariff', *Journal of International Economic Integration*, **4** (1), 1-4.
Jones-Hendrickson, S. B. (1985), *Public Finance and Monetary Policy in Open Economies*, Kingston: ISER.
Kaldor, N. (1955), *An Expenditure Tax*, London: George Allen & Unwin.
______ (1966), *Causes of the Slow Economic Growth of the United Kingdom*, Cambridge: Cambridge University Press.
______ (1970), 'The Case for Regional Policies', *Scottish Journal of Political Economy*, **17** (3), 337-48.
______ (ed.) (1971), *Conflicts in Policy Objectives*, Oxford: Basil Blackwell.
______ (1978a), *Further Essays on Economic Theory*, London: Duckworth.
______ (1978b), *Further Essays on Applied Economics*, London: Duckworth
Kalecki, M. (1937), 'A Theory of Commodity, Income and Capital Taxation', *Economic Journal*, **47**, pp. 444-50.
______ (1971), *Selected Essays on the Dynamics of a Capitalist Economy 1933-1970*, Cambridge: Cambridge University Press.
Kang, T. W. (1989), *Is Korea the Next Japan*?, New York: The Free Press.
Karagiannis, N. (1996), *Fiscal Policy and Development: With Special Reference to the EC Countries*, Ph.D. Dissertation, Leeds: Leeds University Business School.
______ (2002), *Developmental Policy and the State: The European Union, East Asia, and the Caribbean*, Lanham, MD: Lexington Books.
Keen, S. (2002), *Debunking Economics: The Naked Emperor of the Social Sciences*, London & New York: Zed Books.
______ (2007), 'Aggregation Fallacies in the Theory of the Firm', *American Review of Political Economy*, forthcoming.
Keiser, N. F. (1964), *Macroeconomics, Fiscal Policy and Economic Growth*, New York: John Wiley & Sons.
Keng, S. and C.-W. Chen (2004), 'Farewell to the Developmental State? Government and Business in the Kunshan Miracle', Taipei: Chinese Political Science Association, November.
Keohane, R. (1980), *The Theory of Hegemonic Stability and Changes in International Economic Regimes, 1967-1977*, LA: Centre for International and Strategic Affairs.
Keynes, J. M. (1936), *The General Theory of Employment, Interest and Money*, San Diego: Harcourt Brace Jovanovich Publishers.
Kierzkowski, H. (ed.) (1984), *Monopolistic Competition and International Trade*, Oxford: Clarendon Press.
Kim, K.-D. (1988), 'The Distinctive Features of S. Korea's Development', in P. L. Berger and H.-H. M. Hsiao (eds), *In Search of an East Asian Development Model*, pp. 197-219.
Kindleberger, C. P. (1951), 'Group Behaviour and International Trade', *Journal of Political Economy*, **59** (1), 30-46.
______ (1981), 'The Price of Gold and the N-1 Problem', in C. P. Kindleberger (ed.), *International Money*, pp. 76-86.
______ (ed.) (1981), *International Money*, London: George Allen & Unwin.

______ (1986), *The World in Depression: 1929-1939*, Revised and Expanded Edition, Berkeley, CA: University of California Press.

King, R. (1977), 'Recent Industrialisation in Sardinia: Rebirth or Neo-colonialism?', *Erdkunde*, **31**, 87-102.

______ (1987), 'Italy', in H. D. Clout (ed.), *Regional Development in Western Europe*, pp. 129-63.

Kintanar, A. Jr. and T. Loong-Hoe (eds) (1986), *ASEAN-US Economic Relations: An Overview*, Singapore: Institute of Southeast Asian Studies.

Knight, M. D. and P. R. Masson (1988), 'Fiscal Policies, Net Saving and Real Exchange Rates: The United States, the Federal Republic of Germany and Japan', in J. A. Frenkel (ed.), *International Aspects of Fiscal Policies*, Chicago: Chicago University Press, pp. 21-66.

Knox, P. (1995), 'A Global Economy, Yes, But No Thanks to Global Polity', *Toronto Globe and Mail*, 10 June, p. D5.

Kochen, M. and K. W. Deutsch (1980), *Decentralization*, Cambridge, MA: Oelgeschlager, Gunn & Hain.

Kojima, K. (1978), *Direct Foreign Investment: A Japanese Model of Multinational Business Operations*, London: Croom Helm.

Kolb, R. W. (1988), *Principles of Finance*, London: Scott, Foresman & Co.

Kotlin, J. (1992), *Tribes*, New York: Random House.

Kregel, J. A. (1985), 'Budget Deficits, Stabilisation Policy and Liquidity Preference: Keynes' Post-War Proposals', in F. Vicarelli (ed.), *Keynes' Relevance Today*, London: Macmillan.

______ (1994), 'Effective Demand', in P. Arestis and M. C. Sawyer (eds), *The Elgar Companion to Radical Political Economy*, pp. 114-19.

Krueger, A. O. (1974), 'The Political Economy of the Rent-Seeking Society', *American Economic Review*, **64**, June, 291-303.

Krugman, P. R. (1981), 'Trade, Accumulation and Uneven Development', *Journal of Development Economics*, **8**, 149-61.

______ (1984), 'Import Protection as Export Promotion', in H. Kierzkowski (ed.), *Monopolistic Competition and International Trade*, Oxford: Clarendon Press, pp. 180-193.

______ (1991), *Geography and Trade*, Cambridge, Mass: MIT Press.

______ (1992a), 'Imperfect Competition, Increasing Returns, and Differentiated Products in International Trade', in J. M. Letiche (ed.), *International Economic Policies and Their Theoretical Foundations: A Sourcebook*, 2nd edn, pp. 589-660.

Kuznets, S. (1955), 'Economic Growth and Income Inequality', *American Economic Review*, **45**, January, 1-28.

Lang, T. and C. Hines (1993), *The New Protectionism: Protecting the Future Against Free Trade*, New York: The New Press.

Laramie, A. J. (1991), 'Taxation and Kalecki's Distribution Factors', *Journal of Post-Keynesian Economics*, **4**, 583-94.

______ (1994), 'Taxation', in P. Arestis and M. C. Sawyer (eds), *The Elgar Companion to Radical Political Economy*, Aldershot, UK and Brookfield, USA: Edward Elgar.

Laramie, A. J. and D. Mair (1993), 'The Incidence of Business Rates: A Post-Keynesian Approach', *Review of Political Economy*, **5** (1), 55-72.

Lasch, C. (1995), *The Revolt of Elites and the Betrayal of Democracy*, New York: W. W. Norton.

Laxer, J. (1984), *Rethinking the Economy*, Toronto: McClelland & Stewart.

______ (1993), *False God: How the Globalization Myth Has Impoverished Canada*, Toronto: Lester.

Le Grand, J. and R. Robinson (1976), *The Economics of Social Problems*, London: Macmillan.

Leftwich, A. (1995), 'Bringing Politics Back: Towards a Model of the Development State', *Journal of Development Studies*, **31** (3), 400-27.

Lenin, V. I. (1939a), *Imperialism: The Highest Stage of Capitalism*, New York: International Publishers.

______ (1939b), *The State and Revolution*, New York: International Publishers.

Lerner, A. P. (1952), 'Factor Prices and International Trade', *Econometrica*, **19**, 1-15.

Letiche, J. M. (ed.) (1992), *International Economic Policies and Their Theoretical Foundations: A Sourcebook*, 2nd edn, San Diego: Academic Press.

Levitt, K. (1970), *Silent Surrender: The American Economic Empire in Canada*, New York: Liveright Press.

Lewis, S. R. (1984), *Taxation for Development*, New York: Oxford University Press.

Libicki, M. C. (1989), 'What Makes Industries Strategic?', Washington: National Defense University, *McNair Paper No.* **5**, November.

Liebenstein, H. (1966), 'Allocative Efficiency vs. X-Efficiency', *American Economic Review*, **56**, 392-415.

Lim, L. Y. C. (1983), 'Singapore's Success: The Myth of the Free Market Economy', *Asian Survey*, **23**, June, 752-64.

Lin, C.-Y. (1973), *Industrialization in Taiwan, 1946-1972: Trade and Import-Substitution Policies for Developing Countries*, New York: Praeger Books.

Lindahl, E. (1919), *Die Gerechtigkeit der Besteuerung*, Lund.

Lindblom, C. E. (1977), *Politics and Markets: The World's Political-Economic Systems*, New York: Basic Books.

Lindsey, C. W. (1986), 'Transfer of Technology to the ASEAN Region by US Transnational Corporations,' in A. Kintanar Jr. and T. Loong-Hoe (eds), *ASEAN-US Economic Relations: An Overview*, pp. 225-47.

Lipsey, R. G. (1986), 'Sovereignty: Culturally, Economically and Socially,' in J. Crispo (ed.), *Free Trade: The Real Story*, pp. 148-60.

List, F. (1977), *The National System of Political Economy*, S. Lloyd trans., Fairfield, NJ: Augustus M. Kelly.

______ (1983), *The Natural System of Political Economy*, W. O. Henderson trans., London: Frank Cass.

Littlechild, M. (1982), 'Regional Policy in Germany', *Town and Country Planning*, **51**, 155-9.

Losch, A. (1954), *The Economics of Location*, New Haven: Yale University Press.

Lucas, R. E. (1988), 'On the Mechanics of Economic Development', *Journal of Monetary Economics*, **22**, 3-42.

Lutz, F. A. and D. C. Hague (eds) (1961), *The Theory of Capital*, London: Macmillan.

Lybeck, J. A. (1988), 'Comparing Government Growth Rates: The Non-Institutional vs the Institutional Approach', in J. A. Lybeck and M. Henrekson (eds), *Explaining the Growth of Government*, pp. 29-47.

Lysandrou, P. (2005), 'Globalisation as Commodification', *Cambridge Journal of Economics*, **29** (5), 747-67.

MacEwan, A. (1999), *Neoliberalism or Democracy?*, London: Zed Books.

MacInnes, I. (1994), 'A Model for Standard Setting: High Definition Television', *Contemporary Economic Policy*, **12** (4), 67-78.

MacIntyre, D. (1994), 'Oil Firms Criticized For Myanmar Deals', *Financial Post*, 17 September, p. 62.

MacKay, R. R. (1994), 'Automatic Stabilizers, European Union and National Unity', *Cambridge Journal of Economics*, **18**, 571-85.

MacLennan, D. and J. B. Parr (eds) (1979), *Regional Policy*, Oxford: Martin Robertson.

MacPherson, S. and C.-K. Chan (1997), 'Housing and Poverty in Hong Kong', Dept. of Public and Social Administration, City University of Hong Kong.

Maddison, A. (1964), *Economic Growth in the West*, London: George Allen & Unwin.

Madjd-Sadjadi, Z. (1996), *Globalization and the Canadian Provinces*, Ph.D. Dissertation, University of Southern California.

______ (2003), 'Genesis: An Economic Interpretation', *Rethinking Marxism*, **16** (2), 211-14.

Mair, D. (1994), 'Tax Incidence', in P. Arestis and M. C. Sawyer (eds), *The Elgar Companion to Radical Political Economy*, Aldershot, UK and Brookfield, USA: Edward Elgar.

Mair, D. and D. Damania (1992), 'A Post-Keynesian Approach to the Incidence of Taxation', in P. Arestis and V. Chick (eds), *Developments in Post-Keynesian Economics: Essays on Methodology, Pricing, Distribution and Policy*, Aldershot, UK and Brookfield, USA: Edward Elgar.

Mair, D. and A. J. Laramie (1996), 'The Macroeconomic Effects of Taxation in a Federal Europe', *International Review of Applied Economics*, **10** (1), 7-22.

Mandel, E. (1970), *An Introduction to Marxist Economic Theory*, New York: Pathfinder Press.

______ (1978), *Late Capitalism*, London: Verso.

______ (1987), 'Marx, Karl Heinrich (1818-1883)', in J. Eatwell et al. (eds), *The New Palgrave*, Vol. 3, pp. 367-83.

Marglin, S. A. (1967), *Public Investment Criteria*, London: George Allen & Unwin.

Margolis, H. (1982), *Selfishness, Altruism and Rationality*, Cambridge: Cambridge University Press.

Markham, J. and G. Papanek (eds) (1970), *Industrial Organization and Economic Development*, Boston: Hougton Mifflin.

Marshall, A. (1926), *Principles of Economics*, London: Macmillan.

Martin, A. (1986), 'The Politics of Employment and Welfare: National Policies and International Interdependence', in K. Banting (ed.), *The State and Economic Interests*, pp. 157-241.

Martin, R. (1989), 'The New Economics and Politics of Regional Restructuring: The British Experience', in L. Albrechts, F. Moulaert, P. Roberts and E. Swyngedouw (eds), *Regional Policy at the Crossroads*, pp. 27-51.

______ (2001), 'EMU versus the Regions? Regional Convergence and Divergence in Euroland', *Journal of Economic Geography*, **1** (1), 51-80.

Martinelli, F. (1989), 'Business Services, Innovation and Regional Policy: Consideration of the Case of Southern Italy', in L. Albrechts, F. Moulaert, P. Roberts and E. Swyngedouw (eds), *Regional Policy at the Crossroads*, pp. 10-26.

Marx, K. H. (1970), *Capital*, Vols. I, II & III, London: Lawrence & Wishart.

Mason, H. R. (1978), 'Technology Acquisition in the Pacific Basin: Direct Foreign Investment versus Unpackaged Technology', in H. R. Mason (ed.), *International Business in the Pacific Basin*, pp. 117-29.

______ (ed.) (1978), *International Business in the Pacific Basin*, Lanham, MD: Lexington Books.

McCloskey, D. N. (1990), *If You're So Smart: The Narrative of Economic Expertise*, Chicago: University of Chicago Press.

McKean, R. N. (1958), *Efficiency in Government through Systems Analysis*, New York: John Wiley & Sons.

McMenemy, J. (1981), *The Language of Canadian Politics: A Guide to Important Terms and Concepts*, Toronto: John Whiley.

McQuaig, L. (1995), *Shooting the Hippo: Death by Deficit and Other Canadian Myths*, Toronto: Penguin.

Means, G. C. (1935), *Industrial Policies and Their Relative Inflexibility*, 74th Congress, 1st Session, US Senate, *Document* **13**.

Metzler, L. (1949), 'Tariffs, the Terms of Trade and the Distribution of National Income', *Journal of Political Economy*, **57** (1), 1-29.

Michie, J. and J. G. Smith (eds) (1994), *Unemployment in Europe*, London: Academic Press.

Mieszkowski, P. (1987), 'Taxation of Corporate Profits', in J. Eatwell et al. (eds), *The New Palgrave*, Vol. 4, pp. 600-4.

Miliband, R. (1973), *The State in Capitalist Society*, London: Quartet.

Mill, J. S. (1917), *Principles of Political Economy*, London: Longmans & Green.

Ministry of Finance (2000), *Fiscal Investment and Loan Programme Report*, Japan.

Ministry of Finance (2001), *Fiscal Investment and Loan Programme Report*, Japan.

Moore, B. and J. Rhodes (1987), 'Regional Distribution of Economic Activity', in J. Eatwell et al. (eds), *The New Palgrave*, Vol. 4, pp. 113-7.

Morris-Suzuki, T. (1989), *A History of Japanese Economic Thought*, London: Routledge.

Mueller, D. C. (1979), *Public Choice*, Vol. I, Cambridge: Cambridge University Press.

______ (1989), *Public Choice*, Vol. II, Cambridge: Cambridge University Press.

Muirhead, B. W. (1992), *The Development of Postwar Canadian Trade Policy: The Failure of the Anglo-European Option*, Montreal: McGill-Queen's.

Mun, T. (1986), *England's Treasure by Foreign Trade*, Fairfield, NJ: A. M. Kelley.

Munnell, A. (1992), 'Policy Watch: Infrastructure Investment and Economic Growth', *Journal of Economic Perspectives*, **6** (4), 189-98.

Musgrave, R. A. (1959), *The Theory of Public Finance*, New York: McGraw-Hill.

______ (1986), *Public Finance in a Democratic Society*, Vols. I & II, Hemel Hempstead: Harvester Wheatsheaf.

______ (1987), 'Public Finance', in J. Eatwell et al. (eds), *The New Palgrave*, Vol. 3, pp. 1055-60.
Musgrave, R. A. and A. T. Peacock (eds) (1958), *Classics in the Theory of Public Finance*, London: Macmillan.
Musgrave, R. A. and P. B. Musgrave (1973), *Public Finance in Theory and Practice*, New York: McGraw-Hill.
Myrdal, G. (1957), *Economic Theory and Underdeveloped Regions*, London: Duckworth.
______ (1960), *Beyond the Welfare State*, London: Duckworth.
______ (1968), *Asian Drama*, New York: Random House.
Naisbitt, J. (1994), *Global Paradox: The Bigger the World Economy, the More Powerful Its Smallest Players*, New York: William H. Morrow.
National Times (1994), 'The Other American Dream Team', November, p. 4.
Nelson, R. R. and S. G. Winter (1980), 'Firm and Industry Response to Changed Market Conditions: An Evolutionary Approach', *Economic Inquiry*, **18** (2), 179-202.
Nester, W. R. (1990), *Japan's Growing Power over East Asia and the World Economy: Ends and Means*, London: Macmillan.
______ (1991), *Japanese Industrial Targeting*, London: Macmillan.
Newbery, D. M. G. and J. E. Stiglitz (1981), *The Theory of Commodity Price Stabilization: A Study in the Economics of Risk*, Oxford: Oxford University Press.
Nishigaki, N. (2006), 'Recent Fundamental Reform of Public Financial System in Japan: Background and Remaining Problems', *International Journal of Business*, **11** (1), 49-62.
Northover, P. (2001), 'The Role of the State in Caribbean Agriculture in the New Liberal Trade Order', *Caribbean Dialogue*, **7** (3 & 4), 73-98.
Oates, W. E. (1972), *Fiscal Federalism*, New York: Harcourt Brace Jovanovich.
______ (1987), 'Property Taxation', in J. Eatwell et al. (eds), *The New Palgrave*, Vol. 3, pp. 1034-5.
O' Connor, J. (1973), *The Fiscal Crisis of the State*, New York: St Martin's Press.
Odle, M. A. (1976), *The Evolution of Public Expenditure*, Kingston: ISER.
OECD (1968), *Fiscal Policy for a Balanced Economy*, December, Paris.
______ (1969), *Fiscal Policy in Seven Countries: 1955 – 1965*, March, Paris.
______ (1984), *National Accounts 1970 – 1982: Detailed Tables*, Vol. II, Paris.
______ (1985), *Social Expenditure: 1960 – 1990*, Paris.
______ (1991), *Employment Outlook*, July, Paris.
______ (1992a), *Economic Surveys: Sweden 1991/1992*, Paris.
______ (1992b), *Historical Statistics: 1960 – 1990*, Paris.
______ (1993a), *National Accounts 1979 – 1991: Detailed Tables*, Vol. II, Paris.
______ (1993b), *Employment Outlook*, July, Paris.
______ (1994a), *National Accounts 1980 – 1992: Detailed Tables*, Vol. II, Paris.
______ (1994b). *The OECD Jobs Study: Evidence and Explanations*, Parts I & II, Paris.
______ (1994c), *The OECD Jobs Study: Facts, Analysis, Strategies*, Paris.
______ (1994d), *Employment Outlook*, July, Paris.
Ohlin, B. (1933), *Interregional and International Trade*, Cambridge: Harvard University Press.

Ohmae, K. (1990), *The Borderless World: Power and Strategy in the Interlinked Economy*, New York: HarperCollins.
Okimoto, D. I. (1989), *Between MITI and the Market*, Palo Alto: Stanford University Press.
Okun, A. (1975), *Equity and Efficiency*, Washington: Brookings.
Olson, M. (1982), *The Rise and Decline of Nations: Economic Growth, Stagflation, and Social Rigidities*, New Haven: Yale University Press.
Onis, Z. (1991), 'The Logic of the Developmental State', *Comparative Politics*, **24** (1), 109-26.
Palais, J. B. (1996), *Confucian Statecraft and Korean Institutions: Yu Hyongwon and the Late Choson Dynasty*, Seattle: University of Washington Press.
Pangestu, M. E. and I. N. Hasni (1991), 'The EEC Internal Market and the ASEAN Textile and Clothing Industry', in N. Wagner (ed.), *ASEAN and the EC: The Impact of 1992*, Singapore: Institute of Southeast Asian Studies.
Papanek, G. (1988), 'The New Asian Capitalism: An Economic Portrait', in P. L. Berger and H.-H. M. Hsiao (eds), *In Search of an East Asian Development Model*, pp. 27-80.
Pascale, R. T. and A. G. Athos (1981), T*he Art of Japanese Management: Applications for American Executives*, New York: Warner.
Pasinetti, L. L. (1989), 'Ricardian Debt/Taxation Equivalence in the Kaldor Theory of Profits and Distribution', *Cambridge Journal of Economics*, **13**, 26-36.
Pauly, M. V. (1970), 'Optimality, "Public" Goods, and Local Governments: A General Theoretical Analysis', *Journal of Political Economy*, **78**, October, 572-84.
Peacock, A. T. and J. Wiseman (1961), *The Growth of Public Expenditure in the United Kingdom*, Princeton: Princeton University Press.
______ (1979), 'Approaches to the Analysis of Government Expenditure Growth', *Public Finance Quarterly*, **7**.
Peacock, A. T. and G. K. Shaw (1976), *The Economic Theory of Fiscal Policy*, 2nd edn, London: George Allen & Unwin.
Pearce, D. W. (ed.) (1978), *The Valuation of Social Cost*, London: George Allen & Unwin.
Pederson, O. K. (1991), 'Nine Questions to a Neo-institutional Theory in Political Science', *Scandinavian Political Studies*, **14** (2), 125-48.
Peltzman, S. (1980), 'The Growth of Government', *Journal of Law and Economics*, **23**, 209-87.
Peng, I. and J. Wong (2004), 'Growing Out of the Developmental State: East Asian Welfare Reform in the 1990s', *Conference on the Bright and Dark Side of Globalization*, November, Montreal.
Pereira, F. (1993), *The Political-Economic Determinants of ASEAN Regional Economic Cooperation*, Ph.D. Dissertation, University of Southern California.
Perroux, F. (1988), 'The Pole of Development's New Place in a General Theory of Economic Activity', in B. Higgins and D. J. Savoie (eds), *Regional Economic Development*, pp. 48-76.
Perry, G. L. (1987), 'Deficit Financing', in J. Eatwell et al. (eds), *The New Palgrave*, Vol. 1, pp. 762-4.
Peston, M. H. (1987), 'Budgetary Policy', in J. Eatwell et al. (eds), *The New Palgrave*, Vol. 1, pp. 283-5.

Peters, B. G. (1996), *The Future of Governing: Four Emerging Models*, Lawrence, KS: Kansas University Press.

Phelps, D. M. (1936), *Migration of Industry to South America*, New York: McGraw-Hill.

Phillips, P. (1978), *Regional Disparities: Why Ottawa Has So Much and the Others Can't Catch Up*, Toronto: James Lorimer.

Pigou, A. C. (1928), *A Study in Public Finance*, London: Macmillan.

Pitelis, C. (1991a), 'Market Failure and the Existence of the State: A Restatement and Critique', *International Review of Applied Economics*, **5** (3), 325-39.

______ (1991b), *Market and Non-market Hierarchies: Theory of Institutional Failure*, Oxford: Blackwell.

Plummer, A. (1934), *International Combines in Modern History*, London: Pitman.

Polyani, K. (1957), *The Great Transformation: The Political and Economic Origins of Our Time*, Boston: Beacon Press.

Porter, M. (1990), *The Competitive Advantage of Nations*, New York: Free Press.

Poulantzas, N. (1980), *State, Power and Socialism*, London: Verso.

Premchand, A. (1975), 'Budgetary Reforms in Developing Countries', *Finance and Development*, **12** (1).

Price, V. C. (1981), *Industrial Policies in the European Community*, New York: St Martin's Press.

Prices and Income Commission (1969), *Regional Dimensions of Inflation and Unemployment*, Ottawa.

Quesnay, F. (1970), *Physiocratie, ou Constitution Naturelle du Gouvernement le plus Avantageux au Genre Humain*, Tokyo: Society for Reproduction of Rare Books.

Razin, A. and J. Slemrod (eds) (1990), *Taxation in the Global Economy*, Chicago: University of Chicago Press.

Reading, B. (1993), *Japan: The Coming Collapse*, London: Orion.

Regnier, P. (1987), *Singapore: City-State in South-East Asia*, London: Hurst.

Reich, R. (1991), *The Work of Nations*, New York: Vintage.

Reisman, D. A. (2005), 'Exchange and Authority: The Mixed Economy', *American Review of Political Economy*, **3** (2), 1-16.

Reisman, S. (1986), 'The Issue of Free Trade', in D. Cameron (ed.), *The Free Trade Papers*, pp. 33-40.

Ricardo, D. (1911), *The Principles of Political Economy and Taxation*, London: J. M. Dent & Sons, reprinted in 1951 and 1960 by Cambridge University Press.

Richardson, H. (1979), *Regional Economics*, Urbana: University of Illinois Press.

Roberts, P. (1989), 'Local Economic Development: Alternative Forms of Local and Regional Policy for the 1990s', in L. Albrechts, F. Moulaert, P. Roberts and E. Swyngedouw (eds), *Regional Policy at the Crossroads*, pp. 170-79.

Robson, W. A. (1976), *Welfare State and Welfare Society*, London: George Allen & Unwin.

Rodriguez, C. A. (1974), 'The Non-Equivalence of Tariffs and Quotas under Retaliation', *Journal of International Economics*, **4**, 295-8.

Romer, P. (1986), 'Increasing Returns and Long-Run Growth', *Journal of Political Economy*, **94**, 1002-37.

Root, F. R. (1984), *International Trade and Investment*, 6th edn, Cincinnati: South-Western.

Rosensweig, J. A. and E. W. Tallman (1991), 'Fiscal Policy and Trade Adjustment: Are the Deficits Really Twins?', *Working Paper* **91-2**, Atlanda: Federal Reserve Bank of Atlanda.

Ross, R. J. S. and K. C. Trachte (1990), *Global Capitalism: The New Leviathan*, Albany: State University of New York Press.

Rostow, W. W. (1960), *The Stages of Economic Growth: A Non-Communist Manifesto*, Cambridge: Cambridge University Press.

Roubini, N. (1988), 'Current Account and Budget Deficits in an International Model of Consumption and Taxation Smoothing: A Solution to the Feldstein-Horioka Puzzle?', *Working Paper No.* **2773**, Cambridge, MA: National Bureau of Economic Research.

Rowald, B. J. (1976), *Balance of Power or Hegemony: The Interwar Monetary System*, New York: New York University Press.

Rowell-Sirois Commission (1940), *Report of the Royal Commission on Dominion-Provincial Relations*, Ottawa.

Roxborough, I. (1979), *Theories of Underdevelopment*, Atlantic Highlands, NJ: Humanities Press.

Rueff, J. (1972), *The Monetary Sin of the West*, New York: Macmillan.

Samuelson, P. A. (1948), 'International Trade and the Equalisation of Factor Prices', *Economic Journal*, **58**, 163-84.

______ (1949), 'International Factor-Price Equalisation Once Again', *Economic Journal*, **59**, 181-97.

Sant, M. (1975), *Industrial Movement and Regional Development: The British Case*, Oxford: Pergamon Press.

______ (ed.) (1981), *Regional Policy and Planning for Europe*, Hants: Saxon House.

Saul, J. R. (1994), 'Culture and Foreign Policy', in *Canada's Foreign Policy: Principles and Priorities for the Future; the Position Papers*, Ottawa: Special Joint Committee of the Senate and House Reviewing Canadian Foreign Policy.

Savoie, D. J. (ed.) (1986a), *The Canadian Economy: A Regional Perspective*, Agincourt, ON: Methuen Publications.

______ (1986b), *Canada's Regional Development: The Search for Solutions*, Toronto: University of Toronto Press.

Sawyer, M. C. (1985), *The Economics of Michal Kalecki*, London: Macmillan.

______ (ed.) (1988), *Post-Keynesian Economics*, Aldershot, UK and Brookfield, USA: Edward Elgar.

______ (1989), *The Challenge of Radical Political Economy*, Hemel Hempstead: Harvester Wheatsheaf.

______ (1992a), 'Unemployment and the Dismal Science', *Discussion Paper Series* **G92/15**, Leeds: Leeds University Business School.

______ (1992b), 'Reflections on the Nature and Role of Industrial Policy', *Metroeconomica*, **43**, 51-73.

______ (1994), 'The Intellectual and Institutional Requirements for Full Employment', in P. Davidson and J. A. Kregel (eds), *Employment, Growth and Finance*, pp. 3-17.

______ (1995), *Unemployment, Imperfect Competition and Macroeconomics: Essays in the Post Keynesian Tradition*, Aldershot, UK and Brookfield, USA: Edward Elgar.

Scalapino, R. A., Sato, S. and J. Wanandi (eds) (1985), *Asian Economic Development: Present and Future*, Berkeley: Institute of East Asian Studies.

Scaperlanda, A. (1992), 'The European Community and Multinational Enterprises: Lessons in the Social Control of Industry', *Journal of Economic Issues*, June, 421-32.

______ (1993), 'Multinational Enterprises and the Global Market', *Journal of Economic Issues*, June, 605-16.

Schmid, A. A. (1987), *Property, Power, and Public Choice: An Inquiry into Law and Economics*, New York: Praeger Books.

______ (2003), 'Discussion: Social Capital as an Important Lever in Economic Development Policy and Private Strategy', *American Journal of Agricultural Economics*, **85** (3), 716-19.

Schockman, H. E. and Z. Madjd-Sadjadi (1994), 'After NAFTA', *California Policy Choices*, **9**, 95-113.

Schumpeter, J. (1928), 'The Instability of Capitalism', *Economic Journal*, **38** (3), 361-86.

______ (1934), *The Theory of Economic Development: An Inquiry Into Profits, Capital, Credit, Interest and the Business Cycle*, London: Oxford University Press.

Scott, A. M. (1950), 'A Note on Grants in Federal Countries', *Economica*, **17**, November, 416-22.

Sebastiani, M. (ed.) (1989), *Kalecki's Relevance Today*, London: Macmillan.

Seccareccia, M. (1994), 'Socialization of Investment', in P. Arestis and M. C. Sawyer (eds), *The Elgar Companion to Radical Political Economy*, pp. 375-9.

Sesser, S. (1993), *The Lands of Charm and Cruelty: Travels in Southeast Asia*, New York: Alfred A. Knopf.

Shleifer, A. (1986), 'Implementation Cycles', *Journal of Political Economy*, **94** (6), 1163-90.

Silberman, L. (1960), 'Hung Liang-Chi: A Chinese Malthus', *Population Studies*, **13** (2), 257-65.

Simeon, R. (1986), 'Federalism and Free Trade', in D. Cameron (ed.), *The Free Trade Papers*, pp. 187-92.

Simon, H. E. (1983), *Reason in Human Affairs*, Stanford: Stanford University Press.

Simone, V. and A. T. Feraru (1995), *The Asian Pacific: Political and Economic Development in a Global Context*, White Plains, NY: Longman.

Sinden, J. A. and A. C. Worrell (1979), *Unpriced Values*, New York: John Wiley.

Singh, A. (1993), 'Asian Economic Success and Latin American Failure in the 1980s: New Analyses and Future Policy Implications', *International Review of Applied Economics*, **7**, 267-89.

______ (1995), 'Competitive Markets and Economic Development: A Commentary on World Bank Analyses', *International Papers in Political Economy*, **2** (1).

Sleeman, J. F. (1973), *The Welfare State: Its Aims, Benefits and Costs*, London: George Allen & Unwin.

Smith, A. (1976), *The Wealth of Nations*, Chicago: University of Chicago Press.

Smith, B. C. (1985), *Decentralization*, London: George Allen & Unwin.

______ (1996), *Understanding Third World Politics: Theories of Political Change and Development*, Bloomington: Indiana University Press.

Solow, R. (1957), 'Technical Change and the Aggregate Production Function', *Review of Economics and Statistics*, **39**, 312-20.
______ (1991), 'Growth Theory', in D. Greenaway, M. Bleaney and I. Stewart (eds), *Companion to Contemporary Economic Thought*, London: Routledge.
Southard, Jr. F. A. (1931), *American Industry in Europe*, Boston: Houghton-Mifflin.
Sowell, T. (1994), *Race and Culture: A World View*, New York: Basic Books.
Spengler, J. (1964), 'Ssu-Ma Chien, Unsuccessful Exponent of Laissez-Faire', *Southern Economic Journal*, January, 223-43.
Stackhouse, J. (1995), 'The Golden Land's Economic Tiger Awakes', *Toronto Globe and Mail*, 8 April, pp. D1-D2.
Staniland, M. (1985), *What Is Political Economy? A Study of Social Theory and Underdevelopment*, New Haven: Yale University Press.
Stigler, G. J. and G. S. Becker (1978), 'De Gustibus Non Est Disputandum', *American Economic Review*, **67** (2), 76-90.
Stiglitz, J. E. (1988), *Economics of the Public Sector*, 2nd edn, New York: W. W. Norton & Company.
______ (1989), *The Economic Role of the State*, Oxford: Blackwell.
______ (2003), *Globalization and Its Discontents*, New York: W. W. Norton & Company.
______ (2006), *Making Globalization Work*, New York: W. W. Norton & Company.
Stinchcombe, A. L. (1968), *Constructing Social Theories*, New York: Harcourt Brace & World.
Stohr, W. B. (1989), 'Regional Policy at the Crossroads: An Overview', in L. Albrechts, F. Moulaert, P. Roberts and E. Swyngedouw (eds), *Regional Policy at the Crossroads*, pp. 191-7.
Sugiyama, C. (1994), *The Origins of Economic Thought in Modern Japan*, London: Routledge.
Sun, Tzu (1988), *The Art of War*, Cleary T trans., Boston: Shambhala.
Sung, Y.-W. (1989), 'The Hong Kong Model and its Future Evolution: Neoclassical Economics in a Chinese Society', in Y. C. Yao, V. Mok and L.-S. Ho (eds), *Economic Development in Chinese Societies: Models and Experience*.
______ (1994), 'The Economics of the Illegal Trade between Taiwan and Mainland China', Hong Kong: Western Economics Association Pacific Rim Conference.
Thayer, M. A. et al. (1993), 'A Methodology for Valuing Externalities', Reno, Nevada: Western Economics Association Annual Conference.
Thirlwall, A. P. (ed.) (1987), *Keynes and Economic Development*, London: Macmillan.
Thirlwall, A. P. and F. Targetti (eds) (1989), *Further Essays on Economic Theory and Policy: Nicholas Kaldor*, London: Duckworth.
Thurow, L. (1992), *Head to Head: The Coming Economic Battle Among Japan, Europe and America*, New York: William Morrow.
Tiebout, C. M. (1956), 'A Pure Theory of Local Expenditures', *Journal of Political Economy*, **64**, October, 416-24.
Tirole, J. (1988), *The Theory of Industrial Organization*, Cambridge, MA: MIT Press.
Todaro, M. P. (2000), *Economic Development*, 7th edn, Reading, MA: Addison-Wesley.
Toronto Star (1996), 'Fight Continues on Anti-Cuba Law', 8 June, p. E3.

Towse, R. (ed.) (2003), *A Handbook of Cultural Economics*, Cheltenham, UK and Northampton, MA, USA: Edward Elgar.

Toye, J. F. (ed.) (1978), *Taxation and Economic Development*, London: Frank Cass.

Trebilcock, M. J., Chandler, M. and R. Howse (1988), 'Adjusting to Trade: A Comparative Perspective', *Discussion Paper No.* **358**, Ottawa: Economic Council of Canada.

Triffin, R. (1968), *Our International Monetary System*, New York: Random House.

Tullock, G. (1987), 'Public Choice', in J. Eatwell et al. (eds), *The New Palgrave*, Vol. 3, pp. 1040-44.

______ (1992), Statement Made at General Plenary Session of the Western Economic Association International 67th Annual Conference, San Francisco, on 'Economic Integration and the Future of the Nation-State'.

UN (1993), *Trade and Development Report*, UNCTAD.

Vanhove, N. and L. H. Klaassen (1980), *Regional Policy: A European Approach*, Hants, UK: Saxon House.

Vanpelt, L. (1999), 'Mickey Mouse: A Truly Public Character', last visited on 2 June 2005, http://www.public.asu.edu/~dkarjala/publicdomain/

Vasquez, J. (ed.) (1986), *Classics of International Relations*, Englewood Cliffs, NJ: Prentice-Hall.

Veblen, T. (1939), *Imperial Germany and the Industrial Revolution*, New York: Viking Press.

______ (1954), *Absentee Ownership and Business Enterprise in Modern Times*, New York: Viking Press.

Vernon, R. (1966), 'International Investment and International Trade in the Product Cycle', *Quarterly Journal of Economics*, **80**, April, 190-207.

______ (1971), *Sovereignty at Bay*, New York: Basic Books.

Vickrey, W. (1987), 'Progressive and Regressive Taxation', in J. Eatwell et al. (eds), *The New Palgrave*, Vol. 3, pp. 1021-5.

Viner, J. (1950), *The Customs Union Issue*, New York: The Carnegie Endowment for International Peace.

______ (1960), 'The Intellectual History of Laissez-Faire', *Journal of Law and Economics*, **3**, October, 45-69.

Wade, R. (1979), 'Fast Growth and Slow Development in Southern Italy', in D. Seers, B. Schaffer and M. L. Kiljunen (eds), *Underdeveloped Europe*, pp. 197-221.

______ (1980), 'The Italian State and the Underdevelopment of Southern Italy', in R. D. Grillo (ed.), *Nation and State in Europe*, pp. 151-71.

______ (1990), *Governing the Market: Economic Theory and the Role of Government in East Asian Industrialization*, Princeton, NJ: Princeton University Press.

Wagner, N. (ed.) (1991), *ASEAN and the EC: The Impact of 1992*, Singapore: Institute of Southeast Asian Studies.

Wallerstein, I. (1976), *The Modern World-System I*, San Diego: Academic Press.

Walras, L. (1954), *Elements of Pure Economics*, London: George Allen & Unwin.

Wang, S. (2001), *Analysis of the Role of Government in Taiwan's Economic Development and Industrialization*, Ph.D. Dissertation, University of Southern California.

Wang, Z. and Z. Ge (2004), 'Convergence and Transition Auspice of Chinese Regional Growth', *Annals of Regional Science*, **38** (4), 727-39.

Watkins, M. (1963), 'A Staple Theory of Economic Growth', *Canadian Journal of Economics and Political Science*, **29**, 141-58.

______ (1987), 'Ten Good Reasons to Oppose Free Trade', in P. W. Fox and G. White (eds), *Politics: Canada*, 6th edn, Toronto: McGraw-Hill Ryerson, pp. 48-54.

Watson, W. (1995), 'Borders Still Get in the Way of Trade', *Financial Post*, 9 June, p. 11.

Weber, M. (1958), *The Protestant Ethic and the Spirit of Capitalism*, New York: Charles Schribner's Sons.

Webster, D. (2005), 'Long-Term Unemployment, the Invention of "Hysteresis" and the Misdiagnosis of Structural Unemployment in the UK', *Cambridge Journal of Economics*, **29** (6), 975-95.

Wiarda, H. J. (1999), *Non-Western Theories of Development: Regional Norms versus Global Trends*, Fort Worth: Harcourt Brace.

Wibaut, S. (1989), *Tax Reform in Disequilibrium Economics*, Cambridge: Cambridge University Press.

Wicksell, K. (1896), *Finanztheoretische Untersuchungen und das Steuer-wesen Schweden's*, Jena: Gustar Fisher.

Wildavsky, A. (1985), 'A Cultural Theory of Expenditure Growth and (un)balanced budgets', *Journal of Public Economics*, **28**, 349-57.

Wilkinson, M. (1992), *Taxation: Economics Today*, London: Macmillan.

Williams, A. (1966), 'The Optimal Provision of Public Goods in a System of Local Government', *Journal of Political Economy*, **74** (1), 86-90.

Williamson, J. and D. R. Lessard (1987), *Capital Flight: The Problem and Policy Responses*, Washington: Institute for International Economics.

Williamson, O. (1985), *The Economic Institutions of Capitalism*, New York: Free Press.

Woo-Cumings, M. (ed.) (1999), *The Developmental State*, Ithaca: Cornell University Press.

Wolf, Jr. C. (1988), *Markets or Governments: Choosing Between Imperfect Alternatives*, Cambridge, MA: MIT Press.

Wood, P. (1987), 'United Kingdom', in H. D. Clout (ed.), *Regional Development in Western Europe*, pp. 257-83.

World Bank (1993), *The East Asian Miracle: Economic Growth and Public Policy*, New York: Oxford University Press.

______ (1995), *Bureaucrats in Business: The Economics and Politics of Government Ownership*, New York: Oxford University Press.

______ (1997), *World Development Report 1997: The State in a Changing World*, Washington, DC: World Bank.

World Health Organisation (1988), *Economic Support for National Health for All Strategies*, Geneva: WHO.

Wriston, W. (1992), *The Twilight of Sovereignty: How the Information Revolution is Transforming Our World*, New York: Charles Scribner's Sons.

Wu, R.-I (1988), 'The Distinctive Features of Taiwan's Development', in P. L. Berger and H.-H. M. Hsiao (eds), *In Search of an East Asian Development Model*, pp. 179-96.

Xing, L. and J. Hersh (2004), 'The Genesis of Capitalism: The Nexus Between "Politics in Command" and Social Engineering', *American Review of Political Economy*, **2** (2), 99-144.

Yamazawa, I. (1990), *Economic Development and International Trade: The Japanese Model*, Honolulu: East-West Centre.

Yao, Y. C., Mok, V. and L.-S. Ho (eds) (1989), *Economic Development in Chinese Societies: Models and Experience*, Hong Kong: Hong Kong University Press.

Yeager, L. (1976), *International Monetary Relations: Theory, History and Policy*, New York: Harper & Row.

Ziblatt, D. (2006), *Structuring the State: The Formation of Italy and Germany and the Puzzle of Federalism*, Princeton, NJ: Princeton University Press.

Index

ability to pay 113
accelerators 249–50, 268
  see also modern factors
accountability 279
aggregate demand 32, 39, 248–9, 257
Akamatsu, K. 96, 193, 207
allocation 38, 67, 144
Aquinus, Thomas 181
Aristotle 181
Art of War 183
Austria 17
Austrian economics 27, 180
  see also New Right, New Right policy
automatic stabilisers 170, 258
autonomy 25, 245, 246, 247

Baumol formulation 43–44
benefit principle 113
Breton Woods 4
budget 33, 37, 38, 41, 45, 50, 137, 143, 145, 146, 152–4
bureaucracy 23, 42
Bush, George W. 10

Canada xvi, xvii, xxiv, 9, 20, 45, 55, 106, 113, 173, 180, 230, 289, 292
capacity 280
capital accumulation 34
capital manipulation 209–14
capitalism xi, xii, xvi, 34, 56, 72, 73
centralisation 44, 54
Central Provident Fund (CPF) 214–15, 217
centripetalism 240, 257, 274
chaebol 199–200
China xvii, 7, 17, 20, 65, 66, 181–191, 230, 290, 292, 296–7
Chinese economic thought 181–7
Chinese Exclusionary Act of 1872 188
Chuang Tzu 182
Colonialism 99, 107
Commons, J. R. 9, 207
communism xviii, 65, 72
comparative (competitive) advantage xx, 59, 76, 84, 98, 210, 212, 286
Confucianism 181, 185–6, 192–3, 284
  see also Chinese economic thought
copyright 6, 19, 79, 302–3
corporatism 73, 244
Corrupt Practice Investigation Bureau (CPIB) 220
corruption 14, 15, 23, 220, 225
Cowling, K. 160, 161
creative destruction xvi, 304
crowding out 139–40
Cuba xvi
cumulative causation 158–9, 288
  see also Myrdal

decentralisation 44, 251–3, 295
democracy xii, xvii, 41, 59
development x, 50, 51, 59, 97
developmental state xii, xiii, xv, xvi, xxi, 7, 189–93, 225, 229, 234, 235, 236, 237, 240, 242, 243, 244, 247, 255, 258, 263, 264, 270, 272, 283, 285, 301, 303–4
displacement-concentration hypothesis 40
distribution 38, 45, 69, 144

East Asia xi, xii, xv, 7, 66
see also NICs
efficiency 69, 70
endogenous growth xi
entry barriers 10–11
equity 58, 69
European Community/Union (EC/EU) xiii, 81, 135, 136, 150–52, 153, 154, 157-8, 161–3, 163–7, 168, 169, 170, 172, 173, 174–8, 255, 260–74, 281–2
exhaustive government expenditure 37
externalities 8, 31, 285

federalism 44, 294–7
first welfare theorem 8, 12, 63
fiscal policy ix, x, xii, 33, 135, 136, 143, 144, 145, 146, 147
flying geese model 96, 193, 195–7
see also Japanese economic thought
France 17, 20, 113, 126, 127, 164, 167, 169, 266-9
free trade xx–xxii
benefits of xx, 80–87
costs of xx–xxii, 87–95
Fu Xuan 185

General Theory ix, 49
see also Keynes
Germany 20, 88, 92, 113, 167, 230, 264–5
globalisation xii, xix, xx, 55, 57, 58, 59, 60, 75, 76, 99, 101, 102, 107, 172, 276, 303
government ix, x, xi, xii, xviii, xx, xxi, 5, 6, 63, 67, 70, 74, 96, 98, 102, 103, 104, 209, 213, 216, 221, 224, 233, 235, 246, 260, 275, 276, 277, 287, 297, 301, 304
see also state
government capital formation 174–5
government expenditure x, xii, 9, 10, 27, 32, 34, 37, 39, 40, 43, 45, 46, 49, 50, 139, 140, 144, 145, 146, 147, 148–9, 154
on defence 148
on social expenditure 148–9
on economic services 149
Greece 126, 164, 167, 173, 271–4
Gresham's Law 184
growth poles 242, 256, 261
Guan Zi 183–4, 186
Hamilton 87, 230
Helms-Burton xvi
Hong Kong 10, 11, 14, 20, 73, 77, 99, 222-5, 233, 243, 245, 285, 288
huis 188–9
human capital 33, 51
see also modern factors
Hume 80
Hung Liang-Chi 186

imperialism 99, 107
import substitution xvi, 4
Independent Commission Against Corruption (ICAC) 14, 220, 225
industrial development 256
industrial policy xiii, 7, 51, 66, 73, 175–8, 257, 261–75
theoretical perspectives 175
industrial strategy 175, 250
industry standards 10, 13
infant industry argument 19, 92, 93, 287
information asymmetries 8, 11, 13, 41
Institutionalism xii, 21, 22, 46, 62, 105
institutions xix, 22, 35, 61, 63, 276, 277, 280, 281
interest group xviii, 42, 58, 62
internationalisation xii, 99, 107
International Monetary Fund (IMF) xvi, 5
investment 7, 11, 21, 26, 49, 50, 51, 52, 73, 102, 103, 192, 193, 210, 211, 220, 230, 231, 234, 238, 239, 241, 281, 285, 286, 287
Iran 103–4
Italy 20, 127, 164, 167, 169, 269–71

Jamaica 8, 17, 18, 285, 299

Japan xi, xiii, xv, 9, 12, 17, 20, 65, 66, 73, 74, 77, 79, 81, 96, 106, 173, 174-5, 177, 178, 193–9, 230, 231–33, 234, 237, 243, 284, 287, 288
Japanese economic thought 96, 193–8
Jia Yi 184

Kaldor, N. 119, 120, 123, 159, 167, 239, 290
Kalecki, M. 118, 123, 124
keritsu 182, 199–200
Keynes, J. M. ix, 287
Keynesian economics 4, 16, 32, 33, 36, 49, 75, 76, 118, 121, 122, 136, 137, 138, 171, 186
Keynesian policy 146, 179
Korean economic thought 205

labour market 8
labour standards 8
laissez-faire ix, xi, 17, 27, 31, 35, 59, 80, 94, 129, 136, 137, 225, 229, 230, 238
Legalism 181
  see also Chinese economic thought
Leviathan 40
Lindahl, E. 41, 115
linkages 94, 97
List, F. 4, 87–92, 230, 283
Lucas, R. E. 4

Macao 189, 191, 204, 225
Malaysia 189–90, 243
Malthus, T. 186
manufacture 73, 95, 177
market x, xi, xii, xiii, xv, xix, xx, 4, 5, 7, 8, 9, 13, 15, 18, 19, 20, 21, 59, 65, 66, 67, 69, 73, 76, 100, 103, 136, 209, 223, 279, 304
market failure 13, 21, 28, 29, 258, 285
market-friendly approach 285
Marshall, A. 93, 109, 116
Marxist theory 33, 34, 36, 71, 73, 75, 76, 97, 98, 208
megaprojects 167, 274, 297–8
Mencius 184
middle ground 5
Mill, J. S. 93, 114
minimum wages 8
modern factors 192, 273
modernisation 51
Mondragon cooperative 282
monetarism 4, 120, 136, 137, 146, 186
Mo Zi 184
multinational corporations xix, 96–7, 101, 102, 104, 211
multinationalism 99–100, 107
multiplier 33
Mun 80, 181
Myrdal, G. 158–9, 167, 213, 240, 260, 270, 291–2, 293

natural monopoly 11, 184
neoclassical economics xxi, 3, 21, 22, 29, 30, 61, 62, 64, 67, 68, 75, 110, 111, 122, 123, 137, 171, 175, 208, 236, 247, 256, 300
neoclassical policy 179
Neo-institutionalism 73, 74, 75, 301
neoliberal policy 6, 7, 55
neoliberal school 8, 13, 18, 19, 20, 285
new competition 258, 259, 265, 267
New International Economics 87, 93
New Right 31, 32, 146, 236
New Right policy 179, 180
New World Order xii, xv, xvii, 222
Newly Industrialised Countries (NICs) xi, xiii, xv, 10, 14, 17, 23, 66, 74, 181, 202, 203, 204, 213, 219, 225, 231, 237, 287, 288

openness 177–78
optimal tariff 95, 105–6
Organic State view 38
Organisation of Economic Cooperation and Development (OECD) x, xi, 9, 27, 46–9, 51, 112, 113, 125–6
Organisation of Petroleum Exporting Countries (OPEC) 4

Pareto xxii, 40, 63, 95, 109
participation 253
path dependency 13, 105
see also cumulative causation
Perroux, F. 242
Phillips curve 4
Pigou, A. C. 109
planning 7, 11, 51, 233, 240, 259
see also strategic planning
Plato 181
political business cycle 31, 42
Political Constraints model 40
political scientists' views 45
positive non-interventionism 225
Post-Keynesian theory xii, 61, 73, 74, 75, 256, 301
power xii, 3, 22, 55, 56, 57, 58, 67, 72, 73, 79, 95, 98
privatisation 17, 20
profit maximisation 97–8
property rights 6, 9, 18, 19, 20, 38, 59, 65, 68, 70, 301
prosperity 290–92
place prosperity 290–91, 292
people prosperity 290–91
protectionism 94
public administration x, 3, 22
Public Choice 4, 31, 32
public enterprise 10, 11, 12, 14, 15, 16, 17
cross-subsidisation by 11
window on the industry by 11, 13
public expenditure ix, x, 110, 115
see also government expenditure
public finance xii, 109, 110
public goods 29, 37, 41, 42, 66
public sector 7, 14, 15, 38, 41, 44
see also government, state

Quantity Theory of Money 186
Quebec 11, 290
Quesnay, F. 80, 181

rational expectations 4
regional development 102–3, 256
theoretical perspectives 158–61
regional disparities 161–3
regional incentives 164, 166
regional policies xiii, 51, 52, 163–7, 167–70, 257, 261–75
regional problem 291–4
regional trade promotion 298–300
regulation 11, 13, 260
rent-seeking xviii
Ricardian Equivalence Hypothesis (REH) 138, 140, 141, 142, 143
Ricardo, David 83, 84, 85, 86, 87, 115
see also comparative (competitive) advantage
Sang Hongyang 184
Saskatchewan 11
Schumpeter, J. xvi, 21, 22, 304
see also creative destruction
second welfare theorem 8, 12, 21, 63
short-termism 240, 257
see also Cowling
Singapore 10, 14, 17, 20, 77, 214–22, 233, 243, 285
Smith, Adam 4, 9, 28, 81-3, 86, 89, 114, 115, 184
social expenditure 46, 135
on education 47, 48, 51
on health 47, 48, 51
on social security 48
South Korea xv, 10, 14, 17, 20, 73, 77, 193, 199–201, 205, 233, 234, 243, 245, 284, 287
Ssu-ma Ch'ien 182
stabilisation 38, 144
state xvi, xix, xx, xxi, 3, 4, 5, 7, 8, 9, 14, 19, 23, 24, 25, 27, 28, 31, 34, 35, 38, 41, 44, 52, 58, 59, 62, 63, 67, 70, 73, 96, 97, 98, 99, 101, 136, 209, 213, 216, 221, 224, 233, 235, 246, 260, 275, 287, 297, 301, 304
state activity ix, x, xii, xiii, xv, 19, 20, 25, 30, 34, 35, 37, 38, 46, 260, 276, 277
St Louis equation 136–7
strategic partnership 244, 278
strategic planning 74, 240, 279, 286, 288
strategic trade policy 94, 95
structural adjustment programmes 5

Sun Tzu 183
Sun Yat-Sen 202–3

Taiwan xv, 74, 77, 201–4, 233, 234, 243, 245, 285
Taoism 181
  see also Chinese economic thought
taxation ix, xii, 32, 33, 40, 69, 97, 109, 110, 111–3, 115, 117, 121, 122, 125, 126, 127, 128, 129, 135, 138, 145, 146, 215, 296
  aggregate taxation 151–2
  direct taxation 150
  effects of taxation xii
  incidence of taxation xii, 120
  income tax 113, 185
  indirect taxation 151
  profit tax 112
  progressive tax 69, 111, 185
  property tax 112
  regressive tax 111
  wealth tax 113
technological dependence 103, 104
theory of the second best 12, 30
trade x, xvi, xviii, xx, xxi, xxii, xxiv, 4, 5, 9, 10, 65, 67, 79, 80, 81, 82, 83, 85, 86, 87, 93, 94, 95, 96, 98, 101, 300
triad 204
  see also corruption
transaction costs 8, 67, 72, 208
transfer payments 10, 37, 144, 296–7
transnational corporations xviii, 101
transnationalism xii, 240
  see also Cowling
twin deficit hypothesis (TDH) 141, 142, 143

unbalanced growth 289–90
unemployment 171–4
  theoretical perspectives of 171
United Kingdom (UK) x, 15, 19, 27, 45, 99, 100, 113, 127, 163–4, 167, 169, 173, 261–3
United States (USA) xvi, 9, 10, 11, 15, 19, 20, 27, 36, 44, 45, 87, 99, 100, 101, 103–4, 106, 113, 169, 173, 230

Veblenian dichotomy 22, 229, 247, 283, 304
Verdoorn's Law 159

Wagner, A. 38, 39, 44, 128
Wagner's Law 38
  see also Wagner
Walras, L. 116, 117
Wang Mang 185
Washington school 3, 18, 174, 178, 247
Wealth of Nations 9
  see also Smith
welfare state 35, 36, 71, 74, 75, 76
Wicksell, K. 41, 115
World Bank xvi, 5, 19
World Trade Organisation (WTO) xvi, 7
X-efficiency 21, 63, 68, 87
Xun Kuang 183

Yakuza 204
  see also corruption

zaibatsu 182, 199–200